SOCIOLOGICAL THINKING IN CONTEMPORARY ORGANIZATIONAL SCHOLARSHIP

T0384371

RESEARCH IN THE SOCIOLOGY OF ORGANIZATIONS

Series Editor: Michael Lounsbury

RESEARCH IN THE SOCIOLOGY OF ORGANIZATIONS ADVISORY BOARD

RESEARCH IN THE SOCIOLOGY OF
ORGANIZATIONS   VOLUME 90

SOCIOLOGICAL THINKING IN CONTEMPORARY ORGANIZATIONAL SCHOLARSHIP

EDITED BY

STEWART CLEGG
The University of Sydney, Australia

MICHAEL GROTHE-HAMMER
Norwegian University of Science and Technology (NTNU), Norway

and

KATHIA SERRANO VELARDE
Heidelberg University, Germany

United Kingdom – North America – Japan
India – Malaysia – China

Emerald Publishing Limited
Emerald Publishing, Floor 5, Northspring, 21-23 Wellington Street, Leeds LS1 4DL.

First edition 2024

Reprints and permissions service
Contact: www.copyright.com

British Library Cataloguing in Publication Data
A catalogue record for this book is available from the British Library

ISBN: 978-1-83549-591-9 (Print)
ISBN: 978-1-83549-588-9 (Online)
ISBN: 978-1-83549-590-2 (Epub)

ISSN: 0733-558X (Series)

INVESTOR IN PEOPLE

Vale Barbara Czarniawska (December 2, 1948–April 7, 2024) organization scholar and ethnographer, who will be greatly missed by researchers in the sociology of organizations community, especially those who knew and loved not only her work but also the person.

CONTENTS

ABOUT THE EDITORS

Stewart Clegg is Emeritus Distinguished Professor of Management and Organization Studies at the University of Technology Sydney, Australia, as well as Professor of Project Management at the University of Sydney. He is widely acknowledged as one of the most significant contemporary theorists on both power relations and organization studies.

Michael Grothe-Hammer is Associate Professor in Sociology (Organization and Technology) at the Department of Sociology and Political Science of the Norwegian University of Science and Technology, Norway. He is also President of the Research Committee on Sociology of Organizations of the International Sociological Association.

Kathia Serrano Velarde is Professor of Sociology at the Max-Weber-Institute of Sociology at Heidelberg University, Germany. She is also Vice-President of the Research Committee on Sociology of Organizations of the International Sociological Association.

ABOUT THE CONTRIBUTORS

Nadine Arnold, PhD in Sociology, is an Assistant Professor of Organizational Theory at Vrije Universiteit Amsterdam. Her research centers on the organization and valuation of sustainable development efforts, paying particular attention to the role of standards and waste. Her recent work has been published in journals such as *Critical Sociology, Environmental Policy and Governance*, and *International Sociology*.

Christof Brandtner is an Assistant Professor of Social Innovation at EM Lyon Business School, a CIFAR Azrieli Global Scholar, and a Senior Research Fellow at Stanford's Civic Life of Cities Lab. His research examines how institutions and organizations shape the emergence, diffusion, and implementation of social innovations in cities and their civil society. It has appeared in the *American Journal of Sociology, Sociological Theory, Organization Studies, Socio-Economic Review, Urban Studies, Nature Energy*, and the *Journal of Business Ethics*, among others. He received his PhD in Sociology from Stanford University in 2019 and was a Postdoctoral scholar at the University of Chicago's Mansueto Institute for Urban Innovation.

Fagner Carniel is Professor at the Department of Social Sciences at the State University of Maringá, Brazil. He has a PhD in Political Sociology from the Federal University of Santa Catarina, Brazil and the Professional Master's in Sociology in National Network, Brazil. His expertise lies in the field of sociology of education, with a focus on themes related to the teaching of sociology, diversity, and educational inclusion. He has also investigated topics related to disability, biosociabilities, and biopower.

Grégoire Croidieu is Professor of Entrepreneurship at emlyon business school. He recently published a special issue in *Strategic Organization* on category and place co-edited with Candace Jones and Robert David.

Barbara Czarniawska was Professor Emerita at GRI, School of Business, Economics and Law at the University of Gothenburg, Sweden, *Doctor honoris causa* at Stockholm School of Economics, Copenhagen Business School, Helsinki School of Economics, Aalborg University, and Turku School of Economics. She was a member of the Swedish Royal Academy of Sciences, the Swedish Royal Engineering Academy, the Royal Society of Arts and Sciences in Gothenburg, Societas Scientiarum Finnica, and British Academy. She took a feminist and processual perspective on organizing, recently exploring such phenomena as the future of the welfare state, the robotization of work, and personnel management of spies. She was interested in methodology, especially in techniques of fieldwork and in the application of narratology to organization studies. She wrote in Polish, English, Swedish, and Italian; her texts have been translated into Arabic, Chinese, French, Danish, German, and Russian.

Paul du Gay is Professor in the Department of Organization at Copenhagen Business School, Professor and Director of Research Impact in the School of Business and Management at Royal Holloway, University of London, and Visiting Fellow at Kellogg College, University of Oxford. He has a particular interest in bureaucracy and public service, the ethics of public office-holding, and the history and continuing significance of "classical" organization theory. He is the author of, inter alia, *Consumption and Identity at Work* (Sage), *In Praise of Bureaucracy: Weber/Organisation/Ethics* (Sage), *Organizing Identity: Persons and Organisations "After Theory"* (Sage), *For Formal Organisation: The Past in the Present and Future of Organisation Theory* (Oxford University Press, with Signe Vikkelsø), and *For Public Service: State, Office and Ethics* (Routledge, with Thomas Lopdrup Hjorth). His current research focuses on reason of state as a political morality for the present.

Fabien Foureault is a Sociologist, Associate Researcher at the Center for the Sociology of Organizations (Sciences Po) and a Consultant for works councils (Syndex). He specializes in economic sociology, organizations, and social networks. He has published on the financialization of the French economy and on financial elites in two books, several book chapters, and journal articles.

Jorid Hovden is Professor Emerita at the Norwegian University of Science and Technology, Trondheim, Norway. Her research has a main focus on the gendering of sport organizations, how gender power relations are done in sport policy and coaching, and the ways these discriminate and marginalize women.

Brayden G King is the Max McGraw Chair of Management and the Environment and a Professor of Management and Organizations at Northwestern University's Kellogg School of Management. His research focuses on how social movement activists influence corporate social responsibility, organizational change, and legislative policymaking. His recent studies examine the change processes leading to improved corporate environmental and social sustainability. He has published research in the *American Journal of Sociology, Administrative Science Quarterly, American Sociological Review, Organization Science*, and numerous other scholarly journals. From 2012 until 2022, he was a Senior Editor at *Organization Science*. He has been a Guest Editor at *Organization Studies* and *Research in the Sociology of Organizations*.

Annelies Knoppers is Professor emerita at Utrecht School of Governance, Utrecht University in the Netherlands. Her research focus is on the ways gender is done and undone in sport organizations, how these processes shape how women navigate these organizations, and how this gendering marginalizes them in many ways.

Krystal Laryea is a PhD candidate at Stanford University, where she is a member of the Civic Life of Cities Lab and the Ethnography Lab. Her research interests lie at the intersection of culture, identity, and institutions. She uses qualitative methods to examine the microfoundations of inclusion, integration, and equity in organizations and cities. Her work can be found in *American Sociological Review, Sociological Theory, Mobilization, Qualitative Sociology, NVSQ,* and *Global Perspectives.*

Thomas Lopdrup-Hjorth is Associate Professor in the Department of Organization at Copenhagen Business School. His research interests include the history of organization theory as well as contemporary and historical problematizations of bureaucratic expertise and the state. His articles have appeared in numerous journals, including *Organization, European Journal of Cultural and Political Sociology, Journal of Cultural Economy, Foucault Studies,* and *Ephemera.* His most recent work is *For Public Service: State, Office and Ethics,* a book co-authored with Paul du Gay.

Bruno Luiz Americo, PhD in Management (UFES), including a period as a visiting research student (UTS), holds a Tenure-Track Professor position at the Academic Department of Management Sciences, Pontificia Universidad Católica del Perú (PUCP). He is also part of the faculty at the School of Government and Public Policy and at the Doctorate in Strategic Management at PUCP. His interests lie in the social sciences and organization studies.

Lucy V. Piggott is an Associate Professor within the Department of Sociology and Political Science (ISS) at the Norwegian University of Science and Technology (NTNU). Her research interests are broadly centered around equality, diversity, and inclusion in and through sport. This work has had a particular focus on various forms of sport organizations, including national and international sport organizations, esports organizations, and sport for development and peace organizations.

Walter W. Powell is Jacks Family Professor of Education (and) Sociology, Organizational Behavior, Management Science, and Engineering and Communication at Stanford University, and an External Faculty Member of the Santa Fe Institute. His recent books include *The Emergence of Organizations and Markets,* with John F. Padgett (Princeton University Press) and *The Nonprofit Sector,* co-edited with Patricia Bromley (Stanford University Press).

Leopold Ringel is Assistant Professor at the Faculty of Sociology at Bielefeld University. Focusing on the relationship between institutions, fields, discourses, and practices, he has explored themes such as transparency, performance metrics, or expertise. His work has been published in *Distinktion: Journal of Social Theory, Ephemera, Higher Education, Organization Studies,* and *Politics and Governance.*

Werner Schirmer works at the Brussels Institute for Social and Population Studies (BRISPO) at the Vrije Universiteit Brussels VUB. He holds a PhD in Sociology from LMU Munich and a Docent title from Uppsala University. At BRISPO, he teaches courses on classical and contemporary social theory as well as modules on the link between digital technologies and social relations. He has written several articles, book chapters, and books applying Luhmannian systems theoretical thinking to topics such as organizations, interethnic relations, social work and social problems, inclusion/exclusion, international relations, priority setting in healthcare, and loneliness among older people. His current research focuses on the digitalization of everyday lives of older people. A special aspect of his research is the role of emotions in technology adoption and the possibilities and limitations of experiencing a sense of community online.

Mikaela Sundberg is Professor of Sociology in the Department of Sociology, Stockholm University, and Director of Stockholm Centre for Organizational Research. She is the author of *Fraternal Relations in Monasteries: The Laboratory of Love* (Routledge), *A Sociology of the Total Organization: Atomistic Unity in the French Foreign Legion* (Routledge), and numerous articles in both general and specialized sociological journals, such as *Sociology, Current Sociology,* and *Social Studies of Science*. Her present research project "The trajectory of cause of death data: How certainty concerns shape knowledge on causes of death" explores the production of register data from cause of death determination and certification by physicians to registration at the Swedish National Board of Health and Welfare.

FOREWORD: RESEARCH IN THE SOCIOLOGY OF ORGANIZATIONS

Research in the Sociology of Organizations (RSO) publishes cutting-edge empirical research and theoretical papers that seek to enhance our understanding of organizations and organizing as pervasive and fundamental aspects of society and economy. We seek provocative papers that push the frontiers of current conversations, that help to revive old ones, or that incubate and develop new perspectives. Given its successes in this regard, RSO has become an impactful and indispensable fount of knowledge for scholars interested in organizational phenomena and theories. RSO is indexed and ranks highly in Scopus/SCImago as well as in the *Academic Journal Guide* published by the Chartered Association of Business schools.

As one of the most vibrant areas in the social sciences, the sociology of organizations engages a plurality of empirical and theoretical approaches to enhance our understanding of the varied imperatives and challenges that these organizations and their organizers face. Of course, there is a diversity of formal and informal organizations – from for-profit entities to nonprofits, state and public agencies, social enterprises, communal forms of organizing, non-governmental associations, trade associations, publicly traded, family owned and managed, private firms – the list goes on! Organizations, moreover, can vary dramatically in size from small entrepreneurial ventures to large multinational conglomerates to international governing bodies such as the United Nations.

Empirical topics addressed by RSO include the formation, survival, and growth of organizations; collaboration and competition between organizations; the accumulation and management of resources and legitimacy; and how organizations or organizing efforts cope with a multitude of internal and external challenges and pressures. Particular interest is growing in the complexities of contemporary organizations as they cope with changing social expectations and as they seek to address societal problems related to corporate social responsibility, inequality, corruption and wrongdoing, and the challenge of new technologies. As a result, levels of analysis reach from the individual to the organization, industry, community and field, and even the nation-state or world society. Much research is multilevel and embraces both qualitative and quantitative forms of data.

Diverse theory is employed or constructed to enhance our understanding of these topics. While anchored in the discipline of sociology and the field of management, RSO also welcomes theoretical engagement that draws on other disciplinary conversations – such as those in political science or economics, as well as work from diverse philosophical traditions. RSO scholarship has helped push forward a plethora of theoretical conversations on institutions and institutional change, networks, practice, culture, power, inequality, social movements, categories, routines, organization design and change, configurational dynamics, and many other topics.

Each volume of RSO tends to be thematically focused on a particular empirical phenomenon (e.g., creative industries, multinational corporations, and entrepreneurship) or theoretical conversation (e.g., institutional logics, actors and agency, and microfoundations). The series publishes papers by junior as well as leading international scholars and embraces diversity on all dimensions. If you are scholar interested in organizations or organizing, I hope you find RSO to be an invaluable resource as you develop your work.

Professor Michael Lounsbury
Series Editor, *Research in the Sociology of Organizations*
Canada Research Chair in Entrepreneurship & Innovation
University of Alberta

SOCIOLOGICAL THINKING IN CONTEMPORARY ORGANIZATIONAL SCHOLARSHIP

Stewart Clegg[a], Michael Grothe-Hammer[b] and Kathia Serrano Velarde[c]

[a]The University of Sydney, Australia
[b]Norwegian University of Science and Technology (NTNU), Norway
[c]Heidelberg University, Germany

1. INTRODUCTION

The past few years have seen a plethora of debates regarding the nature of theorizing in organization research and the position of sociological theory therein (Besio et al., 2020). Organization studies are nowadays considered an inter- or multidisciplinary research field with organizational sociology being one of the original parent disciplines (Scott, 2020). However, the contemporary role of organizational sociology is increasingly unclear. Organization studies' intellectual lineage drew on a diversity of sources, including sociology; how could it not, with Weber (1978) as a foundational source? However, the divide between organization studies and sociology has widened considerably (Adler et al., 2014; Clegg, 2002; Clegg & Cuhna, 2019; King, 2017; Powell & DiMaggio, 2023). Even though many of the dominant paradigms of organization theory – for example, neo-institutionalism, population ecology, network theory, and resource dependency – originated in sociology (Grothe-Hammer & Kohl, 2020), sociology is no longer a constitutive part of organization studies. The institutional politics and economics of knowledge production have seen a relative decline in the

Sociological Thinking in Contemporary Organizational Scholarship
Research in the Sociology of Organizations, Volume 90, 1–16

ISSN: 0733-558X/doi:10.1108/S0733-558X20240000090001

vibrantly youthful sociological scene of the 1960s, not only as its progenitors aged but also as investments in higher education social science became increasingly focused on economic pursuits, with the ascendancy of business schools marking this shift from the 1980s onward (Augier et al., 2005). Young scholars gravitate to where the jobs are, and increasingly, they were not in sociology but in business schools, booming in neo-liberal times. The once lively dialogue between sociology and organization studies on the social nature, characteristics, and consequences of organizing and organization seemed to come to a halt (Barley, 2010; Clegg, 2002; Davis, 2015; Hinings & Greenwood, 2002). "Organizational sociology" has become a part of the genealogy of organization studies, a classic blast from the past – an occasional reminder that organizational scholarship has "history" (Scott, 2020). The label "organizational sociology" does not mirror the rich and varied scholarship we witness among today's organization scholars. For many, if not most, what the "sociological" is supposed to be or mean in organization studies has become unclear.

If we turn our gaze away from organization studies and toward sociology, we can observe that – as a sociological subfield – organizational sociology seems to be alive and kicking (King, 2024, this volume). This is not particularly surprising, given how modern times are so highly organized (Bromley & Meyer, 2015; Perrow, 1991). Researchers are constantly confronted with organizations in their daily work, whether these are schools, hospitals, universities, social movements, corporations, sports associations, militaries, nongovernmental and public sector bodies, as well as a myriad of organized cultural pursuits. Faced with organizations as a fundament of modern life, manifold works on organizations must be acknowledged as important contributions to sociology (Grothe-Hammer & Jungmann, 2023). For decades, organization-related works have been highly evident in leading sociology journals (Grothe-Hammer & Kohl, 2020). Active communities of organizational sociologists around the globe showcase this with representations in the International Sociological Association, regional networks such as the Ibero-American Association of Research in Sociology of Organizations and Communication (AISOC), or communities in the national sociology associations as, for example, in the United States, Germany, France, and Spain. The book series this piece is published in – *Research in the Sociology of Organizations* – and the newly established *Journal of Organizational Sociology* also underline organizational sociology's continuing relevance to the discipline of sociology. Irrespective of contemporary epistemic debates, as well as the classic canon, we use this volume to provide clues to answering a key question: *what is "organizational sociology" today?*

Our volume seeks to explore the new boundaries of organizational sociology. It sets out to map a community of scholars that transcends disciplinary limitations by following one simple epistemic logic: society happens in, between, across, and around organizations (Powell & Brandtner, 2016). We thereby work with the assumption that dialogue on the social nature of organizing and organization has not vanished but instead shifted its shape to become an integral yet tacit part of the research agenda of organization studies, on the one hand, and sociology, on the other hand (Scott, 2004). Following Grothe-Hammer and Jungmann (2023) in their inaugural editorial for the new *Journal of Organizational Sociology*, we consider organizational sociology today as consisting of "anyone doing sociology with a focus on organization(s)." For while sociological questions and themes are broadly present in the field of organization studies, many organization scholars do not identify as authors of sociological works (Adler et al., 2014). We hope to revitalize the dialogue about future avenues of sociologically minded organization research. We do so by identifying, discussing, and challenging genuinely sociological contributions to and of organization studies.

2. WHAT IS "ORGANIZATIONAL SOCIOLOGY" TODAY?

Organizational sociology is obviously concerned with the study of organizations, but it is more than a synonym for organization studies. The "sociology" makes the difference. As a sub-discipline of sociology, organizational sociology can be defined simply as sociological studies of organizing and organization(s). Hence, to define the boundaries of organizational sociology, we need to determine what characterizes the sociological stance in the study of organizations. The papers we have collected in this volume have allowed us to extract some positions that we see as central to the sociological standpoint in organization studies. Specifically, we identify three positions that differentiate particularly "sociological" works from other works in organization studies.

First, sociologically minded work values the social phenomena under investigation. Organization and management studies are well-known for their "theory fetish" (Hambrick, 2007). The common conviction in this broad field is that the generalizability of findings outranks empirical novelty. The phenomena under study are treated as "cases of" (Langley, 2021). That is, whatever phenomenon is studied, it should only be seen as a case of some larger theoretical concept that is usually of applied relevance for business and management purposes. The result is a publication culture that Tourish (2020) described as follows: "if you use an existing theory to explain an interesting phenomenon, your work will be rejected."

In his empirical analysis of publications in top-tier journals, King (2024, this volume) shows how sociologists often work the opposite way. In contrast to treating empirical phenomena only as cases of a bigger theoretical picture, sociological studies identify interesting and relevant phenomena and value their unique social configuration. The object of investigation, that may or may not include organizations, is of value because the social affordances it exhibits are of a consequence to people. Sociologists then use theory as a tool to understand and explain such phenomena – not the other way around. The paper by Croidieu and Powell (2024, this volume) is a good example of this approach. Their primary analytical focus is to understand the emergence of the cork aristocracy in the Bordeaux wine field in the 19th century. Class and status theories are used to understand and explain the phenomenon, and while the authors make intriguing new theoretical claims, their first objective is to unfold the workings of class struggle in a specific case.

Second, sociologists care about society, both conceptually and empirically. Organization and management studies' preference for middle range theories (Merton, 1949) certainly connects organizations to social undercurrents. Yet, there seems to be a reluctance to connect with larger, macro-theoretical frameworks. When embedding their research in generalist social theory such as "practice theory," "network theory," or "institutionalism," the perspective is – first and foremost – organizational. For organization and management scholars, society becomes visible through the lens of the organization, thus bypassing the possibility of contributing to the explanation and theorization of society.

The "institutional logics" perspective (Lounsbury et al., 2021), for instance, started with the aspiration of "bringing society back in." Friedland and Alford (1991) developed a theory of society-level institutional logics and how these relate to organizations. In spite of notable exceptions such as Gümüsay et al. (2020), this aspiration was quickly abandoned in favor of mapping meso-level dynamics and the identification of yet another logic (cf. Cai & Mountford, 2022), thereby fulfilling the demand of producing "novel" theory (for accounts of this demand, see Bort & Schiller-Merkens, 2011; Tourish, 2020).

It is noteworthy that much research in organization and management studies strives to achieve "societal impact" or solve "societal grand challenges" but shies away from theorizing at a more macro-level. Studies might be interested in inequality or the effects of certain societal domains like politics on organizations; they might even mention terms like "class" and "stratification" (e.g., Amis et al., 2020). Yet, they fall short of leveraging society-level theories of domain-specific differentiation (e.g., Abrutyn & Turner, 2011; Luhmann, 1977; Padgett & Powell, 2012), class distinction and stratification (Bourdieu, 1986; Savage, 2000), or center–periphery dynamics (Knudsen, 2018; Vik et al., 2022) to this end. "Flat ontologies" (Mountford & Cai, 2023; Seidl & Whittington, 2014) are celebrated whereas the macro-level of society is little more than context (cf. Apelt et al., 2017; Sales et al., 2022; Sydow & Windeler, 2020).

Sociology concerns the social construction of social facts, those values, cultural norms and social practices, and structuration that transcend and frame the individual person and organization. It just so happens that, in some cases, social facts are deeply ingrained in organizational fabrics. The order of relevance is thus reversed in the sense that organizations are perceived through the lens of society and take an active part in shaping it. They are the building blocks that mediate between the macrolevel and the microlevel of social life (Alexander, 1992). While organizations are socially constructed, they have an impact not only on individual destinies but also on social life at large (Schirmer, 2024, this volume). To care about society means accounting for the social consequences of organized action. For instance, when Laryea and Brandter (2024, this volume) set out to analyze the human resources (HR) strategies of nonprofits located in Silicon Valley, it is not only to map the reproduction of social inequalities within seemingly communitarian organizations but also to assess their potential to further or hinder social change and inclusion.

Third, while reflexivity is a methodological and normative concern for both disciplines, there is a specific sociological stance to it. Sociological concerns with reflexivity are anchored in broader methodological concerns regarding the level of engagement with the object of study (Holmes, 2010). Being sociological signifies both an act of self-reference and an awareness that leads to rethink one's position as a researcher in and commitment to a researched community as a matter of truly ontological dimensions. Reflexivity becomes the means through which one deploys "sociological imagination" (Mills, 1959) differently, thereby uncovering methodological and social assumptions in the way we apprehend social reality. For instance, current work on "postcolonial" sociology (Go, 2017) or the "decentering" of social theory (Benzecry et al., 2017) calls for a recalibration of theoretical models (Krause, 2022). It is of great interest to observe that several papers in this volume connect issues of reflexivity to emotions. The emotional undercurrent of organizations is described by Schirmer (2024, this volume) as well as Americo and co-authors (2024, this volume), as an additional layer of social meaning that operates within, across, and around organizations. It is as if embracing the emotional reality of organized life would allow us to develop a more comprehensive picture of social action and a possibility to rethink existing theories and social imaginaries (Taylor, 2004) in more abstract terms.

These three characteristics – valuing the social phenomena; caring about society; reflexivity – capture what for this volume is the gist of the sociological contribution to the study of organizations.

3. WHAT DOES THE COMMUNITY OF ORGANIZATIONAL SOCIOLOGISTS LOOK LIKE TODAY?

We tried to mobilize organizational scholarship that takes a specific sociological "stance" (du Gay, 2020), regardless of the disciplinary affiliation of the authors. To this end, we approached established and young scholars that walk the line between disciplines – that is doing sociology in organization and management studies and/or researching organizations in the discipline of sociology. We talked with them about our project to map the community of researchers that understands themselves as sociologically minded organization scholars or organizational sociologists and encouraged them to share their thoughts on the nature of their research. Furthermore, we also organized an open call for papers at the 2022 EGOS colloquium in Vienna under the label "Doing Sociology in Organization Studies" with the hope of detecting new trends originating in this moving target of a research community. Were common themes evident? What might be the relevance of a sociological take on organization for organization and management scholars?

We locate the nature of the sociological contribution to organizational scholarship in a sociological imagination, for which, as Karl Marx wrote in a flamboyant letter to the German philosopher Arnold Ruge, the primary mission is "the ruthless criticism of everything existing." He further elaborated by writing that "the criticism must not be afraid of its own conclusions, nor of conflict with the powers that be" (Marx, 1843/1978). A similar logic has subsequently driven much sociological work, perhaps most notably C. Wright Mills' (1959) "sociological imagination." The question that a sociological imagination implies for organizational scholarship is to ask what constitutes a critical stance, given the following conditions of contemporary sociology's existence? In this volume, this question took the following three main forms:

(i)   In a world in which much of recent scholarship is in business schools, with an inherent mobilization of bias toward normative issues posed by and for business, what is the place and role of a critical sociological imagination?

(ii) What are the various sociological understandings of the "social" and "society," in a world of "modern organizations" (Clegg, 1990)? We are interested in all kinds of sociological notions of society in relation to organizations ranging from macro-theories to the micro-level (Abrutyn & Turner, 2011; Ahrne, 2015; Bauman, 2013; Friedland, 2014; Luhmann, 1994).

(iii) How do organizations contribute to the production and reproduction of social inequalities? When social scientists do situate inequality in a social space, it is too often myopically focused on national markets and cultural processes, thereby ignoring the workings of organizations and their frequently global network implications (Tomaskovic-Devey & Avent-Holt, 2019). We encouraged organization and management scholars to think about society and the natures of social relations and invite sociologists to think more about the organizational consequences of social action.

4. ABOUT THE PAPERS

We present papers from a range of theoretical and methodological approaches that investigate the sociological dimensions of organization and organization studies. Not only do we believe that theoretical and methodological pluralism is a necessary condition to develop an interdisciplinary research agenda – it also prevents this debate from being too tightly linked to a specific community of scholars, a school, or a research niche. Contributions are of three sorts: First, there are papers that unravel and critically discuss the existing (or missing) sociological dimension of contemporary organization research from a theoretical perspective. Second, we included empirical contributions that explicate their sociological stance toward organizational scholarship and provide new avenues for thinking about the interrelation of organization and society. Finally, there are papers that revisit classic sociology and propose new avenues for research on organizational phenomena.

Part 1: The Place of Sociology in Organizational Scholarship

The first part of this volume deals with Organizational Sociology and its place both within sociology and organization and management studies. The authors of these papers adopt different starting points to discuss the epistemic dynamics behind the making of organization and management studies and the supposed unmaking of "family resemblances" (Wittgenstein, 1953) with sociology. By comparing disciplines across time in their practices of theory building (King, 2024, this volume), identity crises (Ringel, 2024, this volume), and critique (Lopdrup-Hjorth & du Gay, 2024, this volume), these authors develop different historical accounts that feature organizations as the boundary objects of scientific pursuits.

In his contribution, King (2024, this volume) claims that contemporary papers on organizations written in sociological high-impact journals fall into two categories: "Organizations within society" papers approach organizations as basic building blocks of social structure. While accomplishing a social purpose, organizations also reproduce basic social inequalities within society. The papers that fall into the "society within organization" category usually analyze organizations as spaces that host social dynamics, thereby reproducing structural inequalities of the macro-order within their boundaries. Drawing on a content analysis of papers published in the *American Journal of Sociology, American Sociological Review*, and *the European Sociological Review*, King argues that current Organizational Sociology has emancipated itself from a narrow understanding of theory building and adopts a distinctively empirical perspective on organizations in its stead. Organizations are, first and foremost, the analytical lens through which sociologists perceive, name, and explain social problems. It is sociology's larger problem-orientation that makes newer organizational sociology irrelevant to business and management scholars, driven by the necessity to frame a distinctive contribution to organizational theory building. Nevertheless, the breadth of sociological analysis and its capacity to grasp the novel, the tragic and the unseen makes it also the perfect starting ground for the identification of future research avenues in organization and management studies.

Adopting a different analytical strategy, Ringel's (2024, this volume) paper explores overlaps and boundaries between organization (and management) studies and organizational sociology. Making use of Abbott's sociology of profession and Eyal's theory of expertise, the author traces epistemic shifts that have taken place in and between these disciplines over time. Starting from the assumption that both organization studies and organizational sociology have a propensity for self-diagnosed crises, Ringel focuses on the factors that sustain these discursive configurations. In the case of organizational sociology, his study argues that although important conceptual tools and analytical perspectives have been developed in what we may call the "golden era" of the decades after World War II, the sub-discipline never managed to stabilize its hold over the intellectual turf that is organization. Rather, organizational sociology has remained a "broad church" (Scott, 2020) and continues to act as an "unintentional donor" whose output contributes to knowledge created in other academic domains. It transpired that organization studies has particularly profited from these "donations:" Increasingly criticized for their practice orientation in the 1950s, business schools sought respectability in the academic pantheon by embracing scientization. Borrowing from established disciplines (especially economics, psychology, and sociology), organization studies was assembled as a scholarly field of practice during the 1970s and 1980s, soon possessing its own social identity, credential system (and control thereof), publication outlets, and institutional arrangements. As a result, business school faculty have effectively built a strongly oligopolistic redoubt concerning the academic study of organizations. Yet, at the same time, the epistemic configuration of organization studies propels an excess of "borrowing" from other disciplines, something that appears to haunt and taunt business school faculty who continue to worry about their ability to engage in basic research.

Lopdrup-Hjorth and du Gay (2024, this volume) share in critically diagnosing organization and management studies as a field. Their paper on the "sense of reality" in organization studies advocates a critical stance, a new type of reflexivity. The field of organization and management studies, they argue, has lost touch with political and social realities that hold few certainties. Driven by a strong economic logic and a fetish for metrics, managers are not taught to deal with the "situation at hand," which is one of recurrent and all-encompassing crises. They forget to exercise their own judgment in situations, relying instead on quantifiable figures and metrics that gloss over the ambiguities of organizational life, lulling them into a false sense of security. To counter these tendencies, the authors propose returning to classic organization theory that predates the professionalization turn so aptly described by Ringel. It is in the work of Max Weber, Philipp Selznick, Chester Bernard, and Isaiah Berlin that an alternative vision of a manager's duty may be found. By educating managers in "statesmanship," they might develop a heightened awareness of the social affordances (and responsibilities) of organizational decision-making. Highlighting the manager's original mission as being to manage a situation based on a sense of reality in regard to which they exercise cautious judgment about what to do and when, du Gay and Lopdrup-Hjorth call for more professional discretion and displays of managerial judgment.

Part 2: Social Stratification in and Through Organizations

A second set of papers is concerned with the organizational dynamics of social stratification, the processes of closure and marginalization in and through organizations. These papers present current work focusing on the intersection between organizational life and society. They describe organizations both as structuring society through the dissemination of social norms of elitism (Croidieu & Powell, 2024, this volume), leadership (Piggott et al., 2024, this volume), professionalism (Layrea & Brandtner, 2024, this volume), and worth (Arnold & Foureault, 2024, this volume), as well as being a social space in which society "happens."

Organizations Within Society: Organizational Perspectives on Status and Distinction

In their contribution on the food waste sector in Switzerland, Arnold and Foureault (2024, this volume) observe how a heterogeneous set of organizations, comprising charities and businesses, plants and tech companies, alternative producers and distributors, as well as public organizations and interest groups, have come to see each other as part of a common endeavor to find a solution for a global problem. Through the combination of a survey and qualitative interviews, the authors mapped an emerging field of organizations dealing with the problem of food waste through a diverse set of strategies. Drawing on this first set of data, they investigated the advisory relations in the field through the means of a quantitative network analysis. By contrasting the findings of the network analysis with qualitative insights into the evaluation of these organizations by food waste charities and government bodies, Arnold and Foureault point to status inconsistencies in the field. While evaluating agencies attribute higher (evaluative) status to those organizations that commercialize food waste, the advisory network of organizations favors expert bodies (such as an interest group or a public research institute). The losers of both status competitions seem to be alternative producers and tech companies. In addition, food waste charities have an unexpectedly low status. The local reinterpretation of a global problem furthers the economic valorization of waste, thereby marginalizing alternative strategies aimed at reallocating what has come to be understood as a resource. In this intriguing piece that sheds light on a new phenomenon, the readers will find traces of a Weberian definition of organizations as drivers of modernity and "green" capitalism.

The contribution by Croidieu and Powell (2024, this volume) expands on that argument and draws on classic works from the Marxian and Weberian traditions to reinterpret the power of organizing. In their historical ethnography of the wine estates of Bordeaux, the authors uncover a covert class struggle. By tracking ownership structures between 1850 and 1929, Croidieu and Powell examine how merchants, financiers, and industrialists competed by entering a status tournament with landed aristocrats, introducing new techniques and managerial practices in their wake. Yet, instead of challenging existing social arrangements, this transformation in ownership proved to be highly conservative. The new elite borrowed its cultural codes from the higher-status aristocratic pedigree of the former owners to expand prestige – both for themselves and their wines. The authors argue that "the transposition of aristocratic trappings into the wine world initially served no practical purpose other than making status claims under the disguise of mimicry. This emulation created a symbolic order that, as it spread, acquired a high-status patina" (Croidieu & Powell, 2024, this volume). Combining Marxian and Weberian analyses, the authors depict wine estates' material and symbolic transformations and the intricate dynamics of social closure. During this 79-year period, the prime vineyards of Bordeaux became a nexus for technical, economic, and social transformation, while expanding their elite status in the wine world. Organizations were the site and vehicle of elite class struggles through status and closure dynamics.

Both papers resonate with the burgeoning literature on rankings and (e)valuation as they elaborate analytical accounts of how the institutional affordances of valorizing food waste and wine develop over time. Studying organizations through the status lens means defining them as nested in social hierarchies that seep into the organizational fabric, the habitus of the owners and members, as well as the handling of the product. It is the porosity of organizations that characterizes the papers in this part, their permeability (Ringel et al., 2018) to the social context they feel part of, whether the context is local (Arnold & Foureault, 2024, this volume; Croidieu & Powell, 2024, this volume), global (Piggott et al., 2024, this volume), or both (Laryea & Brandtner, 2024, this volume). While the first two papers are concerned with social closure and distinction, Laryea and Brandtner, as well as Piggott and co-authors, focus on issues of marginalization and exclusion. The papers address a different type of organizational "nestedness" as they target the multilevel dynamics of social inequality.

Society Within Organizations: Organizational Perspectives on Social Integration and Marginalization

Laryea and Brandtner (2024, this volume) are interested in how nonprofit organizations cope with the challenge of serving a local community while addressing norms of professionalism promoted at the societal level. The paper marshals the insights of a survey of nonprofit organizations operating in the San Francisco Bay Area to identify organizations that combine "social" (*Vergemeinschaftung*) and "systemic" (*Vergesellschaftung*) integration objectives. The study shows that these nonprofits use knowledge about the local community to refine how they implement services and connect to institutions. The authors interviewed leaders and staff to understand how dual integration is managed through organizational practices in day-to-day life. The findings reveal two main organizational strategies that help navigate the gap between communitarian norms and professional rationalization (Hwang & Powell, 2009) that epitomize meso-level processes that reproduce (or not) social inequalities in nonprofits. Many organizations pursuing dual integration adopt a "loose demographic coupling" strategy. While frontline workers are recruited from these nonprofits' communities, the managerial staff mainly comprises White or Asian professional men. These organizations split their activities and hierarchies, making it impossible for frontline workers to advance to higher career levels. Nevertheless, a smaller sample of organizations exhibit a different strategy (community anchoring) that resists systemic pull and creates a continuous career path for frontline workers to be able to move into the organization's upper echelons. Laryea and Brandtner confer a distinctive social function to nonprofits by defining them as "third spaces" fostering community and connecting individuals to complex social systems. Recognizing the meso-level workings of social inequality in a setting that is meant to transcend differences and create cohesion (Clemens, 2006) qualifies this study as an extreme case for the "persistence of inequalities" in and through organizations (Amis et al., 2020).

Much in the same vein, Piggott and co-authors (2024, this volume) identify sports organizations as a special case for the reproduction of binary gender norms and stereotypes. Because of their geographical and social spread that bonds nations, regions, and local societies across divides of class, gender, and race, sport organizations possess ideological power to influence how gender is "done, undone and redone." This integrative function of sport organizations contrasts with a performance norm that equals the male body with leadership, strength, and resilience. The sport organization then becomes a symbolic place in which gendered body norms are mirrored both in formal and informal organizational practices of hiring, promoting, role allocation, and task assignments. The authors discuss existing literature on gender reproduction in sports organizations by tracing the origins of unequal career opportunities to differences in physical performances in a binary sport system. The weakness of the female body is mirrored by organizational structures that marginalize women in hierarchy, culture, and routines. The linkage between sport and constructions of desirable masculinity may also infiltrate conceptualizations of desirable leaders in non-sport organizations and shape gender ratios in positions of leadership in these organizations. Attention, therefore, needs to be paid to the extent to which the gendered sport binary may shape managerial practices in both sport and non-sport organizations. Piggott and co-authors (2024, this volume) make a compelling case to further investigate the symbolic power of sport organizations in societies and call for a "queering" of the binary structuration of sports.

The papers claim that organizations have integrative as well as disintegrative capacities in the sense that they shape social spaces beyond their organizational boundaries. Whether these capacities further societal integration and cohesion depends on the way the organization processes its environment and embodies it in routines of social consequence.

Part 3: Rediscovering Sociological Classics for Organization Studies

The last part is twofold. While the first two papers introduce sociological concepts for organizational analysis, the papers by Schirmer and Czarniawska rediscover classic social theory for organizational analysis.

Reflexivity and Control

The paper by Americo and co-authors (2024, this volume), as well as Sundberg's (2024, this volume) contribution, scrutinize the boundaries between organizational and private life. Both papers deal with issues of reflexivity – but they do so by coming from opposing perspectives.

Americo and co-authors (2024, this volume) advocate the necessity to account for the latent emotional undercurrent of organizational life. Borrowing on the sociology of emotion and the concept of "emotional reflexivity," they picture emotions as relating people to others, to themselves, and – in a surprising posthuman turn of the argument – to "nondiscursive entities." Organizations are then defined as an interrelational space that opens possibilities to become aware of, name, and talk about emotions. By challenging a dominant idea in organization studies that any type of reflexivity is grounded in cognition, the authors sketch the contours of an interesting research agenda that blends emotional sociology, organizational learning, and subjectivity studies for the analysis of organizations. To corroborate their point, Americo and co-authors use narrative fiction and depict the learning path of a young hearing-impaired student in Brazil, who, through membership in an inclusive school that taught him sign language, as well as his adoption of two hearing-impaired dogs, managed to develop a consistent vision about himself, his relation to others and his place in society. In this narrative fiction based on empirically researched materials, the school is an organization that allows Pedro, the young student, to enter a dialogic framework, to develop communicative skills, and finally voice feelings that never surfaced before. The paper explores the emotional landscape of organizations as a hidden layer of meaning behind communication and behavior. It questions our notion that emotions and meanings may only arise from human interaction and calls for a comprehensive view of organizations beyond notions of cognition, discourse, and speech.

Sundberg (2024, this volume) shares the assumption that organizations actively shape the boundaries of what may be said, by whom and to whom – thereby regulating the way emotions may or may not emerge. However, where Americo and co-authors are interested in the opportunities provided by organizations to harness emotions for reflexivity and agency, Sundberg looks at obedience, silence, and subversion. Sundberg's contribution revisits Goffman's concept of "total institution," that is, walled-in-units where people live and work 24/7, such as prisons or asylums. As total institutions contain the "totality" of their resident's lives, they also retain an extraordinary amount of control over them. Whereas organization research mostly equates total institutions with the (de)construction of selves through an organization's role and routines, Sundberg focuses on the maintenance of authority relations and obedience. Following Goffman, she highlights the difference between coercive institutions such as prisons and voluntary total institutions such as oil rigs, the army, or cloistered religious communities. The latter, she argues, make a compelling case for the analysis of authority and obedience since their members actively choose to endorse the organization's goals and values. Their choice comes with a pledge of obedience to communitarian rules, which in the two ethnographic cases presented in the papers – the French Foreign Legion and the French Order of Cistercian monks and nuns – translates into the strict interdiction on talking back to superior officers (even when treated unfairly) or engaging in private conversation with the brothers and sisters of the monastery. Yet, illicit behavior occurs. Soldiers will disappear at night, even without having a formal permission to do so. Sisters and brothers will find discreet confidants among their community. What matters in this case is that the rule of obedience is not breached. Rather, the persons invested in illicit behavior know that they are operating in the grey zones of indifference and that their actions do not represent an open act of subversion calling into question the moral code of their organization or their adherence to it. Soldiers and Cistercians will retain a degree of agency by keeping quiet without falling silent.

Organizing and Organization
The last two papers of this special issue draw attention to a sociological debate that is as old as organizational sociology: the difference between organizing and organization.

In her paper on the relevance of Simmel and Tarde's work for the sociology of organizing, Czarniawska (2024, this volume) points to one of sociology's founding principles: that society is the product of human interaction and that the actual puzzle to solve is why people are drawn together, how they define the unit they feel part of, and how they act with and upon it. The paper draws on Czarniawska's biographical experience of being a sociologically minded organization scholar and challenges perceptions of what classic sociological theory is. By showing the usefulness of Tarde and Simmel's work on fashions, otherness, identity, and the power of innovation for her own research, the author calls for a type of organizational scholarship that is mindful of the social forces behind collective action. For what is organizing if not "the knotting together of people, things, actions?"

In another attempt to comprehend the boundaries of the organizational phenomenon, Schirmer (2024, this volume) proposes a multilevel analysis of organizations in their societal environments borrowing on Luhmann's systems theory. Arguing that organizations are the place where social systems meet agency,

Schirmer defines organization as a bounded unit with clear membership rules and (hierarchical) decision-making structure. As organizations are in more than one social system at any given time, they actively manage societal tensions, thereby producing, reproducing, and innovating society at large. Schirmer delineates a research agenda that bridges with current debates on institutional complexity. By calling attention to the emotional and affective interactional dynamics within organizations, the author also points to future avenues of investigation that link all four papers of this concluding section.

REFERENCES

Abrutyn, S., & Turner, J. H. (2011). The old institutionalism meets the new institutionalism. *Sociological Perspectives, 54*(3), 283–306.

Adler, P. S., du Gay, P., Morgan, G., & Reed, M. (2014). Introduction: Sociology, social theory, and organization studies, continuing entanglements. In P. S. Adler, P. du Gay, G. Morgan, & M. Reed (Eds.), *The Oxford handbook of sociology, social theory, and organization studies: Contemporary currents* (pp. 1–8). Oxford University Press.

Ahrens, G. (2015). The partial organization of intimate relations. *Le Libellio d' AEGIS, 11*, 7–19.

Alexander, J. C. (Ed.). (1992). *The micro-macro link*. University of California Press.

Americo, B. L., Clegg, S., & Carniel, F. (2024). Narrating the disjunctions produced by the sociological concept of emotional reflexivity in organization studies. In S. Clegg, M. Grothe-Hammer, & K. Serrano Velarde (Eds.), *Sociological thinking in contemporary organizational scholarship* (Research in the Sociology of Organizations, Vol. 90, pp. 229–251). Emerald Publishing.

Amis, J., Mair, J., & Munir, K. (2020). The organizational reproduction of inequality. *Academy of Management Annals, 14*(1), 195–230.

Apelt, M., Besio, C., Corsi, G., von Groddeck, V., Grothe-Hammer, M., & Tacke, V. (2017). Resurrecting organization without renouncing society: A response to Ahrne, Brunsson and Seidl. *European Management Journal, 35*(1), 8–14.

Arnold, N., & Foureault, F. (2024). Status in socio-environmental fields: Relationships, evaluations, and otherhood. In S. Clegg, M. Grothe-Hammer, & K. Serrano Velarde (Eds.), *Sociological thinking in contemporary organizational scholarship* (Research in the Sociology of Organizations, Vol. 90, pp. 111–139). Emerald Publishing.

Augier, M., March, J. G., & Sullivan, B. N. (2005). Notes on the evolution of a research community: Organization studies in Anglophone North America, 1945–2000. *Organization Science, 16*(1), 85–95.

Barley, S. (2010). Building an institutional field to corral a government: A case to set an agenda for organization studies. *Organization Studies, 31*(6), 777–805.

Bauman, Z. (2013). *Liquid modernity*. John Wiley & Sons.

Benzecry, C. E., Krause, M., & Reed, I. A. (Eds.). (2017). *Social theory now*. University of Chicago Press.

Besio, C., du Gay, P., & Serrano Velarde, K. (2020). Disappearing organization? Reshaping the sociology of organizations. *Current Sociology, 68*(4), 411–418.

Bort, S., & Schiller-Merkens, S. (2011). Reducing uncertainty in scholarly publishing: Concepts in the field of organization studies, 1960–2008. *Schmalenbach Business Review, 63*, 337–360.

Bourdieu, P. (1986). The forms of capital. In J. G. Richardson (Ed.), *Handbook of theory and research for the sociology of education* (pp. 241–258). Greenwood Press.

Bromley, P., & Meyer, J. W. (2015). *Hyper-organization: Global organizational expansion*. Oxford University Press.

Cai, Y., & Mountford, N. (2022). Institutional logics analysis in higher education research. *Studies in Higher Education, 47*(8), 1627–1651.

Clegg, S. R. (1990). *Modern organizations: Organization studies in the postmodern world*. Sage.

Clegg, S. R. (2002). 'Lives in the balance': A comment on Hinings and Greenwood's 'disconnects and consequences in organization theory?' *Administrative Science Quarterly, 47*(3), 428–441.

Clegg, S. R., & Cuhna, M. P. E. (2019). *Management, organizations and contemporary social theory*. Routledge.

Clemens, E. (2006). The constitution of citizens: Political theories of nonprofit organizations. In W. Powell & R. Steinberg (Eds.), *The nonprofit sector* (pp. 207–220). Yale University Press.

Croidieu, G., & Powell, W. W. (2024). Organizations as carriers of status and class dynamics: A historical ethnography of the emergence of Bordeaux's cork aristocracy. In S. Clegg, M. Grothe-Hammer, & K. Serrano Velarde (Eds.), *Sociological thinking in contemporary organizational scholarship* (Research in the Sociology of Organizations, Vol. 90, pp. 141–174). Emerald Publishing.

Czarniawska, B. (2024). Why organization sociologists should refer to Tarde and Simmel more often. In S. Clegg, M. Grothe-Hammer, & K. Serrano Velarde (Eds.), *Sociological thinking in contemporary organizational scholarship* (Research in the Sociology of Organizations, Vol. 90, pp. 273–285). Emerald Publishing.

Davis, G. F. (2015). Celebrating organization theory: The after-party. *Journal of Management Studies, 52*(2), 309–319.

du Gay, P. (2020). Disappearing 'formal organization': How organization studies dissolved its 'core object', and what follows from this. *Current Sociology, 68*(4), 459–479.

Friedland, R. (2014). Divine institution: Max Weber's value spheres and institutional theory. *Research in the Sociology of Organizations, 41*, 217–258.

Friedland, R., & Alford, R. (1991). Bringing society back. In W. Powell & P. DiMaggio (Eds.), *The new institutionalism in organizational analysis* (pp. 232–263). CUP.

Go, J. (2017). Postcolonial thought and social theory. In C. E. Benzecry, M. Krause, & I. A. Reed (Eds.), *Social theory now* (pp. 130–162). University of Chicago Press.

Grothe-Hammer, M., & Jungmann, R. (2023). A platform for debating the role of organization in, for, and throughout society. *Journal of Organizational Sociology, 1*(1), 1–11.

Grothe-Hammer, M., & Kohl, S. (2020). The decline of organizational sociology? An empirical analysis of research trends in leading journals across half a century. *Current Sociology, 68*(4), 419–442.

Gümüsay, A. A., Claus, L., & Amis, J. (2020). Engaging with grand challenges: An institutional logics perspective. *Organization Theory, 1*(3), 2631787720960487.

Hambrick, D. C. (2007). The field of management's devotion to theory: Too much of a good thing? *Academy of Management Journal, 50*(6), 1346–1352.

Hinings, C., & Greenwood, R. (2002). Disconnects and consequences in organization theory. *Administrative Science Quarterly, 47*(3), 411–421.

Holmes, M. (2010). The emotionalization of reflexivity. *Sociology, 44*(1), 139–154.

Hwang, H., & Powell, W. W. (2009). The rationalization of charity: The influences of professionalism in the nonprofit sector. *Administrative Science Quarterly, 54*(2), 268–298.

King, B. (2017). The relevance of organizational sociology. *Contemporary Sociology, 46*(2), 131–137.

King, B. G. (2024). Revitalizing organizational theory through a problem-oriented sociology. In S. Clegg, M. Grothe-Hammer, & K. Serrano Velarde (Eds.), *Sociological thinking in contemporary organizational scholarship* (Research in the Sociology of Organizations, Vol. 90, pp. 17–54). Emerald Publishing.

Knudsen, J. P. (2018). Towards a new spatial perspective – Norwegian politics at the crossroads. *Norsk Geografisk Tidsskrift-Norwegian Journal of Geography, 72*(2), 67–81.

Krause, M. (2022). *Model cases: On canonical research objects and sites. Chicago scholarship online.* The University of Chicago Press.

Langley, A. (2021). What is 'this' a case of? Generative theorizing for disruptive times. *Journal of Management Inquiry, 30*(3), 251–258.

Laryea, K., & Brandtner, C. (2024). Organizations as drivers of social and systemic integration: Contradiction and reconciliation through loose demographic coupling and community anchoring. In S. Clegg, M. Grothe-Hammer, & K. Serrano Velarde (Eds.), *Sociological thinking in contemporary organizational scholarship* (Research in the Sociology of Organizations, Vol. 90, pp. 175–200). Emerald Publishing.

Lopdrup-Hjorth, T., & du Gay, P. (2024). Facing up to the present? Cultivating Political judgement and a sense of reality in contemporary organizational life. In S. Clegg, M. Grothe-Hammer, & K. Serrano Velarde (Eds.), *Sociological thinking in contemporary organizational scholarship* (Research in the Sociology of Organizations, Vol. 90, pp. 85–108). Emerald Publishing.

Lounsbury, M., Steele, C. W., Wang, M. S., & Toubiana, M. (2021). New directions in the study of institutional logics: From tools to phenomena. *Annual Review of Sociology, 47*, 261–280.

Luhmann, N. (1977). Differentiation of society. *Canadian Journal of Sociology/Cahiers canadiens de sociologie, 2*(1), 29–53.

Luhmann, N. (1994). 'What is the case?' and 'What lies behind It?' The two sociologies and the theory of society. *Sociological Theory, 12*(2), 126–139.

Marx, K. (1843/1978). For a ruthless criticism of everything existing. In R. Tucker (Ed.), *The Marx-Engels reader* (pp. 12–25). Norton.

Merton, R. K. (1949). *Social theory and social structure: Toward the codification of theory and research.* Free Press.

Mills, C. W. (1959). *The sociological imagination.* Oxford University Press.

Mountford, N., & Cai, Y. (2023). Towards a flatter ontology of institutional logics: How logics relate in situations of institutional complexity. *International Journal of Management Reviews, 25*(2), 363–383.

Padgett, J. F., & Powell, W. W. (2012). *The emergence of organizations and markets.* Princeton University Press.

Perrow, C. (1991). A society of organizations. *Theory & Society, 20*, 725–762.

Piggott, L. V., Hovden, J., & Knoppers, A. (2024). Why organization studies should care more about gender exclusion and inclusion in sport organizations. In S. Clegg, M. Grothe-Hammer, & K. Serrano Velarde (Eds.), *Sociological thinking in contemporary organizational scholarship* (Research in the Sociology of Organizations, Vol. 90, pp. 201–226). Emerald Publishing.

Powell, W., & Brandtner, C. (2016). Organizations as sites and drivers of social action. In S. Abrutyn (Ed.), *Handbook of contemporary sociological theory* (pp. 269–291). Springer.

Powell, W. W., & DiMaggio, P. J. (2023). The iron cage redux: Looking back and forward. *Organization Theory, 4*(4), 26317877231221550.

Ringel, L. (2024). Organizational sociology and organization studies: Past, present, and future. In S. Clegg, M. Grothe-Hammer, & K. Serrano Velarde (Eds.), *Sociological thinking in contemporary organizational scholarship* (Research in the Sociology of Organizations, Vol. 90, pp. 55–83). Emerald Publishing.

Ringel, L., Hiller, P., & Zietsma, C. (2018). Toward permeable boundaries of organizations? In L. Ringel, P. Hiller, & C. Zietsma (Eds.), *Toward permeable boundaries of organizations?* (Research in the Sociology of Organizations, Vol. 57, pp. 3–28). Emerald Publishing.

Sales, A., Roth, S., Grothe-Hammer, M., & Azambuja, R. (2022). From play to pay: A multifunctional approach to the role of culture in post-merger integration. *Management Decision, 60*(7), 1922–1946.

Savage, M. (2000). *Class analysis and social transformation. Sociology and social change.* Open University Press.

Schirmer, W. (2024). Organization systems and their social environments: The role of functionally differentiated society and face-to-face interaction rituals. In S. Clegg, M. Grothe-Hammer, & K. Serrano Velarde (Eds.), *Sociological thinking in contemporary organizational scholarship* (Research in the Sociology of Organizations, Vol. 90, pp. 287–308). Emerald Publishing.

Scott, A. (2020). Prodigal offspring: Organizational sociology and organization studies. *Current Sociology, 68*(4), 443–458.

Scott, W. R. (2004). Reflections on a half-century of organizational sociology. *Annual Review of Sociology, 30*, 1–21.

Seidl, D., & Whittington, R. (2014). Enlarging the strategy-as-practice research agenda: Towards taller and flatter ontologies. *Organization Studies, 35*(10), 1407–1421.

Sundberg, M. (2024). The promise of total institutions in the sociology of organizations: Implications of regimental and monastic obedience for underlife. In S. Clegg, M. Grothe-Hammer, & K. Serrano Velarde (Eds.), *Sociological thinking in contemporary organizational scholarship* (Research in the Sociology of Organizations, Vol. 90, pp. 253–269). Emerald Publishing.

Sydow, J., & Windeler, A. (2020). Temporary organizing and permanent contexts. *Current Sociology, 68*(4), 480–498.

Taylor, C. (2004). *Modern social imaginaries, public planet books.* Duke University Press.

Tomaskovic-Devey, D., & Avent-Holt, D. R. (2019). *Relational inequalities. An organizational approach.* Oxford University Press.

Tourish, D. (2020). The triumph of nonsense in management studies. *Academy of Management Learning & Education, 19*(1), 99–109.

Vik, J., Fuglestad, E. M., & Øversveen, E. (2022). Centre–periphery conflicts and alienation in a resource-based economy. *Norsk Geografisk Tidsskrift-Norwegian Journal of Geography, 76*(4), 197–208.

Weber, M. (1978). *Economy and society: An outline of interpretive sociology*. University of California Press.

Wittgenstein, l. (1953). *Philosophical investigations*. Blackwell.

PART 1

THE PLACE OF SOCIOLOGY IN ORGANIZATIONAL SCHOLARSHIP

REVITALIZING ORGANIZATIONAL THEORY THROUGH A PROBLEM-ORIENTED SOCIOLOGY

Brayden G King

Northwestern University, USA

ABSTRACT

Organizations remain a vital sociological topic, but organizational sociology, as a subfield, has evolved significantly since its inception. In this paper, I argue that organization sociology is becoming increasingly disconnected from organizational theory, as currently conceived. The focus of sociological research on organizations has become more empirically grounded in the study of social problems and how organizations contribute to them. Sociologists continue to see organizations as important actors in society that play a role in shaping social order and as contexts in which social processes play out. I propose two main sociological approaches for organizational research, which I describe as "organizations within society" and "society within organizations." The first approach examines the role of organizations as building blocks of social structure and as social actors in their own right. The second approach treats organizations as platforms and locations of social interactions and the building of community. These approaches are somewhat disconnected from the sort of grand theorizing that characterizes much of organizational theory. I argue that the problem-oriented sociology of these two approaches offers a vital way for organizational scholars to expand and theoretically revitalize the field.

Keywords: Organizational sociology; social problems; bureaucracy; social actor; inequality; community

Sociological Thinking in Contemporary Organizational Scholarship
Research in the Sociology of Organizations, Volume 90, 19–54
ISSN: 0733-558X/doi:10.1108/S0733-558X20240000090002

Laments of the decline of organizational sociology have become common in recent years (Gorman, 2014; King, 2017; Scott, 2004). One underlying reason for the supposed demise of organizational sociology is that the subfield has become less theoretically vibrant and less central to the discipline and, consequently, less important to sociology departments themselves (Gorman, 2014). But I contend that our view of organizational sociology's place in the discipline is slanted by looking back nostalgically to an era when the subfield was, arguably, at its peak of theoretical creativity. In the 1970s and 1980s, sociology was fertile ground for offering new theories of organizations, which went on to seed the maturing field of organizational theory. Institutional theory (e.g., Meyer & Rowan, 1977), organizational ecology (Hannan & Freeman, 1977), resource dependence (Pfeffer & Salancik, 1978), and network theory (Burt, 1980) all blossomed during this period. The careers of these theories' progenitors thrived as well, leading some of them (and their students) to emigrate to business schools. Increasingly, scholars who adopted these perspectives found their homes in business schools, and not surprisingly, many of the scholars who used the theories in their own empirical work imbued those theories with a more managerialist orientation. Rather than simply explain how organizations come to be and interact with other elements of society, organizational theories were now meant to also explain how to make organizations better or how to make them better serve the purposes of managers.[1] Sociologists became less interested in these theories as they mutated.

But that is just one narrative of what happened to the subfield of organizational sociology. Another way to read the history of organizational sociology is one of success. Organizational sociologists developed uniquely sociological views of organizations, which departed in important ways from economics-oriented approaches; those perspectives proved useful for management scholars, and they incorporated key insights into their own research about how organizations behave (or ought to behave). Management scholars borrowed extensively from sociology, and the new field of organizational theory thrived as a result (Lounsbury & Beckman, 2015; Whetten et al., 2009). Organizational sociology succeeded precisely because it had practical and applied implications! But a consequence of this success was that organizational theory began to develop a life of its own, distinct from the discipline of sociology.

Another consequence of vibrancy of organizational theory was a distancing from the founding discipline of sociology (and we can include anthropology and psychology among the disaffected disciplines). Organizational theory (or organization studies) became its own settled field, as Leopold Ringel (2024) argues in this volume. Even though organizational theory will always be profoundly influenced by the early importation of sociological theories, it has since evolved into a distinctive field and grown distant from the discipline of sociology, as the ongoing theoretical concerns of sociologists seem to differ from what organizational theorists care about. This is the story we often hear, at least.

But I will argue that sociologists have not moved on from organizational sociology at all or at least not from "a sociology of organizations" (Lammers, 1981). Organizations continue to be a concern of much theoretical and empirical sociology. Due to their prominent role in most societal dynamics, sociologists need to theorize what organizations do, how they influence societal dynamics, and how they serve as social contexts for groups and individual behavior. The kinds of organizational phenomena that sociologists analyze range from the sources of economic and social inequality to the drivers of political participation. And of course, the forms of organizations that sociologists study are equally varied, including voluntary associations, schools, and the business establishments that management scholars typically study. Moreover, sociologists are increasingly interested in organizations because they see them as contributors to social problems (Hilgartner & Bosk, 1988), such as inequality or climate change, as well as offering the tools for interventions that can help alleviate those problems.

Organizations matter because they are fundamental building blocks of society. Perrow's (1991) and Coleman's (1982) basic observation that organizations facilitate much of social life still remains true. We rely on organizations to accomplish our collective endeavors, not to mention our personal ones. Organizations are as relevant as ever. The question that organizational scholars should ask is not, is organizational sociology in decline? But rather, they should ask, what does organizational sociology look like today? What is its relationship to the broader field of sociology?

In this paper, I offer a reading of contemporary organizational sociology based, somewhat selectively, on research published in the traditionally most important journals in US-based sociology and one European journal: *American Sociological Review* (*ASR*), *American Journal of Sociology* (*AJS*), and *European Sociological Review* (*ESR*). Searching the keywords, titles, and abstracts of articles for mentions of "organization" and "organizational," I identify 118 articles published about organizations in these top sociology journals during a 10-year time span from 2012 to 2021. By selecting exclusively only those articles published in elite sociology journals, the group of articles is an idiosyncratic subset but one that, I believe, accurately reflects how organizations are represented in mainstream sociology. When organizational theorists say that sociologists no longer care about organizations, they usually say this in reflection of journals like *ASR, AJS*, and *ESR*. Although there is some engagement with organizational theory as typically conceived, most of these articles are not written with organizational theorists as their primary audience. But they are, undoubtedly, organizational in their focus. The articles touch on a variety of sociological themes, ranging from culture to employment discrimination.

Based on my reading of these articles, I identify two approaches to organizational sociology that currently thrive in the discipline: "organizations within society" and "society within organizations." The first approach examines the role of organizations as building blocks of social structure and as social actors in their own right. The second approach treats organizations as contexts of social interactions and the building of community. Both approaches allow for the study of organizations as part of society and, importantly, as both drivers of and solutions for the pressing social problems of society.

A common theme within these articles is understanding the role of organizations in creating and magnifying important social problems. This theme, I will argue, is rooted in a long sociological tradition in understanding the causes and implications of social problems and is now the orienting perspective within main-stream sociology (e.g., Schneider, 1985). Rather than starting from a common theoretical orientation – as is true with economics' adherence to rational choice – or a methodological approach – as is true of psychology's embrace of experimental positivism – what sets sociology apart is its interest in explaining and potentially offering solutions to social problems, such as inequality. Sociologists often find that organizations take center stage in their explanations for these social problems. The approach that sociologists take to study organizations depends on whether they cast the organization as a unit within society or as a social structure or platform that is worth interrogating on its own.

Articles that capture the *organizations within society* approach cast organizations as basic building blocks of social structure. Some organizations, such as corporations or grassroots movements organizations, are created to accomplish some social purpose, like generating wealth for owners or pursuing a social jus-tice cause. Organizations, whether they intend to or not, also create, reproduce, and amplify basic inequalities within society, as when a business organization enables wealth generation for an elite few. Another type of article in this genre of organizational sociology focuses on the organization as a social actor. That is, it conceives of the organization as pursuing some purpose and emphasizes the agentic qualities of the organization. Research in political sociology, for example, often analyzes organizations as powerful entities that put their goals and interests above those of individuals in mass society. Analyses of this type depict organiza-tions as bodies of concentrated resources that are able to leverage institutional mechanisms of control to wield their power. Other studies in this vein highlight the extent to which organizations serve as gateways to larger institutions or as the purveyors of public goods, as was the case of Lipsky's (2010) "street-level bureaucracy."

Articles that capture a *society within organizations* approach usually analyze organizations as platforms and spaces that host the social dynamics that interest the authors. This kind of research recognizes that many of society's meaningful interactions, such as the building of community, take place within the boundaries of formal organizations. Often, these studies focus on the workplace. Scholarship on occupations, professions, and work focuses on organizations because that is where people do their jobs. In this sense, organizations are primary sites of other fundamental social processes that sociologists care about, including processes of conflict, cooperation, and creativity. But this genre of sociology also emphasizes organizations as locations where elite reproduction takes place. Much of this research examines internal stratification of resources among competing groups and individuals.

What is our understanding of organizational sociology if we consider articles from this sample as the foundation of the subfield? I will argue in this paper that it gives us a more empirically grounded view of organizational sociology that is rooted in an effort to understand society itself and the problems within that soci-ety. But empirically grounded research is not necessarily theoretically vacuous. In fact, this type of research, which begins with an exploration of an empirical problem or puzzle, creates the seeds for new theoretical insights. Beginning with an empirical puzzle was the starting place for most of the theoretically fruitful papers that shaped the period of high creativity in organizational sociology in the 1970s and 1980s. Scholars like John Meyer and Brian Rowan (1977) did not begin writing about "rationalized myths" in an effort to revolutionize organizational sociology and found a new theoretical literature on institutions. Rather, their analysis was an effort to understand the empirical puzzle of why schools adopted the language of rationalization without any real behavioral commitment to the formal structures left in its wake. They were trying to understand a basic social problem that persisted in educational organizations. This insight led to a theoretical breakthrough that not only changed the way we conceive of Weberian bureaucracy and rationalization processes but also reoriented our study of institutions in organizations (Scott, 1992).

As mentioned before, the purpose of much contemporary organizational sociology is to shed light on basic social problems. This type of organizational research, while fundamental to sociology, is somewhat different from the way that organizational theorists have come to approach research, in which the question of "theoretical contribution" reigns supreme and motivates the impetus for the study. Rather than seek theoretical insights from developing a better explanation of a social problem or empirical puzzle, organizational theorists usually begin by finding a theoretical puzzle and trying to find an ideal organizational setting in which to resolve that puzzle (or at least that is the way papers are written). This difference in framing research creates distance between the body of contemporary organizational sociology and organizational theory, at the current moment.

In this paper, I discuss the implications of taking organizational sociology on its own terms. I argue that the potential for developing novel theoretical insights is still there, but creating a fruitful dialogue between the two fields may require loosening our expectations about what constitutes a theoretical contribution and focusing more on the problem-oriented nature of empirical research.

ORGANIZATIONAL RESEARCH IN SOCIOLOGY

In pursuing a grounded approach to understanding the contemporary state of organizational sociology, I selected all articles in the *ASR* that included "organization" or "organizational" as a keyword or word in the title of the paper. The same search in the *ESR* yielded zero articles, and the *AJS* does not include a keyword search. To create comparable results for these journals, I expanded the search to include all articles with the word "organization" in the abstract. I eliminated articles that used the term "organization" to describe a structure other than a formal organization, as for example, when an article describes the "social organization" of a neighborhood. *AJS* yielded the greatest number of articles with 52, *ASR* had 47, and *ESR* had 18. These represent roughly 15% of all articles published in *AJS*, 10% of articles in *ASR*, and 3% of articles in *ESR*.

I coded key features of each article that came up in the search. *Organizational form* refers to the type of organization(s) analyzed in the research. Forms can be as abstract as a general kind of organization, as is the case with Ray's (2019) theory of "racialized organizations," or quite specific, as in the of Fligstein et al.'s (2017) research on the Federal Reserve Bank. The most typical form was "employer." In this case, the kind of organizational form likely varied, as it was often self-reported by an individual survey participant simply as the organization that employed them.

Theory refers to the primary theoretical orientation(s) that the authors use to motivate their analysis. In some cases, it was stated quite clearly, but in many cases, especially in work that is more problem oriented, the theoretical orientation refers to a broad literature on the topic that has built-in assumptions about the behavior or social dynamic in question. *Method* refers to the type of analysis applied in the study. In most cases, I simply note the most prominent method used, but when multiple methods were applied equally, I listed both methods.

Outcome of interest is the object of the study design. In quantitative studies, outcome refers to the dependent variable of the analysis, but in many qualitative studies, the outcome is a process or dynamic the authors are seeking to shed light on. *Unit* refers to the unit of analysis that the authors are interested in examining. In quantitative studies, the unit of analysis is relatively straightforward, but in qualitative studies, it is not always clear. I chose the unit of analysis that seemed most relevant to the research question posed by the authors.

Finally, I coded each article by the *organizational approach* evident in the paper. The approach is a categorization of the author's interest in organizations. To code these approaches, I first created two subcodes: level of theorizing and organizations' role in the theorizing. For the level of theorizing, I focused on the primary mechanisms used by the authors to generate an explanation for their outcome of interest. The second subcode, organizations' role, was more specifically about where the organization resided in the authors' chain of theorizing.

If the authors are interested in organizations as structures or actors that they want to explain or as structures or actors that influence broader society in some way, I categorize their approach as "organizations within society." In these studies, the main theoretical lens explains how organizations shape the broader society in which they are a part or how they operate and function as social units. Studies of this type are generally quite "macro" in their flavor. Individuals may be present in the study, but organizations operate as actors in their own right alongside individuals. For example, consider the case of an organization seeking to shape the mindset of policymakers and thereby shape legislation (Best, 2012). The focus of studies like this is about the existence and impact of organizations on broader societal, and more specifically legislative, outcomes; hence, I refer to this approach as organizations within society.

If the authors are interested in organizations as contexts in which societal dynamics play out, I categorize their approach as "society within organizations." Sociologists often study organizations simply because this is the place where society happens. Individuals rely on organizations for forming a community, getting jobs and income, and doing a variety of other things that require collective endeavors. For many of these studies, the main interest of the authors is not the organizations themselves, but rather the outcomes that take place within organizations. For instance, if a scholar is interested in explaining why some occupations have a greater gender pay gap than others, they are likely to turn to organizations as a location for their study (e.g., van Hek & van der Lippe, 2019). Many of these studies include organizational practices, rules, or other dynamics as key variables in their analysis, but not all do. These studies tend to be more "micro" in that they are interested in outcomes experienced at the individual level of analysis. For example, Qvist et al. (2018) focus on voluntary organizations as a setting to understand better why certain individuals dedicate more hours to volunteering than others.

Tables 1 and 2 display the coded variables for each article found in my search. Table 1 includes all articles that use an "organizations within society" approach, and Table 2 includes all articles using the "society within organizations" approach. There are 32 articles using an "organizations within society" approach and 51 articles using a "society within organizations" approach.

One of the most notable aspects of the papers represented here is the sheer diversity of theoretical perspectives represented. Whereas many organizational scholars associate sociology with one of the core theories exported from sociology to organizational research, such as institutional theory or organizational ecology, these theories are not well represented in the mix of articles. Institutional theory only appears as a primary theoretical orientation in five articles, with an additional three articles framed around diffusion theory (a strong corollary of institutional theory). Organizational ecology or resource partitioning theory is only a primary orientation in four articles, with an additional article motivated by "social ecology" (which is a Chicago school of sociology theory about local ecologies of relationships between organizations and individuals). And interestingly, two of the articles using an ecological framework are derived from the network-based approach to ecology as originated by Miller McPherson and associated with the concept of Blau Space (Brashears et al., 2017; Shi et al., 2017). This version of ecology is far less common in studies published in organizational or management journals.

The most common theory represented in the studies is social movement theory, which is a primary motivating theory for 11 articles. The presence of so many social movement-related papers is indicative of the strong interest that sociologists have in bottom-up theories of social change, often represented in the form of collective action taken by activists. Much of this research is organizational inasmuch as one of the core theories – resource mobilization theory – is about how organizations provide infrastructure and other resources for the emergence and mobilization of movements. Moreover, in recent years, there has been a surge of research that uses insights from social movement theory to explain corporate and market outcomes (e.g., Bartley & Child, 2014; McDonnell et al., 2015). Organizations are often both the targets of movement mobilization and inputs for anti-corporate campaigns.

The broad mix of remaining theoretical orientations reflects, in my view, the social problem orientation. Rather than seeking to contribute to a particular theoretical perspective, this paper sets out to better understand a problem. In what follows, I will discuss the theoretical ambiguity of organizational sociology and what it says about the discipline and its relationship to organizational theory.

Table 1. Articles Using an "Organizations Within Society" Approach.

Author(s)	Year	Title	Published	Organization Form	Theory	Method	Outcome of Interest	Unit
S. Y. P. Choi; R. David	2012	Lustration systems and trust: evidence from survey experiments in the Czech Republic, Hungary, and Poland	AJS	Government agencies	Lustration systems	Survey research	Trust in government	Citizens
D. J. Wang; S. A. Soule	2012	Social movement organizational collaboration: networks of learning and the diffusion of protest tactics, 1960–1995	AJS	Social movement organization	Diffusion theory	Network analysis; protest data	Tactical diffusion between organizational dyads	Dyad
H. R. Greve; H. Rao	2012	Echoes of the past: organizational foundings as sources of an institutional legacy of mutualism	AJS	Nonprofit organizations; cooperatives	Imprinting theory; institutional theory	Panel data; longitudinal analysis	Founding of cooperative stores	Norwegian communities
I. B. Vasi; B. G. King	2012	Social movements, risk perceptions, and economic outcomes: the effect of primary and secondary stakeholder activism on firms' perceived environmental risk and financial performance	ASR	Public corporations	Social movement theory; sociology of risk	Longitudinal analysis	Risk perceptions	Company/year
R. K. Best	2012	Disease politics and medical research funding: three ways advocacy shapes policy	ASR	Advocacy organizations	Political agenda setting	Longitudinal analysis	Funding and legislative attention to diseases	Disease as treated in congress/year

Authors	Year	Journal	Title	Organization type	Theory	Method	Variable	Unit of analysis
J. Alcacer; P. Ingram	2013	AJS	Spanning the institutional abyss: the intergovernmental network and the governance of foreign direct investment	Intergovernmental organizations	Relational theory	Gravity models	Foreign direct investment flows	Country network dyads
A. Goldstein; H. A. Haveman	2013	ASR	Pulpit and press: denominational dynamics and the growth of religious magazines in Antebellum America	Religious organizations (as represented by religious magazines)	Social movement theory; economic theories of religion	Longitudinal analysis	Magazine foundings	Denomination/ year
E. d. Graauw; S. Gleeson; I. Bloemraad	2013	AJS	Funding immigrant organizations: suburban free riding and local civic presence	Immigrant service organizations	Social construction theory; civil society	Interviews	Source of funding for organization; how organizations procured funding	Immigrant organization
G. Negro; F. Perretti; G. R. Carroll	2013	AJS	Challenger groups, commercial organizations, and policy enactment: local lesbian/ gay rights ordinances in the United States from 1972 to 2008	Commercial organizations linked to gay/lesbian	Social movement theory; organizational ecology	Longitudinal; hazard models	Policy passage of anti-discriminatory policy	Municipality
M. T. Heaney; F. Rojas	2014	AJS	Hybrid activism: social movement mobilization in a multimovement environment	Social movement organizations	Social movement theory; organizational identity	Survey research	Movement organization membership	Individual activist

(Continued)

Table 1. (*Continued*)

Author(s)	Year	Title	Published	Organization Form	Theory	Method	Outcome of Interest	Unit
D. Riley; J. J. Fernández	2014	Beyond strong and weak: rethinking postdictatorship civil societies	*AJS*	Political parties; cooperative organizations	Civil society	Archival research	Organizational membership	Parties and organizations
J. P. Steil; I. B. Vasi	2014	The new immigration contestation: social movements and local immigration policy making in the United States, 2000–2011	*AJS*	Social movement organizations	Social movement theory	Archival research	Adoption of pro-immigrant ordinances	Local municipality
D. Strang; R. J. David; S. Akhlaghpour	2014	Coevolution in management fashion: an agent-based model of consultant-driven innovation	*AJS*	Firms	Management fads; diffusion	Computational experiments; agent-based modeling	Adoption of management fads	Firms
A. J. Sharkey	2014	Categories and organizational status: the role of industry status in the response to organizational deviance	*AJS*	US firms	Status theory; social evaluation	Financial analysis	Investor reaction to earnings restatements (car)	Firms at time of earnings restatements
A. Wimmer	2014	Nation building. a long-term perspective and global analysis	*ESR*	Voluntary and civic organizations	Theory of state formation	Longitudinal analysis	Number of voluntary associations	Nation-state
G. C. Gray; S. S. Silbey	2014	Governing inside the organization: interpreting regulation and compliance	*AJS*	Business organizations	Institutional theory; regulatory compliance theory	Ethnography	Perceptions of regulatory control and compliance	Individual managers; organizational perspective

Author(s)	Year	Title	Journal	Actor	Theory	Method	Outcome	Historical process
G. C. Mora	2014	Cross-field effects and ethnic classification: the institutionalization of Hispanic panethnicity, 1965 to 1990	ASR	State agencies; Hispanic civic organizations	Field theory; social construction of categories	Archival and interviews	Emergence of new ethnic category	
G. Negro; F. Visentin; A. Swaminathan	2014	Resource partitioning and the organizational dynamics of "fringe banking"	ASR	Payday lenders	Resource partitioning theory	Longitudinal analysis	Entry and exit rates of payday lenders	Wisconsin county
T. Bartley; C. Child	2014	Shaming the corporation: the social production of targets and the anti-sweatshop movement	ASR	Multinational firms	Social movement theory; power analysis	Longitudinal analysis	Firms become target of an anti-sweatshop campaign	Firm/year
M.-H. McDonnell; B. G. King; S. A. Soule	2015	A dynamic process model of private politics: activist targeting and corporate receptivity to social challenges	ASR	Firms	Social movement theory	Longitudinal analysis	Receptivity to activists	Firm/year
J. J. Savelsberg; H. N. Brehm	2015	Representing human rights violations in Darfur: global justice, national distinctions	AJS	Media companies	Media and ideological bias	Archival research; content analysis	Reporting of violent crimes	Media frames
M. Smångs	2016	Doing violence, making race: southern lynching and white racial group formation	AJS	Southern democratic party	Collective identity; resource mobilization	Event history analysis	Public lynchings	County
A. De Wit; R. Bekkers; M. Broese van Groenou	2016	Heterogeneity in crowding-out: when are charitable donations responsive to government support?	ESR	Nonprofit organizations	Welfare state regime theory	Survey research	Donations to nonprofit	Individuals

(Continued)

Table 1. (Continued)

Author(s)	Year	Title	Published	Organization Form	Theory	Method	Outcome of Interest	Unit
B. Eidlin	2016	Why is there no labor party in the United States? Political articulation and the Canadian comparison, 1932 to 1948	ASR	Political parties	None	Comparative historical analysis	Formation and endurance of labor party	Country
H. R. Greve; J.-Y. Kim; D. Teh	2016	Ripples of fear: the diffusion of a bank panic	ASR	Banks	Diffusion theory	Longitudinal analysis	Bank experiencing a run	Bank
J. R. Levine	2016	The privatization of political representation: community-based organizations as nonelected neighborhood representatives	ASR	Nonprofit community organizations	Political sociology	Ethnography	Political role of community organizations	Community organizations
N. Fligstein; A. F. Roehrkasse	2016	The causes of fraud in the financial crisis of 2007 to 2009: evidence from the mortgage-backed securities industry	ASR	Mortgage securities issuers	Theories of white collar crime	Longitudinal analysis	Settlements over alleged fraud	Firm
S. Liu; H. Wu	2016	The ecology of organizational growth: Chinese law firms in the age of globalization	AJS	Chinese law firms	Social ecology	Longitudinal	Organizational growth	Law firm
A. D. Çakmaklı; C. Boone; A. v. Witteloostuijn	2017	When does globalization lead to local adaptation? the emergence of hybrid Islamic schools in Turkey, 1985–2007	AJS	Turkish high school organizations	Globalization theory	Longitudinal analysis	Founding rate of hybrid organizations	School district

Authors	Year	Journal	Title	Subject	Theory	Method	Topic	Unit of analysis
J. A. Kitts; A. Lomi; D. Mascia; F. Pallotti; E. Quintane	2017	AJS	Investigating the temporal dynamics of interorganizational exchange: patient transfers among Italian hospitals	Italian hospitals	Exchange theory; network analysis	Network analysis	Patient transfers between hospitals	Hospital dyads
J. Murray	2017	AJS	Interlock globally, act domestically: corporate political unity in the 21st century	G500 firms	Elite and class theory	Longitudinal analysis; network analysis	Common political donations	Firm dyads
K. Tsutsui	2017	AJS	Human rights and minority activism in Japan: transformation of movement actorhood and local-global feedback loop	Social movement organizations	World polity theory; organizational institutionalism	Interviews	Movement dynamics	Three Japan-based movement organizations
C. Tuğal	2017	AJS	The uneven neoliberalization of good works: Islamic charitable fields and their impact on diffusion	Islamic charitable organizations	Political economy; neoliberal diffusion	Interviews	Transformation of charity organizations	Turkish and Egyptian charitable fields
J. Jourdan; R. Durand; P. H. Thornton	2017	AJS	The price of admission: organizational deference as strategic behavior	Market finance organizations	Category theory; symbolic interactionism	Longitudinal analysis	Deference on social capital	Firm-year
K. Pernell; J. Jung; F. Dobbin	2017	ASR	The hazards of expert control: chief risk officers and risky derivatives	Banks	Institutional theory; moral licensing	Longitudinal analysis	Adoption of risky financial derivatives	Bank-year

(Continued)

Table 1. (Continued)

Author(s)	Year	Title	Published	Organization Form	Theory	Method	Outcome of Interest	Unit
Y. Shi; F. A. Dokshin; M. Genkin; M. E. Brashears	2017	A member saved is a member earned? the recruitment-retention trade-off and organizational strategies for membership growth	ASR	Organizations (general)	Organizational ecology	Formal model/ simulation	Organizational growth	Organization
E. M. McDonnell	2017	Patchwork leviathan: how pockets of bureaucratic governance flourish within institutionally diverse developing states	ASR	State organizations in developing countries	Bureaucracy theory	Comparative historical; interviews	Coexistence of bureaucratic and non-bureaucratic features	State organization
C. Arndt	2018	White-collar unions and attitudes towards income inequality, redistribution, and state–market relations	ESR	Labor unions	Labor and industrial relations	Survey research	Attitudes about economic redistribution	Individual union members
D. Clifford	2018	Neighborhood context and enduring differences in the density of charitable organizations: reinforcing dynamics of foundation and dissolution	AJS	Charitable organizations	Organizational ecology	Longitudinal analysis	Organizational foundings and dissolution	Neighborhoods
M. A. Kadivar	2018	Mass mobilization and the durability of new democracies	ASR	Social movement organization	Social movement theory; democratization	Mixed; longitudinal and case study	Democratic breakdown	Nation-state

Author	Year	Title	Journal		Theory	Method		Unit of analysis
Y. Long	2018	The contradictory impact of transnational AIDS institutions on state repression in China, 1989–2013	AJS	Chinese health organizations	Institutional theory; social movement theory	Multi-site field research	State repressions of aids activists	Government organizations
M. Ruef; A. Grigoryeva	2018	Jim Crow, ethnic enclaves, and status attainment: occupational mobility among U.S. blacks, 1880–1940	AJS	Self-employment	Ethnic enclave theory; ecology	Archival; longitudinal analysis	Self-employment; income attainment	Census tracts
M.-H. McDonnell; B. G. King	2018	Order in the court: how firm status and reputation shape the outcomes of employment discrimination suits	ASR	Employers	Status and reputation; social evaluation theory	Cross-sectional analysis	Liability in lawsuits; punitive damages	Employment discrimination lawsuit
D. J. Wang; H. Rao; S. A. Soule	2019	Crossing categorical boundaries: a study of diversification by social movement organizations	ASR	Social movement organization	Social movement theory	Longitudinal analysis	Social movement organization diversification	Social movement organization
R. A. Benton; J. A. Cobb	2019	Eyes on the horizon? Fragmented elites and the short-term focus of the American corporation	AJS	Corporations	Elite theory; social networks	Social network analysis; longitudinal analysis	Corporate short-termism	Firm-year
J. E. Fiel; Y. Zhang	2019	With all deliberate speed: the reversal of court-ordered school desegregation, 1970–2013	AJS	School districts	Racial composition theory	Longitudinal analysis	Dismissal of desegregation orders	District-year

(*Continued*)

Table 1. (Continued)

Author(s)	Year	Title	Published	Organization Form	Theory	Method	Outcome of Interest	Unit
B. Reinsberg; A. Kentikelenis; T. Stubbs; L. King	2019	The world system and the hollowing out of state capacity: how structural adjustment programs affect bureaucratic quality in developing countries	*AJS*	State bureaucracies	Weberian bureaucracy theory; world systems	Longitudinal analysis	Bureaucratic quality	Nation-state bureaucracies
J. Go	2020	The imperial origins of American policing: militarization and imperial feedback in the early 20th century	*AJS*	Police departments	Imperialism	Comparative case analysis; archival analysis	Militarization of police	Police departments
N. P. Marwell; E. A. Marantz; D. Baldassarri	2020	The microrelations of urban governance: dynamics of patronage and partnership	*AJS*	Nonprofit organizations	Urban governance	Social network analysis; event history	Tie formation and dissolution	City council member and nonprofit dyads
C. M. Smith	2020	Exogenous shocks, the criminal elite, and increasing gender inequality in Chicago organized crime	*ASR*	Organized crime organization	Network analysis; organizational restructuring	Network analysis; case study	Changes in network and its consequences	Organizational network
J. Rözer; H. G. van de Werfhorst	2020	Three worlds of vocational education: specialized and general craftsmanship in France, Germany, and the Netherlands	*ESR*	Vocational educational programs	Occupational training	Variance decomposition	Training program education-to-work link	Training program

Author	Year	Title	Journal	Empirical setting	Theory	Method	Dependent variable	Unit of analysis
L. B. Doering; K. McNeill	2020	Elaborating on the abstract: group meaning-making in a Colombian microsavings program	ASR	Banks	Organizational theory; microsociology	Cross-sectional analysis and interviews	Financial interest	Savings group participants
T. Shiff	2021	A sociology of discordance: negotiating schemas of deservingness and codified law in U.S. asylum status determinations	AJS	Asylum agencies	Institutional theory; practice theory	Archival research; interviews	Determination of asylum	Asylum officers
A. Wimmer	2021	Domains of diffusion: how culture and institutions travel around the world and with what consequences	AJS	Organizations (in general)	Diffusion; institutional theory; globalization	Theory development	Diffusion of organizational templates	Organizations

Table 2. Articles Using a "Society within Organizations" Approach.

Author(s)	Year	Published	Organization Form	Theory	Method	Outcome of Interest	Unit
F. Varese	2012	ESR	Organized crime organizations	Social networks	Network analysis; content analysis	Organizational structure of a mafia cell	Social network
C. Turco	2012	AJS	Nonprofit organization	Institutional theory; conflict	Ethnography	Employee resistance	Employee groups
K. Karpinska; K. Henkens; J. Schippers	2013	ESR	Employers	Rational choice theory	Vignette study; surveys	Perceptions of early retirement	Managers
J. Rydgren; D. Sofi; M. Hällsten	2013	AJS	Civil society organizations	Network theory; relational analysis	Network analysis	Friendship ties	Individual networks
N. Gerstel; D. Clawson	2014	AJS	Workplaces	Class theory; gender	Survey; interviews; observations	Temporal flexibility in work	Individual employees
P. Lichterman; N. Eliasoph	2014	AJS	Housing advocacy organizations	Civil society	Ethnography	Styles of civic action	Civic projects
A. Kalev	2014	ASR	US firms	Bureaucracy theory; institutional theory	Longitudinal analysis	Minority representation in managerial jobs	Firms
A. Lara-Millán	2014	ASR	Public emergency rooms	Stigma theory; criminology	Ethnography	How er professionals decide which patients are deserving of pain medication	Er unit

Titles:
- F. Varese, 2012: The structure and the content of criminal connections: the Russian mafia in Italy
- C. Turco, 2012: Difficult decoupling: employee resistance to the commercialization of personal settings
- K. Karpinska; K. Henkens; J. Schippers, 2013: Retention of older workers: impact of managers' age norms and stereotypes
- J. Rydgren; D. Sofi; M. Hällsten, 2013: Interethnic friendship, trust, and tolerance: findings from two north Iraqi cities
- N. Gerstel; D. Clawson, 2014: Class advantage and the gender divide: flexibility on the job and at home
- P. Lichterman; N. Eliasoph, 2014: Civic action
- A. Kalev, 2014: How you downsize is who you downsize: biased formalization, accountability, and managerial diversity
- A. Lara-Millán, 2014: Public emergency room overcrowding in the era of mass imprisonment

Authors	Year	Journal	Title					
B. A. Rissing; E. J. Castilla	2014	ASR	House of green cards: statistical or preference-based inequality in the employment of foreign nationals	Department of labor; regulatory agency	Employment discrimination models	Logistic regression of certification approval	Application approval	Application from foreign-national
A. D. Reich	2014	AJS	Contradictions in the commodification of hospital care	Hospitals	Commodification and moral markets	Ethnography; interviews	Commodification of hospital care	Hospitals
B. Klandermans; J. van Stekelenburg; M.-L. Damen; D. van Troost; A. van Leeuwen	2014	ESR	Mobilization without organization: the case of unaffiliated demonstrators	Social movement organization	Social movement theory	Survey research	Protest participation	Individual activist
C. Noelke; D. Horn	2014	ESR	Social transformation and the transition from vocational education to work in Hungary: a differences-in-differences approach	Employers; schools	Comparative economy	Difference-in-difference	Individuals' unemployment	Individuals
E. L. Kelly; P. Moen; J. M. Oakes; W. Fan; C. Okechukwu; K. D. Davis; L. B. Hammer; E. E. Kossek; R. B. King; G. C. Hanson; F. Mierzwa; L. M. Casper	2014	ASR	Changing work and work-family conflict: evidence from the work, family, and health network	Employer	Employee work-life balance	Randomized field experiment	Flexible work arrangements	Individual employee

(Continued)

Table 2. (*Continued*)

Author(s)	Year	Title	Published	Organization Form	Theory	Method	Outcome of Interest	Unit
J. B. Sørensen; A. J. Sharkey	2014	Entrepreneurship as a mobility process	ASR	Employers	Organizational demography; entrepreneurship	Longitudinal analysis	Rate of entrepreneurship entry	Individual employee
P. Wiepking; R. H. F. P. Bekkers; U. O. Osili	2014	Examining the association of religious context with giving to non-profit organizations	ESR	Religious organizations	Rational choice theory; religious competition model	Survey research	Religious donation	Individuals
R. Braunstein; B. R. Fulton; R. L. Wood	2014	The role of bridging cultural practices in racially and socioeconomically diverse civic organizations	ASR	Civic organizations	Diversity research	Ethnography	Processes that enable participant diversity without destroying cohesion	Faith based organizational coalition
D. Baldassarri	2015	Cooperative networks: altruism, group solidarity, reciprocity, and sanctioning in Ugandan producer organizations	AJS	Ugandan producer organizations	Group processes; network theory	Field experiment	Cooperation between groups	Groups
F. Dobbin; D. Schrage; A. Kalev	2015	Rage against the iron cage: the varied effects of bureaucratic personnel reforms on diversity	ASR	Employers	Bureaucracy theory; job autonomy; accountability theories	Longitudinal analysis	Changes in managerial diversity	Firms
J. Berger; A. Diekmann	2015	The logic of relative frustration: Boudon's competition model and experimental evidence	ESR	Employers	Game theory	Lab experiments	Frustration with promotion opportunities	Individual
J. Rosenfeld; P. Denice	2015	The power of transparency: evidence from a British workplace survey	ASR	Employers	Transparency theory	Survey research	Wages	Individuals

Authors	Year	Title	Journal	Organizations	Theory	Method	Outcome	Unit of analysis
T. Anttila; T. Oinas; M. Tammelin; J. Nätti	2015	Working-time regimes and work-life balance in Europe	ESR	Employers	Comparative economy	Survey research	Work–life balance	Individual employee
J.-P. Ferguson	2015	The control of managerial discretion: evidence from unionization's impact on employment segregation	AJS	Employers	Inequality; discrimination theories	Regression discontinuity	Occupational and establishment segregation	Employing firm
S. B. Srivastava; E. L. Sherman	2015	Agents of change or cogs in the machine? Reexamining the influence of female managers on the gender wage gap	AJS	Employers	Inequality; gender theories of discrimination	Longitudinal analysis	Gender wage gap	Individual employee
D. Tomaskovic-Devey; M. Hällsten; D. Avent-Holt	2015	Where do immigrants fare worse? Modeling workplace wage gap variation with longitudinal employer-employee data	AJS	Employers	Inequality; wage discrimination; power	Cross-sectional analysis of workplaces	Immigrant-native wage gaps	Employer establishment
P. Catron	2016	Made in America? Immigrant occupational mobility in the first half of the twentieth century	AJS	Employers	Assimilation theory	Longitudinal analysis of employment histories	Occupational mobility	Immigrant employees
A. Goldberg; S. B. Srivastava; V. G. Manian; W. Monroe; C. Potts	2016	Fitting in or standing out? The tradeoffs of structural and cultural embeddedness	ASR	Employers	Cultural sociology; network analysis	Longitudinal analysis	Individual attainment	Individual employee
D. Minkoff	2016	The payoffs of organizational membership for political activism in established democracies	AJS	Political and civic organizations	Social movement theory; civil society	Survey research; propensity score matching	Political activism	Individuals

(Continued)

Table 2. (*Continued*)

Author(s)	Year	Title	Published	Organization Form	Theory	Method	Outcome of Interest	Unit
P. Moen; E. L. Kelly; W. Fan; S.-R. Lee; D. Almeida; E. E. Kossek; O. M. Buxton	2016	Does a flexibility/support organizational initiative improve high-tech employees' well-being? Evidence from the work, family, and health network	*ASR*	Employer	Worker well-being	Field experiment	Changes in worker well-being	Individual employee
A. E. Kentikelenis; L. Seabrooke	2017	The politics of world polity: script-writing in international organizations	*ASR*	International nongovernmental organizations	World-culture theory; power-political theory	Archival data	Script writing about capital allocation	Transcripts of board meetings
C. Herring	2017	Is diversity still a good thing?	*ASR*	Business establishments	Diversity research	Cross-sectional analysis	Firm performance (various)	Establishment
D. Stojmenovska; T. Bol; T. Leopold	2017	Does diversity pay? A replication of Herring (2009)	*ASR*	Business establishments	Diversity research	Cross-sectional analysis	Firm performance (various)	Establishment
F. C. Wezel; M. Ruef	2017	Agents with principles: the control of labor in the Dutch East India Company, 1700 to 1796	*ASR*	Dutch east India company	Agency theory	Longitudinal analysis	Desertion	Individual seafarers
M. E. Brashears; M. Genkin; C. S. Suh	2017	In the organization's shadow: how individual behavior is shaped by organizational leakage	*AJS*	School clubs/teams	Organizational ecology	Cross-sectional analysis	Similarity in behaviors	Individual students
N. Fligstein; J. Stuart Brundage; M. Schultz	2017	Seeing like the fed: culture, cognition, and framing in the failure to anticipate the financial crisis of 2008	*ASR*	Federal reserve bank	Framing theory; culture and cognition	Topic modeling	Frames used to make sense of the financial collapse	Meeting transcripts

Author	Year	Title	Journal	Setting	Theory	Method	Dependent variable	Unit of analysis
Y. Lu; R. Tao	2017	Organizational structure and collective action: lineage networks, semiautonomous civic associations, and collective resistance in rural China	AJS	Civic associations	Collective action theory; social movement theory	Longitudinal analysis	Petitions	Rural Chinese villages
E. Hirsh; Y. Cha	2018	For law and markets: employment discrimination lawsuits, market performance, and managerial diversity	AJS	Employers	Institutional theory; law and society	Longitudinal analysis	Gender and racial representation in management	Employer establishments
V. J. Roscigno; C. Sauer; P. Valet	2018	Rules, relations, and work	AJS	German employers	Bureaucracy theory	Survey research	Job satisfaction and fairness perceptions	Individual employee
H.-P. Y. Qvist; L. S. Henriksen; T. Fridberg	2018	The consequences of weakening organizational attachment for volunteering in Denmark, 2004–2012	ESR	Voluntary organizations	Organizational attachment	Longitudinal analysis	Hours spent volunteering	Individual volunteers
J.-P. Ferguson; R. Koning	2018	Firm turnover and the return of racial establishment segregation	ASR	Business establishments	Occupational segregation theory	Longitudinal analysis	Racial composition	Establishment
N. Wilmers	2018	Wage stagnation and buyer power: how buyer-supplier relations affect U.S. workers' wages, 1978 to 2014	ASR	Publicly traded companies	Wage premium and buyer power theory	Longitudinal analysis	Wages	Firm-year
A. Saatcioglu; T. M. Skrtic	2019	Categorization by organizations: manipulation of disability categories in a racially desegregated school district	AJS	School district	Categories and inequality	Mixed; longitudinal and interviews	Excess costs for disability categories	Disability categories

(Continued)

Table 2. (*Continued*)

Author(s)	Year	Title	Published	Organization Form	Theory	Method	Outcome of Interest	Unit
J. L. Nelson	2019	How organizational minorities form and use social ties: evidence from teachers in majority-white and majority-black schools	AJS	Secondary schools	Race and networks	Multi-site ethnography	How white and black teachers form social ties with other teachers	Relationship
L. Smith-Doerr; S. Alegria; K. H. Fealing; D. Fitzpatrick; D. Tomaskovic-Devey	2019	Gender pay gaps in U.S. federal science agencies: an organizational approach	AJS	Government agencies	Gender pay gap theory	Longitudinal analysis	Gender pay gap	Individual employee
M. Giesselmann; S. Bohmann; J. Goebel; P. Krause; E. Liebau; D. Richter; D. Schacht; C. Schröder; J. Schupp; S. Liebig	2019	The individual in context(s): research potentials of the socio-economic panel study (SOEP) in sociology	ESR	Employers	None	Survey analysis	None	Individual linked to organizational
M. van Hek; T. van der Lippe	2019	Are female managers agents of change or cogs in the machine? An assessment with three-level manager–employee linked data	ESR	Employers	Gender pay gap theory	Cross-sectional; cross-national	Gender pay gap	Individual employee

Year	Author	Journal	Title	Context	Theory	Method	Outcome	Level of analysis
2019	R. Taiji; M. C. Mills	ESR	Non-standard schedules, work–family conflict, and the moderating role of national labour context: evidence from 32 European countries	Employers	Flexible work arrangements	Cross-sectional; cross-national	Work-family conflict	Individual employee
2019	V. Ray	ASR	A theory of racialized organizations	Organizations (general)	Race theory	Theory building	Racialized practices in organizations	Organization
2019	L. A. Rivera; A. Tilcsik	ASR	Scaling down inequality: rating scales, gender bias, and the architecture of evaluation	University	Gender evaluation theory	Field experiment	Performance ratings	Instructor-course
2020	A. D. Reich; S. J Prins	AJS	The disciplining effect of mass incarceration on labor organization	Labor organizations	Labor market theory	Longitudinal analysis	Membership in labor organization	Individual employee
2020	A. H. Wingfield; K. Chavez	ASR	Getting in, getting hired, getting sideways looks: organizational hierarchy and perceptions of racial discrimination	Health care organizations	Racial discrimination theory	Interviews	Perceptions of racial discrimination	Individual employee
2020	A. Ranganathan; A. Benson	ASR	A numbers game: quantification of work, auto-gamification, and worker productivity	Garment manufacturing factory	Quantification of work	Natural experiment	Worker productivity	Individual employee
2020	A. Storer; D. Schneider; K. Harknett	ASR	What explains racial/ethnic inequality in job quality in the service sector?	Employers	Flexible work arrangements	Survey data	Job quality	Individual employee
2020	D. R. Schaefer; D. A. Kreager	ASR	New on the block: analyzing network selection trajectories in a prison treatment program	Prison based therapy organization	Network theory	Network analysis	Network tie selection	Individual prisoner

(Continued)

Table 2. (Continued)

Author(s)	Year	Title	Published	Organization Form	Theory	Method	Outcome of Interest	Unit
F. Bernardi; C. J. Gil-Hernández	2020	The social-origins gap in labour market outcomes: compensatory and boosting advantages using a micro-class approach	ESR	Employers	Effectively maintained inequality theory	Cross-sectional regression	Occupational status and net income	Individual employee
G. Altomonte	2020	Exploiting ambiguity: a moral polysemy approach to variation in economic practices	ASR	Post-acute care unit; health care	Ethnography; interviews	Moralization of economic goals	Organization	
J. M. Calarco	2020	Avoiding us versus them: how schools' dependence on privileged "helicopter" parents influences enforcement of rules	ASR	Public elementary school	Organizational theory; cultural capital	Ethnography	Homework rule enforcement	Teachers
S. Gorleer; P. Bracke; L. Hustinx	2020	The organizational field of blood collection: a multilevel analysis of organizational determinants of blood donation in Europe	ESR	Blood donation organizations	Organizational field theory	Survey analysis	Lifetime prevalence of blood donation	Individual blood donors
S. J. Correll; K. R. Weisshaar; A. T. Wynn; J. D. Wehner	2020	Inside the black box of organizational life: the gendered language of performance assessment	ASR	Fortune 500 tech company	Viewing and Valuing Social Cognitive Processing Model	Content analysis; cross-sectional analysis	Performance rating	Performance evaluation
T. Kristal; Y. Cohen; E. Navot	2020	Workplace compensation practices and the rise in benefit inequality	ASR	Employers	Workplace compensation practices	Longitudinal analysis	Hourly inequality	Employer-job

Author	Year	Title	Journal	Unit	Theory	Method	Outcome	Level
J. Chu	2021	Cameras of merit or engines of inequality? College ranking systems and the enrollment of disadvantaged students	*AJS*	Colleges and universities	Rankings systems	Longitudinal analysis	Disadvantaged student enrollment	College-year
L. Zhang	2021	Shaking things up: disruptive events and inequality	*AJS*	Employers	Disruptive events and inequality	Longitudinal analysis; difference-in-difference	Change in occupational composition & segregation	Firm-year
F. Zimmermann	2021	Managing the gender wage gap – how female managers influence the gender wage gap among workers	*ESR*	Employers	Gender pay gap theory	Longitudinal analysis	Gender wage gap	Employer-employee
J. Laurence	2021	The impact of youth engagement on life satisfaction: a quasi-experimental field study of a UK national youth engagement scheme	*ESR*	Clubs and voluntary associations	Subjective well-being literature	Difference-in-difference	Life satisfaction	Individual youth
N. Wilmers; C. Aeppli	2021	Consolidated advantage: new organizational dynamics of wage inequality	*ASR*	Employers	Wage inequality theory	Longitudinal analysis	Wage inequality	Occupation-workplace

THEORETICAL AMBIGUITY AND
PROBLEM-ORIENTED SOCIOLOGY

Many scholars' views of organizational sociology reflect their training in semi-nal texts, such as Clegg (1989), Scott (1992), or Aldrich and Ruef (2006), that seek to lay out a coherent perspective of organizations as a social phenomenon, usually finding their roots in classic sociological theory. These perspectives bring together various strands of theoretical and empirical work into a cohesive frame-work. Within the perspective, one can deduce theoretical expectations and even-tually hypotheses. The sociological perspectives, perhaps intentionally so, were developed as alternatives to economic perspectives that had become dominant but that sociologists viewed as too normative and not consistent with the social constructionist lens that runs throughout most sociology. Numerous cohorts of organizational scholars, of which I was a part, viewed these texts as the baseline for their training and as ideal models for how to theorize and conduct empirical work. Theoretical contributions, we were taught, were meant to be in conver-sation with these guiding frameworks. When a new framework emerged, you could do good scholarship by tagging on your own ideas to it in a generative fashion. This is what organizational scholars think of as a theoretical contribu-tion when they do research. How do I contribute to an existing framework by adding a new idea, a new mechanism, modifying the boundary conditions of the theory, etc.?

But it is apparent from reading the articles listed here that this is not the only way to do organizational research, and it is certainly not the most common way to do organizational sociology. Rather, a different way of doing organizational soci-ology is what I will refer to as "problem-oriented" sociology (Prasad, 2021). The main purpose of this kind of sociological research is to identify social problems and then shed light on them, explain why they exist, and analyze what accounts for variation in exposure or consequences from those problems. Some research is even framed as an attempt to solve those problems (see, e.g., Prasad, 2021).

Problem-oriented sociology, of course, relies on scholars sharing an under-standing of what important problems are. As sociologists, we take for granted that problems are inherently socially constructed, but nevertheless the problems that motivate the discipline's interest tend to have high agreement among sociolo-gists as being problems and they receive a high proportion of public attention (Hilgartner & Bosk, 1988). The "social problems" perspective has a long history in sociology, with an early emphasis on crime and deviance and gradually mor-phing into programmatic research on various forms of inequality (e.g., Schneider, 1985; Spector & Kitsuse, 2017). In many cases, research seeks to understand the negative consequences of various social phenomena (e.g., wealth inequality; racial bias), which further justifies the phenomena as a problem worth solving. When there is high agreement about the phenomenon as having negative con-sequences, scholars are "studying what is popularly seen as a social problem" (Prasad, 2021, p. 33).

After reading the articles sampled for this paper, one can see the authors' inter-ests in the topics as emanating from their desire to label, understand, and, if fortunate, add insights about how to solve a particular social problem. The best example of this type of research, of which there are numerous in the list of articles, is related to social and economic inequality, whether based on race, gender, or some other form of group membership. Ridgeway (2014) captured well the sociological urge to study inequality in her presidential address for the American Sociological Association:

> Sociologists want to do more than describe social inequality. We want to understand the deeper problem of how inequality is *made* and, therefore, could potentially be unmade. What are the mechanisms? How do we uncover them?

Ridgeway goes on to urge sociologists not just to consider how resources and power shape inequality but also status – or signifiers that convey respect or prestige – influence inequality between groups.

Naturally, organizations are an ideal place in which to study all three of Weber's (1968) sources of inequality – resources, power, and status – because it is in organizations that they accrue. Some have argued that the pursuit of these three kinds of resources motivates most organizational actions (King & Walker, 2014). Organizations are made up of various kinds of resources, bundled together in structures and routines. Organizations convey power on groups or individuals through their control of those resources and ability to exert authority on who else has access to them. And organizations are carriers of status and grant status to individuals, although not equally to all groups (see, e.g., Croidieu & Powell, 2024, this volume). Thus, as scholars seek to study the problem of inequality, they easily find their way to organizations as an object or at least context for their analyses.

Types of inequality abound in organizations. Studies of inequality end up being one of the main types of papers in the "society within organizations" approach. Scholars recognize that inequality, bias, and discrimination abound in society and that we can better understand their sources by looking inside organizations where they are reproduced. In some papers, scholars portray organizations as the mechanism that accounts for inequalities, creating the structural fabric that allows certain kinds of discrimination to persist (e.g., Smith-Doerr et al., 2019). Many papers listed here relate to gender inequality and, even more specifically, to the causes of the "gender pay gap" (e.g., Rivera & Tilcsik, 2019; Smith-Doerr et al., 2019) or gender bias as manifest in organizational evaluation practices (Correll et al., 2020). In most of this work, gender inequality is not only viewed as a problem to explain but also one that can be alleviated if we used organizational interventions consistent with the findings of the analysis. Much inequality research links problem identification with problem solving. If society happens inside organizations and we want to fix society's problems, naturally we turn to organizations as both the culprits and the potential saviors.

Inequality is not the only social problem that raises its head in the problem-focused research found in these papers, but it is the most common one, especially in the papers using a society within organization approach. Other problems include employee well-being and life satisfaction, worker productivity, performance ratings, and cooperation.

Much problem-oriented sociology is characterized by a loose theoretical orientation. By loose, I mean that the paper is not driven by a theoretical question at all. Instead, theory is in the background, offering expectations about what is contributing to the problem under investigation. In many cases, the theoretical background is not even a coherent theoretical framework but rather a literature of prior research and its associated findings. Consider, for example, Wilmers' (2018) article about wage stagnation. Rather than turn to a single theory about why wages stagnate, he instead looks at all of the available research on wages and market structure and uses that to generate hypotheses about how buyer power influences suppliers' wage-setting practices and ultimately wage differentials between firms. Reading theory this way can be shocking for an organizational theorist who is accustomed to having their feet held to the fire by reviewers demanding a theoretical contribution! There's no attempt to draw on resource dependence theory or formulate different types of Weberian power. Instead, Wilmers focuses squarely on "buyer power" as a practical construct that has relevance for the problem at hand – explaining wage differences across firms. In the conclusion, the author describes how the paper tests and extends economic segmentation theory, but prior to mentioning it in the conclusion the term "economic segmentation" is only mentioned twice. To be fair, there isn't a great need to describe the theory in detail. It is obvious from his description of buyer power what the theory is about.

Many of the "organizations within society" papers also tackle social problems, examining the role of organizations in formulating policy change (or resisting policy change) that might help resolve an existing social problem or by exploring the dynamics by which organizations contribute to or even create intermediate solutions to systemic problems. Steil and Vasi (2014), as an example of organizations contributing to policy changes, find that the presence of immigrant community organizations facilitated the passage of pro-immigrant ordinances in cities. Fiel and Zhang (2019), in contrast, show that the politics of local school districts influence the reversal of desegregation orders, a policy measure used to combat racial inequality in the education system. As an example of organizations creating intermediate solutions to social problems, McDonnell (2017) demonstrates that Ghanaian state organizations often have unique bureaucratic structures in order to adapt to the cultural and social needs of the communities in which they are embedded.

Not all problem-oriented papers are as loose with theory, as illustrated by some of the papers using an "organizations within society" approach. These papers use theory explicitly as a way to explain the problem at hand and generate hypotheses. For example, Pernell et al. (2017) seek to explain why banks begin adopting risky financial derivatives, a practice that they associate with the global financial crisis of the 2000s. To generate theoretical expectations, they draw from institutional theory as well as psychological theory on moral reasoning. In their conclusion, they contrast the implications of their study with what one would expect if deriving policy from agency theory. Thus, in the paper's conclusion, they offer generalizable policy solutions that would potentially combat dangerous risk-taking. The paper's theoretical contributions, as often conceived of by organizational theorists, are quite modest, but they nevertheless use theory deftly to diagnose the problem and find potential solutions.

It is clear from reading many of the problem-oriented papers that they embrace theoretical ambiguity. Rather than see that the purpose of the paper is to build or generate new theoretical insights, they instead allow theory to sit lightly in the background, or they draw liberally from various theories to shed light on a social problem. Doing this helps them get greater leverage over what is actually contributing to the problem. They are open to the idea that a single theoretical framework might not be sufficient to explain the problem. Moreover, their entire focus on the organization – as its own unit of analysis or as a context in which the problem is occurring – is to get better leverage in targeting the problem. The organization is often the problem itself, and that is why they are driven to study them.

This approach to scholarship is quite different from what we see in a typical publication in an organization theory journal, where the emphasis is placed on theoretical novelty. The reason for doing a study – at least as expressed by reviewers – is to make a theoretical contribution. Usually, we know if someone has made a theoretical contribution because they have identified a "theoretical gap" prior to doing the study and then they seek to address the gap with the new study, often by inventing a new concept or mechanism of explanation. Addressing problems or practical implications usually only enter the discussion on the back end of a paper and may even find their home in a section of the paper designed for that purpose. Showing the managerial implications of one's research is a bonus for any study, but even this aspect of organizational research is quite different from what we see in contemporary organizational sociology. Drawing out the implications for managers is not warranted and may even be looked down upon by sociologists. The problems that interest sociologists derive from a different set of assumptions about why scholars engage in research and are usually focused on improving the collective good rather than simply benefitting the organization itself or a subset of elites within that organization.

ENGAGING WITH SOCIAL PROBLEMS AND THEORETICAL DEVELOPMENT

One could conclude from reading the above description of contemporary organizational sociology that the field has entered a stage of normal science. We have enough theory now that we can use it as a tool to incrementally arrive at the answers to societal and organizational problems. And I would certainly agree that much of the research has embraced the spirit of normal science. But I think that characterizing the entire field in that way leads us to ignore the potential for creativity and idea generation had by organizational sociology. Moreover, I think we sometimes dismiss normal science as being theoretically vacuous when, I would argue, it can be the basis for important new theoretical insights.

In the last part of this paper, I focus on this theme: studying organizations as actors and sites where society plays out gives us unique opportunities to develop theory. One reason for this is that it frees scholars from being entirely bound by the constraints of existing theory and getting caught up in siloed conversations about theory that have little relevance to scholars outside that theoretical tradition. When the entire purpose of research is to contribute to theoretical frameworks, over time, research in that area becomes narrower in its focus and offers more obscure innovations that can only be appreciated by the most ardent fans of the theory. Theory becomes its own goal and becomes delinked from the pressing empirical issues that call our attention to organizational research in the first place.

In contrast, when we approach empirical research as an attempt to better understand and (potentially) offer solutions to a social problem, we wear less opaque theoretical blinders. Seeing research through the lens of "social problems" gives scholars the opportunity to offer up new explanations and in the process rethink why organizations operate and function as they do.

As I mentioned at the beginning of this paper, some of the most important theoretical innovations made in organizational theory came about because scholars were trying to better understand an empirical puzzle or problem. Meyer and Rowan (1977) and DiMaggio and Powell (1983), two of the most important starting points of institutional theory, began as attempts to explain why organizations adopted practices and formal structures that did not always make logical sense. From the point of view of Meyer and Rowan, the schools they studied may have even looked quite dysfunctional, even if they purported to do things for rational purposes. The theory of institutions they helped create came from a genuine struggle to understand social problems that previous theories fell short of explaining.

Not all organizational sociology seek to do this, but there are some good examples of theoretical development that emerge out of empirical puzzles and grappling with real social problems happening within those organizations. I provide two examples. The aforementioned McDonnell's (2017) investigation of pockets of high performing bureaucracies alongside highly dysfunctional organizations in Ghanaian government yields a theorization of a new type of bureaucracy – interstitial bureaucracy. By trying to shed light on why these highly effective bureaucracies exist, she is also able to help explain what is absent in the less effective bureaucracies next to them. Through interviews and comparative case analysis, she identifies the microfoundations of bureaucracy through which individuals tie together local culture and institutions to the ideal type of Weberian bureaucracy. Her approach – contrasting the ideal type with the reality she observes in her data – identifies adaptive characteristics local bureaucrats used given their interstitial position. McDonnell's study and a series of other papers related to the administration of public services (e.g., Lara-Millán, 2014; Seim, 2017) breathe new life into bureaucratic theory and rejuvenate interest in variation in bureaucratic forms. These studies also remind us of organizational sociology's intellectual connections to urban and community sociology and public administration research.

Another example of theoretical development that came about through a problem-oriented focus is Ray's (2019) theory of racialized organizations. The problem that Ray seeks to explain is why seemingly race-neutral organizations are quite critical to the reproduction of racial disparities in society. His theoretical innovation is to bring Du Boisian critical race theory into conversation with organizational theory to develop a theory about how race becomes instantiated and reproduced in organizational structure. Organizations, Ray (2019, p. 26) writes "are racial structures" inasmuch as "race is constitutive of organizational foundations, hierarchies, and processes." He goes on to develop a set of assumptions and mechanisms to support this idea, as well as proposing an agenda for future research.

Both of these studies offer innovative ways of viewing organizations. And although it is clear that the authors were well read in organizational theory, they did not begin their papers as seeking to work within the constraints of a given theoretical framework. Instead, they approach their research by pointing to an existing social problem and then wrestle with existing theory that cannot easily account for the problems they are trying to explain and solve. It is the contradiction and tension that their empirical problems have with existing theory that gives impetus to new theory. In the case of Ray (2019, p. 46), he proposes that "organizational theorists should abandon the notion that organizational formations, hierarchies, and processes are race-neutral." Organizational theory should incorporate insights from race theory about how organizations are manifestations of racial structures that reproduce and reinforce inequalities. His theorizing opens the door for a new way to theorize organizations and race. Given organizational theorists' interest in conceiving of "organizational practices ... as being central to the reproduction of inequality" (Amis et al., 2020, p. 195), it makes sense that organizational scholars would heed Ray's urging to integrate race theory with our own understanding of organizations. Theoretical innovation is likely to come from tackling these problems empirically.

Sociology's gravitation around social problems also encourages scholars to study a broader variety of organizations. Whereas the tendency in organizational research is to study for-profit businesses,[2] sociological research on organizations is more inclusive, including research on nonprofit organizations, schools, social movement organizations, and government agencies. Organizational variety allows scholars to push against long-held theoretical assumptions about organizations, which may be only true of the for-profit organizations that management scholars study, and opens the door for comparative organizational research (King et al., 2009). In short, by expanding the variety of organizations studied, scholars will be able to test the scope conditions of existing theory and create new opportunities for theoretically generative analysis.

CONCLUSION

Organizational sociology, despite reports of its demise, is alive and well and regularly published in top sociology journals. And yet, it does seem to be the case that organizational sociology has grown somewhat distant from the broader community of organizational scholars. I have sought to understand this by looking more closely at the research that sociologists have published about organizations in the past decade.

One of the main implications of this paper is that the distance between organizational sociology is partly a function of very different approaches to doing organizational research. Whereas much research in management and organizational specialist journals is motivated by identifying theoretical gaps or puzzles to resolve, much of the organizational sociology published in sociology journals is problem oriented. Explaining organizations and why they do what they do or how people behave in them is not the primary purpose of this research. Rather, sociologists are more likely to try to explain and identify solutions to social problems by studying organizations' roles in those problems. This research is in conversation with a "social problems perspective" of sociological research that seeks to identify, explain, and conceive of solutions for society's pressing problems. Organizations, because of their prominent role in society as either social actors or rich social contexts, are naturally caught up in those problems. They are often conceptualized as a source of the problem, although organizational interventions may also offer potential solutions as well.

The two approaches to studying organizations in sociology reflect the problem-oriented nature of research. An organizations within society approach implies that organizations are important actors and structures through which resources, power, and status are channeled. Organizations may impede change, especially when it is in the interest of the elites guiding them. But organizations can also be powerful agents for shaping the future of society, as we see in the case of Best (2012) in which she studies how interest groups draw attention to new diseases and advocate for federal funding to fight them. Many of the social movement theory papers in the sample are very much about organizations as drivers of social change. The second approach is more about what happens inside organizations. A society within organizations approach implies that organizations are contexts in which social dynamics play out, for good or bad. Many of society's problems therefore can only be understood and combated by studying how organizations work and what role they play in the perpetuation of those problems.

Research of this type is often theoretically ambivalent, choosing those theoretical tools that give them the best leverage in understanding the problem. But it doesn't always have to be that way. In fact, I would argue that some of the most innovative theoretical development comes when tackling an empirical problem that existing theory cannot easily explain. This is where the real potential for theoretical innovation lies.

For organizational scholars, more generally, organizational sociology offers a potential model for our own development. If we continue down the current path of publishing, in which theoretical contribution is valued above all, scholars will continue to be incentivized to do research that primarily addresses theoretical gaps or resolves theoretical puzzles, but perhaps at the expense of doing work that has broader social relevance. Moreover, given complaints about how much organizational theory has become more specialized, more jargon-filled, and less innovative, perhaps there is room for a different approach to organizational scholarship – one more grounded in real-world problems and connected to a broad variety of social settings.

As I have argued in this paper, studying organizations where we find problems does not have to be vacant of theoretical development. In fact, we may find that grounding organizational analysis in social problems will trigger new innovations and change how we think about theoretical contributions to focus more on explanation, rather than situating findings within an umbrella theoretical framework. Generating theoretical insights from the study of social problems has the potential to unleash organizational analysis from the stifling conformity imposed by dominant theoretical paradigms, find ways out of theoretical silos, and lead scholars to rethink what constitutes a theoretical contribution. Finally, the approach laid out by organizational sociology will encourage organizational scholars to expand their view of what constitutes an organization and consider the organization's place in the broader social world. Undoubtedly, this repositioning of organizations will open up new theoretical possibilities.

NOTES

1. Many organizational theory journals now encourage authors to include a section about managerial implications at the end of their articles.
2. Granted, not all departments where organizational research takes place today are as management-dominated as American business schools. European schools of organizational studies or nonprofit management departments introduce key sources of heterogeneity in the kind of organizational research that is done, and of course as I show here, sociology departments continue to be a bastion of organizational research, although less likely to be labeled as such.

ACKNOWLEDGMENTS

I am grateful to participants in the EGOS sub-theme on Doing Sociology in Organization Studies for their helpful feedback. I also appreciate Omar Lizardo for reading a previous draft and sharing his insights.

REFERENCES

Aldrich, H. E., & Ruef, M. (2006). *Organizations evolving* (Edited by Anonymous). Sage.
Amis, J. M., Mair, J., & Munir, K. A. (2020). The organizational reproduction of inequality. *Academy of Management Annals, 14*(1), 195–230.
Burt, R. S. (1980). Cooptive corporate actor networks: A reconsideration of interlocking directorates involving American manufacturing. *Administrative Science Quarterly, 25*, 557–582.
Clegg, S. (1989). *Frameworks of power*. Sage.
Coleman, J. S. (1982). *The asymmetric society* (Edited by Anonymous). Syracuse University Press.
Croidieu, G., & Powell, W. W. (2024). Organizations as carriers of status and class dynamics: A historical ethnography of the emergence of Bordeaux's cork aristocracy. In S. Clegg, M. Grothe-Hammer, & K. Serrano Velarde (Eds.), *Sociological thinking in contemporary organizational scholarship* (Research in the Sociology of Organizations, Vol. 90, pp. 141–174). Emerald Publishing.
Gorman, E. (2014). *The end of 'organizational sociology' as we know it?* Retrieved January 10, 2022, from https://workinprogress.oowsection.org/2014/11/20/the-end-of-organizational-sociology-as-we-know-it/
Hannan, M. T., & Freeman, J. (1977). The population ecology of organizations. *American Journal of Sociology, 82*(5), 929–964.
Hilgartner, S., & Bosk, C. L. (1988). The rise and fall of social problems: A public arenas model. *American Journal of Sociology, 94*(1), 53–78.

King, B. G. (2017). The relevance of organizational sociology. *Contemporary Sociology*, *46*(2), 131–137.

King, B. G., Felin, T., & Whetten, D. A. (2009). Comparative organizational analysis: An introduction. In B. King, T. Felin, & D. Whetten (Eds.), *Studying differences between organizations: Comparative approaches to organizational research* (pp. 3–19). Emerald Group Publishing Limited.

Lammers, C. J. (1981). Contributions of organizational sociology: Part I: Contributions to sociology – A liberal view. *Organization Studies*, *2*(3), 26–86.

Lara-Millán, A. (2014). Public emergency room overcrowding in the era of mass imprisonment. *American Sociological Review*, *79*(5), 866–887.

Lipsky, M. (2010). *Street-level bureaucracy: Dilemmas of the individual in public service*. Russell Sage Foundation.

Lounsbury, M., & Beckman, C. M. (2015). Celebrating organization theory. *Journal of Management Studies*, *52*(2), 288–308.

Meyer, J. W., & Rowan, B. (1977). Institutionalized organizations: Formal structure as myth and ceremony. *The American Journal of Sociology*, *83*(2), 340–363.

Perrow, C. (1991). A society of organizations. *Theory and Society*, *20*(6), 725–762.

Pfeffer, J., & Salancik, G. R. (1978). *The external control of organizations: A resource dependence perspective* (Edited by Anonymous). Stanford Business Books.

Prasad, M. (2021). *Problem solving sociology: A guide for students*. Oxford University Press.

Ridgeway, C. L. (2014). Why status matters for inequality. *American Sociological Review*, *79*(1), 1–16.

Ringel, L. (2024). Organizational sociology and organization studies: Past, present, and future. In S. Clegg, M. Grothe-Hammer, & K. Serrano Velarde (Eds.), *Sociological thinking in contemporary organizational scholarship* (Research in the Sociology of Organizations, Vol. 90, pp. 55–84). Emerald Publishing.

Seim, J. (2017). The ambulance: Toward a labor theory of poverty governance. *American Sociological Review*, *82*(3), 451–475.

Scott, W. R. (2004). Reflections on a half-century of organizational sociology. *Annual Review of Sociology*, *30*, 1–21.

Scott, W. R. (1992). *Organizations: Rational, natural, and open systems* (3rd ed.) Prentice-Hall.

Schneider, J. W. (1985). Social problems theory: The constructionist view. *Annual Review of Sociology*, *11*(1), 209–229.

Spector, M., & Kitsuse, J. I. (2017). *Constructing social problems*. Routledge.

Weber, M. (1968). *Economy and society: An outline of interpretive sociology*. Bedminster.

Whetten, D. A., Felin, T., & King, B. G. (2009). The practice of theory borrowing in organizational studies: Current issues and future directions. *Journal of Management*, *35*(3), 537–563.

ORGANIZATIONAL SOCIOLOGY AND ORGANIZATION STUDIES: PAST, PRESENT, AND FUTURE

Leopold Ringel

Bielefeld University, Germany

ABSTRACT

Organizational sociology and organization studies have a long history together, while also sharing a proclivity to self-diagnose crises. Instead of taking these assessments at face value, this paper treats them as an object of study, asking what conditions have fueled them. In the case of organizational sociology, there are indications of a connection between rising levels of discontent and community building: self-identified organizational sociologists have progressively withdrawn from general debates in the discipline and turned their attention to organization studies, which, they suspect, has seen dramatic levels of growth at their expense. Organization studies, on the other hand, are still haunted by "a Faustian bargain": leaning heavily on the authority of the social sciences, business school faculty were able to facilitate the emergence of a scholarly field of practice dedicated to the study of organizations, which they control. However, in doing so, they also set organization studies on a path of continued dependence on knowledge produced elsewhere: notably, by university disciplines such as sociology.

Keywords: Business schools; expertise; organization studies; sociology; scholarly practice

Sociological Thinking in Contemporary Organizational Scholarship
Research in the Sociology of Organizations, Volume 90, 55–83

ISSN: 0733-558X/doi:10.1108/S0733-558X20240000090003

INTRODUCTION

Over the past 100 years, the academic study of organizations has become a popular endeavor in the social sciences and several interdisciplinary fields of study, some largely oblivious of their neighbors, others connected by common interests, intellectual spillovers, and networks of mutual exchange. Organizational sociology (OrgSoc hereafter), a subdiscipline of sociology, and organization studies (OS hereafter), an interdisciplinary field of study, arguably belong in the second category (Haveman, 2022): not only are their epistemic cultures closely entwined, but they also share a proclivity to self-diagnose crises – which is the main topic of interest in this paper. Instead of participating in these debates, I intend to approach them from a sociology of knowledge perspective and treat self-diagnosed crises in OrgSoc and OS as objects of inquiry. Specifically, I am interested in the conditions that have fueled and sustained them.

Starting with sociology, it seems that those with a vested interest in the subdiscipline OrgSoc are struck by a growing "sense of depression" (Besio et al., 2020, p. 411). Take a session held at the Annual Conference of the American Sociological Association (ASA) in 2014 as an example. Its premise: OrgSoc is facing a profound and perhaps even existential crisis. The participants, therefore, were asked to discuss if we are currently witnessing "the end of 'organizational sociology' as we know it." Another vivid example can be found in a paper titled "The decline of organizational sociology? An empirical analysis of research trends in leading journals across half a century," which ponders the question: "Is organizational sociology becoming obsolete?" (Grothe-Hammer & Kohl, 2020, p. 420). The basic storyline around which OrgSoc has coalesced goes like this: "Centrifugal forces" (Thoenig, 1998, p. 307) have been pulling apart the foundations of OrgSoc, which is not only on the verge of extinction in terms of its relevance "outside of the discipline" (Besio et al., 2020, p. 412), but also "no longer appears to have any specific location [...] within sociology itself" (du Gay, 2020, p. 460).

When discussing the "external conditions" (Holmwood, 2010, p. 640) that have caused the downward spiral of OrgSoc, sociologists often blame OS. They argue that although sociology has "played a central role in shaping many aspects of this wide-ranging field" (Scott, 2004, p. 4), OS, by differentiating "itself from other fields and from the social science disciplines" (Augier et al., 2005, p. 87) has appropriated significant resources that are now missing elsewhere. Business schools are said to have played a key role in this process: instilled with a sudden appetite for academic credibility in the 1960s and 1970s, they vigorously supported their faculty in demarcating fields of study and making them their own. The OrgSoc community, meanwhile, feeling itself to be an increasingly marginalized group in the larger realm of organizational scholarship, occasionally pays a visit to what it sees as territory that has been lost. Organizational sociologists participate in conferences such as the annual colloquium, hosted by the European Group of Organization Science (EGOS), and sometimes even get to publish an article in one of the esteemed journals such as *Administrative Science Quarterly* (*ASQ*), *Organization Science* (*OrgSc*), the *Academy of Management Journal*

(*AMJ*), or *Organization Studies* (*OrgStudies*). But, rest assured, these visits are just temporary. Organizational sociologists have concluded, for better or worse, that the scientific study of organizations is now dominated by business school faculty.

In a surprising twist, the apparent victor, far from thumping its chest, is also consumed by doubts and equally prone to indulge in self-diagnosed crises, albeit of a different kind. As early as 1959, two influential reports on the general state of management education – one commissioned by the Ford Foundation, the other by the Carnegie Foundation – concluded that, despite their lavish resources, business schools lacked quality: "the central problem confronting this branch of higher education," one of the reports concluded, "is that academic standards need to be materially increased" (Pierson, 1959, p. ix). Decades later, after much money spent and countless reforms implemented, business school faculty still face a "crisis of confidence" (Harley, 2019, p. 286). Reporting conditions such as an "impostor syndrome" (Bothello & Roulet, 2019, p. 854), they experience a creeping feeling that their authority is always in danger of being revealed as nothing but "surface bluster" (Starkey & Tiratsoo, 2007, p. 35). The title of a recently published book, *Management Studies in Crisis: Fraud, Deception and Meaningless Research* (Tourish, 2019), vividly captures this anxiety. Unlike in OrgSoc, where the default position is that an otherwise healthy field (OrgSoc) has fallen prey to a powerful opponent (OS), problems are not externalized but perceived as being internal in origin.

OS scholars frequently express worries about their dependence on imports from university disciplines such as economics, psychology, and sociology (Agarwal & Hoetker, 2007; Holmwood, 2010; Lockett & McWilliams, 2005). They concede that the knowledge provided by university disciplines is a valuable source of inspiration. Sociology, for example, was "foundational in shaping [OS] in its earliest years" and continues "to be an important influence" (Adler, 2009, p. 5). But we are told, by being too reliant "on borrowed concepts and theories from neighboring disciplines," OS has incurred a "balance of trade deficit" (Whetten et al., 2009, pp. 537–538) which ultimately hurts the field. The university disciplines "often discount the scientific rigor of management research" and consider "the business school [...] a necessary evil to subsidize other faculties, rather than a legitimate source of knowledge and scientific creation" (Bothello & Roulet, 2019, p. 857).

To understand why OrgSoc is struck by a "sense of depression" and why OS remains an "ungainly giant," my analysis proceeds in two steps. First, I trace the transformation of OrgSoc and OS into bounded fields of practice or "settlements" (Abbott, 1988, 2001). On that basis, OS does control vast resources, while OrgSoc struggles to keep afloat. But the story becomes more complicated when, in a second step, the perspective is extended from how actors create and enforce the boundaries of settlements to the assemblage of bundles of tasks and problems into networks of expertise (Eyal, 2013). As we will see, the very foundations of OS expertise have been assembled using bits and pieces from several university disciplines, among them sociology. This is why the field is naturally drawn to, and continues to depend on, knowledge created elsewhere, no matter how settled it might be.

58 LEOPOLD RINGEL

CONCEPTUAL CONSIDERATIONS

The conceptual tools used to analyze OrgSoc and OS are drawn from the sociology of professions and the sociology of expertise. The former, as outlined by Andrew Abbott, focuses on struggles between occupational groups to be the designated experts for specific bundles of tasks and problems. Building on and extending Abbott's view, Gil Eyal turns his attention to how bundles of tasks and problems are assembled into areas of expertise. I briefly discuss both positions in this section.

Calling for a "history of tasks and problems," Abbott (1988, p. 314) foregrounds the processes by which occupational groups fashion links between themselves and bundles of tasks and problems. These processes are referred to as *jurisdictional claims*, which, to be successful, must be rooted in knowledge that reaches a sufficient level of *abstraction*. Jurisdictional claims can result in stable jurisdictions "anchored by formal and informal social structure" (Abbott, 1988, p. 20). Under these conditions, occupational groups, once they become the designated professionals, work on their own terms and decide who may or may not join them. The sociology of professions, Abbott argues, is well advised to take into account that there is always a larger context to any given "case." He refers to this context as the interdependent *system of professions*, where jurisdictional disputes and struggles abound and the gains of one professional group inevitably come at another's expense.

Abbott (2001) more recently adapted his sociology of professions for the study of science. The goal again is to trace how groups define and lay claim to bundles of tasks and problems, or, in this case, "bodies of potential academic work" (Abbott, 2001, p. 137). Fields of scholarly practice or *disciplinary settlements* develop an internal system of credentials, a distinct culture, and stable relations with their audience or multiple audiences; they are delineated as intellectual domains, though less clearly than professional jurisdictions; and they occupy positions in a larger *system of disciplines*, where they constantly vie for advantage. Moves made by the members of one settlement have a direct impact on the boundaries of other settlements: "No discipline gains or loses authority in an area without displacing or enticing other disciplines" (Abbott, 2001).

Abbott is mainly interested in disciplines (e.g., sociology, biology, economics, medicine). But he also recognizes the large number of problem-driven fields of research or *studies* (e.g., gender studies, area studies, social studies of science, or OS) that have emerged throughout the 20th century. Despite their popularity, he questions the ability of *studies* to truly challenge the dominant role of traditional disciplines. First, *studies* cannot reach the same levels of institutionalization as disciplines, which, organized in departments, are deeply entrenched in the academic labor market. Second, due to their problem orientation, *studies* are, as Abbott (2001, p. 135) puts it, "insufficiently abstract," which is why they depend "on specialized disciplines to generate new theories and methods. Interdisciplinarity presupposes disciplines." In sum, modern science has "a structure of flexibly stable disciplines, surrounded by a perpetual hazy buzz of interdisciplinarity" (Abbott, 2001, p. 136).

Eyal (2013, p. 872) distinguishes the "question of jurisdiction" from the "question of expertise, namely, what arrangements must be in place for a task to be accomplished." Taking a relational view, he defines *expertise* as "a network connecting together not only the putative experts but also other actors [...], devices and instruments, concepts, and institutional and spatial arrangements" (Eyal, 2013). This has several consequences for the study of experts and professional work. Of these, two are particularly interesting for our purposes:

- Because experts and their jurisdictional claims are just one element in a larger network, attention is drawn to that network itself: rather than simply taking bundles of tasks and problems for granted, studies should explore the practices and conditions that allow these bundles to be assembled in the first place.
- Deviating from the common postulate that authority is a function of monopoly, Eyal argues that successful jurisdictional claims depend on a certain degree of leniency or *generosity*. Networks of expertise remain small if the putative experts wield too much control over roles, standards, goals, etc. They can only grow once the perspectives of others are taken into account. This means that "a network of expertise [...] becomes more powerful and influential by virtue of its capacity to craft and package its concepts, its discourse, its modes of seeing, doing, and judging" in such a way that "they can be grafted onto what others are doing, thus linking them to the network and eliciting their cooperation" (Eyal, 2013, pp. 875–876).

Now that this section has (a) shown that jurisdictional claims over a bundle of tasks and problems are a defining marker of expert work, (b) conceptualized academic fields as settlements within a larger system of disciplines and *studies*, and (c) extended the scope of analysis from experts to networks of expertise, we can turn our attention to OrgSoc and OS. Each field is discussed in turn.

FROM "ACCIDENTAL OUTCOMES" TO "ORGANIZATIONAL SOCIOLOGY IN A NARROW SENSE"

Landmark publications by towering figures such as Max Weber and Robert Michels notwithstanding, "organizations did not exist as a distinct field of sociological inquiry" (Scott, 1998, p. 8) before World War II. Sociologists occasionally studied organizations, but, conceptually, their interests lay elsewhere, for example, in modernity's iron cage (Weber) or the subversion of democratic procedures (Michels). Using a distinction made by Krause (2021), we may say that organizations constituted a *material research object*, a site of empirical investigation, without being elevated to the status of an *epistemic target*. "The sociological study of organizations is," in this sense, "much longer standing than organizational sociology as a more or less institutionalized subdiscipline" (Lammers, 1981a, p. 268).

It was only after the war and in the United States that a larger number of social scientists – many of them immigrants from Europe[1] and driven by genuinely academic interests – tried to grasp organizations conceptually (Augier et al., 2005;

March, 2007). Over the next decades, several university disciplines – political science, social psychology, anthropology, economics, sociology – generated "siloed" stocks of knowledge and were motivated by different (and to some degree incommensurable) epistemic targets. Although these scholars did not necessarily ignore their colleagues in other departments, they were mainly concerned with the questions emerging within and not across disciplinary boundaries.

Sociologists like Robert K. Merton, Alvin Gouldner, Philip Selznick, Peter M. Blau, and Michel Crozier made vital contributions to debates in sociology and, in addition, received recognition beyond disciplinary confines. While it is true that it was more and more common to theorize "organizations as a distinctive social phenomenon" (Grothe-Hammer & Kohl, 2020, p. 421), the sociologists in question for the most part followed the path laid down by the classics like Weber and Michels: organizations were not an epistemic target by virtue of their existence but in many ways still just a means to achieve another goal – "understanding modernity" (Parker, 2000, p. 141). These authors, then, showed an interest in organizations because of the larger questions they were asking, which, occasionally, drew them toward organizational phenomena, empirically and conceptually. Having no identity attached to the study of organizations, they would usually not align "their efforts with just one speciality or even with any speciality at all" (Lammers, 1981a, p. 279).

During the 1960s, sociology as a discipline saw rising levels of internal divisions of labor, which also changed how sociologists studied organizations. A new class of younger (and predominantly US-American) sociologists ceased to approach organizations in the disinterested manner of their predecessors. Now self-identifying as *organizational sociologists*, they showed great dedication to institutionalizing OrgSoc as a subdiscipline, pitted against other subdisciplines such as industrial sociology (Lammers, 1981a, 1981b). An early indication of this changing attitude is the foundation of the section on Organizations and Occupations in the ASA in 1969 (ASA, 1970), later renamed the Section on Organizations, Occupations, and Work (OOW). The OOW would grow significantly in the decades to come, and, as the following quote reveals, made community building one of its priorities:

> A variety of membership suggestions for potential activities – the publishing of a journal or a newsletter, the sponsorship of regional workshops, the development of mechanisms for recognizing distinguished work of younger scholars – are currently being debated and explored. (ASA, 1971, p. 366)

The OOW "sought to fill the void between Annual Meetings of the ASA" (ASA, 1972, p. 32) by acting as a facilitator of regular interaction between its members at in-person meetings but also via the section's newsletter: "As more of our members develop the habit of corresponding with (our secretary, Marie Haug) or other officers, we can expect the Newsletter to grow in usefulness" (ASA, 1972). Recognition by sociological peers was another goal that the OOW clearly embraced: "Our most visible activity remains 'Section Day' at the ASA meeting," which, the reader is told, could be used "to focus on research needs or opportunities rather than the reading of research papers" (ASA, 1972). Finally, the section also raised the issue of funding:

the membership continues to request that the Section sponsor regional workshops, or dissertation prizes, or other activities. In recognition of the fact that these cost money and that our current Section dues go entirely to ASA for services provided to us, we are conducting a referendum about the possibility of an increase in Section dues. (ASA, 1972)

In the decades that followed, the OOW consolidated itself as the main hub for OrgSoc in the United States. It would organize events such as conference sessions or workshops, issue a newsletter that was sent to members regularly, and publish an influential book series, *Research in the Sociology of Organizations* (RSO), that continues today. The OOW has indeed contributed to building a community of self-identified organizational sociologists. At the same time, the section's name itself reveals that there are certain limits within sociology to constituting a subdiscipline around the epistemic target "organization" that is distinct from other epistemic targets such as "work" or "occupation."

At the international level, OrgSoc was able to achieve marginal levels of institutionalization within the larger realm of sociology (Hiller & Pohlmann, 2015). Founded in 1957, Research Committee 17: Sociology of Organizations (RC17) represents OrgSoc in the International Sociological Association. RC17 preceded the OOW by a decade, but, with a membership base that barely reaches triple digits, is not nearly as influential. The European Sociological Association does not have a section or committee dedicated to OrgSoc. There are 13 national OrgSoc associations (ISA, 2023) with varying degrees of institutionalization: In some countries, such as Great Britain (Holmwood, 2010; Parker, 2000; Rowlinson & Hassard, 2011), OrgSoc is all but extinct, whereas it has succeeded in retaining a stable foundation in others such as Germany (Hiller & Pohlmann, 2015).

It is not easy to assess whether OrgSoc is a settlement in Abbot's sense. On a long "march toward sophistication" (Suchman, 2014), a community of sociologists has worked hard to make "organizations" an epistemic target worthy of being a subdiscipline. Compared to their predecessors, self-identified organizational sociologists have shown less interest in general sociological debates cutting across subdisciplinary boundaries. Despite successful community building and its stabilization as an identity project, OrgSoc has only been partially embedded into sociology in a structural sense. For one thing, tenured positions solely dedicated to the sociological study of organizations are scarce, even in countries such as Germany where OrgSoc is said to have a strong foothold (Hiller & Pohlmann, 2015). Moreover, the influence of OrgSoc on national and international sociology associations is moderate at best, which also holds true for general debates in sociology and sociological publishing.

Organizational sociologists give the impression that they are fighting what seems like a war on two fronts: in sociology, where OrgSoc has "been increasingly positioned as a more and more marginal subdiscipline" (Parker, 2000, p. 126), and with business school faculty, who are perceived as an even bigger threat. Those who subscribe to this view paint "a gloomy future for the sociology of organizations" and worry that they will be "overtaken [...] by the research performance of business schools" (Besio et al., 2020, p. 412). Scott (2020, p. 444), for example, argues that sociology "has been very productive in spawning new disciplinary fields" (such as OS) but suffers from its inherent "weakness of monopolistic claims." Fields like OS, he continues, have profited from this weakness and been able to "establish themselves as separate subdisciplines or 'studies'." Echoing this sentiment, Holmwood (2010, p. 646) points out that "it is not only individuals and frameworks, concepts and methodologies that migrate, but also entire sub-fields," which "are then reproduced within the 'applied' subject area." Sociology's "bread and butter," he concludes, "is vulnerable to be taken off our plates to become a full meal in an importer subject" (Holmwood, 2010, p. 648).

It appears that "sociologists" and "business school faculty" are considered stable categories. Simply put, according to these narratives, people *are* sociolo-gists or business school faculty – by virtue of training, self-identification, or a little of both. Organizational sociologists might retain their identity after cross-ing disciplinary boundaries, as implied by the title of a subtheme at the annual EGOS Colloquium in 2022 ("Doing sociology in organization studies"). Yet, we are reminded that these qualities, though stable, should not be mistaken for being completely immutable. According to the following quote from a blog post, organizational sociologists who have joined the ranks of business school faculty are liable to feel more and more pressure to adapt:

> In business schools [...] sociologists constitute a rather small component of the larger inter-disciplinary field of management or organization studies [...]. Business-school based sociolo-gists, too, have moved away from the traditional topics and themes of organizational sociology. (Gorman, 2014)

The blog post further illustrates the sense of homelessness that may afflict self-identified organizational sociologists. In the following quote, the author ponders the difficulties she experienced when she wanted to update a syllabus for a gradu-ate course on organizational sociology:

> I found myself puzzled about what to include. On the one hand, there were active research conversations that seemed to be taking place almost entirely among management faculty and in management journals – and thus arguably outside the disciplinary boundaries of sociology [...]. On the other hand, there was no shortage of sociological research involving organizations in some way, but most of it seemed better classified under (and was often clearly intended to speak to) another subfield of the discipline [...]. Work that could be uniquely identified as "organiza-tional sociology" seemed to have largely disappeared. (Gorman, 2014)

What is noteworthy about this streak in OrgSoc discourse is that it rallies around a framing that bears resemblance to Abbott's view of settlements: groups of actors (organizational sociologists and business school faculty) com-pete over the prerogative to study organizations, with gains made by one group inevitably coming at their competitor's expense. Other accounts pursue a differ-ent line of reasoning, one that has more in common with Eyal's (2013) defini-tion of expertise. Instead of actors, jurisdictions, and resources, their focus lies mainly on the structure of sociological knowledge about organizations. An early review article concludes that "organizational sociology has been and remains an important asset for general sociology and for a variety of sociological sister spe-cialities" (Lammers, 1981b, p. 361). Published a few years later, another article mentions that "the areas of organization and stratification crosscut most of the empirical subfields of sociology and are amenable to theoretical analysis into a compact and coherent body of principles" (Collins, 1986, p. 1346). And, more recently, studies have found that articles published in sociology journals consistently apply theoretical frameworks that either conceptualize organizations or are sensitive to organizational phenomena (Grothe-Hammer & Kohl, 2020; Jacobs, 2007).

The bottom line for this second view is that, as a discipline, sociology generally accepts that organizations are key to a better understanding of society. There is reason to believe that OrgSoc has been so successful that it now must succumb to what Merton (1988, p. 622) calls "obliteration by integration," which he defines as "the obliteration of the sources of ideas, methods, or findings by their being anonymously incorporated in current canonical knowledge." In this spirit, Thoenig (1998) concedes that OrgSoc has made valuable contributions to the sociological tool kit and proved to be a great asset in furthering our knowledge of "basic societal mechanisms or processes, such as trust, power, capitalism, institutions, social exchange, stratification, action, order." Somewhat provocatively, he ponders whether we have already discovered everything we need to know about organizations, which, he continues, might be the reason why OrgSoc "can no longer be identified as a bounded and specialized knowledge-production programme" (Thoenig, 1998, p. 314). Suchman (2014, p. 42) makes a related point when he argues that decades of research have revealed that "organizations are not as distinctive as one might naively expect." He has no doubt that organizations *could be* key pieces in sociological puzzles, but we are well advised to consider that "the study of organizations is [...] not as indispensible [*sic.*] for understanding teams, industries, politics and beliefs as we, in our more grandiose moments, might claim" (Suchman, 2014).

Each of these views draws attention to different aspects. The first view suggests that OrgSoc was established as a sociological subdiscipline, but remains, in Abbott's terms, a weak settlement; after initial periods of growth, it is bound to lose its "bread and butter" to a hyper-muscular opponent – OS. The second view foregrounds sociological knowledge about organizations – a broader and fuzzier category than "organizational sociology in a narrow sense" (Grothe-Hammer & Kohl, 2020, p. 421) – which appears to have left its mark on sociology and beyond. Either way, it has become clear that to fully grasp developments in OrgSoc, we must explore its relationship with OS.

FROM PROFESSIONALIZATION TO SCIENTIZATION: A BRIEF HISTORY OF THE BUSINESS SCHOOL

The history of OS is inextricably entwined with the changing nature of business schools, the place where "most organization studies are now conducted [...] and from which organization studies is now inseparable" (Grey, 2010, pp. 677–678). This section traces the delegitimization of an organizational template that we may refer to as the *profession-oriented business school*, which lasted from the late 19th century until the 1950s, and subsequent reforms in the 1960s and 1970s, which led to the institutionalization of the *science-oriented business school*.

From the 19th century until the mid-20th century, the core mission of (US-American) business schools, and eventually their key source of legitimacy, was to facilitate the professionalization of management, which implied an orientation toward (managerial) practice (Khurana, 2007).[2] Take the Wharton School of the University of Pennsylvania. In 1881, industrialist Joseph Wharton donated a large sum of money to the University of Pennsylvania for the purpose of founding a business school where students could receive an education that was steeped in scientific principles, but for a very specific reason: to make them better managers (Sass, 1982). Seeking to elevate management into the sacred status of a profession by providing what they saw as vitally needed higher education, these profession-oriented business schools were determined to foster ties between higher education and the business community, arguably their most important stakeholder in that period. Faculty was, therefore, chosen mainly on the basis of practical experience and encouraged to continue offering consulting services even after being granted tenure. As a result, business schools held a "subordinate position in the academic pantheon" (Starkey & Tiratsoo, 2007, p. 13), which, however, they did not mind. To be treated "as the equals of other 'professional faculties'" (Alajoutsijärvi et al., 2015, p. 280) had little value for them because they did not seek recognition within the academy; their attention lay elsewhere.

Overall, business school faculty created knowledge according to four core premises: (1) The *object of study* was a specific type of organization, the corporation, and conceived of as a "closed-rational system" (Scott, 1998, p. 108); (2) the *goal* was to "discover those procedures that would produce the maximum output with the minimum input of energies and resources" (Scott, 1998, p. 38), resulting in countless accounts "of how management could maximise productivity and thus profits" (Tourish, 2019, p. 9); (3) *formal hierarchies*, the preferred style of organizational governance, would unite "all control of the labour process in the hands of [management]" and furthermore ensure "that a worker had no more knowledge or skill than was needed to perform the particular task" (Tourish, 2019, p. 12); (4) knowledge production predominantly reflected the *interests of management* and was, as such, inherently biased – workers needed to be dealt with but, since their concerns were interpreted as "an irrational pathology that required treatment," they were not thought of as having a legitimate voice of their own; meanwhile, it was unthinkable "that managers might sometimes act irrationally" (Tourish, 2019, p. 17).

The profession-oriented model of business schools encountered a surge in public criticism in the 1950s, followed by that model's gradual replacement. A crucial factor was undoubtedly an influx of new students in the wake of economic growth and the GI Bill, which poured large sums of money into higher education and especially the business school sector. This turned out to be a blessing and a curse. Business schools gained in resources, personnel, and numbers, but at the same time, the stakes were raised. Facing heightened scrutiny by prospective students, politicians, funding bodies, and journalists, their growth and expansion also "imperiled [their] meager academic legitimacy" (Khurana, 2007, p. 235). A purported cure was soon found and promoted vigorously throughout the 1950s by a coalition of scholars, deans, university presidents, politicians, government agencies, philanthropic organizations, and journalists: "scientification" (Alajoutsijärvi et al., 2015, p. 280). The Ford Foundation was at the center of this movement. Its direct involvement, while spanning only a brief period from the 1950s until the early 1960s, was of critical importance (Augier & March, 2011; Khurana, 2007; Starkey & Tiratsoo, 2007).

The reformers exerted influence through direct engagement, whereby they exposed business school faculty to the standards of research and teaching that hailed from traditional university departments. The following quote illustrates the magnitude and comprehensive nature of the investments undertaken by the Ford Foundation:

> In total, the foundation spent over $35 million in its programs to improve business schools and management education [...]. The major categories of grants included $12 million that went to general institutional support, $8 million to research support, $6 million to doctoral and faculty fellowships, and $4 million to workshops and seminars designed to improve the teaching and research in specific areas [...]. Altogether, 1,500 faculty members from nearly 300 different institutions participated. Thirty-eight (64 percent) of the workshops were organized by one of the top eight schools using faculty drawn primarily from those schools. (Augier & March, 2011, pp. 111–112)

The reformers also promoted their vision of scientification in the public domain to create a favorable climate for change. An article by James D. Thompson – a sociologist by training – illustrates the main thrust of these calls for action. Published in the first issue of *ASQ*, the article is a devastating account of knowledge production at business schools:

> Much of our literature is lore, spelling out how a procedure or technique is carried out in current practice or proclaiming that "this is the way" to do it. This material contains rather bold and often implicit assumptions about the relationships between the procedure or technique under consideration and other things which take place within the organization [...]. The pressure for immediately applicable research results must be removed from a large part of our research. It is this pressure which, in part, leads to the formulation of common-sense hypotheses framed at low levels of abstraction, without regard for general theory. (Thompson, 1956, pp. 105, 110)

Business schools were usually benchmarked against universities, with traditional disciplines serving as role models. The following quote by Thomas Carroll, head of the Ford Foundation's influential program on Economic Development and Administration, is a typical expression of this sentiment: "Certain influential business educators regard social psychology, cultural anthropology, sociology, mathematics, and statistics, as well as economics, as the business analogues of the medical students' anatomy, biochemistry, pathology, and physiology" (Carroll, 1958, p. 6).

Standing out in the avalanche of critical assessments are two reports, one commissioned by the Carnegie Foundation (Pierson, 1959), the other by the Ford Foundation (Gordon & Howell, 1959), both described as "key events in the records of business school history" (Augier & March, 2011, p. 113). The authors of the report issued by the Ford Foundation – which is usually seen as having had the biggest impact on public debates – make their case in no uncertain terms:

Collegiate business education is [...] a restless and uncertain giant in the halls of higher education [...], gnawed by doubt and harassed by the barbs of unfriendly critics [...]. It is aware of its
ungainly size and views apprehensively the prospect of still further growth. (Gordon & Howell,
1959, p. 4)

As they turned to "the halls of higher education," reformers such as the
authors of the Ford Foundation's report adopted the habit of discrediting the
profession-oriented business school: what had thus far been perceived as the
noble goal of transforming management into a legitimate profession was now
called "(t)he vocational approach," which, according to the report, "has all too
often characterized these schools in the past" and must be "considered inade-
quate" (Gordon & Howell, 1959, p. v). Business schools, the report concludes,
should truly embrace the scientific ideal, both in their research and teaching:

While there is need for improvement in all the dimensions of quality, the primary needs are
quite clear. They are to create in the business schools a more stimulating intellectual atmosphere, to bring the less progressive faculty members up to date with the latest scientific literature
and business practice in their own and related fields, and to generate the capacity and desire to
ask more probing questions and to engage in more significant research. In this sort of environment, academic standards will necessarily be high, the achievement of more effective teaching
should not be difficult, and the ability of the business schools to serve the business community
and society at large will be enormously increased. (Gordon & Howell, 1959, p. 357)

Exposed to public criticism of this kind throughout the 1950s, business school
faculty gradually saw their past in a different light and were more inclined to
reconsider the value of the professionalization project. For instance, in the 1960s,
Herbert Simon (1967), who migrated from a university department to a business
school early on in his career, was already being skeptical of efforts "to get as close
to the actual practice and environment of business as possible" (pp. 6–7). Later in
his career, he would famously characterize profession-oriented business schools
as "a wasteland of vocationalism" (Simon, 1991, p. 138). Many share this view.
For example, Dennis Tourish (2019), in a recently published book, laments that
knowledge "lacked theoretical or methodological sophistication and was as likely
to be wrong as it was to be right" (p. 8).

Under the impression of a changing discursive landscape, business schools
initiated lasting reforms in the 1960s and 1970s (Khurana, 2007). Increasingly
caring about "respectability and approval on their campuses" (Pfeffer & Fong,
2002, p. 92), science-oriented business schools turned to new hiring practices,
implemented scientific standards in research and teaching, and reassessed their
traditional forms of evaluation.

(1) To be perceived as "serious academic institutions" (Augier et al., 2005,
p. 90), business schools first and foremost needed credible personnel, which is why,
in the pursuit of respectability, they pressured "less progressive faculty members" (Gordon & Howell, 1959, p. 357) to adapt by, for instance, obtaining a PhD.
Alternatively, those labeled "less progressive" were gradually replaced with scholars from university departments. Hiring from the social sciences (economics,
sociology, philosophy, political science, anthropology) became so widespread that
university departments were forced to fight for their talent. Yet, business schools

often had the upper hand simply because they could offer "high pay compared with that in faculties of arts and sciences" (Khurana, 2007, p. 307; Rowlinson & Hassard 2011; Scott, 2004).[3] Stockpiling their ranks with graduates from traditional university departments further increased "the scholarly pretensions of many business schools" (Augier & March, 2011, p. 180) – and their faculty, who felt that they "deserved to be accorded higher status, and especially a greater degree of recognition from their peers" (Starkey & Tiratsoo, 2007, p. 130).

(2) Business schools also chose a new approach to research and teaching. Facing higher "expectations with respect to academic research" (Augier & March, 2011, p. 179), faculty were endowed with "generous research budgets" and "relatively light teaching loads" (Khurana, 2007, p. 307). Vocational courses and case-study teaching, hallmarks of traditional business education, lost relevance and new study programs touted "research-based teaching." While it would be an overstatement to say that business schools abandoned their traditional ways of teaching, they did come under increased pressure to offer a larger share of courses focusing on "scientifically valid procedures" (Alajoutsijärvi et al., 2015, p. 280).

(3) Business schools adopted evaluation procedures that valorized research articles published in peer-reviewed journals. As Starkey and Tiratsoo (2007, pp. 130, 132) put it, faculty "now wrote what they termed 'papers', which, like those in natural science journals, featured specialist language and a rigidly prescribed format." Thanks to the promise of "academic respectability" (Starkey & Tiratsoo, 2007), research articles quickly came into fashion and the number of specialized academic journals exploded (Agarwal & Hoetker, 2007; Khurana, 2007). Some of the traditional journals, like the *Sloan Management Review* (published since 1959), tried to maintain a balance between this new vision of scientific rigor and relevance for the management profession, but the majority turned to (natural) scientific forms of scholarly publishing, particularly those that would eventually be designated the "few primary outlets" (Augier et al., 2005, p. 87) such as *AMJ* and *ASQ* (Strang & Siler, 2017). This sudden appetite for research articles targeting an expert audience was intimately connected to institutional reforms of the criteria for hiring faculty and awarding tenure, which "began to attach greater weight to the number of publications in leading journals and the number of times an individual's work was cited by other academics" (Khurana, 2007, p. 307).

The changes described in this section are neither uniform or universal. Not all business schools in the United States have committed to the same level of "scientification." Arguably, the so-called elite institutions have been the most prolific reformers, but the further we move down the hierarchy, the more traces of "practical relevance" we still find. In a similar vein, the global diffusion of the science-oriented business school is a complex process with considerable variations in the template's national implementation. While acknowledging these variations, I would maintain that the science-oriented business school has effectively become the dominant model in contemporary higher education and continues to crowd out competing models.

OS AS A SETTLEMENT

The spread of the science-oriented business school coincided with, and brought about changes in, multiple fields of scholarly practice such as economics, finance, organizational psychology – and what would be known as OS. Emerging in the 1970s, OS became a settled field of scholarly practice with "its own community, its own institutions, its own standards, and its own language" (Augier et al., 2005, p. 93). Having established jurisdiction by enforcing several "mechanisms of control," business school faculty define "what is included and taken as legitimate and proper and what is excluded and deemed to be improper and illegitimate" (Westwood & Clegg, 2003, p. 13) in OS. A review of the research literature, essays, editorials, and other material reveals the following mechanisms: (1) fostering relationships (with key stakeholders), (2) valorizing research articles (published in a specific set of journals), and (3) monopolizing influential positions.[4]

(1) *Fostering relationships.* Compared to most university departments, business schools have access to a wealth of resources that they use to secure the lion's share of tenured positions dedicated to the academic study of organizations for themselves. This puts disciplines such as sociology, which compete for the same resources, at a clear disadvantage. Moreover, the tenured positions that sociology awards to those who are specialized in organizations usually have more than one epistemic target ("Gender and Organization," "Organization and Work"). All of this makes OS a far more reliable provider of "financial and occupational bases for organization studies" (March, 2007, p. 17; see also Hinings, 2010) than sociology.

To obtain funds on such a scale, business schools seek to convince different stakeholders that OS is useful and should be under their purview. University administrators have been identified as key stakeholders because they "control the immediately crucial resources of faculty lines" (Abbott, 1988, p. 141). Perceiving business schools as the proverbial "cash cow" (Bothello & Roulet, 2019, p. 857), administrators see investing in them as "a particularly attractive option" (Starkey & Tiratsoo, 2007, p. 32). Regulators and regulatory agencies are also stakeholders. In higher education systems with merit-based evaluation procedures, such as the REF in Great Britain, business schools and their faculty seem well versed in funneling the stream of resources their own way, thus putting university disciplines such as sociology at a disadvantage (Holmwood, 2010). Other stakeholders that business schools (though not necessarily business school faculty) try to sway are prospective students and their parents. Although the day-to-day life of OS scholarship is primarily driven by research and publishing, business schools cunningly lure clients in by touting their strengths in teaching, as evidenced by the "copious material on courses, virtual tours round state-of-the-art teaching and learning facilities, and panegyrics about the alleged benefits of this or that qualification" (Starkey & Tiratsoo, 2007, p. 115).

(2) *Valorizing research articles.* Once the research article had been defined as "an important currency of standing" (Augier & March, 2011, p. 180) in the 1970s, it eventually became *the* yardstick for quality in OS. Virtually all journals – at least, those that "count" – nowadays subscribe to similar criteria: a "good article" should comply with a highly standardized format (Strang & Siler, 2017), contain

sufficient references to the OS literature (Agarwal & Hoetker, 2007; Augier et al., 2005), make ritualistic claims to a theoretical contribution – the "stylized holy grail" (McGrath, 2007, p. 1371) of OS – and be written in English, "the language of 'top' quality scholarship" (Boussebaa & Tienari, 2021, p. 62). Business schools impose rigid "tenure and promotion mechanisms" (Grey, 2010, p. 684) on their faculty who live and die by being able to publish research articles in "top journals." Any other type of scholarly activity – editing volumes or anthologies, writing books, advocacy, teaching, or simply being a "good local" by taking on administrative tasks – is of no practical use to one's career.

While, to a degree, most higher education institutions, disciplines, and fields of study are subject to change of the above kind, business schools have certainly taken a position at the forefront. Resembling the higher education institutions that Paradeise and Thoenig (2015) call "Wannabes," they treat academic work as a game. The preparation of faculty is "a substantive concern" (Starkey & Tiratsoo, 2007, p. 118) and starts early on. PhD students are kept "busy writing their first journal articles" (Grey, 2010, p. 684), which, they learn, are the one and only "currency on the job market" (Bothello & Roulet, 2019, p. 856). To this end, they receive "formalized research training" (Grey, 2010, p. 684) tailored to their needs, have a steady supply of workshops on themes such as "how to get published in an A+ journal," amass "best practice" PowerPoint slides, are taught important acronyms signaling membership, and profit from close guidance by advisors who are usually themselves seasoned OS experts and privy to the "tricks of the trade." By contrast, scholars who work at sociology departments do not enjoy the same privileges when it comes to their initiation into OS, which is why they have to deal with a tilted table from the beginning. In addition, by belonging to other academic settlements, they are bound to address scholarly debates, use theories, apply methods, and ask research questions in ways that might put them at a disadvantage in OS.

We should note that publishing research articles is as much "a demanding form of identity work" (Boussebaa & Tienari, 2021, p. 63) as it is about strategic action, meaning that being published in a "top journal" also attests one's belonging in the OS settlement and is thereby "enmeshed within the making of modern business schools as legitimate academic entities" (Grey, 2010, p. 684). This sheds new light on the findings of studies on citation patterns (Lockett & McWilliams, 2005; Vogel, 2012). Business school faculty have "constructed a history [...], a set of loosely connected stories" (Augier et al., 2005, p. 87) signifying that OS knowledge production is more than just derivative. By increasingly referring to each other's work and by constructing narratives that downplay the importance of university disciplines, OS scholars define theirs as a field that is "*not* organizational sociology, or industrial relations and so on [...]. It is precisely by neglecting its prehistory that organization studies can come into being" (Parker, 2000, p. 140 – italics in original).

On closer inspection, business school faculty show such dedication to what they see as scientific rigor that they often lose sight of another major requirement for fields of study: building a productive relationship with stakeholders outside of academia who are provided with "extensive applied knowledge" (Abbott,

2001, p. 140). Not only is relevance less of a concern than in the first half of the 20th century (Bothello & Roulet, 2019; Hambrick, 1994), but business school faculty worry that their community's style of writing is obscure even by academic standards: "only a handful of devotees can understand most of our ideas, and fewer still can find any application for them" (Tourish, 2019, p. 8; see also Grey & Sinclair, 2006). It seems that the administrative staff of business schools work tirelessly to navigate the obscurity of OS publishing and to maintain the impression there is a real-world benefit to be had from the extensive funding of tenure track positions with a focus on organizations.

(3) *Monopolizing influential positions.* Business school faculty have assumed control over influential positions in the field, so that they act as gatekeepers and fulfill elementary self-governing functions. Specifically, they monopolize positions (3a) on executive boards of associations and (3b) on the editorial boards of "top journals."

(3a) Professional associations are important tools in the governance of academic settlements for several reasons (Heilbron, 2014). They might be used as levers for collective action, critical interventions, and the diffusion of standards, but they also present opportunities to celebrate and affirm shared identities. Prestigious conferences organized by professional associations are sites where junior and senior scholars ceremonially present themselves as worthy members of the community (Westwood & Clegg, 2003, p. 14). In this sense, March (2007, p. 10) interprets EGOS "as a broad association of scholars" who are united by their belief in what he refers to as "the myth of organization studies."

Some professional associations were always dominated by business school faculty but eventually turned to scientific credibility in the 1970s, often at the expense of practical relevance (Hambrick, 1994). A well-known example is the Academy of Management (AOM), which, according to its own website, "has evolved from an organization of 10 members to an organization of over 18,000 members from nearly 120 countries" (AOM, 2022). In other cases, professional associations that previously had a mixed membership base gradually limited access to scholars working at university departments. EGOS, for instance, was "inspired and set up by sociologists, not scholars in management" (Greenwood et al., 2010, p. 653). As one founding member details:

> originally our idea was to constitute some kind of association to promote the mutual exchange of information and insights between, and eventually joint research efforts by, sociologists engaged in organizational research across Europe. At our first meeting in Paris, which later on turned out to have been the originating assembly of EGOS, it was in my recollection Jean-Claude Thoenig who insisted that we should not deter those who had no training in sociology, but who, nevertheless, were approaching the subject from other social science points of view. Therefore, the S of EGOS came to stand for "studies" rather than "sociology." (Lammers, 1998, p. 884)

Yet, over time, the executive board gradually closed its ranks. Stacked with business school faculty, it shifted the position of EGOS in academia, so that it eventually became a part of the OS settlement (Hiller & Pohlmann, 2015, pp. 57–58).

Business school faculty have access to privileged information, for instance, which conferences must be attended, and they know how to write abstracts in compliance with the field's conventions. Junior faculty can count on their advisors – who also happen to be part of the group dominating OS – to act as co-authors, which lowers the threshold for inclusion substantially compared to their peers from university departments, whose advisors are more likely to be oriented toward other settlements, such as sociology.

(3b) Like professional associations, OS journals either have always been dominated by business school faculty or were eventually absorbed into the settlement. The *AMJ*, seen as one of the leading outlets in OS, has attracted the attention of business school faculty since it came into existence. *OrgStudies*, on the other hand, founded in 1980 by EGOS, was in large part conceived by sociologists from different European countries and, in its early years, emphasized inclusiveness (Lammers, 1998). The following quote from the first editorial exemplifies this sentiment:

> Since one of the demands which spurred the launching of Organization Studies was for a journal that would be flexible in content and style, open to a diversity of paradigms, and to any and all of the disciplines which contribute to organization theory, we hesitate to define its scope more than is already done by the dedication on the cover and the aims stated on the inside front cover. To define which ideas are "in" is also to define those which are "out." To define who is "in" is also to define who is "out." (Hickson et al., 1980, p. 2)

But the make-up of the journal's editorial board has changed dramatically over the decades. With the share of business school faculty growing, the journal was gradually pulled into the OS settlement, just like EGOS. Today *OrgStudies* subscribes to the same standards as any other journal within the boundaries of the OS settlement. Relatedly, a study of *ASQ* reveals a steady increase in articles by business school faculty since the journal's first launch (Strang & Siler, 2017). The trajectory of RSO is probably the most intriguing case in point. Nominally still issued by the OOW section in the ASA, most volumes published in the series are edited by scholars working at business schools and comply with the standards and norms of the OS settlement.

Journal editors are powerful gatekeepers, even more so in settlements such as OS where the research article is the gold standard. As Pfeffer (2007, p. 1339) observes, editors in OS (and quite likely elsewhere too) "have a tendency to engage in coproduction, to 'help' an author write the paper they want to see or the paper they might have written had they done the particular study." By virtue of affiliation with OS, then, editors presumably act on behalf of the settlement and, in doing so partake in reproducing its norms and values. While perhaps seeing themselves as neutral arbiters, editors have been described as enforcers of "the dominant and orthodox position within OS" and acting "almost as holders of the citadels of publishing power, to the extent that they have control and manipulation of key journal publication processes" (Westwood & Clegg, 2003, pp. 13–14). Besides presiding over the legitimacy of theories, concepts, methodologies, topics, or research questions, editors enshrine English as the settlement's *lingua franca* – to the extent that most OS scholars decide against publishing their work in any other language. Unsurprisingly, the editorial boards of the "top journals" are dominated by scholars who work for, or are affiliated with, business schools in

English-speaking countries and who themselves publish only or mainly in English (Meyer & Boxenbaum, 2010).

In sum, business schools and their faculty sustain jurisdiction over OS by fostering relationships with key stakeholders, valorizing research articles, and monopolizing influential positions. These activities appear to be mutually reinforcing: being subject to initiation rituals early on in their careers and supported by powerful gatekeepers, business school faculty are likely to dominate the "top journals" in OS, which, in turn, ensures that tenure track positions are awarded to scholars from among their ranks.

OS AS A NETWORK OF EXPERTISE

After analyzing OS as a settled field of scholarly practice in Abbott's sense, this section explores its characteristics as a network of expertise, thereby drawing attention to a recurring theme: the chronic dependance on "borrowing" (Whetten et al., 2009, p. 538) analytical tools. I specifically discuss why OS, a matured and bounded settlement, has not put an end to intellectual "imports," a practice that has the potential to damage its reputation and credibility, as we are often told by those on the inside. I am going to argue that what is perceived as excessive "borrowing" is intimately connected to the epistemic configuration of OS expertise.

To get a better sense of the practice of "borrowing," we must go back to when OS was yoked together as a network of expertise. Instilled with a taste for the kind of basic research that is decoupled from external concerns such as the professionalization project, business school faculty entered uncharted territory in the 1960s. Craving, or feeling expected to crave, ownership over a respectable academic field, they found themselves unable to build on the work of their predecessors, who, according to the new paradigm of the science-oriented business school, were much too practice oriented. For this reason, they turned to "linking" (Whetten et al., 2009) with university disciplines such as economics, social psychology, and sociology, which presented them with the opportunity "to gain legitimacy and a relevant resource base" (Agarwal & Hoetker, 2007, p. 1305).

It seems that not much has changed: until today, "a primary source of novelty in organization studies has been importation from outside" (March, 2007, p. 16), which creates considerable unrest in OS as many wonder why such "strong ties between the applied study of organizations and the core social science disciplines" (Whetten et al., 2009, p. 538) continue to exist – a question asked by none other than business school faculty themselves. Using the analogy of the "Faustian bargain," Agarwal and Hoetker (2007, p. 1304) worry that OS has been committed to an "evolutionary path" (p. 1305) of continuously importing "different cognitive frameworks and capabilities," each containing "core research questions of interest, underlying assumptions, and conceptualizations of organizations" (p. 1307). In analytical terms, by linking with multiple university disciplines, business school faculty have shown "generosity" (in the sense of Eyal, 2013), as they allowed different epistemic cultures to be grafted onto OS expertise. This means that irrespective of who holds jurisdiction over the OS settlement, as a form of expertise, it inevitably gravitates toward theories, concepts, methodologies, methods, and research themes conceived outside its realm.

We should note that "borrowing" is far from unusual in the academic system. It is common for settlements to lean on the output of others, which they repackage or reinvent and subsequently present as being of their own making (Abbott, 2001). But in one respect, OS is indeed exceptional: the dominant group of experts is inherently drawn toward questioning its heavy engagement in "borrowing" which it sees as an indication of a lack of scientific maturity and the inability to produce knowledge on one's own terms. Thus, while every settlement "borrows," only some, OS in particular, are prone to critical self-examination. We may suspect that the high level of unease in OS is related to the epistemic configuration of its expertise, which, as already mentioned, is a patchwork of elements from multiple university disciplines. For the purposes of this article, the analysis of OS expertise is limited to what Lammers (1981b, p. 362) has called the sociological "touch": a number of principles that were grafted onto OS expertise and continue to influence knowledge production in the field.

There is considerable evidence for a sociological "touch." *Sociological theories and concepts* are key elements of OS. This holds true for the formative years, as illustrated by the abundance of references to the likes of Max Weber or by the title of Gibson Burrell and Gareth Morgan's seminal textbook published in 1979 (*Sociological Paradigms and Organizational Analysis*), which has been described as "one of the most referenced works in organization theory" (Hassard & Wolfram Cox, 2013, p. 1701). But sociological theories and concepts have also played a crucial role more recently. Taking stock, Lounsbury and Beckman (2015, p. 288) discuss five areas "where there are flourishing and generative developments" in OS: institutional logics, categorization, networks, performance feedback, and strategy-as-practice. Except for performance feedback, theorizing in these areas is firmly rooted in sociological thinking. OS also imports its fair share of *sociological methodologies and methods* (Buchanan & Bryman, 2009). Grounded theory, for example, has become a standard reference in qualitative research; the same holds true for network analysis in quantitative research. Lastly, *research themes* often originate in sociology. Case in point: countless studies on quantification, rankings, and valuation, all of which stand on the shoulders of sociological publications (e.g., Espeland & Sauder, 2007; Lamont, 2012).

Conventional approaches to measuring impact have only limited utility in this case. The problem with the most popular method, citation analysis, is that "not all published works that have actually guided an author's research are necessarily included in bibliographies" (Vogel, 2012, p. 1022). In other words, it is likely for sociology to exert influence over OS without necessarily receiving its share of citations. In turn, "authors may reference publications that they have not, in fact, drawn on" (Vogel, 2012), most likely because they feel that they must pay tribute to esteemed colleagues: increasingly self-referential citation networks in OS could therefore be mistaken for manifestations of rising levels of independence in knowledge production. This means that citation network analyses, while arguably shedding light on the boundedness of settlements, should not be taken at face value in the study of expertise. Rather, the task at hand is to trace the flow of *sociological bits and pieces* to OS expertise, however altered, doctored, modified, hidden, insufficient, transformed, or disfigured they might appear from the organizational sociologist's point of view. With this in mind, we now turn to four ways in which sociology has touched OS according to Lammers (1981b) – and, we might add, continues to do so.

(1) Sociological knowledge production is rooted in the idea of contributing to a deeper understanding of stability and change in modern societies. This is why sociologists gravitate toward contextualizing even the most mundane research objects (taking an elevator, crossing the street, organizing a party, etc.) by approaching them with more general questions in mind – at least in principle. Lammers (1981b) argues that sociologists who study organizations have done so in precisely this spirit: by analyzing organizations not as if they existed in a social vacuum but as "part and parcel of society," sociology has contributed "more than any other discipline" to our knowledge about "the interrelations between organizations and their societal surroundings" (p. 363).

This principle evidently left its mark on OS in the early days: "diverse theoretical developments followed one another in rapid succession during the 1960s and 1970s," each emphasizing "the richness of the environment and [...] its importance for organizational structures and processes" (Scott, 2004, p. 7). The population ecology approach and institutional theory are prime examples. Popular ecology, dating back to an article published in the *American Journal of Sociology* (*AJS*) (Hannan & Freeman, 1977), has received a great deal of attention in OS (Barley, 2016). Institutional theory, nowadays a hallmark of OS expertise and referred to in countless publications (Vogel, 2012), also dates to an article published in the *AJS* (Meyer & Rowan, 1977). Another foundational contribution to institutional theory (DiMaggio & Powell, 1983) is the most-cited paper ever to be published in the *American Sociological Review* (*ASR*), which also speaks to the relevance of organizational phenomena in sociology (Jacobs, 2005).

Clearly, OS has always been drawn toward conceptualizations of organizations as open systems that are "embedded in [...] the environments in which they operate" (Scott, 1998, p. 28). This might explain why "the study of organizations is scarcely imaginable without the aid of [...] sociological theory" (Whetten et al., 2009, p. 539). The sociological attitude of approaching research objects by asking general questions related to stability and change in modern society is likely one of the drivers of critical self-examinations to the effect that OS "today focuses too little on the big issues of our own times" (Adler, 2009, p. 5) and should "look outward and ask how organizations are altering our society" (Barley, 2016, p. 7).

(2) Another principle of sociological inquiry is that epistemic targets (class, occupation, network, family, and so forth) are conceptualized as having a "life of their own" rather than being the product of conscious design. Because sociologists take it for granted that their epistemic targets emerge organically, they are natural skeptics (though not necessarily opponents) of interventions. After all, something that has "a life of its own" is likely to be complex, meaning that we can never fully anticipate what will happen if we try to change it. Aware that purposeful action breeds unintended consequences, sociologists are liable to approach

organizations as "recalcitrant tools" that are basically "unmanageable," which is why they prioritize "such processes as goal displacement, oligarchic tendencies, the partly unintended consequences of vested interests, and of power struggles between dominant elites" (Lammers, 1981b, pp. 362–363).

In the 1970s, a growing number of business school faculty began to question what their predecessors held as self-evident: that they should provide "deep knowledge about organizations for improving managerial practice" (Khurana, 2007, p. 312). Casting doubts on the possibility of improvement by reform, these scholars withdrew their commitment to the "normative structure" of organizations and turned to the "behavioral structure" (Scott, 1998, pp. 17–18). What is more, by extending the scope of analysis from corporations to organizations in general, they soon discovered topics other than profitmaking (Khurana, 2007). The theme of the 38th EGOS Colloquium, "Organizing: The Beauty of Imperfection," encapsulates how contemporary OS is taking it for granted that the object of study has a life of its own and escapes managerial stewardship:

> The 38th EGOS Colloquium's theme engages with the dynamic and complex nature of organizing by questioning idealized images of 'perfection' as being rooted in order, efficiency, symmetry, and predictability. Rarely, if ever, do our theories and methods, or the contexts and organizations we study, conform to such idealized images. (EGOS, 2022)

(3) The third principle of sociological inquiry that found its way into OS expertise is what might be called "a gaze below the surface." Concepts such as frame of reference, symbol, institution, social construction, communication, or practice all hold the promise of revealing to us the subtle fabric of everyday life, that which cannot be seen straight away but is, in actual fact, of the essence for the analysis of social order. Clearly adopting this principle, classical sociological studies on organizational phenomena saw the formal structure as little more than "a decorative canopy" (Scott, 1998, p. 26) and laid their focus on "cultural aspects and determinants of organizational forms and processes" (Lammers, 1981b, p. 364) instead.

Organizational culture is arguably one of the first successful manifestations of this principle in OS scholarship. Parker (2000, p. 127) describes how "the explosion of interest was phenomenal. Academic management journals fell over each other to have a special issue on symbolism or culture." Constructivism is another good example. Besides their epistemological implications, constructivist theories also promote a critical attitude that eventually took hold in business schools (Khurana, 2007). Over the years, OS expertise broadened its analytical scope and developed an interest in such diverse themes as discourses, symbols, communication, and, recently, sociomateriality. This inevitably draws attention away from the formal structure and managerial concerns, which worries not only those among business school faculty who still hold practical relevance in high esteem. For instance, an article published in *Current Sociology* discusses a decision made by the editors of *OrgStudies* to add a section titled "X and Organization Studies" dedicated to unexplored areas of organizational life. "[T]he idea, explicitly articulated in the 'X and Organization Studies' call [...], and implicit in much contemporary scholarship in organization studies," the author complains, is "that one can get a better purchase on the intelligibility of matters organizational by looking beyond 'formal organization'" (du Gay, 2020, pp. 460, 462).

(4) A last principle is that there seems to be a "normative aspect of socio-logical inquiry" (Abbott, 2018, p. 159). Although it would be a mistake to think of sociology as a discipline that is inherently normative (Turner, 2016), we can-not ignore that many sociologists subscribe to what is essentially a progressive political agenda. Some are explicitly normative, which they highlight by making heavy use of adjectives like "critical," while in other cases the norm is implied (Stinchcombe, 1984) and remains in the (moral) background (Abend, 2014). Either way, there is no shortage of sociologists inclined to side with those who suffer from inequality and injustice, which has also always been a major con-cern for sociologists who study organizations: "in many of the best sociological studies of organizations there lurks a concern with social or human problems which are generated or aggravated by organizations" (Lammers, 1981b, p. 365). These studies, Lammers (1981b) continues, were "seldom undertaken with an eye towards helping management," which set their authors apart from those working at a profession-oriented business school.

Infused with the sociological habit of championing the powerless and under-privileged, OS scholarship nowadays recognizes inequality as an important issue while, on the other hand, ostentatiously neglecting leadership-related themes. As Khurana (2007, p. 357) explains, leadership has become such a marginal issue that "[e]ven established scholars who study the subject later in their careers risk academic marginalization and cynical accusations of having 'sold out.'" But more than simply neglecting the needs and concerns of management, OS might actu-ally have become openly antagonistic to it. Research on rankings is an intriguing example: following the path laid out by sociologists (Espeland & Sauder, 2007), many studies in OS seem determined to shine the light on the negative conse-quences of rankings but have little to say about how organizations could improve their positions. All of this is remarkable insofar as, despite the abundance of grandiose gestures and references to "global challenges," "social responsibil-ity," "ethics," and so on in mission statements, leaflets, or on websites, the main purpose of business schools is still to prepare students for leadership positions, mostly in for-profit organizations.

CRISES REVISITED

This paper started with a simple observation: both OrgSoc and OS have a pen-chant for self-diagnosed crises, albeit for different reasons. Organizational sociol-ogists, worried about losing influence and seeing their livelihood endangered, are struck by a "sense of depression" (Besio et al., 2020, p. 411). They lay the blame for this development on the growth of OS, nowadays a matured and bounded field of scholarly study that is dominated by business school faculty. The latter, however, far from bursting with self-confidence, continuously indulge in soul-searching and seem concerned about being perceived as "ungainly" (Gordon &

Howell, 1959, p. 4). I have approached these assessments as objects of study by asking what conditions fuel and sustain them. To answer this question, I have analyzed OrgSoc and OS as settlements, in Abbott's (1988, 2001) sense, and networks of expertise, in Eyal's (2013).

OrgSoc has, as we have seen, "become increasingly sophisticated over the years" (Suchman, 2014) and, thanks to extensive community building, been able to render organizations an epistemic target worthy of sociological attention (Krause, 2021). But, at the same time, it has only reached marginal levels of structural embeddedness in the discipline of sociology. There is then a mismatch between the spread of OrgSoc as a scholarly identity, one that numerous sociologists find attractive, and the (in)ability of the OrgSoc community to accumulate sufficient resources and gain influence. According to organizational sociologists, their subdiscipline is in a dire state because of the rampant growth of OS since the 1970s, a claim for which an analysis that conceptualizes academic fields as settlements shows some support.

Over the past decades, business school faculty have been able to draw a boundary around OS by limiting access to:

- tenured positions dedicated to the academic study of organizations,
- "top journals" such as the *ASQ, AMJ*, or *OS*, and
- and associations such as AOM or EGOS.

Under these conditions, organizational sociologists, apparently, can either start "navigating the business school job market" (Bariola, 2020) and effectively relinquish their affiliation with sociology or attempt cross-border skirmishes to tip the scales in their favor (for instance, by claiming or retaking a "top journal"). Neither option seems particularly promising. The first amounts to a mass exodus from sociology, which could have adverse effects on the discipline's intellectual output. The second, a kind of boundary work that might be summarized as "getting back what's ours," is futile because of the firm jurisdictional control that business school faculty hold over OS. But more than that, it draws organizational sociologists away from debates in the discipline of sociology. As a result, OrgSoc ends up "less interesting to non-organizational sociologists" (Suchman, 2014) *and* "less relevant to the broader discipline of which it is a part" (King, 2017, p. 132).[5]

The analysis of OrgSoc and OS as settlements has certainly helped us understand the conditions that fuel self-diagnosed crises in OrgSoc. The widespread unease in OS, on the other hand, forces us to extend the analytical scope: from experts and boundary work to networks of expertise. Criticized as being "ungainly" and an "uncertain giant" (Gordon & Howell, 1959, p. 4) in the 1950s, business schools began abandoning the project of transforming management into a profession and pushed faculty toward treating knowledge production in similar terms to those that operate in university departments: as something that is done for its own sake. In order to assemble scientized forms of expertise such as OS, business school faculty turned to the established university disciplines. This process has been described as "a Faustian bargain" (Agarwal & Hoetker, 2007,

p. 1304): by drawing on the disciplines' authority, business school faculty tacitly accepted that several existing epistemic cultures were grafted onto OS expertise. This set OS on a path of extensively borrowing theories, concepts, methodologies, methods, and research themes, irrespective of how vigorously business school faculty police its boundaries.

As a matter of fact, some version of a "trade deficit" (Whetten et al., 2009, p. 538) between disciplines and *studies* can be expected and is, to a degree, an organic feature of modern science (Abbott, 2001). But for at least two reasons, we may suspect that OS will continue to practice borrowing in a way that stirs controversy and raises doubts internally.

First, unlike *studies*, which are comfortable with their client orientation, OS embraces an ideal of scientific rigor that undermines the notion of utility or practical relevance (Bennis & O'Toole, 2005; Hambrick, 1994; Khurana, 2007). The most obvious manifestation of this sentiment are the hiring criteria for tenure track positions in OS, which, above all, favor research articles published in a limited number of "top journals." In stark contrast, the "utilitarian morality" (Augier & March, 2011, p. 223) deeply engrained in business schools still pushes faculty to be aware that, at least in principle, they should also be "useful" and "relevant" to managers. This inevitably creates tensions and, we may suspect, impinges on the production of scientific knowledge. Furthermore, entrapped in a complicated relationship with their employers and anxious about being perceived by their academic peers as lacking "scientific rigor," OS scholars presumably do not make the most of their unique access to corporations and managers (Khurana, 2007).

Second, the valorization of the research article (published in a "top journal") undermines the potential for innovation within OS. Research articles, it is said, engender incremental novelty (Barley, 2016; Pfeffer, 2007); meanwhile, books and book chapters offer space for experimental styles of writing, bolder claims, and more extensive discussions. Unlike sociology, which still sees value in books (Jacobs & Habinek, 2023), OS is only beholden to the research article, which deprives its members of other means of science communication. Moreover, the universal demand that all research articles should make a theoretical contribution – an obscure feature of OS publishing – fuels "a great deal of faux theorizing" (Tourish, 2020, p. 100). Finally, journals in OS coalesce around a format that strips research articles of the space necessary to develop rich empirical narratives or to flesh out intellectually stimulating conceptualizations. A study by Strang and Siler (2017) on *ASQ* found that articles typically have extensive sections on literature, theory, methods, data, and discussion – all at the expense of the author's original contribution, which has to be "squeezed in."

If OS is likely to remain dependent on "borrowing," then what exactly do the sociological bits and pieces in its epistemic configuration have in common? A shared feature of the examples given in the previous section is that they are for the most part not framed as contributions to "organizational sociology in a narrow sense" (Grothe-Hammer & Kohl, 2020, p. 421) or OS for that matter. Instead, we might think of them as carrying on the tradition of classical sociologists, whose insights on organizations were "accidental outcomes" (Scott, 2020, p. 447). Bruno Latour is one of the most intriguing cases of a sociologist who has had an accidental, yet significant impact on OS:

> I believe that it is precisely because Bruno Latour never intended to conduct organization studies that his work made us see beyond the iron cage of our own discipline. Interested in science and technology, he saw beyond the ossified structures of formal organizations, ignored the micro and macro hierarchies, and depicted a flat world, where connections between hybrid entities are constantly built and stabilized. (Czarniawska, 2014, p. 102)

This adds another layer to the self-proclaimed crisis in OrgSoc. Not only does OS fail to recognize self-identified organizational sociologists as potential *trading partners* who are owed something in return (a chance to get published in "top journals" or access to influential positions). But, almost adding insult to injury, OS frequently "borrows" from general sociology rather than "organizational sociology in a narrow sense" (Grothe-Hammer & Kohl, 2020, p. 421). If anything, sociology is an *unintentional donor* to OS expertise, not a trading partner.

In closing, I want to invoke an article by Jean-Claude Thoenig (1998) titled "How far is a sociology of organizations still needed?" published more than 20 years ago. Those among us who allege that there is such a need and who wish to save OrgSoc from extinction could draw inspiration from the undertone of Thoenig's article. The goals would then be threefold: first, to maintain a solid foundation in sociology so as to expose OrgSoc to the discipline's gravitational pulls and pushes; second, to disengage from skirmishes with business school faculty, which, besides being futile, also absorb time and energy that could be used toward more productive goals; and, finally, to never stop asking the question "why should I study organizations?" (Suchman, 2014), which ensures that OrgSoc does not become a bloodless version of itself.

NOTES

1. See Heilbron et al. (2008) for the impact of migration on scientific knowledge production.
2. Drumming up basic levels of support for business schools in the 19th century to admit them into the category of "higher education institutions" while also convincing future managers that they would benefit from becoming "college men" was, in fact, a complex process (Abend, 2014, chapter 5).
3. The existence of events with titles such as "Sociology PhDs Navigating the Business School Job Market" (Bariola, 2020) speaks volumes.
4. The reader should keep in mind that these mechanisms are not necessarily a matter of conscious choice or deliberation but more likely a by-product of social practice.
5. There are notable exceptions such as recent calls for ties to be renewed between OrgSoc and the larger discipline (Arnold et al., 2021).

ACKNOWLEDGMENTS

I acknowledge support for the publication costs by the Open Access Publication Fund of Bielefeld University and the Deutsche Forschungsgemeinschaft (DFG).

For their invaluable feedback on earlier drafts of this paper, I would like to thank the editors of this volume – Stewart Clegg, Michael Grothe-Hammer, Kathia Serrano Velarde – and the anonymous reviewers, as well as Gabriel Abend, Jelena Brankovic, Nils Brunsson, Raimund Hasse, Maximilian Heimstädt, Robert Jungmann, Sven Kette, Anne K. Krüger, Stefan Kühl, Thomas Mtüller, Martin Petzke, Georg Reischauer, Charlotte Renda, Michael Sauder, Andreas Schmitz, and Friedrich Stratmann.

REFERENCES

Abbott, A. (1988). *The system of professions: An essay on the division of expert labor.* University of Chicago Press.

Abbott, A. (2001). *Chaos of disciplines.* University of Chicago Press.

Abbott, A. (2018). Varieties of normative inquiry: Moral alternatives to politicization in sociology. *The American Sociologist, 49*(2), 158–180.

Abend, G. (2014). *The moral background: An inquiry into the history of business ethics.* Princeton University Press.

Adler, P. S. (2009). Introduction: A social science which forgets its founders is lost. In P. Adler (Ed.), *The Oxford handbook of sociology and organization studies* (pp. 4–19). Oxford University Press.

Agarwal, R., & Hoetker, G. (2007). A Faustian bargain? The growth of management and its relationship with related disciplines. *The Academy of Management Journal, 50*(6), 1304–1322.

Alajoutsijärvi, K., Juusola, K., & Siltaoja, M. (2015). The legitimacy paradox of business schools: Losing by gaining? *Academy of Management Learning & Education, 14*(2), 277–291.

AOM. (2022). *The history of the Academy of Management.* Retrieved September 11, 2022, from https://aom.org/about-aom/history

Arnold, N., Hasse, R., & Mormann, H. (2021). Organisationsgesellschaft neu gedacht: Vom Archetyp zu neuen Formen der Organisation. *Kölner Zeitschrift für Soziologie & Sozialpsychologie, 73*(3), 339–360.

ASA. (1970). Official reports and proceedings. *The American Sociologist, 5*(4), 396–428.

ASA. (1971). Official reports and proceedings. *The American Sociologist, 6*(4), 335–366.

ASA. (1972). Official reports and proceedings. *The American Sociologist, 7*(7), 24–32.

Augier, M., & March, J. G. (2011). *The roots, rituals, and rhetorics of change: North American business schools after the Second World War.* Stanford Business Books.

Augier, M., March, J. G., & Sullivan, B. N. (2005). Notes on the evolution of a research community: Organization studies in Anglophone North America, 1945–2000. *Organization Science, 16*(1), 85–95.

Bariola, N. (2020). *Call for participants: AOM OMT virtual cafe: Sociology PhDs navigating the business school job market.* https://oowsection.org/2020/08/07/call-for-participants-aom-omt-virtual-cafe-sociology-phds-navigating-the-business-school-job-market/

Barley, S. R. (2016). 60th anniversary essay: Ruminations on how we became a mystery house and how we might get out. *Administrative Science Quarterly, 61*(1), 1–8.

Bennis, W. G., & O'Toole, J. (2005). How business schools lost their way. *Harvard Business Review, 83*(5), 96–154.

Besio, C., du Gay, P., & Serrano Velarde, K. (2020). Disappearing organization? Reshaping the sociology of organizations. *Current Sociology, 68*(4), 411–418.

Bothello, J., & Roulet, T. J. (2019). The imposter syndrome, or the mis-representation of self in academic life. *Journal of Management Studies, 56*(4), 854–861.

Boussebaa, M., & Tienari, J. (2021). Englishization and the politics of knowledge production in management studies. *Journal of Management Inquiry, 30*(1), 59–67.

Buchanan, A., & Bryman, A. (Eds.). (2009). *The Sage handbook of organizational research methods.* Sage.

Carroll, T. H. (1958). Education for business: A dynamic concept and process. *The Accounting Review*, *33*(1), 3–10.

Collins, R. (1986). Is 1980s sociology in the doldrums? *American Journal of Sociology*, *91*(6), 1336–1355.

Czarniawska, B. (2014). Bruno Latour: An accidental organization theorist? In P. Adler, P. Du Gay, G. Morgan, & M. Reed (Eds.), *The Oxford handbook of sociology, social theory & organization studies. Contemporary currents* (pp. 87–105). Oxford University Press.

DiMaggio, P., & Powell, W. (1983). The iron cage revisited: Institutional isomorphism and collective rationality in organizational fields. *American Sociological Review*, *48*(2), 147–160.

du Gay, P. (2020). Disappearing "formal organization": How organization studies dissolved its "core object," and what follows from this. *Current Sociology*, *68*(4), 459–479.

EGOS. (2022). *General theme*. https://egos.org/2022_Vienna/General-Theme

Espeland, W., & Sauder, M. (2007). Rankings and reactivity: How public measures recreate social worlds. *American Journal of Sociology*, *113*(1), 1–40.

Eyal, G. (2013). For a sociology of expertise: The social origins of the autism epidemic. *American Journal of Sociology*, *118*(4), 863–907.

Gordon, R. A., & Howell, J. E. (1959). *Higher education for business*. Columbia University Press.

Gorman, E. (2014). *The end of "organizational sociology" as we know it?* https://workinprogress.oowsection.org/2014/11/20/the-end-of-organizational-sociology-as-we-know-it/

Greenwood, R., Brown, A. D., Lounsbury, M., & Wilson, D. (2010). Organization studies 30th anniversary special issue. *Organization Studies*, *31*(6), 653–658.

Grey, C. (2010). Organizing studies: Publications, politics, and polemic. *Organization Studies*, *31*(6), 677–694.

Grey, C., & Sinclair, A. (2006). Writing differently. *Organization*, *13*(3), 443–453.

Grothe-Hammer, M., & Kohl, S. (2020). The decline of organizational sociology? An empirical analysis of research trends in leading journals across half a century. *Current Sociology*, *68*(4), 419–442.

Hambrick, D. C. (1994). What if the academy actually mattered. *Academy of Management Review*, *19*(1), 11–16.

Hannan, M. T., & Freeman, J. (1977). The population ecology of organizations. *American Journal of Sociology*, *82*(5), 929–964.

Harley, B. (2019). Confronting the crisis of confidence in management studies: Why senior scholars need to stop setting a bad example. *Academy of Management Learning & Education*, *18*(2), 286–297.

Hassard, J., & Wolfram Cox, J. (2013). Can sociological paradigms still inform organizational analysis? A paradigm model for post-paradigm times. *Organization Studies*, *34*(11), 1701–1728.

Haveman, H. A. (2022). *The power of organizations: A new approach to organizational theory*. Princeton University Press.

Heilbron, J. (2014). The social sciences as an emerging global field. *Current Sociology*, *62*(5), 685–703.

Heilbron, J., Guilhot, N., & Jeanpierre, L. (2008). Toward a transnational history of the social sciences. *Journal of the History of the Behavioral Sciences*, *44*(2), 146–160.

Hickson, D., Agersnap, F., Ferraresi, F., Hofstede, G., Kieser, A., Lammers, C., & Thoenig, J.-C. (1980). Editorial. *Organization Studies*, *1*(1), 1–2.

Hiller, P., & Pohlmann, M. (2015). Organisationssoziologie in Deutschland. In M. Apelt & U. Wilkesmann (Eds.), *Zur Zukunft der Organisationssoziologie* (pp. 47–72). Springer VS.

Hinings, C. R. (2010). Thirty years of organization studies: Enduring themes in a changing institutional field. *Organization Studies*, *31*(6), 659–675.

Holmwood, J. (2010). Sociology's misfortune: Disciplines, interdisciplinarity and the impact of audit culture. *British Journal of Sociology*, *61*(4), 639–658.

ISA. (2023). *The world of organizational sociology*. https://organizational-sociology.com/world-of-organizational-sociology

Jacobs, J. A. (2005). ASR's greatest hits. *American Sociological Review*, *70*(1), 1–4.

Jacobs, J. A. (2007). Further reflections on ASR's greatest hits. *The American Sociologist*, *38*(1), 99–131.

Jacobs, J. A., & Habinek, J. (2023). The enduring role of books in sociology publishing. *Contemporary Sociology*, *52*(1), 5–9.

Khurana, R. (2007). *From higher aims to hired hands: The social transformation of American business schools and the unfulfilled promise of management as a profession*. Princeton University Press.

King, B. (2017). The relevance of organizational sociology. *Contemporary Sociology, 46*(2), 131–137.

Krause, M. (2021). *Model cases: On canonical research objects and sites*. University of Chicago Press.

Lammers, C. J. (1981a). Contributions of organizational sociology: Part I: Contributions to sociology – A liberal view. *Organization Studies, 2*(3), 267–286.

Lammers, C. J. (1981b). Contributions of organizational sociology: Part II: Contributions to organizational theory and practice – A liberal view. *Organization Studies, 2*(4), 361–376.

Lammers, C. J. (1998). An inside story: The birth and infancy of EGOS: Memories in tribute to Franco Ferraresi. *Organization Studies, 19*(5), 883–888.

Lamont, M. (2012). Toward a comparative sociology of valuation of evaluation. *Annual Review of Sociology, 38*(1), 201–221.

Lockett, A., & McWilliams, A. (2005). The balance of trade between disciplines: Do we effectively manage knowledge? *Journal of Management Inquiry, 14*(2), 139–150.

Lounsbury, M., & Beckman, C. M. (2015). Celebrating organization theory. *Journal of Management Studies, 52*, 288–308.

March, J. G. (2007). The study of organizations and organizing since 1945. *Organization Studies, 28*(1), 9–19.

McGrath, R. G. (2007). No longer a stepchild: How the management field can come into its own. *The Academy of Management Journal, 50*(6), 1365–1378.

Merton, R. K. (1988). The Matthew effect in science, II: Cumulative advantage and the symbolism of intellectual property. *Isis, 79*(4), 606–623.

Meyer, J. W., & Rowan, B. (1977). Institutionalized organizations: Formal structure as myth and ceremony. *American Journal of Sociology, 83*(2), 340–363.

Meyer, R. E., & Boxenbaum, E. (2010). Exploring European-ness in organization research. *Organization Studies, 31*(6), 737–755.

Paradeise, C., & Thoenig, J. C. (2015). *In search of academic quality*. Palgrave McMillan.

Parker, M. (2000) The sociology of organizations and the organization of sociology: Some reflections on the making of a division of labour. *The Sociological Review, 48*(1), 124–146.

Pfeffer, J. (2007). A modest proposal: How we might change the process and product of managerial research. *Academy of Management Journal, 50*(6), 1334–1345.

Pfeffer, J., & Fong, C. T. (2002). The end of business schools? Less success than meets the eye. *Academy of Management Learning & Education, 1*(1), 78–95.

Pierson, F. C. (1959). *The education of American businessmen*. McGraw-Hill.

Rowlinson, M., & Hassard, J. (2011). How come the critters came to be teaching in business schools? Contradictions in the institutionalization of critical management studies. *Organization, 18*(5), 673–689.

Sass, S. A. (1982). *The pragmatic imagination: A history of the Wharton School 1881–1981*. University of Pennsylvania Press.

Scott, A. (2020). Prodigal offspring: Organizational sociology and organization studies. *Current Sociology, 68*(4), 443–458.

Scott, W. R. (1998). *Organizations: Rational, natural, and open systems*. Prentice-Hall.

Scott, W. R. (2004). Reflections on a half-century of organizational sociology. *Annual Review of Sociology, 30*(1), 1–21.

Simon, H. A. (1967). The business school: A problem in organizational design. *Journal of Management Studies, 4*(1), 1–16.

Simon, H. A. (1991). *Models of my life*. MIT Press.

Starkey, K., & Tiratsoo, N. (2007). *The business school and the bottom line*. Cambridge University Press.

Stinchcombe, A. L. (1984). The origins of sociology as a discipline. *Acta Sociologica, 27*(1), 51–61.

Strang, D., & Siler, K. (2017). From "just the facts" to "more theory and methods, please": The evolution of the research article in *Administrative Science Quarterly*, 1956–2008. *Social Studies of Science, 47*(4), 528–555.

Suchman, M. (2014). *Why before how: "Distinctive and indispensable" beats "sophisticated but superfluous."* https://workinprogress.oowsection.org/2014/11/19/why-before-how/#more-2583

Thoenig, J. C. (1998). Essai: How far is a sociology of organizations still needed? *Organization Studies*, *19*(2), 307–320.

Thompson, J. D. (1956). On building an administrative science. *Administrative Science Quarterly*, *1*(1), 102–111.

Tourish, D. (2019). *Management studies in crisis: Fraud, deception and meaningless research*. Cambridge University Press.

Tourish, D. (2020). The triumph of nonsense in management studies. *Academy of Management Learning & Education*, *19*(1), 99–109.

Turner, J. H. (2016). Academic journals and sociology's big divide: A modest but radical proposal. *The American Sociologist*, *47*(2), 289–301.

Vogel, R. (2012). The visible colleges of management and organization studies: A bibliometric analysis of academic journals. *Organization Studies*, *33*(8), 1015–1043.

Westwood, R., & Clegg, S. (2003). The discourse of organization studies: Dissensus, politics, and paradigms. In R. Westwood & S. Clegg (Eds.), *Debating organization: Point-counterpoint in organization studies* (pp. 1–43). Blackwell.

Whetten, D. A., Felin, T., & King, B. G. (2009). The practice of theory borrowing in organizational studies: Current issues and future directions. *Journal of Management*, *35*(3), 537–563.

FACING UP TO THE PRESENT? CULTIVATING POLITICAL JUDGMENT AND A SENSE OF REALITY IN CONTEMPORARY ORGANIZATIONAL LIFE

Thomas Lopdrup-Hjorth and Paul du Gay

Copenhagen Business School, Denmark

ABSTRACT

Organizations are confronted with problems and political risks to which they have to respond, presenting a need to develop tools and frames of understanding requisite to do so. In this article, we argue for the necessity of cultivating "political judgment" with a "sense of reality," especially in the upper echelons of organizations. This article has two objectives: First to highlight how a number of recent interlinked developments within organizational analysis and practice have contributed to weakening judgment and its accompanying "sense of reality." Second, to (re)introduce some canonical works that, although less in vogue recently, provide both a source of wisdom and frames of understanding that are key to tackling today's problems. We begin by mapping the context in which the need for the cultivation of political judgment within organizations has arisen: (i) increasing proliferation of political risks and "wicked problems" to which it is expected that organizations adapt and respond; (ii) a wider historical and contemporary context in which the exercise of judgment has been undermined – a result of a combination of economics-inspired styles of

Sociological Thinking in Contemporary Organizational Scholarship
Research in the Sociology of Organizations, Volume 90, 85–108
ISSN: 0733-558X/doi:10.1108/S0733-558X20240000090004

theorizing and an associated obsession with metrics. We also explore the nature of "political judgment" and its accompanying "sense of reality" through the work of authors such as Philip Selznick, Max Weber, Chester Barnard, and Isaiah Berlin. We suggest that these authors have a weighty "sense of reality"; are antithetical to "high," "abstract," or "axiomatic" theorizing; and have a profound sense of the burden from exercising political judgment in difficult organizational circumstances.

Keywords: Organization theory; organizational sociology; metrics; political judgment; political risks; sense of reality

INTRODUCTION

Executives in the upper echelons of public and private organizations have to navigate problems that have a "political" component. While this is hardly a novel comment (March, 1962; Pfeffer, 1992; Selznick, 1957), recent decades have nevertheless accentuated the political nature of problems in a number of interrelated ways. On the one hand, this tendency has become manifest in the manner in which organizational environments are increasingly mined with a number of "political risks" that in the blink of an eye can cause significant problems and therefore call for swift and imaginative responses (Brands & Edel, 2019; Kitsing, 2022; Rice & Zegart, 2018; Zhang & Duschesne, 2022). On the other hand, problems pertaining to how to act appropriately in the face of major crises such as accelerated climate change, the Covid-19 pandemic, rising inequality, new security threats, populism, and a devastating war in Ukraine also challenge organizations in significant ways and necessitate reflexive organizational conduct with a keen awareness of political threats and possibilities (e.g., Council on Foreign Relations, 2023; EY, 2022; Grant et al., 2022; Office of the Director of National Intelligence, 2023; The National Intelligence Council, 2021). As a response to the latter, recent discussions within organizational theorizing have suggested that organization scholars better face up to reality by theorizing how to respond to, navigate, and/or alleviate such major, indeed even potentially "existential" (Ord, 2020), risks and problems (Adler et al., 2023; Creed et al., 2022). Given the nature of the political challenges facing organizations today, it is therefore deemed necessary that managers and leaders are capable of not only exercising good judgment (DeRose & Tichy, 2008; Tichy & Bennis, 2007) but also of fostering the ability to exercise "political judgment" with a keen sense of reality, if they are to act responsibly in the face of the manifold problems they can expect to encounter (du Gay, 2023).

While the ability to exercise political judgment is in high demand, it is less clear whether and to what extent organizational theorists have much to contribute to sharpening and articulating the relevant capacities and dispositions that go with this. Indeed, rather than having a solid foundation from which to fashion concepts and frames of understanding requisite for intervening in organizational settings, there are reasons to believe that a number of problems within the field of organizational analysis currently prohibit a proper cultivation of a "sense of reality" and the "political judgment" that goes with it. First of all, there is the obstacle of adequately grasping what such judgment and its accompanying "sense of reality" consists in and where one can go looking for some of their crucial characteristics. Second, several deep-seated practical and theoretical hindrances work counter to, and reduce the conditions necessary for, the exercise of responsible judgment with a "sense of reality." Having a proper understanding of these obstacles, too, represents an additional crucial step for creating the conditions under which the exercise of political judgment can be developed.

In this article, we argue for the necessity of cultivating "political judgment" with a "sense of reality," especially at the higher echelons of organizations. As will become evident in this article, where you find the one, you inevitably find the other; and, conversely, where one is absent, the other will be weak or missing too. As a stepping stone to advancing this proposition, this article has two objectives: On the one hand, to highlight how over recent decades a number of interlinked developments within organizational analysis and practice have contributed to problematizing and undermining judgment and its associated "sense of reality." On the other hand, to (re)introduce some canonical works that, although currently less than fashionable, provide both a source of wisdom and frames of understanding that can be fruitfully deployed in facing up to today's major problems in organizational analysis and practice. The argument proceeds as follows: First, we map the context in which the need for the cultivation of political judgment within organizations has arisen. We locate two trajectories: an increasing proliferation of political risks and major "wicked problems" to which it is expected that organizations adapt and respond, and a wider historical and contemporary context in which the exercise of judgment has been undermined. In regard to the latter, we focus especially on economics-inspired strands of theorizing and indicate how these have been interconnected with the proliferation of metrics within organizational life. Second, we flesh out the specific nature of "political judgment" and its accompanying "sense of reality" by mining the work and stance adopted by authors such as Philip Selznick, Max Weber, Chester Barnard, and Isaiah Berlin. In spite of their immediate differences, these authors, we suggest, have a weighty "sense of reality"; are antithetical to "high," "abstract," or "axiomatic" theorizing; and furthermore have a profound sense of the burdens that go with exercising political judgment in difficult organizational circumstances. Finally, we discuss the implications of this article and map its contributions, including how these advance and add to existing lines of research within organizational theorizing.

JUDGMENT UNDERMINED AMID POLITICAL RISKS AND PROBLEMS

The quality of judgments made in the upper echelons of organizations are a significant contributing factor to whether organizations are successful or not (Barnard, 1968a; Berlin, 2019a, 2019b; Selznick, 1957; West et al., 2020). Countless organizational successes and failures throughout history have as their overriding determinant the proper use (or lack thereof) of judgment – whether in business, politics, or military affairs. Judgment is usually understood to come into play, when there is a certain indeterminacy, a lack of clear evidence supporting a definitive approach or decision (Likierman, 2020; Tichy & Bennis, 2007), and a general openness pertaining to the context within which an assessment and/or decision has to be made, sometimes under considerable time constraints (Schumpeter, 1911/2011). Hence, the situations within which judgments are called for in organizations are not the equivalent of situations resembling an arithmetic puzzle, but, more often than not, an ambiguous and highly complex setting in which a large number of only partly intelligible, interrelated processes and variables are present (Geuss, 2009). As such, situations demanding judgment are different from situations amenable to mere calculation, or so-called "optimization." As recent research shows, decisions based upon judgment often outperform decisions made on the basis of analytical and logical foundations (Gigerenzer, 2015; West et al., 2020). As Acar puts it:

> Under extreme uncertainty, managers, particularly those with more experience, should trust the expertise and instincts that have propelled them to such a position. The nous developed over the years as a leader can be a more effective tool than an analytical tool which, in situation of extreme uncertainty, could act as a hindrance rather than a driver of success. (Lambert, 2021, n.p.)

Judgment is therefore at the heart of responsible organizational conduct, especially at the higher strata of organizations, where the quality, or lack thereof, of judgment can have significant consequences for organizational survival and flourishing (Brown, 1974, pp. 71–72). Indeed, judgment is said to be "the essence of leadership" (DeRose & Tichy, 2008, p. 26), because when "a leader shows consistently good judgement, little else matters. When he or she shows poor judgment, nothing else matters" (Tichy & Bennis, 2007, p. 94).

It is therefore not surprising that judgment is considered to be of vital importance. As we will highlight below, however, the exercise of judgment in organizations is challenged on several fronts. On the one hand, judgment, and especially political judgment, is currently in high demand. On the other hand, major tendencies in recent decades have contributed to undermining the exercise of judgment. In the remainder of this section, we will first signpost a number of rising political problems that call for the necessity of developing the prudential use of judgment. We will then seek to highlight how the conditions for the exercise of such judgment have been increasingly undermined.

Facing Political Risks and Problems

Throughout the last couple of years, it has become increasingly apparent that the wheels of history are turning again, and that the relative political stability and security provided by the breakdown of Communism in Eastern Europe and the Soviet Union is a thing of the past (Brands & Edel, 2019). From the beginning of the 21st century onward, a number of events and trajectories have ushered in a new and increasingly uncertain environment, where risks and threats have been accumulating. 9/11, the financial crisis of 2008, a surge in populist discontents, climate catastrophe, and increasing polarization within and across many societies have all contributed to turbulent organizational environments, where new risks and threats appear to be constantly emerging. Whether one looks at the academic literature (Brands & Edel, 2019; du Gay & Lopdrup-Hjorth, 2022; Gewen, 2020; Kitsing, 2022; Zhang & Duschesne, 2022), threat assessments and documents from intelligence organizations (e.g., Office of the Director of National Intelligence, 2023; The National Intelligence Council, 2021), or reports from the large consulting houses and think tanks (e.g., Council on Foreign Relations, 2023; EY, 2022; Grant et al., 2022), the picture painted across the board is unanimously bleak, indicating an increased number of political risks facing organizations. Such risks can be of a varied nature and scope (encompassing everything from war, espionage, and geopolitical rivalry to the actions of disgruntled employees, for instance), affecting, among other things, consumer demand, public perceptions, supply chains, and macroeconomic conditions. While the Russian invasion of Ukraine and the intensified geopolitical competition between the United States and China have obviously accentuated the intensification of recent political risks facing organizations, such risks, however, have been on the rise for quite some time (Rice & Zegart, 2018). In their practitioner-oriented book on how organizations can cope with political risks, Condoleeza Rice and Amy Zegart (2018) outline numerous examples of what such risks can look like, and how they might emerge seemingly out of nowhere. From hacker attacks to "shit-storms" on social media, Rice and Zegart highlight a number of different ways in which a plethora of organizations have had to face up to a wide variety of political risks, sometimes bringing them to the verge of bankruptcy or disintegration. Indeed, as the authors stress, navigating such risks is not merely something to take seriously for organizations operating in volatile and often hostile political environments. Rather, as several of their examples illustrate, it is something that organizations as diverse as SeaWorld, Sony Pictures, Ford, and Boeing, among others, have had to navigate – with greater or lesser success.[1] To provide merely one example, in 2014, a hacker group attacked Sony Pictures and released bundles of confidential information (comprising personal information about employees, copies of unreleased films, information about salaries, emails, plans for future films, etc.). The hackers additionally demanded that Sony Pictures should withdraw the movie *The Interview*, a comedy about a plot to assassinate North Korean leader Kim Jong-Un. This demand was accompanied by threats about possible terrorist attacks to be directed at cinemas screening the movie (Rice & Zegart, 2018, p. 52). Although a state actor (North Korea), in this instance, in all likelihood, was responsible, that is by no means always the case. Indeed, political risks can come from within the organization too, as recent #MeToo incidents at the *New York Times* and *Uber* attest to (Rice & Zegart, 2018, p. 53). No matter their origin, however, the intensification of political risks should be seen in conjunction with recent decades' surge of so-called "wicked problems," the consequences of which have already proved disastrous for numerous organizations. The financial crisis of 2008 and its repercussions (Tooze, 2018), the accelerating, multifaceted climate catastrophe (Wallace-Wells, 2019), the Covid-19 pandemic (Tooze, 2021), increasing inequalities, and political polarization within and across several countries (Moore, 2018; Nagle, 2017) all accentuate the need for sound judgment with an eye to the political implications of decisions and conduct. Exercising judgment and having "a sense" of one's organization and its environment therefore becomes *sine qua non* in navigating "hard to quantify" political risks (Rice & Zegart, 2018, p. 93).

Although there is no simplistic causal relation between the prescriptions inherent in organization and management theories disseminated via business schools, on the one hand, and managers and leaders' practical exercise of judgment, on the other hand, it would also be misleading to assume that there is a no relation at all. In particular, the economics-based governance and agency models that came to proliferate from the 1980s onward, with business schools as the key disseminators (Khurana, 2010), are deemed to have had remarkably damaging effects for how managers exercise judgment (Dobbin & Jung, 2010; Ghoshal, 2005; Stout, 2014). The prevalence and propagation of these economics-based models and theories has had a number of pernicious effects (Ghoshal, 2005; Stout, 2012) including a gradual undermining and mistrust of managers' ability to act responsibly and exercise judgment in a host of organizational settings (Donaldson, 2002; Muller, 2018). For that reason, any attempt at strengthening the ability to exercise judgment in the face of the numerous political challenges outlined above necessitates both a recognition of the less than benign impact unleashed by a number of interrelated conditions that have contributed to the undermining of judgment in organizations, and an associated recognition of which kinds of alternative conceptions might prove more useful in facing up to the organizational and societal realities of today. While several early figures in the history of organizational analysis pointed to the indispensability of judgment in organizational life, a number of, allegedly, more "scientific" and "rigorous" approaches have represented these authors and the maxims they developed as anachronistic and increasingly redundant.

Undermining Judgment Through "Rigor" and "Science"

Across its various exemplars (such as, for instance, Henri Fayol, Mary Parker Follett, Chester Barnard, Lyndall Urwick, Luther Gulick, and Wilfred Brown), "classical organizational theory" is characterized by

> a pragmatic call to experience, an antithetical attitude to "high" or transcendental theorizing, an admiration for scientific forms of enquiry (in the Weberian sense of the "disciplined pursuit of knowledge," and as such not reducible to the laboratory sciences, nor to the content of the sciences per se), a dissatisfaction and devaluation of explanation by postulate, and, not least, a practical focus on organizational effectiveness, for instance, born of a close connection to "the work itself," or (…) "the situation at hand." (du Gay & Vikkelsø, 2014, p. 737)

While this antipathy toward high theorizing and an associated preoccupation with practical experience allowed several of the classical theorists to supply frameworks and concepts adapted to real-life concerns in organizations, it did, however, also make many of its exponents vulnerable to a number of critiques of not being sufficiently based on "science." Thus, toward the end of the 1950s and the beginning of the 1960s, a set of, allegedly, more scientific and systematic ways of practicing organization were deployed against the classical theorists' "proverbs," as Herbert Simon (1946) dismissively portrayed them. Against the approach adopted by several of the classical theorists, a new "management science" began to emerge, one that purported to teach students a science-based methodology for decision-making. "Instead of being taught to rely on judgment (...), students could develop a more analytical competence by being immersed in quantitative methods and decision theory" (Freedman, 2015, pp. 516–517). Fueling these efforts were two reports issued in 1959 by the Ford Foundation and the Carnegie Corporation, respectively (Khurana, 2010; Waring, 1991; Wren, 2005). In these reports, a strong case was made for the necessity of dispensing with preexisting conceptualizations and understandings of organizational analysis and business school education. Rather than a pragmatic call to experience, and a close connection with the work itself, the new "management science" was to be anchored in quantitative methodologies and the new behavioral sciences. The scientific approach that was to emanate from this "would allow managers to make decisions solely on analytical and rational grounds, without recourse to fuzzy notions such as intuition and judgment" (Khurana, 2010, p. 271). To realize these purposes, however, it was also deemed necessary to bring a new set of requisite analytical competencies into business schools – something that in the United States entailed an influx of, especially, economists into the latter's ranks. With this turn, a new ideal of the manager also materialized. Rather than one steeped in the practicalities of distinct industries and specific work practices, the "general manager" emerged as a category of person who would apply a set of context-independent techniques and quantitative methodologies that could be deployed in any organizational setting. However, in committing "themselves to omniscient rationality" and simultaneously omitting practice, judgment, and the specific contexts within which these allegedly universal techniques would be set to work, "economists and other hard management science advocates" ended up producing "a science divorced from reality" (Locke & Spender, 2011, p. 17).

While these developments did provoke concerns and critiques, their proponents nevertheless maintained a strong belief in the possibility of turning management and business school education from a "wasteland of vocationalism into a science based profession," as Herbert Simon memorably expressed it (quoted in Freedman, 2015, p. 517). Such a stance was exacerbated in the 1970s and 1980s, when a new cluster of economically inspired organization theories made rapid forays into, and eventually became dominant within, business schools (Ghoshal, 2005; Khurana, 2010). Of major significance in this regard was "agency theory," a strand of theorizing initiated by a group of economists at The University of Chicago (Jensen, 1983; Jensen & Meckling, 1976; see also Khurana, 2010, pp. 313–326; Perrow, 1986, pp. 224–236). With the casual modesty of an economist, Michael Jensen proclaimed a "revolution in the science of organisations" – a field he considered was "still in its infancy" (Jensen, 1983, p. 324). While Jensen and his colleagues shared with their earlier business school colleagues the ambition to turn management and organization theory into a true science, they were even more skeptical of managerial judgment than their predecessors. Indeed, they not only mistrusted any reliance upon managers' judgment, they mistrusted managers per se, because they were opportunistic by default and could not be relied upon to look out for anyone but themselves. Inspired by Milton Friedman, and building upon "the efficient market" hypothesis, Jensen and Meckling brought a set of controversial theoretical economic postulates into the world of organizations. As Justin Fox remarked:

> "the rational market idea" moved from "theoretical economics into the empirical subdivision of finance." There it "lost in nuance and gained in intensity." It was now seeking to use the "stock market's collective judgment to resolve conflicts of interest that had plagued scholars, executives, and shareholders for generations. (quoted in Freedman, 2015, p. 526)

By taking this route, agency theory sought to erase previous conceptions of organizations, and with them preceding theorizing about the nature of responsibility pertaining to the function of management. Now, it was claimed that organizations were nothing but "legal fictions which serve as a nexus for a set of contracting relationships among individuals" (Jensen & Meckling, 1976, p. 310). The implication of this was that a form or other form of organization was simply

> a legal fiction which serves as a focus for a complex process in which the conflicting objectives of individuals (...) are brought into equilibrium within a framework of contractual relations. In this sense the "behavior" of the firm is like the behavior of a market, that is, the outcome of a complex equilibrium process. (Jensen & Meckling, 1976, p. 310)

The key assumptions and operating concepts of agency theory therefore implied that "an organization's history and culture were irrelevant, staffed by people who might as well be strangers to each other" (Freedman, 2015, p. 528). Due to this, organizations, in the memorable phrasing of Oliver Williamson (1991), could essentially be considered as "a continuation of market relations, *by other means*" (p. 162). With this frame of understanding, managers became reconceived as opportunistic actors in need of market discipline, since they could not be expected to think and act beyond their narrow self-interest. "Managers being trained in this theory would offer no loyalty and expect none in return. Their task was to interpret the markets and respond to incentives. Little scope was left for the exercise of judgment and responsibility" (Freedman, 2015, p. 528).

Undermining Judgment Through Metrics

The practical implication of agency theory has not merely been an even greater wariness toward managerial "judgment" than that exhibited by earlier advocates of "management science," it also implied a generalized suspicion toward management practice that – in several registers – has proved toxic to organizations and societies. Indeed, while some scholars have pointed to the ways in which agency theory's central tenets were directly implicated in the Financial Crisis of 2008 (Dobbin & Jung, 2010; Robé, 2011), others have highlighted how the key doctrines of the theory have been hugely damaging as its ideas spread from business schools into organizations. Ghoshal (2005) and Donaldson (2002), for instance, have indicated how agency theory has undermined more or less well-functioning management practices. Muller (2015, 2018), too, has emphasized how the increasing proliferation of metrics in organizations should be seen as intimately linked with the dominance that agency theory came to have over the last three to four decades. This mode of theorizing, he argues, articulates in abstract terms the general suspicion that those employed in institutions are not to be trusted; that their activity must be monitored and measured; that those measures need to be transparent to those without firsthand knowledge of the institutions; and that pecuniary rewards and punishments are the most effective way to motivate "agents." (Muller, 2018, p. 49)

In this sense, agency theory has theoretically legitimized and been one (albeit not the only) driver paving the way for the onslaught of the metrics fixation framing the proliferation of what Michael Power (1997) termed the "audit society." In line with agency theory, this metrics fixation can be characterized by the belief that the most fair and effective way of managing organizations is to replace judgment based on experience and in-depth practical know-how with numbers, the belief that such numbers should be "transparent," and the belief that those subject to such numbers should be motivated via penalties and rewards in regard to their "objective" performance (Collini, 2018; Muller, 2015, 2018). The problem, however, as Collini highlights, is that as

[...] soon as numbers come into play, we are all liable to fall into what Oscar Wilde called "careless habits of accuracy." A number holds out the promise of definiteness, exactness and objectivity. But a number is a signifier like any other, a way of representing something (...). The digital revolution has brought with it a huge increase in quantifiable information, the very existence of which provides a constant temptation to metric misbehaviour. If there are numbers to be had, we come to feel that we must have them, even though they may mislead us into thinking we have solid information about something important when in reality all we have is the precise and selective misrepresentation of something insignificant. (Collini, 2018, n.p.)

The retort to such a critique by agency theorists, and others predisposed to the same kind of thinking, has been that without determinate and clear indicators, managers cannot make responsible decisions. As one of the pioneers of agency theory, Michael Jensen has argued,

Any organization must have a single-valued objective as a precursor to purposeful or rational behavior .... It is logically impossible to maximize in more than one dimension at the same time .... Thus, telling a manager to maximize current profits, market share, future growth profits, and anything else one pleases will leave that manager with no way to make a reasoned decision. In effect it leaves the manger with no objective. (quoted in Stout, 2014, p. 108)

As Jensen puts it, "[t]he solution is to define a true (single dimensional) score for measuring performance for the organization" (quoted in Stout, 2014, p. 108). However, as Stout (2014) goes on to argue, such an approach neglects the fundamental human "capacity to balance, albeit imperfectly, competing interests and responsibilities (...). Balancing interests – decently satisfying several sometimes-competing objectives, rather than trying to 'maximize' only one – is the rule and not the exception in human affairs" (pp. 107–108). This is essentially what judgment is about. However, with the excessive use of metrics across any number of organizations – universities, the police, schools, hospitals, businesses, the military, etc. (for case studies pertaining to these, see Muller, 2018) – the capacity for organizational members to exercise prudent and balanced judgment has been significantly reduced. And no wonder. The central traits and bases of agency theory and like-minded approaches that underpin "trust in numbers" have consisted in setting up abstractions and models bent on escaping the messiness of reality (Espeland, 2001; Skidelsky, 2021).

In his review and critique of the economists' reductive approach to organization, Charles Perrow writes about "the challenge" that agency theorists have presented organizational analysis and practice. This challenge, Perrow states, "evokes the menace of the novel and film *The Invasion of the Body Snatchers*, in which aliens occupy human forms, but all that we value about human behavior (…) has disappeared" (Perrow, 1986, p. 257). The ability to make prudent judgment has been one of the casualties of this foray. On the one hand, it has been compromised by a set of ideas that from the 1950s onward have progressively discredited and undermined practical judgment; on the other hand, it has been challenged by the closely associated proliferation of "metrics" that have colonized public as well as private organizations. As Muller (2015, pp. 1–2) states, the "characteristic feature of the" metrics fixation and its underlying ideas "is the aspiration to replace judgment with standardized measurement"; the virtues of these metrics "have been oversold and their costs are underappreciated."

So far, we have sought to argue that judgment, and especially political judgment, is in high demand today, not least as a result of the proliferation of "political risks" we discussed above. At the same time, however, the conditions for cultivating and exercising judgment have been weakened. As we have attempted to indicate, this development is in no small part the result of the proliferation of theoretical approaches bred within the modern business school and the related tendency to rely increasingly upon metrics in contemporary organizational life. However, in stating this, it would be misleading to pretend that this is a unitary and total history, where problematizations of judgment within specific kinds of theories translate one-to-one into organizational practices. Indeed, the history of quantification and its relationship to how judgment is exercised in organizations has more nuances and details than what we have been able to cover here.[2] However, our ambition has also been more modest: to highlight how a number of emerging political risks necessitates the cultivation of prudential judgment in organizations, at the same time as the conditions for the exercise of the latter has been weakened by the proliferation of economics-inspired modes of theorizing (Ghoshal, 2005; Khurana, 2010; Perrow, 1986) and its associated metrics fixation (Muller, 2015, 2018).

RE-ENTER "POLITICAL JUDGMENT" AND A "SENSE OF REALITY"

We now turn to the second part of our argument, namely, that in attempting to face up to the plethora of "wicked problems" and political risks in the present, inculcating a "sense of reality" and the "political judgment" that goes with it, might be a more requisite stance for those in the senior echelons of organizations to develop. Our task is therefore to explore what such a stance entails. We do so by returning to the work of Chester Barnard, Max Weber, Philip Selznick, and Isaiah Berlin. In spite of their evident differences, these thinkers (i) share a certain disposition toward (organizational) reality, (ii) highlight the importance of (political) judgment, (iii) are antithetical toward deriving practical conduct and judgment from a "rigorous" and science-based foundation, and (iv) have an appreciation of tragedy.[3] We can begin to get a sense of what this stance entails by outlining contours of its constituent components in Selznick, Barnard, and Weber's theorizing to begin with. We will then turn to Berlin. We proceed in this manner because Berlin's thinking, while adding important nuances to the insights developed by the former authors, is considerably less well known within the orbit of organizational theorizing.

Political Judgment and Sense of Reality in Organizational Sociology and Theory

In his book, *Leadership in Administration*, the organizational sociologist Philip Selznick draws on what, at first sight, appears to be a curious analogy pertaining to the responsibility of those exercising authority in the upper echelons of organizations. Their role and responsibility, Selznick claims, is to act like "statesmen," no matter whether their particular role happens to be located in a public or a private organization (Selznick, 1957, p. 37). Thus, they might be heads of state, senior public officials, or managing large commercial enterprises. By describing the activities of those leading public institutions and private enterprises as involving statesmanship [*sic*.], Selzick wants us to recognize that there are certain responsibilities pertaining to such roles that transcends the parameters of what he conceives of as a constricted business stance. The narrowness that he attempts to warn his readers against is the outlook of those executives who – blinded as they are by a technical point of view – are less than well grounded in reality than the office for which they have assumed responsibility necessitates. As he writes:

> To be ... "just a businessman" is inconsistent with the demands of statesmanship. It is utopian and irresponsible to suppose that a narrow technical logic can be relied on by men who make decisions that, though they originate in technical problems, have larger consequences for the ultimate evolution of the enterprise and its position in the world. (Selznick, 1957, p. 148).

According to Selznick, the "statesman" must first and foremost be attuned to the organizational realities within which s/he is placed. Only by being grounded in this way is it possible to exercise judgment in a responsible manner. Thus, there is an intimate connection between the responsible use of the statesman's political judgment and having a firm grasp of reality. Indeed, facing up to reality in a requisite way can be considered the foundation and first step in exercising judgment. To illustrate this point, Selznick quotes the Prussian general and theorist of war, Carl von Clausewitz:

> the greatest and the most decisive act of the judgment which a statesman ... performs is that of correctly recognizing the kind of war he is undertaking, of not taking it for, or wishing to make it, something which by the nature of the circumstances it cannot be. (quoted in Selznick, 1957, p. 78)

As we have already indicated, Selznick is not alone in making this connection. Max Weber and Chester Barnard came to similar conclusions, and for not entirely unrelated reasons. Both of them also argued for the tight-knit connection between the responsible use of judgment and a profound sense of the realities of distinct, though widely differing, organizational contexts. And they recognized some of the same dangers, too. By not being receptive to reality, by insisting upon holding on to a set of ideas (metrics, frameworks, etc.) that abstracts from the "total situation," people in positions of authority are prohibited from exercising judgment in a responsible manner. Indeed, this is one of the chief dangers Weber warns of in his famous lecture, *The Profession and Vocation of Politics*. Here, he highlights that "*responsibility* requires ... *judgement*, the ability to maintain one's inner composure and calm while being receptive to realities" (Weber, 1994, p. 353). What matters most in a leader, Weber claims, is "the trained ability to look at the realities of life with an unsparing gaze, to bear these realities and be a match for them inwardly" (Weber, 1994, p. 367). While definitely being less sanguine about the prospects for humankind than Selznick, Weber nevertheless expresses a stance that is not entirely unrelated to Selnick's view of the states-man's responsibility, especially when Selznick expresses this via Clausewitz, with whom Weber has an even closer intellectual affinity. Weber, too, worries about the erosion of political judgment and responsibility that arises when statesmen and leaders lose their sense of reality by seeking to represent it in a manner that makes it into something it cannot be. As da Mata argues, "Weber clearly realizes that disconnection to reality leads to the decline of political judgment and, with this, a conscious and responsible engagement." For him, much like Clausewitz, "specific intellectual fashions have the potential of leading social actors to take the way of a 'mystical escape of the world' (*mystische Weltflucht*) so that they are not 'a match for the world as it really is'" (da Mata, 2019, p. 607).

This is also one of the chief dangers Chester Barnard addresses, not only in his magnum opus, *The Functions of the Executive* (1968a) but also in articles and public speeches (see, e.g., Barnard, 1968b). While Barnard's warnings about this are not drawn from the study of 18th- and 19th-century warfare, like Clausewitz, nor from political and societal debates of 19th- and 20th-century Germany, like Weber, they persistently move across a terrain of problems where overreliance on utopian and abstract ideas are linked to the erosion of responsible conduct. As with Selznick, who approvingly quotes Barnard (see, e.g., Selznick, 1957, p. 36), and Weber before him, Barnard highlights judgment as dependent upon a sense of reality that is not amenable to "scientific" or "rigorous" representation. Contrary to agency theorists, such as Jensen, Barnard (1968a, 1968b) points to the necessity of having a "sense for the whole situation" as the indispensable foundation for the exercise of judgment (Barnard, 1938a, p. 235). And he insists that grasping the reality pertaining to "the whole," and the forming of judgment in relation to this whole, has to be described in the registers of "intimate experience," "sensing," and "having a feel for," rather than through a terminology emphasizing logical and analytical processes of thought (Barnard, 1968a, p. 235). In particular, he warns against the irresponsibility and utopianism implicated in the abstractions associ-ated with economics-based approaches to executive decision-making (Barnard, 1968a, p. 239; Selznick, 1957, p. 148), something which Weber was familiar with, too (Hennis, 2000, pp. 40–41, 125–126, 200–201).

In a lecture given at Princeton in 1936, Barnard illustrates the manner in which a central component of most leadership roles exactly consists in exercising fac-ulties that are not logical, nor grounded in science. As he says to his audience:

"be careful not to be logically arithmetical about organization" (Barnard, 1968b, p. 316).

> You cannot get organization by adding up the parts. They are only one aspect of it. To understand the society you live in, you must *feel* organization – which is exactly what you do with your non-logical minds – about your nation, the state, your university. (Barnard, 1968b, p. 317)

He emphasizes that the often denigrated "intuitional" and "non-logical" thought processes tend to be *the most important* – albeit not the only ones necessary – across a number of different occupations, such as, for instance, the statesman, the junior and senior executives, as well as the politician. Conversely, in the accountant and the engineer, logical processes tend to dominate (Barnard, 1968b, p. 320). Hence, it is not a question of one set of competences or thought processes being more important than others per se. Barnard's more general point is that we can only determine the importance of distinct thought processes when we view them in relation to a particular context, on behalf of which they *then* can be seen to be more or less important. In other words, such capacities should be assessed as a function of the distinctive offices an individual occupies (du Gay et al., 2019). Nevertheless, Barnard (1968b) argues that the "failure observed in many concrete instances to take into account all the elements of the situation as a whole" is "promoted by a specialization in thinking that arises in part from the specialization of the sciences" (p. 290).

> In the common-sense, everyday, practical knowledge necessary to the practice of the arts, there is much that is not susceptible of verbal statement – it is a matter of know-how (...). It is necessary to doing things in concrete situations. It is nowhere more indispensable than in the executive arts. It is acquired by persistent habitual experience and is often called intuitive. (Barnard, 1968b, p. 291)

The same point is reiterated in his book *The Functions of the Executive*:

> the essential aspect of the process [of organization] is the sensing of the organization as a whole and the total situation relevant to it. It transcends the capacity of merely intellectual methods, and the techniques of discriminating the factors of the situation. The terms pertinent to it are "feeling," "judgment," "sense," "proportion," "balance," "appropriateness." It is a matter of art rather than science, and it is aesthetic rather than logical. For this reason it is recognized rather than described and is known by its effects rather than by analysis. (Barnard, 1968a, p. 235)

Just like Weber before him, Barnard is of the opinion that cultivation of the requisite exercise of judgment at the top of organizations require experience, practical training, and development; hence, Weber's overriding preoccupation with the distinctive life orders, such as the bureaucracy, the parliament, the political party, etc., wherein appropriate office-based comportment was to be shaped and perfected (Hennis, 2000). "It seems to me clear," Barnard (1968b) says, "that, whatever else may be desirable, it is certainly well to develop the efficiency of the non-logical processes. How can this be done?" (p. 321).

> No direct method seems applicable. The task seems to be one of "conditioning" the mind and to let nature do what it then can. The conditioning will consists of stocking the mind properly and in exercising the non-logical faculties. The mind will be stocked by experience and study. Experience means doing things, action, the taking of responsibility. It is the process by which an immense amount of material is unconsciously acquired for the mind to use (...). Study

supplements that process by introducing facts, concepts, patterns that would fail of perception through undirected experience. Action or experience at the same time gives the opportunity for practice. There seems to be no substitute for using the mind, applying it, working it, to develop its power. (Barnard, 1968b, p. 321)

This training for the responsible use of judgment grounded in real circumstances is about as far away as one can get from the abstract approach proposed by the early "management science" proponents and their later, even more "rigorous," agency-theoretical successors.

We have now elaborated a number of common themes and shared dispositions across such different classical organization theorists as Philip Selznick, Chester Barnard, and Max Weber. Although they differ in a number of important respects,[4] they nevertheless coalesce in their persistence that responsible leadership requires the cultivation of (political) judgment, and that this in turn requires being receptive to reality. This is what acting as a "statesman" entails. This is what acting as a responsible politician entails. And this is what acting as a top executive entails. They furthermore agree that abstract theorizing, technical logics, and the intellectual frameworks that go with these (whether numbers or utopian ideas) tend to move leaders further away from, rather than closer to, reality. Being guided by these results in what Weber called a "mystical escape of the world," that is, the route traveled by economics-based theories of organization and the related metrics fixation that now dominates the ways in which public and private organizations are managed.

Isaiah Berlin: "Sense of Reality" and "Political Judgment"

By outlining the common concerns linking Selznick, Barnard, and Weber, we can begin to see the contours of a common stance; one that, we believe, is of considerable importance to our present circumstances. To more fully articulate this stance, we now turn to the work of Isaiah Berlin. While in no sense an "organizational theorist," Berlin traveled across an intellectual terrain where he encountered problems that contain more than faint echoes of what we have attended to above. While not easily categorizable within anyone tradition, Berlin has for good reasons been called a "realist" or "proto-realist," a position which brings him in close contact with Weber, for instance.[5] For our purposes, however, the important thing is the way in which Berlin circles around like-minded concerns to those explored by Selznick, Weber, and Barnard – although, obviously, from a different angle of attack. Most notable, perhaps, is the insistence on the tight-knit interconnection between having a "sense of reality" and what Berlin refers to as "political judgment." Like Weber and Barnard before him, Berlin, had a profound understanding of how the world works – hence his association with "realism." As John Gray (2013) states, the reason for this has to do with biographical details of Berlin's life:

Unlike that of the majority of philosophers in his time, and nearly all at present, Berlin's work was not shaped primarily by an academic agenda. Much of his life, including much that was formative of his thinking, occurred outside the seminar room. Moving among writers and musicians, working for the British government in Washington during the Second World War, talking with diplomats and political leaders about international issues, not always in public, he gained a sense of how the world works that is painfully absent from much academic writing on ethics and politics. These practical involvements are one reason for the vivid sense of reality that informs Berlin's work. (p. 33)

Berlin laid out his thinking on these matters in speeches and lectures given as early as the 1950s (Hardy, 2019, pp. xxx–xxxi). In particular, in the two thematically overlapping texts, "Political Judgment" and "Sense of Reality," Berlin emphasizes what having "a sense of reality" implies for the making of "political judgment," and, additionally, how this dimension is inescapably located beyond clear-cut theoretical delineations and modeling attempts. Failing to act in accordance with "reality" has dire consequences. Indeed, as Berlin (2019a, 2019b) stresses, several catastrophes throughout human history are attributable to leaders who failed to exercise political judgment with a sense of reality.

So what does this "sense of reality" consist in and what are its key characteristics? And if it is not liable to modeling and clear-cut theoretical delineations, then how is it knowable? Before providing us with an answer to these questions, Berlin, like Weber, Barnard, and Selznick, emphasizes how judgment can be let astray, if it relies excessively on science and techniques, especially in the hands of those who do not have a "sense of reality." Furthermore, Berlin (2019b) emphasizes that the optimism with which some advance a scientific approach to the conduct of human affairs, whether in business, politics, or elsewhere, has deep historical roots in the 17th, 18th, and 19th centuries (e.g., Spinoza, Holbach, Helvétius):

It was argued (...) that just as knowledge of mechanics was indispensable to engineers or architects or inventors, so knowledge of social mechanics was necessary for anyone – statesmen, for example – who wished to get large bodies of men to do this or that. (p. 51)

The optimism with which many hoped to uncover the laws governing human behavior, however, has been unwarranted, according to Berlin. While no skeptic of science per se, he nevertheless draws attention to how the various advances made within science and technology do not necessarily entail the advancement of civilization more generally, especially in the domains of human conduct:

The techniques of modern civilization, so far from guaranteeing us against lapses into the past or violent lunges in unpredictable directions, have proved the most effective weapons in the hands of those who wish to change human beings by playing on irrational impulses and defying the framework of civilised life according to some arbitrary pattern of their own. (Berlin, 2019a, p. 14)

In this sense, Berlin is skeptical toward the attempt to grasp political and social reality through numbers, formulas and/or rigorous frameworks. Indeed, he thinks that attempts so to do are not only utopian, but they also lead us astray in grasping reality. However, as he indicates, there is more than one way in which this can happen:

It would be generally agreed that the reverse of a grasp of reality is the tendency to fantasy or Utopia. But perhaps there exits more ways than one to defy reality. May it not be that to be unscientific is to defy, for no good logical or empirical reason, established hypotheses and laws; while to be unhistorical is the opposite – to ignore or twist one's view of particular events, persons, predicaments, in the name of law's, theories, principles derived from other fields, logical, ethical, metaphysical, scientific which the nature of the medium renders inapplicable? For what else is it that is done by those theorists who are called fanatical because their faith in a given pattern is not overcome by their sense of reality? For this reason the attempt to construct a discipline which would stand to concrete history as pure to applied, no matter how successful the human sciences may grow to be – even if, as all but obscurantists must hope, they discover genuine, empirically confirmed, laws of individual and collective behaviour – seems an attempt to square the circle. It is not a vain hope for an ideal beyond human powers, but a chimera, born of a lack of understanding of the nature of natural science, or of history, or of both. (Berlin, quoted in Gray, 2013, p. 111)

If we cannot gain a "sense of reality" necessary for the exercise of political judgment through a scientific method, how can we then approach this, still, some-what vaguely formulated, reality? Berlin (2019a) now moves closer to an answer to these questions by indicating how a medical chart or diagram differs from the qualitative knowledge he seeks to articulate the contours of:

A medical chart or diagram is not the equivalent of a portrait such as a gifted novelist or human being endowed with adequate insight – understanding – could form; not equivalent not at all because it needs less skill or is less valuable for its own purposes, but because if it confines itself to publicly recordable facts and generalisations attested by them, it must necessarily leave out of account the vast number of small, constantly altering, evanescent colours, scents, sounds, and the physical equivalents of these, the half noticed, half inferred, half gazed at, half uncon-sciously absorbed minutia of behaviour and thought and feeling which are at once too numer-ous, too complex, too fine and too indiscriminable from each other to be identified, named, ordered, recorded, set forth in neutral scientific language. And more than this, there are among them pattern qualities – what else are we to call them? – habits of thought and emotion, ways of looking at, reacting to, talking about experiences which lie too close to us to be discriminated and classified – of which we are not strictly aware as such, but which, nevertheless, we absorb into our picture of what goes on, and the more sensitively and sharply aware of them we are, the more understanding and insight we are rightly said to possess. (p. 29)

This, Berlin continues (sounding remarkably like Barnard), "is what under-standing human beings largely consists in. To try to analyze and clearly describe what goes on when we understand in this sense is impossible," he says, "not because the process in some way 'transcends' or is 'beyond' normal experience, is some special act of magical divination not describeable in the language of ordi-nary experience," but rather

for the opposite reason, that it enters too intimately into our most normal experience, and is a kind of automatic integration of a very large number of data too fugitive and various to be mounted on the pin of some scientific process, one by one, in a sense too obvious, too much taken for granted, to be enumerable. (Berlin, 2019a, p. 29)

Berlin (2019b) now goes on to stress how the characteristics of the kinds of knowledge he has just described is what those at the upper echelons of organiza-tions need to master, or, more generally, those who wish "to get large bodies of men to do this or that" (p. 51), such as, for instance, "industrialists," "social wel-fare officers or statesmen" (p. 55). Hence, statecraft, leadership, and the sense of reality and judgment implicated here "is unlike either the erudition of scholars or scientific knowledge" (Berlin, 2019a, p. 39). In contrast to those who master the (natural) sciences, the statesman or leader "cannot communicate their knowledge directly, cannot teach a specific set of rules, cannot set forth any propositions they have established in a form in which they can be learned easily by others"; nor can they "teach a method which, after them, any competent specialist can practice without needing the genius of the original inventor or discoverer" (Berlin, 2019a, p. 41). "What is called wisdom in statesmen, political skill" rather relies upon political judgment, and this requires "understanding rather than knowledge – some kind of acquaintance with the relevant facts of such a kind that it enables" leaders in the upper echelons of organizations

> to tell what fits with what: what can be done in given circumstances and what cannot, what means will work in what situations and how far, without necessarily being able to explain how they know this or even what they know. (Berlin, 2019a, p. 41)

If we look for the key to unlocking the secret, to grasping the sense of reality and the accompanying political judgment, Berlin says that we will be disappointed. For the truth of the matter is that "there is no key" (Berlin, 2019a, p. 41).

> Botany is a science but gardening is not; action and the results of action in situations where only the surface is visible will be successful, partly, no doubt, as the result of luck, but partly owing to "insight" on the part of the actors, that is, the kind of understanding of the relations of the "upper" to the "lower" levels, the kind of semi-instinctive integration of the unaccountable infinitesimals of which individual and social life is composed (…), in which all kinds of skills are involved – powers of observation, knowledge of facts, above all experience […] [I]n short the kind of human wisdom, ability to conduct one's life or fit means to ends, with which, as Faust found, mere knowledge of facts – learning, science – was not at all identical […] [T]here is an element of improvisation, of playing by ear, of being able to size up the situation, of knowing when to leap and when to remain still, for which no formulae, no nostrums, no general recipes, no skill in identifying specific situations as instances of general laws can be a substitute. (Berlin, 2019a, p. 41)

This sense of reality and the political judgment that goes with it, however, is not reducible to "the celebrated distinction drawn by Gilbert Ryle between knowing that and knowing how. To know how to do something" does not, in most instances, "imply an ability to describe why one is acting as one is; a man who knows how to ride a bicycle," for instance, "need not be able to explain what he is doing or why his behaviour leads to the results he desires" (Berlin, 2019a, p. 42). "But a statesman faced with a critical situation and forced to choose between alternative courses (…) does," in contrast to the cyclist "judge the situation" and assess it in such a way so that she/he "can answer objectors, can give reasons for rejecting alternative solutions" (Berlin, 2019a, p. 42). The statesman, though, "cannot demonstrate the truth of what" is said "by reference to theories or systems of knowledge, except to some inconsiderable degree – certainly not in a sense in which scientists or scholars must be ready to do it" (Berlin, 2019a, p. 42).

DISCUSSION AND CONCLUDING REMARKS

From its very inception, organizational theorizing has been marked by strife and critique about what constitutes the field's *raison d'être* (Westwood & Clegg, 2003, p. 3; see also Ringel, 2024, this volume). However, from the 1960s and onward, a number of developments have cumulatively added to promoting a style of theorizing that in its attempt to emulate the natural sciences has contributed to undermining a distinctive practical stance in which the exercise of (political) judgment was considered premium. As we head into a very uncertain third decade of the 21st century, this latter stance might be worth reviving. Instead of "maximizing," "optimizing," and relying upon allegedly objective metrics, managers in the upper echelons of organizations ought rather to cultivate a "sense of reality" and "political judgment" as the requisite dispositions via which they could attempt to face up to the problems of the present. Although we have only been able to scratch the surface of the works of Max Weber, Chester Barnard, Philip Selznick, and Isaiah Berlin, we nevertheless hope to have made it evident that key elements of such a practical stance runs through their otherwise diverse works. In this final section, we will discuss how the argument we have set forth contributes to ongoing discussions within organizational theorizing. We shall do so by emphasizing two points in particular: looking forward via the past and educating responsible practitioners.

Like other scholars in our field (e.g., Adler et al., 2023; Creed et al., 2022), we are also of the conviction that theorizing ought to be engaged with responding to major contemporary problems. And although it is perfectly reasonable to seek to bring about new syntheses and concepts tailored to our particular contemporary predicaments, a less explored route – and the one we advocate here – consists in pausing to ponder if already existing – but now largely forgotten, belittled and "old fashioned" – organizational principles and stances, can (still) be of assistance in tackling the problems of responsible organizational conduct in the face of political risks and dangers. In arguing for the latter, we aim to contribute to a distinctive turn within organizational theorizing, which, over the last couple of decades, has had as its ambition to show the continuing relevance of some of the classical works within our field (e.g., Casler, 2020; du Gay & Vikkelsø, 2014, 2017; Lopdrup-Hjorth, 2015; O'Connor, 2012). As Hinings et al. (2018, p. 341) have recently argued, it is perhaps time to skip the "unhealthy obsession with the recent and the novel," which to a large extent dominates contemporary organizational theorizing, and instead consider reconnecting with history and the wisdom that some of the classical works of our field has to offer. In this article, we have attempted to follow this route by highlighting how threads of a distinctive practical stance that places judgment, and its accompanying sense of reality, center stage can be found in works as diverse as Weber's, Selznick's, Barnard's, and Berlin's. We have attempted to argue that not only is this stance of continuing relevance for organizational theorists and practitioners but also that this stance, throughout the last five decades, has been problematized and belittled, as newer and, allegedly, more "rigorous" quantitative frameworks have been on the ascent within both theory and practice. In making this argument, our ambition has been to suggest that key resources for conceiving and understanding what exercising judgment with a sense of reality amounts to can be lifted directly off the pages of the works we have dealt with here. This, however, is not to suggest that elements of such a stance are only to be found in these works. Rather, additional resources for revitalizing such a stance might equally draw from the works of, among others, Mary Parker Follet, Wilfred Brown, and/or Robert Michels, too.

Here, though, we have sought to indicate how four very different theorists shared a preoccupation with thinking through the requirements of what exercising judgment in a responsible manner amounts to, and, not least, how executive conduct might be let astray if managers and leaders overemphasize the extent to which actions can have a solid foundation in "rigorous" metrics-based frameworks at the expense of a "sense of reality." By reconnecting with the thoughts of these and other classics, it is worth following Thomas Hobbes, who, in the introductory pages to his translation of Thucydides' The Peloponnesian War, argued that "the principal and proper work of history" is "to instruct and enable men, by the knowledge of actions past, to bear themselves prudently in the present and providently towards the future" (quoted in du Gay & Lopdrup-Hjorth, 2022, p. 157).

This leads us to discuss how our argument contributes to ongoing discussions pertaining to the education of responsible organizational practitioners. This theme has been extensively debated in the slipstream of the corporate scandals of 1990s and 2000s and further accentuated in the aftermath of the financial crisis of 2008 (e.g., Dobbin & Jung, 2010; Ghoshal, 2005). Whereas some have argued that several of the most influential organization and management theories of the last four to five decades are essentially anti-management (Donaldson, 1995) and therefore undermine the whole purpose of management education (Donaldson, 2002), others have highlighted how especially economics-based theories have colonized the business school curriculum and – directly or indirectly – contributed to the destruction of otherwise more or less well-functioning management practices (Ghoshal, 2005; Khurana, 2010). While we are largely in agreement with most of these diagnoses, we have sought to highlight some other pathways to addressing these ills. Whereas Donaldson (1995) argue for revitalizing structural contingency theory as the dominant paradigm within management and organizational theorizing, Ghoshal (2005) has urged management and organizational scholars to dispense with what he terms "ideology based gloomy vision" and instead (guided and inspired by the turn toward "positive psychology" within the discipline of psychology) to pursue "positive organizational scholarship." This, in combination with more diversity in dean's hiring practices within business schools, is Ghoshal's proposal for countering how "bad management theories destroys management practices." Finally, Nohria and Khurana (2008) have proposed installing an "oath of management" in order to make management more like the professions (medicine, law, etc.), with all the attending ethical guidelines and sanctions that go with a process of professionalization. While these suggestions might have some traction, we have suggested here that organizational theorists and practitioners ought rather to (re)familiarize themselves with the classics of our field and to utilize the wisdom accumulated in these works as a potential remedy for tackling contemporary political risks and wicked problems. The authors we have attended to here, in their diverse ways, wrote against a background where tragedy was never too far away. In spite of the fact that they lived and wrote within largely divergent contexts, and through only partly overlapping historical periods, there might be more than faint echoes between their differing circumstances and our own less than optimal societal, political, climatic, and economic prospects today. If our own "end of history" moment is finally over, and tragedy and difficult choices explicitly force themselves upon us (Brands & Edel, 2019; Gewen, 2020), it might be worth resuscitating ideas and outlooks stemming from before this moment became prevalent, not least because several of the concepts and frames of understanding outlined by Weber, Barnard, Selznick, and Berlin were penned on a canvas where tragedy, turmoil, and political risks were prominent, too. It is thus worth remembering that Weber in his lecture *The Profession and Vocation of Politics* spoke against the background of a devasting World War, a worrying lack of responsible leaders and statesmen, and, not least, political disorder and revolutionary fervor. Barnard, too, sought to cultivate and express his stance on responsible leadership against the background of tragedy in the form of devastating economic and social turmoil. Written in the midst of the Great Depression in the 1930s, *The Functions of the Executive* opens with an emphasis on the fragility of organizational life. In spite of the fact that what we find "reliable, foreseeable, and stable" is accomplished by organizations, Barnard argues, "successful cooperation in or by" organizations "is the abnormal, not the normal, condition. What are observed from day to day are the successful survivors among innumerable failures. The organizations commanding attention, almost all of which are short-lived at best, are the exceptions, not the rule" (Barnard, 1968a, pp. 4–5). Berlin, too, witnessing the Russian Revolution in 1917 and fleeing the Bolshevik mobs with his family, always kept an eye on tragedy and the harms that humans do to each other in the name of "higher truths." He probably would have agreed with Selznick (1994) who, in his major work, *The Moral Commonwealth*, drew on political realists such as Niebuhr when he wrote: "The most important evils are those we generate ourselves, from ourselves, rather than those imposed upon us by external conditions. This is a lesson liberals and radicals have been slow to learn and loath to accept" (p. 175). While history never repeats itself, it certainly often rhymes, as Mark Twain is believed to have said (MacMillan, 2020, p. 14). And although students within business schools do not learn to become responsible managers and leaders solely by reading books and articles, their outlooks and their professional "persona in spe" is nevertheless shaped to a significant extent by what they read and are taught. Here, as Cummings and Bridgman (2011) have argued, exposing students to classical theorists within our field is one way in to fashion more reflective and responsible practitioners.

NOTES

1. In this context, we are less concerned with whether and to what extent the frameworks proposed by Rice and Zegart (2018) to counter political risks are adequate in regard to the problems they diagnose, just as we shall abstain from entering into discussions about whether one of the authors (Rice) might herself have contributed to an increase in political risks by being part of an administration exhibiting remarkable few restraints in its foreign policy ambitions in combination with a notable inability to think "tragically" (Brands & Edel, 2019; Gewen, 2020). What concern us here is solely the fact that such political risks have been on the rise – something that can be seen in the scholarly literature, in documents from intelligence agencies, and in reports from think tanks and large consulting houses, all of which we have cited above.

2. For instance, the trajectory outlined above has abstained from relating to inquiries of a more encompassing historical scope, whether in the form of the development of statistical

reasoning (Desrosières, 1998), the formation of the overwhelming appeal of quantification in the modern world (Porter, 1995), and the even more encompassing philosophical history of the relationship between numbers and humanity (Nirenberg & Nirenberg, 2021). Equally, we have also abstained from entering into close dialogue with more recent discussions within valuation studies, where debates about how organizations respond to metrics, rankings, and quantitative assessments paint a considerably more nuanced and multifaceted picture (see, e.g., Chun & Sauder, 2022; Dahler-Larsen, 2012; Espeland & Sauder, 2007; Greenwood et al., 2011; Mennicken & Espeland, 2019; Pollock et al., 2018; Strathern, 1997) than what we have been able to provide here. Also, due to limited space, we have only mentioned Herbert Simon and the Carnegiee School in passing, although they play a rather crucial role.

3. Concerning the latter point (i.e., iv), see the final section "Discussion and Concluding Remarks."

4. We will here only highlight one such difference, although there are numerous. Distinguishing between "organization" and "institution" is, for instance, one major difference between Selznick and Barnard. Whereas Selznick insists on this distinction, Barnard (1968a, p. 235, 1968b, p. 317), as we have seen, continually speaks about the necessity of "sensing the organization as a whole" and of the important ability to "*feel* organization." Such phrasings make little sense in Selznick's (1957) conceptual universe, where organizations are defined as "expendable," "technical instruments" that "are judged on engineering premises" (p. 21). In essence, several of the positive qualities that are retained within Barnard's (more expansive) understanding of organization is in Selznick's theory relocated under the conceptual umbrella of "institution," thereby leaving organization – relatively speaking – as a more stripped down, technical, engineering entity – hence its "expendability."

5. The question as to whether Berlin is a "true realist" is of less importance for us. Moreover, although "there exists considerable discrepancy between the amount of ink spilled on [Bernard] William's and [Raymond] Geuss' thought *vis-à-vis* (…) Berlin's," much of Berlin's work can nevertheless be described as "proto realist" (Vogler & Tillyris, 2019, p. 20 (n. 5)). "Proto-realist," however, is not just a label used to describe Berlin, since it is also used to describe, among others, Max Weber and Hans Morgenthau (see Maynard, 2022).

REFERENCES

Adler, P. S., Adly, A., Armanios, D. E., Battilana, J., Bodrožić, Z., Clegg, S., Davis, G. F., Gartenberg, C., Glynn, M. A., Aslan Gümüsay, A., Haveman, H. A., Leonardi, P., Lounsbury, M., McGahan, A. M., Meyer, R., Phillips, N., & Sheppard-Jones, K. (2023). Authoritarianism, populism, and the global retreat of democracy: A curated discussion. *Journal of Management Inquiry, 32*(1): 3–20. https://doi.org/10.1177/10564926221119395

Barnard, C. (1968a). *The functions of the executive.* Harvard University Press.

Barnard, C. (1968b). Mind in everyday affairs. A Cyrus Foff Brackett lecture before the engineering faculty and students of Princeton University, March 10, 1936. In C. Barnard (Ed.), *The functions of the executive* (pp. 299–322). Harvard University Press.

Berlin, I. (2019a). The sense of reality. In I. Berlin (Ed.), *The sense of reality: Studies in ideas and their history* (2nd ed, pp. 1–49.). Princeton University Press.

Berlin, I. (2019b). Political judgement. In I. Berlin (Ed.), *The sense of reality: Studies in ideas and their history* (2nd ed, pp. 50–66.). Princeton University Press.

Brands, H., & Edel, C. (2019). *The lessons of tragedy: Statecraft and world order.* Yale University Press.

Brown, W. (1974). *Organization.* Penguin (Pelican Library of Business and Management).

Casler, C. (2020). *Reconstruction in strategy and organization: For a pragmatic stance* [PhD Series No. 14.2020, Copenhagen Business School].

Chun, H., & Sauder, M. (2022). The logic of quantification: Institutionalizing numerical thinking. *Theory and Society, 51*(2), 335–370.

Collini, S. (2018). Kept alive for thirty days. *London Review of Books, 40*(21). https://www.lrb.co.uk/the-paper/v40/n21/stefan-collini/kept-alive-for-thirty-days

Council on Foreign Relations. (2023). *Preventive priorities survey 2023*. https://cdn.cfr.org/sites/default/files/report_pdf/CFR_CPA_PPS23.pdf?_gl=1*1xx4mit*_ga*MzU4OTQ0MzEwLjE2ODAxNjY4OTQ.*_ga_24W5E70YKH*MTY4MDE2Njg5NC4zLjEuMTY4MDE2NjkxMC4wLjA.uMA

Creed, D., Gray, B., Höllerer, M. A., Karam, C., & Reay, T. (2022). Organizing for social and institutional change in response to disruption, division, and displacement: Introduction to the special issue. *Organization Studies*, *43*(10), 1535–1557. https://doi.org/10.1177/01708406221122237

Cummings, S., & Bridgman, T. (2011). The relevant past: Why the history of management should be critical for our future. *Academy of Management Learning & Education*, *19*(1), 77–93.

Dahler-Larsen, P. (2012). *The evaluation society*. Stanford University Press.

da Mata, S. (2019). Realism and reality in Max Weber. In E. Hanke, L. Scaff, & S. Whimster (Eds.), *The Oxford handbook of Max Weber* (pp. 596–614). Oxford. https://doi.org/10.1093/oxfordhb/9780190679545.013.39

DeRose, C., & Tichy, N. M. (2008). Leadership judgment: Without it nothing else matters. *Leader to Leader*, *48*, 26–32. https://doi.org/10.1002/ltl.277

Desrosières, A. (1998). *The politics of large numbers: A history of statistical reasoning*. Harvard University Press.

Dobbin, F., & Jung, J. (2010). The misapplication of Mr. Michael Jensen: How agency theory brought down the economy and why it might again. In M. Lounsbury & P. M. Hirsch (Eds.), *Markets on trial: The economic sociology of the U.S. financial crisis: Part B* (pp. 29–64). Emerald Group.

Donaldson, L. (1995). *American anti-management theories of organization: A critique of paradigm proliferation*. Cambridge University Press.

Donaldson, L. (2002). Damned by our own theories: Contradictions between theories and management education. *Academy of Management Learning & Education*, *1*(1), 96–106.

du Gay, P. (2023). Reason of state as a stance for organizing the world as we find it. *Organization Studies*, *44*(2), 343–346.

du Gay, P., & Lopdrup-Hjorth, T. (2022). *For public service: State, office and ethics*. Routledge.

du Gay, P., Lopdrup-Hjorth, T., Pedersen, K. Z., & Roelsgaard, A. O. (2019). Character and organization. *Journal of Cultural Economy*, *12*(1), 36–53.

du Gay, P., & Vikkelsø, S. (2014). What makes organization? Organizational theory as a "practical science." In P. Adler, P. du Gay, G. Morgan, & M. Reed (Eds.), *Oxford handbook of sociology, social theory and organization studies: Contemporary currents* (pp. 736–758). Oxford University.

du Gay, P., & Vikkelsø, S. (2017). *For formal organization: The past in the present and future of organization theory*. Oxford University Press.

Espeland, W. N. (2001). Value-matters. *Economic and Political Weekly*, *36*(21), 1839–1845.

Espeland, W. N., & Sauder, M. (2007). Rankings and reactivity: How public measures recreate social worlds. *American Journal of Sociology*, *113*(1), 1–40.

EY. (2022). *2023 Geostrategic outlook: How to build a robust strategy for a volatile world*. https://assets.ey.com/content/dam/ey-sites/ey-com/en_gl/topics/geostrategy/geostrategy-pdf/ey-2023-geo-strategic-outlook.pdf

Freedman, L. (2015). *Strategy: A history* (1st paperback ed.). Oxford University Press.

Geuss, R. (2009). What is political judgement? In R. Bourke & R. Geuss (Eds.), *Political judgement* (pp. 29–46). Cambridge University Press.

Gewen, B. (2020). *The inevitability of tragedy: Henry Kissinger and his world*. W.W. Norton & Company.

Ghoshal, S. (2005). Bad management theories are destroying good management practices. *Academy of Management Learning and Education*, *4*(1), 75–91.

Gigerenzer, G. (2015). *Risk savvy – How to make good decisions*. Penguin Books, Ltd.

Grant, A., Haider, Z., & Mieszala, J.-C. (2022). *How to build geopolitical resilience amid a fragmenting global order*. https://www.mckinsey.com/capabilities/risk-and-resilience/our-insights/how-to-build-geopolitical-resilience-amid-a-fragmenting-global-order#/

Gray, J. (2013). *Isaiah Berlin: An interpretation of his thought*. Princeton University Press.

Greenwood, R., Raynard, M., Kodeih, F., Micelotta, E. R., & Lounsbury, M. (2011). Institutional complexity and organizational responses. *Academy of Management Annals*, *5*(1), 317–371.

Hardy, H. (2019). Editor's preface. In I. Berlin (Ed.), *The sense of reality: Studies in ideas and their history* (2nd ed, pp. xxix–xxxvi.). Princeton University Press.

Hennis, W. (2000). *Max Weber's central question* (2nd ed., K. Tribe, Trans.). Threshold Press Ltd.

Hinings, C. R., Greenwood, R., & Meyer, R. (2018). Dusty books? The liability of oldness. *Academy of Management Review, 43*(2), 333–343.

Jensen, M. C. (1983). Organization theory and methodology. *The Accounting Review, 8*(2), 319–337.

Jensen, M. C., & Meckling, W. H. (1976). Theory of the firm: Managerial behavior, agency costs and ownership structure. *Journal of Financial Economics, 3*(4), 305–360.

Khurana, R. (2010). *From higher aims to hired hands: The social transformation of American business schools and the unfulfilled promise of management as a profession.* Princeton University Press.

Kitsing, M. (2022). Geopolitical risk and uncertainty: How transnational corporations can use scenario planning for strategic resilience. *Transnational Corporations Review, 14*(4), 339–352.

Lambert, L. (2021). *Going with your gut can result in better decision-making than using detailed data methods, study shows.* Retrieved August 2, 2022, from https://www.bayes.city.ac.uk/news-and-events/news/2021/june/going-with-your-gut-can-result-in-better-decision-making-than-using-detailed-data-methods-under-high-uncertainty

Likierman, A. (2020). The elements of good judgement. *Harvard Business Review, 98*(1), 103–111.

Locke, R. R., & Spender, J.-C. (2011). *Confronting managerialism: How the business elite and their schools threw our lives out of balance.* Zed Books.

Lopdrup-Hjorth, T. (2015). Object and objective lost? Organization-phobia in organization theory. *Journal of Cultural Economy, 8*(1), 439–461.

MacMillan, M. (2020, October). Which past is prologue? Heeding the right warnings from history. *Foreign Affairs.* https://www.foreignaffairs.com/articles/united-states/2020-08-11/history-which-past-prologue

March, J. G. (1962). The business firm as a political coalition. *The Journal of Politics, 24*(4), 662–678.

Maynard, J. L. (2022). Political realism as methods not metaethics. *Ethical Theory Moral Practice, 25*(3), 449–463.

Mennicken, A., & Espeland, W. N. (2019). What's new with numbers? Sociological approaches to the study of quantification. *Annual Review of Sociology, 45,* 223–245.

Moore, M. (2018). *Democracy hacked: Political turmoil and information warfare in the digital age.* Oneworld.

Muller, J. Z. (2015). The costs of accountability. *The American Interest, 11*(1), 1–23.

Muller, J. Z. (2018). *The tyranny of metrics.* Princeton University Press.

Nagle, A. (2017). *Kill all normies: Online culture wars from 4Chan and Tumblr to Trump and the Alt-Right.* Zero Books.

Nirenberg, D., & Nirenberg, R. L. (2021). *Uncountable. A philosophical history of number and humanity from antiquity to the present.* The University of Chicago Press.

Nohria, N., & Khurana, R. (2008). It's time to make management a true profession. *Harvard Business Review, 86*(10), 70–77.

O'Connor, E. S. (2012). *Creating new knowledge in management: Appropriating the field's lost foundation.* Stanford University Press.

Office of the Director of National Intelligence. (2023). *Annual threat assessment of the U.S. intelligence community.* https://www.odni.gov/files/ODNI/documents/assessments/ATA-2023-Unclassified-Report.pdf

Ord, T. (2020). *The precipice: Existential risk and the future of humanity.* Hachette Books.

Perrow, C. (1986). *Complex organizations: A critical essay.* McGraw Hill.

Pfeffer, J. (1992). *Managing with power: Politics and influence in organizations.* Harvard Business School Press.

Pollock, N., D'Adderio, L., Williams, R., & Leforestier, L. (2018). Conforming or transforming? How organizations respond to multiple rankings. *Accounting, Organizations and Society, 64,* 55–68.

Porter, T. M. (1995). *Trust in numbers: The pursuit of objectivity in science and public life.* Princeton University Press.

Power, M. (1997). *The audit society: Rituals of verification.* Oxford University Press.

Ringel, L. (2024). Organizational sociology and organization studies: Past, present, and future. In S. Clegg, M. Grothe-Hammer, & K. Serrano Velarde (Eds.), *Sociological thinking in contemporary organizational scholarship* (Research in the Sociology of Organizations, Vol. 90, pp. 55–84). Emerald Publishing.

Rice, C., & Zegart, A. B. (2018). *Political risk: How businesses and organizations can anticipate global insecurity*. Twelve Hachette Book Group.

Robé, J. P. (2011). The legal structure of the firm. *Accounting, Economics and Law*, *1*(1), 1–86.

Schumpeter, J. S. (1911/2011). The entrepreneur. In M. C. Becker, T. Knudsen, & R. Swedberg (Eds.), *The entrepreneur: Classic texts by Joseph A. Schumpeter*. Stanford Business Books.

Selznick, P. (1957). *Leadership in administration. A sociological interpretation*. University of California Press.

Selznick, P. (1994). *The moral commonwealth: Social theory and the promise of community* (First paperback ed.). University of California Press.

Simon, H. A. (1946). The proverbs of administration. *Public Administration Review*, *6*(1), 53–67.

Skidelsky, R. (2021). *What's wrong with economics: A primer for the perplexed*. Yale University Press.

Stout, L. (2012). *The shareholder value myth: How putting shareholders first harms investors, corporations, and the public*. Berrett-Koehler.

Struthers, M. (1997). Improving ratings: Audit in the British university system. *European Review*, *5*(3), 305–321.

The National Intelligence Council. (2021). *Global trends 2040. A more contested world*. https://www.dni.gov/files/ODNI/documents/assessments/GlobalTrends_2040.pdf

Tichy, N. M., & Bennis W. G. (2007). Making judgment calls. The ultimate act of leadership. *Harvard Business Review*, *85*(10), 94–102.

Tooze, A. (2018). *Crashed: How a decade of financial crises changed the world*. Viking.

Tooze, A. (2021). *Shutdown: How Covid shook the world economy*. Viking.

Vogler, G., & Tillyris, D. (2019). Arendt and political realism: Towards a realist account of political judgement. *Critical Review of International Social and Political Philosophy*, *24*(6), 821–844.

Wallace-Wells, D. (2019). *The uninhabitable earth: Life after warming* (1st ed.). Tim Duggan Books.

Waring, S. P. (1991). *Taylorism transformed: Scientific management theory since 1945*. The University of Carolina Press.

Weber, M. (1994). The profession and vocation of politics. In M. Weber (Ed.), *Political writings* (1st ed., pp. 309–369). Cambridge University Press.

West, D. C., Acar, O. A., & Caruana, A. (2020). Choosing among alternative new product development projects: The role of heuristics. *Psychology & Marketing*, *37*(11), 1511–1524.

Westwood, R., & Clegg, S. (2003). The discourse of organization studies: Dissensus, politics, and paradigms. In R. Westwood & S. Clegg (Eds.), *Debating organization: Point-counterpoint in organization studies* (pp. 1–42). Blackwell.

Williamson, O. (1991). Economic institutions: Spontaneous and intentional governance. *Journal of Law, Economics and Organization*, *7*, 159–187.

Wren, D. A. (2005). *The history of management thought*. John Wiley & Sons Inc.

Zhang, X., & Duchesne, É. (2022). Introduction for the special issue geopolitical risks and transnational corporations: The case of the Ukrainian crisis. *Transnational Corporations Review*, *14*(4), 333–338.

PART 2

SOCIAL STRATIFICATION IN AND THROUGH ORGANIZATIONS

Organizations within Society: Organizational Perspectives on Status and Distinction

STATUS IN SOCIO-ENVIRONMENTAL FIELDS: RELATIONSHIPS, EVALUATIONS, AND OTHERHOOD

Nadine Arnold[a] and Fabien Foureault[b]

[a]Vrije Universiteit Amsterdam, The Netherlands
[b]Sciences Po, France

ABSTRACT

Status distinctions matter among heterogeneous organizations within a socio-environmental field. This is exemplified in the food waste field, where six types of organizations employ different excess strategies to address the issue. Theoretically, we propose that status is constructed internally through advice relationships and externally through evaluations. We posit that organizations conducting evaluations and advocating legitimate principles based on expertise (i.e., Others) are status winners. Our mixed-method study confirms that Others hold privileged positions and identifies status inconsistencies. By critically illuminating these status dynamics, we contribute to a better understanding of the roles of organizations and status in tackling socio-environmental issues.

Keywords: Organization; food waste; network; Others; excess; organizational field

Sociological Thinking in Contemporary Organizational Scholarship
Research in the Sociology of Organizations, Volume 90, 111–139
ISSN: 0733-558X/doi:10.1108/S0733-558X20240000090005

1. INTRODUCTION

Status is considered one of the most sociological concepts (Podolny, 2005, p. 11), encompassing esteem, admiration, and deference given to or achieved by an actor (Boudon & Bourricaud, 1992). It is used to explain social order and to critically reflect on social differences and inequalities (Ridgeway, 2014). Notably, Max Weber explained that social positions in society are not only based on economic power but also honor, respect, and deference (or defiance, dishonor, and disrespect), resulting in the formation of privileged and marginalized groups.[1] These status hierarchies are neither naturally given nor objectively justified, as status is self-reinforcing (Merton, 1968), and one can observe strategies of distinction and conflicts over social positions (Bourdieu, 1987). Consequently, in sociological thinking, the notion status helps to investigate critically the construction of social order.

Complementarily, organizational scholars have demonstrated the value of "status" in enhancing our understanding of organizational life and survival as well as interorganizational collaborations and relationships (Chen et al., 2011; Piazza & Castellucci, 2014; Sauder et al., 2012). The construct has gained a foothold in organizational research due to Podolny's (2005) seminal work applying status to markets and detailing that market participants in situations of uncertainty rely on producers' status to make inferences about the products' and services' quality. The identification of status effects on organizations is a core topic in organizational research, with particular emphasis placed on its associated benefits (Chen et al., 2011).[2] Hence, organizational scholars put emphasis on the desired effects of status on organizations, such as reducing uncertainty, facilitating transactions, accessing better opportunities, or minimizing costs (Sauder et al., 2012).

However, in light of sociologists' critical analysis of status, it is essential to acknowledge that status does not solely generate desirable effects but establishes order among organizations by constructing privileged and marginalized groups. The objective of this paper is to delve into the role of status in creating such hierarchical orders within socio-environmental fields that are burgeoning in response to escalating awareness of social and planetary boundaries (e.g., Rockström et al., 2009). These fields are characterized by a variety of organizations that unite around a socio-environmental issue (Hoffman, 1999; Wooten & Hoffman, 2017). As they emerge and grow, these organizations develop a shared understanding of the field's purpose and relationships with one another (Fligstein & McAdam, 2012). To date, interorganizational status differences have typically been examined between similar organizations such as wineries (Croidieu & Powell, 2024, in this volume; Malter, 2014), colleges and universities (Bühlmann et al., 2022; Chu, 2021; Sauder, 2006), or restaurants (Borkenhagen & Martin, 2018). Thus, there is limited knowledge of how status establishes order among heterogeneous organizations. Against this backdrop we ask: what are the determinants of organizational status in a heterogeneous socio-environmental field? Which organizations are the privileged ones, and which are the marginalized ones? In answering these questions, we will provide findings that are of interest to sociologists and organizational scholars concerned with the role of organizations and status in addressing socio-environmental issues, specifically determining the types of organizations that inhabit the dominant center of the field.

In the empirical spotlight of this paper is the specific socio-environmental issue of food waste. Following Abbott (2014), food waste can be considered a problem of excess, as most will agree that it is "too much" when approximately one-third of all food produced in the world is lost or wasted every year (FAO, 2019). Looking at the emerging food waste field in Switzerland, we will demonstrate that heterogeneous organizational types (*food save charities, food save businesses, plants and tech companies, alternative producers, and distributors* as well as *public and political organizations* and *interest groups*) are proposing different excess strategies to tackle the issue. Nevertheless, driven by a national policy push, they interact and exchange. To explore the status dynamics among these organizations, we will draw from sociological literature on status (especially Lazega et al., 2012; Sauder et al., 2012) and assume that status is constructed endogenously through advice relations among field inhabitants (i.e., relational status), as well as exogenously through evaluations (i.e., evaluative status). In addition to this conceptual distinction, we will pay specific attention to those organizations that advocate abstract, legitimate principles based on expertise (referred to as Others) because, according to institutional theory, these organizations are held high in esteem in current society (Meyer & Jepperson, 2000).

Our empirical results from a mixed-method study will confirm that Others (*public and political organizations* and *interest groups*) inhabit a privileged position in the food waste field compared to other types of organizations that distribute food waste and avoid this by establishing alternative value chains or transforming waste into new food products and energy. As we critically illuminate Others' status-laden position, we will also uncover status inconsistencies and spillover effects of Others' status-relevant evaluations that create additional disadvantage for people who rely on food supplies from *food save charities*. These findings will support the relevance of studying status in socio-environmental fields and, more importantly, indicate where to shift analytical focus when grappling with interorganizational status dynamics in the context of socio-environmental challenges.

Next, we will develop our conceptual framework and introduce our case and methods in Section 3. In Section 4, we present empirical findings sequentially, focusing first on the relational and then on the evaluative status hierarchy. We discuss our findings in Section 5 and conclude with a brief reflection on the implications for further studies on organizational status dynamics in socio-environmental fields.

2. STATUS AND SOCIO-ENVIRONMENTAL ISSUES

The contemporary world faces manifold socio-environmental challenges such as massive pollution, overfishing, waste accumulation, or deforestation. As these problems worsen and attract growing attention, individuals, businesses, non-profit organizations, and governments are taking responsibility to mitigate them. Addressing socio-environmental issues can enhance social status, as evidenced by ethical consumption (Fifita et al., 2020) or the awarding of environmental certifi-cates (Carlos & Lewis, 2018). At the same time, however, these issues also lead to the formation of new fields inhabited by multiple, heterogeneous organizations (Hoffman, 1999; Wooten & Hoffman, 2017). Status flows on these interorgani-zational relations, and we elucidate hereafter how to grasp these status construc-tions and distinctions analytically.

Using different terms, authors refer to two fundamental components in the construction of status hierarchies (e.g., Gould, 2002; Sauder et al., 2012; Sharkey, 2014), which we distinguish with the terms *evaluative* and *relational* status. In both cases, organizations do not achieve status on their own, because status is an attribution by other actors. An organization's status can emerge endogenously from field relationships with other organizations (i.e., relational status) and be exogenously imposed by the evaluation of other actors (i.e., evaluative status). Looking at socio-environmental fields, we address these two forms of status in turn by directing attention to their underlying social process, their social basis, and their operationalization. In doing so, we assume that evaluative and rela-tional status dynamics are not necessarily congruent and may differ, resulting in status inconsistencies (Sauder et al., 2012; Zhao & Zhou, 2011). Table 1 summa-rizes the key assumptions of our conceptual framework.

In any field, a status order emerges endogenously from the relations between its inhabitants. In this sense, relational status highlights the fact that an organization's status is dependent on with whom the organization is connected to and with whom it builds relationships (Sauder et al., 2012). Given that "status leaks through linkages" (Podolny, 2005, p. 15), actors seek linkages to those with high status in hopes of benefiting from their prestige and esteem. That is why high status brings benefits and advantages, as pointed out by the seminal Matthew effect (Merton, 1968). We know that status flows through exchange relationships, but who the specific organizational status winners and losers are in the context of socio-environmental challenges needs to be explored (Blau, 1964; Lazega et al., 2012). Determining who gives and seeks advice is beneficial to illuminate how status is distributed in networks of relationships (Podolny, 2005). Against

Table 1.   Types of Organizational Status in Fields Formed Around Socio-Environmental Issues.

	Relational Status	Evaluative Status
Social process	Endogenous, emergent from field relationships (Blau, 1964; Lazega et al., 2012; Podolny, 2005)	Exogenous, typically imposed by Others that evaluate organizational performance and quality (Correll et al., 2017; Sauder et al., 2012)
Social basis	Perceived competence in taking responsibility for the socio-environmental issue	Conformity to policy expectations relevant to the socio-environmental issue
Operationalization	Interorganizational networks (esp. advice networks)	Evaluative devices (e.g., rankings, ratings, standards, certificates)

Source: Authors' own.

this background, we assume that those organizations that are considered to be competent in taking responsibility for socio-environmental issues are asked for advice by other organizations and gain relational status. To acquire a more precise understanding of the dynamics of relational status, one must therefore study interorganizational networks, especially advice networks (Lazega et al., 2012).

By searching for organizations that are asked for and giving advice, we hypothesize that status winners are those organizations that possess knowledge and expertise and are specialized in gathering information and making recommendations. Identifying the types of organizations that are relational status winners is congruent with arguments from institutional theory about actorhood (Meyer, 2010, 2019; Meyer & Jepperson, 2000). Meyer and Jepperson (2000, p. 106) explain that the "capacity for responsible agency" is central to the construction of actorhood, whereby actors (including organizations) construct agency not only for themselves and other actors but also for abstract principles and cultural standards. In the latter case, otherhood is observed, meaning that actors do not act as self-interested agents for their individual concerns and priorities, but serve abstract and theoretical principles that are mobilized to guide and orient action. These actors are labeled as Others – a term that identifies a particular way of being an actor that requires education, training, and knowledge. In modern, globalized society, these Others receive the highest status, because "otherhood, rather than successfully interested actorhood, ranks at the top of the prestige system, worldwide" (Meyer, 2010, p. 10). That is, "the most admired actors in contemporary society are mostly such Others, carrying disinterested commitment to very general goods, and transmitting these" (Meyer, 2019, p. 283, own capitalization of the term "Others"). In the case of socio-environmental issues, the organizational Others are those that advocate legitimate principles and standards that help protect the planet and society (e.g., environmental protection and justice, biodiversity, solidarity, and fairness).

However, status differences do not result solely from the dynamics of field relationships. Others also evaluate organizations in a status-relevant way (Correll et al., 2017; Sauder et al., 2012). Others typically assume their intermediary function in an expertise-based way and with references to societally legitimate principles (Meyer, 2019). To evaluate these parties, for example, Others develop ratings and rankings, award prizes and certificates, or publish indicators that assess organizations' performance and quality. Consequently, we assume that formal evaluations matter for the construction of evaluative status, although informal evaluations may also influence status dynamics. However, it is formal evaluations that have intensified in the organizational world (Dahler-Larsen, 2011), and they also enjoy high acceptance in dealing with socio-environmental challenges. For example, an increasing variety of standards and certificates assess the socio-environmentally relevant actions and inactions of organizations (Carlos & Lewis, 2018; Loconto & Arnold, 2022), while indicators measure organizations' contribution to a socio-environmental transition (Bexell & Jönsson, 2017). Typically, these evaluative devices check conformity with policy expectations relevant to the particular issue, with good and positive evaluations increasing status and poor evaluations working in the other direction. Given that evaluative status depends on how much value is attributed to organizational performance and quality, it is exogenous, and we assume that Others are relevant evaluators. Yet, their evaluations are not objective but contingent, and the high status of those being evaluated may positively influence the evaluation (Lamont, 2012). Consequently, evaluations can produce status hierarchies that tend to reproduce themselves.

In a nutshell, we assume that a status order in a socio-environmental field is constructed endogenously by advice relations and exogenously by evaluations. Therein, Others play a key role because, on the one hand, they rank at the top of the societal status hierarchy, and, on the other hand, they shape status differences through their formal evaluations.

3. THE SWISS FOOD WASTE FIELD

As a socio-environmental issue, food waste started to receive global attention when the Food and Agriculture Organization (FAO) of the United Nations unveiled that about one-third of all food produced worldwide for human consumption is wasted (Gustavsson et al., 2011). This quantification has provoked lively scientific and policy debates (Reynolds et al., 2020), for example, being reflected in the setting of the UN Sustainable Development Goal 12.3, which states that food waste must be dramatically reduced by 2030. However, food waste continues to accumulate and the 931 million tons of food that end up in the garbage annually is indisputably too much (FAO, 2019). Hence, food waste is undoubtedly an "excess problem" (Abbott, 2014), but it is based on other problems of excess. In particular, excessive consumption (Evans, 2014; Packard, [1960] 2011) and exorbitant standards that define expectations about the quality, safety, and appearance of the food drive its accumulation (Arnold, 2022). Both excessive consumption and standards are pronounced in Western industrialized countries such as Switzerland where we put our empirical focus.

In Switzerland, 330 kg of food is wasted per year per citizen (Foodwaste.ch, 2019). The food waste debates are still young, but they are gaining continuous momentum, making Switzerland a suitable setting for examining status dynamics in an emerging field. Specifically, the food waste debates started no more than 10 years ago, when the Federal Office for Agriculture called for a stakeholder dialogue on the issue in 2013, opening a conversation among all actors interested in the issue. This stakeholder dialogue can be considered a major field-configuring event, as various organizations have exchanged their ideas and perspectives on the issue and started to build relationships (Lampel & Meyer, 2008). While Switzerland has been committed to the sustainable development goals (SDGs) (including food waste reduction) since the beginning, the Swiss government did not become active until a corresponding postulate was submitted and officially accepted by the Swiss Parliament in March 2019 (Die Bundesversammlung, 2018). Following this, a nationwide action plan was adopted in 2022, which provides a two-step plan on how to achieve the goal of halving food waste by first taking voluntary measures, which, if they are not effective enough, can then be supplemented by government measures (Schweizerische Eidgenossenschaft, 2022).

For our research purpose, the Swiss food waste field is appealing, because a growing number of organizations, heterogeneous in nature, are involved in addressing the problem. Our first empirical goal and challenge were to track and identify the organizational field inhabitants before turning to their status hierarchies. To do so, we used a mixed-methods approach, in which we collected first qualitative and then quantitative data in two phases (Leech & Onwuegbuzie, 2009). The identification of all organizations that take responsibility for food waste was a crucial part of both approaches. This undertaking has garnered the interest of policymakers, who utilized our information to ensure they have not overlooked any pertinent actors for their stakeholder dialogue in developing the food waste action plan. The limited knowledge of policymakers about who is part of the field underscores that the Swiss food waste field is thoroughly emergent and hardly stabilized (Fligstein & McAdam, 2012). In line with our sequential approach, we next present our methods and emphasize that our subsequentially obtained data iteratively enriched each other during data interpretation. Thus, the sequential approach has dissolved during the research process.

4. METHODS

4.1. Drawing the Field Boundaries

In 2018, we started to conduct semi-structured interviews with key players in the Swiss Food Waste field to learn which organizations address this issue, what approaches they propose, and with whom they collaborate and/or compete. To start a snowball sampling process, we conducted the first interview with a natural scientist who quantifies Swiss food waste volumes and raises broad attention from the media. At the end of each interview, we asked for other key players. With this snowball system approach, we reached 29 interviewees with an average duration of 60 minutes as of April 2023. Interviewees included politicians, chefs, consultants and lobbyists, activists, biogas plant operators, as well as managing directors of food banks and consumer organizations. Alongside the interviews, we conducted participant observations in different organizational settings (e.g., food waste restaurants, food banks, food saving activities, urban food waste events) to observe and familiarize ourselves with what taking responsibility for food waste means in everyday life.

The qualitative data were used to set up a database of Swiss food waste organizations. By triangulating information from interviews with information from newspaper articles, we identified a total of 102 organizations. These organizations can be categorized into six different organizational types, all of which can be assigned to one of Abbott's (2014) four excess strategies (defensive, reactive, adaptive, and creative).

- The first group combines those organizations that apply a defensive strategy. That is, they do not solve the problem, but they "transform it (excess) into a problem of scarcity" (Abbott, 2014, p. 18). These include *food save charities* (1) that redistribute food waste for human consumption to those in need. By redistributing food waste for free or very cheap, these organizations generate a high demand for such waste, rendering food waste a scarce resource. *Food save businesses* (2) save and mostly process food waste to sell it in conventional markets for human consumption. This introduction in conventional markets is a classic defensive strategy that aims at taming the problem. Similarly, *plants and tech companies* (3) that generate energy from food waste make food waste a scarce supply for energy production.

- Those organizations with a reactive strategy form the second group. Like the first group, these organizations also aim to reduce excessive food waste, but instead of making it scarce, they seek to create order in excess, for example, through prioritization or hierarchization. *Public and political organizations* (4) that study food waste, provide information, and work toward regulation belong to this group. Additionally, *interest groups* (5), who campaign privately to reduce food waste, provide information, and make policies, apply a reactive strategy. Both organizational types (*public and political organizations* and *interest groups*) are Others because their strategies are based on expertise, education, and training and give guidance and evaluation of what should be done with food waste.
- The third group consists of those organizations that use an adaptive strategy that "focuses less on ignoring or reducing excess [as the defensive and reactive strategy do] than on finding it more desirable and less disturbing" (p. 20). This group includes only one organizational type, *the alternative producers and distributors* (6), which create new, inclusive production and trade chains. In doing so, *alternative producers and distributors* scale excess as they produce and trade even more food (waste).

Although we do not observe the fourth, creative strategy, the listing above proves the heterogeneity of organizations and their strategies in the food waste field.[3] When stressing the heterogeneity, it is important to add that these organizations can be compared because they all take responsibility for food waste and are therefore concerned with food safety issues and logistics, as well as standards and regulations, relevant to food production and trade. Further, they actually know each other and engage in mutual exchange, as we will show later.

4.2. Designing the Survey

Our database on heterogeneous organizations provided an excellent opportunity to invite the organizations to participate in a self-completion survey that collected systematic information about their characteristics and relationships. In May 2020, we invited persons with good organizational knowledge (e.g., owners, founders, managers) to fill out the survey on behalf of their organization. Two respondents informed that their organizations no longer exist, eight clarified that their activities have nothing to do with food waste, and two explained that their organizations formally constitute one organization. As a result, we corrected our reference population to 91 organizations. In total, 84 completed our survey, giving us an outstanding response rate of 92% (84/91). We achieved this by sending personalized letters and then motivating non-respondents (first by email and then by phone) to complete the survey online (Qualtrics) via a QR code or by hand on paper.

Questions in the survey addressed three domains: *organizational characteristics* (year of foundation, industry, canton, specialization, number of employees/volunteers, funding, legal form, target audience), *organizational practices* (quantity and types of food processed), and *attitudes* (definition of the food waste problem). Most importantly for this study, the survey included a sociometric module about relations of awareness, advice, exchange of food and personnel, taking inspiration from the interorganizational networks literature (DiMaggio, 1986; Lazega, 2014; Lazega et al., 2012). Given that status refers to the accumulated acts of deference that are intangible per se, organization scholars generally infer status from exchange relations, such as syndication, strategic alliances, patent citations, or PhD exchanges (cf. Sauder et al., 2012).

4.3. Conceptualizing and Measuring Status

Lazega et al. (2012) proposed to measure status via the exchange of advice and resulting relationships. We follow this suggestion for three main reasons. First, inferring relational status from advice relationships is significant, because we can explain the origins of status with social exchange theory, considering that advice givers exchange advice for status (Blau, 1955) and accumulate it as capital (Blau, 1964). Second, advice-seeking implies deference. When reaching for advice, advice seekers signal their deference to more competent actors (Lazega et al., 2012). Third, numerous studies confirm that actors tend to seek advice from those perceived to have higher status, as evidenced by Lazega et al.'s (2012, p. 2) citation of 19 relevant studies. While some literature simply argues that advice is sought from status winners, we follow Lazega et al. (2012) and approach seeking advice as a way to measure status. The specific measure of status we used for the quantitative analysis is the response to the following question from the sociometric module: "Would you [i.e. ego] call this [i.e. alter] organization if you needed advice?" To account for the elements of desire and admiration in the concept of status, we formulated the question in a conditional mode and did not ask who has been asked for advice in a past period of time, as Lazega et al. (2012) did in their study.

In a next step, we concatenated each bilateral advice relation among all organizations to get an advice network. Indegree centrality refers to the number of ties received by an organization in this network. This variable was taken as a measure of status: the more central an organization is in terms of indegree in the advice network, the more status it has. This operationalization of status has external validity, as we asked a supplementary question in the survey to capture organizational status in another way: "List the three most important organizations that deal with the issue of food waste in Switzerland." The answers given to this question corresponded to our results from the network analysis, giving us high confidence in our measure of status with indegree centrality in the advice network (see the Appendix).

Building on our network analysis, which confirmed Others' dominant position in the food waste field, we finally compared our empirical findings on the relational status hierarchy with the status-relevant evaluations in the field. Specifically, we used our qualitative data to analyze how Others evaluate existing food waste strategies while influencing status distinctions in the field. For this purpose, information from the interviews with those organizations that provide field-relevant evaluations was particularly helpful. Of our 29 interviews, we conducted 7 interviews with members of *public and political organizations* and 3 interviews with employees from *private interest groups*. These 10 interviews, along with information given by the dominant Others (especially BAFU and Foodwaste.ch) on their websites, were helpful in identifying their formal, hierarchizing evaluations of food waste approaches and understanding how they shape the evaluative status hierarchy in the food waste field.

5. STATUS HIERARCHIES IN THE FOOD WASTE FIELD

Following our framework, we detail what organizations receive and are given high/low status through relationships and formal evaluations given by Others. Table 2 summarizes our results and anticipates that status differences are not consistently constructed. Given that Others are the evaluators rather than the ones being evaluated, Others' evaluative status is not specified in Table 2.

5.1. Relational Status

Despite their heterogeneity, the organizations present in the food waste field mutually know each other and actively exchange food, personnel, and advice. This is shown by the upper network in Fig. 1, which provides evidence that we are dealing with, indeed, an organizational *field* (Panel a). However, given our research question, we zoom in on the advice relationships as they provide information about status (Panel b).

When examining advice relationships, we find that organizations taking responsibility for food waste form a dense network. The lower network in Fig. 1 shows that all organizations are connected via advice seeking, meaning that all organizations are sending or receiving at least one advice tie to or from another.

Table 2.   Status Hierarchies in the Swiss Food Waste Field.

	Relational Status	Evaluative Status
Not specified		Public sector organizations; interest groups
High	Interest groups	Food save business; alternative producers and distributors
Intermediary	Public sector organizations; food save charities; food save businesses, plants and tech companies	Food save charities
Low	Alternative producers and distributors	Plants and tech companies

Source: Authors' own.

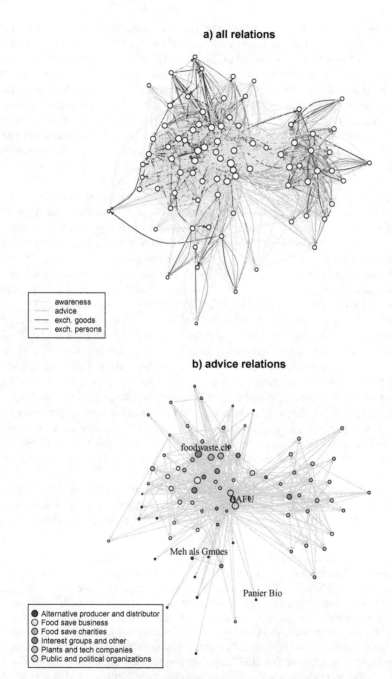

a) all relations

awareness
advice
exch. goods
exch. persons

b) advice relations

foodwaste.ch?

BAFU

Meh als Gmües

Panier Bio

● Alternative producer and distributor
○ Food save business
○ Food save charities
● Interest groups and other
○ Plants and tech companies
○ Public and political organizations

Fig. 1. The Network of Relationships in the Food Waste Field.
Source: Food waste survey ($n = 84$, $l = 2,503$). *Notes*: This figure represents the
network of relations in the Swiss food waste field among the 84 organizations that

The two most sought-after organizations are Foodwaste.ch (*interest group*) and the Federal Office for the Environment – BAFU (*public and political organization*). The Swiss Federal Institute of Technology – ETH Zürich (*public and political organization*, not shown in the figure) is less central (20 incoming ties) but has a "star-like" relational profile because it sends a lot of ties to diverse parts of the network. Crucially, these organizations that inhabit the center belong to the organizational groups *public and political organizations* and *interest groups*. Building on their reactive strategy to excessive food waste, they construct otherhood by providing knowledge-based guidance and advice on how to approach and manage food waste excess in a way that benefits society, the environment, and the climate.

The dispersion of relational status among Others is shown in Fig. 2, which highlights that Others do not all have high scores of indegree centrality. This implies that *public and political organizations* and *interest groups* do not systematically have very high indegree scores. Nearly 50% of *public and political organizations* have quite a low score of indegree. Among those who are not popular in terms of advice are political parties and some interest groups, such as La Fédération Romande d'Agriculture Contractuelle de Proximité (FRACP), which is the network of French-speaking contract farming initiatives.

If we focus on the top of the relational status hierarchy, we notice that it is dominated by two Others: Foodwaste.ch (*interest group*) and the BAFU (*public and political organization*). However, some *food save charities and business*es also have a very high relational status: Äss-Bar, Tischlein deck dich, and Schweizer Tafel/Table Suisse. This means that the status elite is composed of both Others and a subset of rather large-size and well-known *food save businesses and charities* (see Table 3). This status elite forms a dense network of advice giving and receiving, of which *plants and tech companies and alternative producers and distributors* are excluded. While *plants and tech companies* form their dense network aside, the *alternative producers and distributors* (e.g., Panier Bio or Meh als Gmües) are at the margins of the network (see Fig. 1).

As a measure of status received from relationships, we took the number of advice ties received by an organization (indegree centrality). This variable is unequally distributed: although all organizations receive at least one advice tie, only

---

responded to the survey. Panel a represents the network of all 2,503 relations of: awareness in yellow ($l = 1,464$), advice in green ($l = 582$), exchange of goods in red ($l = 245$), and exchange of persons in orange ($l = 212$). White nodes represent organizations. The size of nodes is proportional to their overall degree. Panel b displays the network of advice relations only. The color of nodes in Panel b depends on their organizational type, and their size is proportional to their (advice) indegree.

In Panel b, we observe that BAFU (public and political organization) and Foodwaste.ch (interest group) are central organizations, in contrast to Meh als Gmües and Panier Bio (alternative producers and distributors), which appear peripheral in the network. Color descriptions are *not* present in the figure, and the digital version contains color figures.

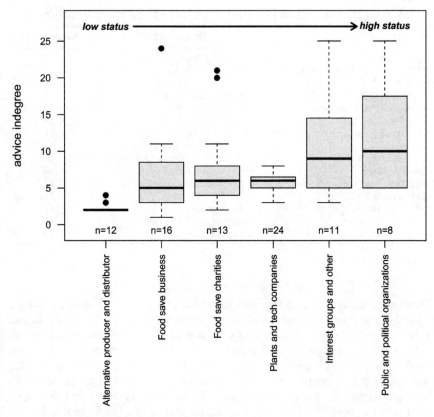

Fig. 2. Distribution of Relational Status According to Organizational Type.
Source: Food waste survey (*n* = 84). *Notes:* This figure presents a boxplot that
displays the distribution of status among organizational types. The variable used to
measure status is the indegree of each node (i.e., organization) within the advice network. Indegree refers to the number of ties a node receives from other nodes. Each
box displays summary statistics for the distribution of this variable for each type of
organization: the first decile (lower line), the second quartile (lower end of the box),
the median (thick line in the middle of the box), the third quartile (upper end of the
box), and the last decile (upper line). Outlier values are represented as points outside
the boxes. The median value orders the types of organizations from lower status
to higher status. We can see that status is relatively concentrated for certain types
(i.e., plants and tech companies) and more dispersed for others (public and political
organizations).

15 organizations (18%) receive more than 10 advice mentions, while 57 (or 68%)
receive less than 7 mentions. When comparing indegree among organizational
categories (see Fig. 2), the results indicate that relational status is concentrated
among *public and political organizations* and *interest groups*, whereas *alternative
producers and distributors* are given very low status through advice relationships.

Table 3.   Relational Status Hierarchy in the Swiss Food Waste Field (Top 15).

Name of the Organization	Organizational Type	Advice Indegree
Foodwaste.ch	Interest groups and other	25
BAFU (Sektion Konsum und Produkte)	Public and political organization	25
Äss-Bar	Food save business	24
Tischlein deck dich	Food save charities	21
Schweizer Tafel/Table Suisse	Food save charities	20
ETH Zürich	Public and political organization	20
OGG (Ökonomische Gemeinschaft Bern)	Interest groups and other	17
Pusch	Interest groups and other	15
Berner Fachhochschule	Public and political organization	15
Biomasse Suisse	Interest groups and other	14
Fachhochschule Nordwestschweiz	Public and political organization	14
Zum guten Heinrich	Food save business	11
Slow Food Youth	Food save organization	11
United against waste	Interest groups and other	11
Mein Küchenchef Restaurant	Food save business	10

Source: Authors' own.

Other organizational categories, such as *food save businesses, food save charities,* as well as *plants and tech companies,* have intermediary scores in terms of indegree (see Fig. 2). As shown in the Appendix, these findings on the most central organizations (*interest groups* and *public and political organizations*) in the advice network correspond with the ranking of "most important" organizations in the field, as declared in the questionnaire. This means *interest groups* and *public and political organizations* are on top of both lists. In particular, these include Foodwaste. ch (ranked 13 times #1, five times #2, and four times #3), the Federal Office for the Environment – BAFU (ranked seven times #1 and four times #2), or United against waste (ranked six times #1, two times #2, and two times #3). When other types of organizations are rated as important to the field, they are primarily food save charities (e.g., Tischlein Deck Dich, Schweizer Tafel) or food save businesses (e.g., Too good to go, Grassrooted, Mein Küchenchef). They are not plants and tech companies nor alternative producers and distributors.

To test this finding and understand which factors most explain the distribution of status resulting from advice relationships, we performed a Poisson regression on indegree, with organizational categories as the main independent variable. Given that *food save charities* have an intermediary status, we made them our reference category. In Table 4, Model 1 analyzes the impact of *organizational type* (e.g., *public and political organization, interest groups*) on status, without controls; Model 2 has control variables that could be correlated with the dependent variable (for example, the high status of *public and political organizations* could be due to its public funding or its location in urban areas). One should note the extremely good fit of the models: in Model 1, we can describe almost 70% of the variation of relational status by only five modalities of the same variable. In Model 2, some observations are dropped due to missing values, but the quality of the model improves, as its fit increases by 10 points.

a) all relations

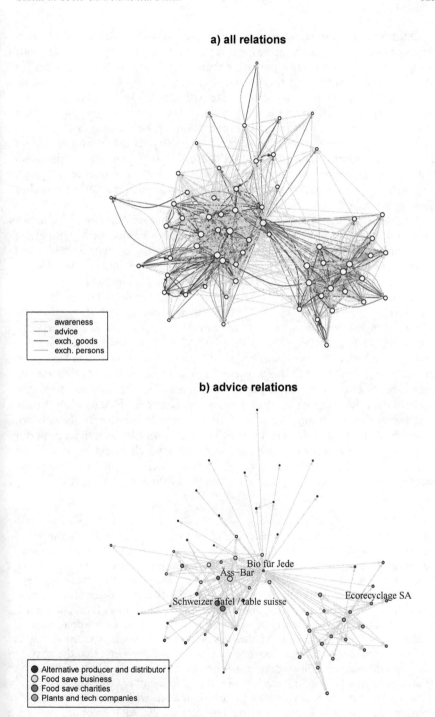

Fig. 3. The Network of Relationships Without Others (Interest Groups and Public and Political Organizations). *Source*: Food waste survey ($n = 65, l = 1,090$).

One result of major relevance is consistent across both models: being an *alternative producer and distributor* has a negative impact on relational status while being an *interest group* has a positive impact. *Public and political organizations* also receive high status, but their impact becomes nonsignificant when we control for other variables (e.g., funding, size, language). The fact that *public and political* organizations receive less esteem than the *interest groups* might reflect that the Swiss prioritize private initiatives for solving socio-environmental issues over public government-initiated attempts (Steinberg, 2015). However, *interest groups* are the winners: according to Model 2 for instance, they have suppress two times more in-coming ties compared to *food save charities* (reference category). *Alternative producers and distributors* have 42% fewer incoming ties compared to those organizations.

While *interest groups* are the relational status winners in the field, it is important to note that their relevant role in the field goes beyond being sought for and giving advice. Together with the *public and political organizations*, the *interest groups* have a real impact on the structure of the network and the field formation process. By removing the *public and political organizations* and *interest groups* from the network, our data show Others' impact on the field. This is shown in Fig. 3, in which all the nodes belonging to the *public and political organizations* and *interest groups* are removed. On the top (Panel a), we see that the network is much more fragmented between the *plants/tech companies*, on the one hand (exemplified here by Ecorecyclage SA), and the *food save charities and businesses,* on the other hand (Table Suisse/Schweizer Tafel). These two worlds are aware of each other but do not exchange persons, food, or advice. This is seen more precisely in Panel b when we display only the advice relations. If we take out Bio für Jede (which has the strange behavior of asking everyone for advice), the network would be disconnected. Others are therefore status winners as well as powerful integrators and organizers of this food waste field, which would be fragmented into two worlds if they were not involved. Thus, the social role of Others and their reactive strategies lies in integrating the field (Fligstein & McAdam, 2012).

Notes: This figure represents the network of relations in the Swiss food waste field after excluding the 19 organizations classified as public and political organizations, as well as interest groups. This results in a network with 65 nodes. Panel a represents the network of all 1,090 relations of: awareness in yellow ($l = 618$), advice in green ($l = 222$), exchange of goods in red ($l = 126$), and exchange of persons in orange ($l = 124$). White nodes represent organizations. The size of nodes is proportional to their overall degree. Panel b represents the network of advice relations only. The color of the nodes in Panel b depends on its organizational type and its size is proportional to its (advice) indegree. In Panel a, we can observe that the graph is polarized into two subnetworks in the absence of public and political organizations and interest groups. In Panel b, we see that plants and tech companies (such as Ecorecyclage SA) are relatively disconnected from food save business and food save charities (such as Table Suisse/Schweizer Tafel and Bio für Jede). Color descriptions are *not* present in the figure, and the digital version contains color figures.

Table 4. Poisson Regression of Indegree on Selected Variables.

	Model 1	Model 2
(Intercept)	2.05***	5.88**
	(0.10)	(2.16)
Alternative producer and distributor	−1.24***	−0.87**
	(0.22)	(0.27)
Food save business	−0.18	0.26
	(0.14)	(0.17)
Interest groups and other	0.30*	0.88***
	(0.14)	(0.22)
Plants and tech companies	−0.29*	0.17
	(0.13)	(0.21)
Public and political organization	0.42**	0.03
	(0.14)	(0.24)
Year of founding		−0.00*
		(0.00)
City area		−0.25
		(0.20)
Rural area		−0.07
		(0.23)
French-speaking canton		−0.39*
		(0.18)
German-speaking canton		−0.05
		(0.11)
Size ($\log_{10}$)		0.28***
		(0.07)
No funding		−0.10
		(0.16)
Private funding		0.41*
		(0.19)
Public funding		−0.11
		(0.22)
N	84	73
AIC	500.61	407.28
BIC	515.20	441.63
Pseudo R^2	0.69	0.79

Source: Authors' own.
***$p < 0.001$; **$p < 0.01$; *$p < 0.05$.

5.2. Evaluative Status

Given the excess of food waste and the multiple organizations and strategies to tackle it, the systematizing efforts of Others to establish order and hierarchy in the field are appreciated. In this vein, an interviewee highlighted the need for orientation and systematization, explaining that they "desired a prioritization of what should be done with the [food] leftovers" (interview, March 21, 2018). To provide this guiding evaluation, Others (*public and political organizations* and *interest groups*) draw strong inspiration from the international debates around the so-called waste hierarchy, which is a policy that has diffused throughout Europe and is implemented locally (Hultman & Corvellec, 2012). This means Others reproduce the food waste policy that evaluates waste-relevant interventions in a hierarchical order from desirable to avoidable (Arnold, 2021; Papargyropoulou et al., 2014). One of the many reproductions of this evaluative policy is published by the Federal Office for the Environment (BAFU) – the organization that is at the very center of the advisory network:

> For ecological and social reasons, it makes more sense to primarily avoid food waste. If, exceptionally, this is not possible, *we recommend, in this order*, giving away food that is not needed, feeding it to animals, fermenting it to produce biogas, composting it, and only lastly incinerating it. (Website BAFU, May 22, 2022, own emphasis)

Similarly, the private *interest group* Foodwaste.ch, which also boasts high status, proclaims on one of its educational posters for Swiss citizens: "1) Avoid food waste. 2) If you do have food waste, feed your pets, compost it or dispose of it in the organic waste garbage. 3) Avoid incineration and sewage" (Foodwaste.ch, 2023). While the BAFU refers to both "ecological and social reasons," ecological considerations dominate the prioritization given by Foodwaste.ch, as Foodwaste.ch does not account for the possibility of sharing or giving food surplus to others. This exemplifies that food waste is mainly assessed as an ecological issue that "leads to unnecessary CO_2 emissions, biodiversity loss, and land and water consumption," as the status-laden public organization BAFU announces on its website (BAFU, 2023). The dominant Others, therefore, evaluate which organizations and strategies take responsibility for food waste in the most ecologically valuable way. This is also reflected in the latest national action plan that evaluates and grades interventions for their "current range, environmental potential, scaling potential" (Schweizerische Eidgenossenschaft, 2022), passing over social benefits and potential. Thus, ecological considerations inform Others' evaluations, which result in an evaluative status hierarchy that negatively affects the *food save charities*, as we explain after having named the evaluative status winners.

Evaluative status winners are those organizational groups (*food save businesses* and *alternative producers and distributors*) that help avoid food waste by ensuring that food waste is purchased and consumed by humans. In this sense, a well-known natural science food waste researcher from a public organization praised the chef of the first Swiss food waste restaurant (*food save business*), which also operates a small store selling food waste products. The scientist acknowledges the chef's remarkable cooking skills that make excessive food waste scare and valuable, expressing admiration in the following manner:

> The zero-food-waste chef [...] is really good. The menus are sealed in plastic bags, vacuumed, and cooked in them [...]. This gives the opportunity, firstly, to avoid food waste by sourcing directly and processing the products that do not meet the standards [...] or the market does not demand. And secondly, [the vacuumization enables] durable products [...]. It can be kept for one, two, three months. (Interview, January 30, 2018)

Apart from *food save businesses* that receive high evaluative status by valorizing discarded food in consumption markets, *alternative producers and distributors* also rank high in the evaluative status hierarchy. From an evaluative perspective, *alternative producers and distributors* receive high status because they prevent food waste by creating trade and sales channels for humans that include food that would otherwise be discarded. The underlying reason why the two organizational types meet with outstanding positive responses is that their strategies help to establish food systems that prevent waste. In the words of the managing director of an interest group, their approaches are best evaluated because they develop a "fundamental idea of making a transformation" (interview, February 12, 2018). On a higher level of abstraction, we can summarize that an adaptive strategy to the problem of excess is evaluated best.

Interestingly, the high evaluative status of *alternative producers and distributors* contradicts their marginalized position in the hierarchical network of relationships that we illuminated earlier in this paper. An explanation for this inconsistency is that *alternative producers and distributors* are small, young, and receive no funding, whereas size, age, and funding are associated with status in this particular field (see Table 3). However, these factors are not sufficient to explain their marginalization, because being an *alternative producer and distributor* has an independent effect from these other causes (see Table 3). One fundamental reason is that this organizational group has obvious difficulties in determining the number of kilos of food saved due to their adaptive strategy, which is, notably, a strategy of scaling rather than reducing (Abbott, 2014). While *alternative producers and distributors* can hardly quantify the waste they reduce, because they prevent it by establishing more alternative food value chains, other organizational groups (especially *food save businesses* and *organizations*) invest a lot in quantifying the food volumes they save. For example, a bakery that sells bread from the previous day, announces that thanks to their approach, "several *hundred tons* have already been 'saved'" (Website Ässbar, May 21, 2021, emphasis on website). Reduction-oriented strategies that allow for quantification thus make organizations well-recognized advisors for how to tackle food waste in the field, while, on the other hand, adaptive strategies bring little recognition and low relational status, even though this approach is given the highest admiration through Others' formal evaluations.

While one might expect that giving food waste to marginalized people and groups is status enhancing (Meyer & Jepperson, 2000), *food save charities,* which follow this approach, receive only intermediary evaluative status. Paradoxically, the reason for this lies in what the *food save charities* themselves are proud of, namely "to collect and redistribute for free, [as] it is not about making a profit on unsold goods" (interview, March 21, 2018). This free distribution is not a priority by the Others in the food waste field and the internationally adopted food waste policy (Papargyropoulou et al., 2014). Following the belief "what costs nothing is worth nothing," it is assumed that giving away food for free further reduces the value of food and thus further drives waste (Arnold, 2021). Rather, food and also food surpluses should have a (high) price so that consumers value and appreciate it instead of discarding it. This is a dominant formal evaluation in the field from which an employee of a public organization interestingly distanced herself informally. Emphasizing that this is her own, personal standpoint, she explained:

This [whether food waste must have a price] is a discussion that has to be conducted at the political level and binding instruments suitable for the masses have to be found [...]. You can not burden this discussion on an individual and certainly not on one [...] with a small budget. (Interview, October 7, 2022)

This quote illustrates that evaluations are contingent and could always turn out differently (Lamont, 2012). Nevertheless, the fact that *food save charities* obtain only an intermediary (evaluative and relational) status already negatively affects their work. During a field trip, an experienced regional manager of a food bank stated:

> The food bank will no longer exist in this form in 20 years [...]. There are fewer and fewer boxes from the supermarkets because they are working better and better. There is less and less surplus food. (Field protocol, March 13, 2019)

This means, the loss of status that *food save charities* experience due to the status-relevant formal evaluations by Others appears to be causing a reduction in surplus food that *food save charities* redistribute to those in need. A recent newspaper article underpins:

> Every year, thousands of people with demonstrably little money benefit from the work of the Swiss food bank. The demand for saved food is at an all-time high [...]. To meet the increasing demand, the foundation made some investments in 2021 [...]. Nevertheless, the share of processed fresh products directly from the retail trade, the largest food donor, declined – the reason was, among other things, commercial organizations that also process surplus food. (Newspaper *Tagblatt*, March 15, 2022)

Thus, our data indicate that food save organizations' intermediary status materializes in a reduction of food volumes that they can distribute to those in need.

For the sake of completeness, we add that Others give least evaluative esteem and admiration to the *plants and tech companies*. By typically generating energy (biogas) from food waste, these evaluative status losers (*plants and tech companies*) are taking responsibility for food waste as they are saving it from incineration. In doing so, they reduce food waste and make it a scarce resource for "green" energy production. However, this approach is little appreciated by the formal food waste policy. In this sense, a researcher from a public organization highlights in an exemplary manner: "I do not think that [biogas] is a solution. It's just damage control. It is nothing more than that" (interview, February 11, 2019). This evaluation is reflected in legal guidelines from the public organization BAFU, which only allow the transformation of food into energy if the food cannot be used in any other way. The biogas *plants and tech companies* accept that the transformation of food to energy achieves little admiration and do not show any efforts to climb up the evaluative status ladder (Arnold, 2021). However, in the advice network, *plants and tech companies* receive intermediary relational status (see Fig. 2), because they often represent the last possible option to obtain something from waste (i.e., energy) and are therefore consulted. However, when we look at the network graph, especially when removing Others, we see that they are exchanging advice mostly among themselves, forming a small world of their own (see Fig. 3).

6. DISCUSSION AND CONCLUSION

Driven by the motivation to better understand status distinctions between heterogeneous organizations committed to a shared socio-environmental concern, we explored the construction of status hierarchies in the Swiss food waste field.

Conceptually, we assumed that one can distinguish between evaluative and relational status and hypothesized that organizations that engage in otherhood (i.e., Others) are status winners while shaping evaluative status hierarchies. Indeed, our study provided empirical evidence that Others (*public and political organizations, interest groups*) inhabit the privileged position and integrate the emerging field. Drawing on Abbott's (2014) excess strategies, we thus find that Others deploying a reactive strategy, which reduces excess by hierarchizing and ordering it, occupy the field center. Other organizations (*food save charities, food save businesses*, and *plants and tech companies*) that also tame excess but use a defensive strategy that does not tackle the problem, per se, receive less status. Lowest relational status, however, is given to *alternative producers and distributors* that apply an adaptive strategy and "rescale excess [...] in a subtle and nuanced way" (Abbott, 2014, p. 20). Although this approach achieves high evaluative status, the *alternative producers and distributors* experience only low relational status, positioning them at the periphery of the field. Hence, an adaptive strategy may be judged as profitable and valuable, but it seems to lack direction-setting influence in the field, as the organizations employing it (*alternative producers and distributors*) are rarely sought for advice. Building on these empirical findings, we first discuss the status-laden role of Others and then outline the implications of studying interorganizational status relations in socio-environmental fields.

Our study empirically substantiates that Others rank at the top of the status hierarchy (Meyer, 2010; Meyer & Jepperson, 2000). While it has been argued that high status positively influences evaluation and vice versa (Lamont, 2012), our results suggest that those who evaluate and avoid evaluation (i.e., Others) are the true status winners. In this sense, the food waste literature hardly evaluates the strategies of Others but tends to adopt their standpoint and investigates the actions of other organizational types such as *food save businesses or charities* (e.g., Reynolds et al., 2020). This provokes the question of who evaluates the status winners and holds them accountable, a question one can assume the winners avoid because of accountability-induced status anxiety (Jensen, 2006). We thus encourage sociologists and organizational researchers to critically examine the role of Others, while paying close attention to how evaluations shape the construction of status in a socio-environmental setting – a focus that is required because evaluations are not only relevant in the area of food waste but are proliferating in general in the context of organizations and socio-environmental problems (Dahler-Larsen, 2011; Ratner, 2004).

Moreover, capturing the prestigious role of Others can help explain why socio-environmental transformation is not progressing as desired. Blühdorn et al. (2020) argue that despite an intensification of discourse around socio-environmental challenges and the countless efforts of various organizations (political parties, social movements, and civil society organizations, etc.), the necessary transformation does hardly occur. Rather, these efforts sustain the unsustainable, as stated in Blühdorn et al.'s (2020) line of argument. The strategy in which Others take responsibility for socio-environmental issues tends to fit into this picture; with reference to well-accepted abstract principles and based on knowledge and expertise, Others try to induce socio-environmentally friendly changes without directly tackling the issue. Specifically, in the case of food waste, Others do not get their hands dirty and take indirect responsibility for the issue (e.g., researching, campaigning, lobbying, and policy-making). If we seriously believe that this approach receives the most esteem, one must critically question the extent to which calls for more responsibility and accountability contribute to solving socio-environmental issues (e.g., Arnold et al., 2022). At best, these demands motivate existing actions to be more socially and environmentally friendly or lead to regulations that force change. In the worst case, the calls for more responsibility only lead to more otherhood, as this promises the highest status.

At this point, we should reiterate that Others do not achieve their privileged position by themselves, since status always results from relationships (Boudon & Bourricaud, 1992). Consequently, the study of status contributes to understanding that not only do organizations matter in society (Besio et al., 2020) but also that their societal influence unfolds through their relationships with one another (DiMaggio & Powell, 1983; Wooten & Hoffman, 2017). In socio-environmental fields, these relationships concern organizational heterogeneity, which we could capture and systematize in our study based on Abbott's (2014) excess strategies. The extent to which these strategies are also helpful in other fields in order to grasp heterogeneity and differences needs to be examined. However, and more importantly, accounting for the role and impact of interorganizational relationships between heterogeneous organizations can complete existing research that prioritizes the study of a particular type of organization – that is, for example, businesses' role in socio-environmental (non-)transformations (e.g., Ergene et al., 2021). Examining heterogeneous interorganizational relationships allows us to draw a bigger picture of what is going on in a socio-environmental field, which in the case of food waste includes status inconsistencies and spillover effects – two themes with which we conclude.

The fact that status inconsistencies occur in socio-environmental fields has been exemplified by the case of *alternative producers and distributors*. In particular, our data showed that the *alternative producers and distributors* who achieve high esteem in the evaluations occupy marginalized positions in the advice network (relational status). One possible reason for this status inconsistency could be that we examined an emergent field for which we know that stability and order turn out to be low (Fligstein & McAdam, 2012). Future research, therefore, should illuminate the long-term changes in organizational status hierarchies to illuminate how evaluative and relational status relate to each, and whether there are stabilization and consistency trends. Of particular interest would be to better understand whether and how exogenous status attributions through evaluations (e.g., rankings, standards, and certificates) translate into endogenous status hierarchies. In the case of food waste, this means examining whether the *alternative producers and distributors* will receive higher status from relationships in the longer term as a consequence of their good, status-enhancing evaluations.

Finally, we have to reckon with the relevant spillover effects of Others' status-relevant evaluations in socio-environmental fields. This has been indicated by the case of *food save charities*. The lack of priority given to *food save charities* as advisors, and the limited evaluative recognition they receive for distributing valuable food surplus for free, has significant consequences. Particularly, non-intended consequences result from the evaluations (Lamont, 2012) that are given by Others and prioritize environmental concerns. The *food waste charities* have reduced food waste volumes by distribution which negatively impacts those people who rely on cheap or even free food. Organizational status dynamics might thus trickle down to the individual level and do not only materialize bottom-up in organizational structures (Ridgeway, 2014). Others have pointed to these spillover effects of organizational status dynamics (Borkenhagen & Martin, 2018; Chu, 2021), and they require special attention in socio-environmental fields because prioritizing environmentally motivated strategies risks fueling social inequalities. In the context of food, this brings into focus the relationship between environmentally sound food, on the one hand, food security and justice, on the other hand, and the question of how status dynamics affect this relationship. A sociologically informed look at the status relations between organizations will have much to contribute to this.

NOTES

1. The marginalized low-status groups, for example, are studied by Nancy Fraser (2000), who argued that individuals with low status are negatively affected by misrecognition and maldistribution. The privileged groups, on the other hand, are examined by Thorstein Veblen (1992), for example, who stated that individuals achieve social status through conspicuous consumption that signals wealth.

2. For example, we know that high status helps organizations to be selected as a trading partner (Jensen & Roy, 2008), allows them to price their products higher (Malter, 2014), positively impacts jurisdiction (McDonnell & King, 2018), or might stimulate collective learning (Bunderson & Reagans, 2011).

3. An example of the creative strategy was to be found at the climate conference in Glasgow COP26, where an installation rendered food waste visible (Chaplin, 2021).

ACKNOWLEDGEMENTS

We thank the organizers and participants of the Workshop "Field Analysis" at TU Berlin 2023, the INTRANSIT seminars at the University of Oslo 2022, the EGOS track "Doing Sociology in Organization Studies" 2022, the editors, and an anonymous reviewer for their valuable feedback. Special thanks to Kathia Serrano Velarde for her guidance. We are also grateful to Jennifer Widmer, Salome Rüttimann, and Noemi Wolf for their dedicated assistance in identifying and contacting food waste organizations.

REFERENCES

Abbott, A. (2014). The problem of excess. *Sociological Theory*, *32*(1), 1–26. https://doi.org/10.1177/0735275114523419

Arnold, N. (2021). Avoiding competition: The effects of rankings in the food waste field. In S. Arora-Jonsson, N. Brunsson, R. Hasse, & K. Lagerström (Eds.), *Competition: What it is and why it happens* (pp. 112–130). Oxford University Press. https://doi.org/10.1093/oso/9780192898012.003.0007

Arnold, N. (2022). Standards and waste: Valuing food waste in consumer markets. *Worldwide Waste: Journal of Interdisciplinary Studies, 5*(1), 2. https://doi.org/10.5334/wwwj.84

Arnold, N., Brunori, G., Dessein, J., Galli, F., Ghosh, R., Loconto, A., & Maye, D. (2022). Governing food futures: Towards a 'responsibility turn' in food and agriculture. *Journal of Rural Studies, 89*, 82–86. https://doi.org/10.1016/j.jrurstud.2021.11.017

BAFU. (2023). *Lebensmittelabfälle.* Retrieved May 10, 2023, from https://www.bafu.admin.ch/bafu/de/home/themen/thema-abfall/abfallwegweiser-stichworte-a-z/biogene-abfaelle/abfallarten/lebensmittelabfaelle.html

Besio, C., du Gay, P., & Serrano Velarde, K. (2020). Disappearing organization? Reshaping the sociology of organizations. *Current Sociology, 68*(4), 411–418. https://doi.org/10.1177/0011392120907613

Bexell, M., & Jönsson, K. (2017). Responsibility and the United Nations' sustainable development goals. *Forum for Development Studies, 44*(1), 13–29. https://doi.org/10.1080/08039410.2016.1252424

Blau, P. M. (1955). *The dynamics of bureaucracy: A study of interpersonal relations in two government agencies.* University of Chicago Press.

Blau, P. M. (1964). *Exchange and power in social life.* John Wiley.

Blühdorn, I., Butzlaff, F., Deflorian, M., Hausknost, D., & Mock, M. (2020). *Nachhaltige Nicht-Nachhaltigkeit: Warum die ökologische Transformation der Gesellschaft nicht stattfindet* (2nd ed.). Transcript.

Borkenhagen, C., & Martin, J. L. (2018). Status and career mobility in organizational fields: Chefs and restaurants in the United States, 1990–2013. *Social Forces, 97*(1), 1–26. https://doi.org/10.1093/sf/soy024

Boudon, R., & Bourricaud, F. (1992). *Soziologische Stichworte: Ein Handbuch.* VS Verlag für Sozialwissenschaften.

Bourdieu, P. (1987). *Die feinen Unterschiede: Kritik der gesellschaftlichen Urteilskraft* (4th ed.). Suhrkamp.

Bühlmann, F., Schoenberger, F., Ajdacic, L., & Foureault, F. (2022). Elite recruitment in US finance: How university prestige is used to secure top executive positions. *The British Journal of Sociology, 73*(4), 667–684. https://doi.org/10.1111/1468-4446.12971

Bunderson, J. S., & Reagans, R. E. (2011). Power, status, and learning in organizations. *Organization Science, 22*(5), 1182–1194. https://doi.org/10.1287/orsc.1100.0590

Carlos, W. C., & Lewis, B. W. (2018). Strategic silence: Withholding certification status as a hypocrisy avoidance tactic. *Administrative Science Quarterly, 63*(1), 130–169. https://doi.org/10.1177/0001839217695089

Chaplin, H. (2021). *Hellmann's and artist Itamar Gilboa put food waste issue front and centre at COP26.* Retrieved May 17, 2023, from https://www.circularonline.co.uk/news/hellmanns-and-artist-itamar-gilboa-put-food-waste-issue-front-and-centre-at-cop26/

Chen, Y.-R., Peterson, R. S., Phillips, D. J., Podolny, J. M., & Ridgeway, C. L. (2011). Introduction to the special issue: Bringing status to the table – Attaining, maintaining, and experiencing status in organizations and markets. *Organization Science, 23*(2), 299–307. https://doi.org/10.1287/orsc.1110.0668

Chu, J. (2021). Cameras of merit or engines of inequality? College ranking systems and the enrollment of disadvantaged students. *American Journal of Sociology, 126*(6), 1307–1346. https://doi.org/10.1086/714916

Correll, S. J., Ridgeway, C. L., Zuckerman, E. W., Jank, S., Jordan-Bloch, S., & Nakagawa, S. (2017). It's the conventional thought that counts: How third-order inference produces status advantage. *American Sociological Review, 82*(2), 297–327. https://doi.org/10.1177/0003122417691503

Croidieu, G., & Powell, W. W. (2024). Organizations as carriers of status and class dynamics: A historical ethnography of the emergence of Bordeaux's cork aristocracy. In S. Clegg, M. Grothe-Hammer, & K. Serrano Velarde (Eds.), *Sociological thinking in contemporary organizational scholarship* (Research in the Sociology of Organizations, Vol. 90, pp. 141–174). Emerald Publishing.

Dahler-Larsen, P. (2011). *The evaluation society.* Stanford University Press.

Die Bundesversammlung. (2018). *18.3829 Postulat.* Retrieved May 10, 2023, from https://www.parlament.ch/de/ratsbetrieb/suche-curia-vista/geschaeft?AffairId=20183829

DiMaggio, P. J. (1986). Structural analysis of organizational fields: A blockmodel approach. *Research in Organizational Behavior, 8*, 335–370.

DiMaggio, P. J., & Powell, W. W. (1983). The iron cage revisited: Institutional isomorphism and collective rationality in organizational fields. *American Sociological Review, 48*, 147–160.

Ergene, S., Banerjee, S. B., & Hoffman, A. J. (2021). (Un)Sustainability and organization studies: Towards a radical engagement. *Organization Studies, 42*(8), 1319–1335. https://doi.org/10.1177/0170840620937892

Evans, D. (2014). *Food waste: Home consumption, material culture and everyday life*. Bloomsbury Publishing.

FAO. (2019). *Moving forward on food loss and waste reduction*. Food and Agriculture Organization of the United Nations.

Fifita, I. M. E., Seo, Y., Ko, E., Conroy, D., & Hong, D. (2020). Fashioning organics: Wellbeing, sustainability, and status consumption practices. *Journal of Business Research, 117*, 664–671. https://doi.org/10.1016/j.jbusres.2019.01.005

Fligstein, N., & McAdam, D. (2012). *A theory of fields*. Oxford University Press.

Foodwaste.ch. (2019). *Was is food waste?* Retrieved August 29, 2022, from https://foodwaste.ch/was-ist-food-waste/

Foodwaste.ch. (2023). *Wo entsorgen wir unseren food waste?* Retrieved May 10, 2023, from https://foodwaste.ch/was-ist-food-waste/

Fraser, N. (2000). Rethinking recognition. *New Left Review, 3*, 107.

Gould, R. V. (2002). The origins of status hierarchies: A formal theory and empirical test. *American Journal of Sociology, 107*(5), 1143–1178. https://doi.org/10.1086/341744

Gustavsson, J., Cederberg, C., & Sonesson, U. (2011). *Global food losses and food waste: Extent, causes and prevention*. Food and Agriculture Organization of the United Nations.

Hoffman, A. J. (1999). Institutional evolution and change: Environmentalism and the U.S. chemical industry. *Academy of Management Journal, 42*(4), 351–371. https://doi.org/10.5465/257008

Hultman, J., & Corvellec, H. (2012). The European waste hierarchy: From the sociomateriality of waste to a politics of consumption. *Environment and Planning A, 44*(10), 2413–2427.

Jensen, M. (2006). Should we stay or should we go? Accountability, status anxiety, and client defections. *Administrative Science Quarterly, 51*(1), 97–128. https://doi.org/10.2189/asqu.51.1.97

Jensen, M., & Roy, A. (2008). Staging exchange partner choices: When do status and reputation matter? *Academy of Management Journal, 51*(3), 495–516. https://doi.org/10.5465/amj.2008.32625985

Lamont, M. (2012). Toward a comparative sociology of valuation and evaluation. *Annual Review of Sociology, 38*(1), 201–221. https://doi.org/10.1146/annurev-soc-070308-120022

Lampel, J., & Meyer, A. D. (2008). Field-configuring events as structuring mechanisms: How conferences, ceremonies, and trade shows constitute new technologies, industries, and markets. *Journal of Management Studies, 45*(6), 1025–1035. https://doi.org/10.1111/j.1467-6486.2008.00787.x

Lazega, E. (2014). Appropriateness and structure in organizations: Secondary socialization through dynamics of advice networks and weak culture. In D. J. Brass, G. Labianca, A. Mehra, D. S. Halgin, & S. P. Borgatti (Eds.), *Contemporary perspectives on organizational social networks* (Research in the Sociology of Organizations, Vol. 40, pp. 381–402). Emerald Group Publishing Limited. https://doi.org/10.1108/S0733-558X(2014)0000040019

Lazega, E., Mounier, L., Snijders, T., & Tubaro, P. (2012). Norms, status and the dynamics of advice networks: A case study. *Social Networks, 34*(3), 323–332. https://doi.org/10.1016/j.socnet.2009.12.001

Leech, N. L., & Onwuegbuzie, A. J. (2009). A typology of mixed methods research designs. *Quality & Quantity, 43*(2), 265–275. https://doi.org/10.1007/s11135-007-9105-3

Loconto, A. M., & Arnold, N. (2022). Governing value(s) and organizing through standards. *International Sociology, 37*(6), 601–611. https://doi.org/10.1177/02685809221133055

Malter, D. (2014). On the causality and cause of returns to organizational status: Evidence from the Grands Crus Classés of the Médoc. *Administrative Science Quarterly, 59*(2), 271–300. https://doi.org/10.1177/0001839214532428

McDonnell, M.-H., & King, B. G. (2018). Order in the court: How firm status and reputation shape the outcomes of employment discrimination suits. *American Sociological Review, 83*(1), 61–87. https://doi.org/10.1177/0003122417747289

Merton, R. K. (1968). The Matthew effect in science. *Science, 159*(3810), 56–63. https://doi.org/10.1126/science.159.3810.56

Meyer, J. W. (2010). World society, institutional theories, and the actor. *Annual Review of Sociology*, *36*(1), 1–20. https://doi.org/10.1146/annurev.soc.012809.102506

Meyer, J. W. (2019). Reflections on rationalization, actors, and others. In H. Hwang, J. A. Colyvas, & G. S. Drori (Eds.), *Agents, actors, actorhood: institutional perspectives on the nature of agency, action, and authority* (pp. 275–285). Emerald Publishing Limited. https://doi.org/10.1108/S0733-558X20190000058015

Meyer, J. W., & Jepperson, R. L. (2000). The 'actors' of modern society: The cultural construction of social agency. *Sociological Theory*, *18*(1), 100–120. https://doi.org/10.1111/0735-2751.00090

Packard, V. ([1960] 2011). *The waste makers*. Ig Publishing.

Papargyropoulou, E., Lozano, R. Steinberger, J. K., Wright, N., & Ujang, Z. B. (2014). The food waste hierarchy as a framework for the management of food surplus and food waste. *Journal of Cleaner Production*, *76*, 106–115. https://doi.org/10.1016/j.jclepro.2014.04.020

Piazza, A., & Castellucci, F. (2014). Status in organization and management theory. *Journal of Management*, *40*(1), 287–315. https://doi.org/10.1177/0149206313498904

Podolny, J. M. (2005). *Status signals: A sociological study of market competition*. Princeton University Press.

Ratner, B. D. (2004). "Sustainability" as a dialogue of values: Challenges to the sociology of development. *Sociological Inquiry*, *74*(1), 50–69. https://doi.org/10.1111/j.1475-682X.2004.00079.x

Reynolds, C., Soma, T., Spring, C., & Lazell, J. (2020). *Routledge handbook of food waste*. Routledge.

Ridgeway, C. L. (2014). Why status matters for inequality. *American Sociological Review*, *79*(1), 1–16. https://doi.org/10.1177/0003122413515997

Rockström, J., Steffen, W., Noone, K., Persson, Å., Chapin, F. S. I., Lambin, E., … Foley, J. (2009). Planetary boundaries: Exploring the safe operating space for humanity. *Ecology and Society*, *14*(2). https://doi.org/10.5751/ES-03180-140232

Sauder, M. (2006). Third parties and status position: How the characteristics of status systems matter. *Theory & Society*, *35*(3), 299–321. https://doi.org/10.1007/s11186-006-9005-x

Sauder, M., Lynn, F., & Podolny, J. M. (2012). Status: Insights from organizational sociology. *Annual Review of Sociology*, *38*(1), 267–283. https://doi.org/10.1146/annurev-soc-071811-145503

Schweizerische Eidgenossenschaft. (2022). *Aktionsplan gegen die Lebensmittelverschwenudng*. Retrieved May 12, 2023, from https://www.newsd.admin.ch/newsd/message/attachments/70975.pdf

Sharkey, A. J. (2014). Categories and organizational status: The role of industry status in the response to organizational deviance. *American Journal of Sociology*, *119*(5), 1380–1433. https://doi.org/10.1086/675385

Steinberg, J. (2015). *Why Switzerland?* 3rd edition. Cambridge University Press.

Veblen, T. (1992). *The theory of the leisure class*. Routledge.

Wooten, M., & Hoffman, J. (2017). Organizational fields: Past, present and future. In R. Greenwood, C. Oliver, T. B. Lawrence, & R. E. Meyer (Eds.), *The SAGE handbook of organizational institutionalism* (pp. 130–148). SAGE.

Zhao, W., & Zhou, X. (2011). Status inconsistency and product valuation in the California wine market. *Organization Science*, *22*(6), 1435–1448. https://doi.org/10.1287/orsc.1100.0597

APPENDIX: ANSWERS TO THE QUESTION ABOUT "MOST IMPORTANT" ORGANIZATION IN THE FOOD WASTE FIELD

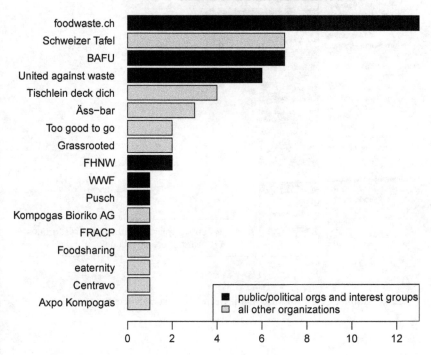

Fig. A1. Number of Times an Organization Is Ranked as First Most Important.

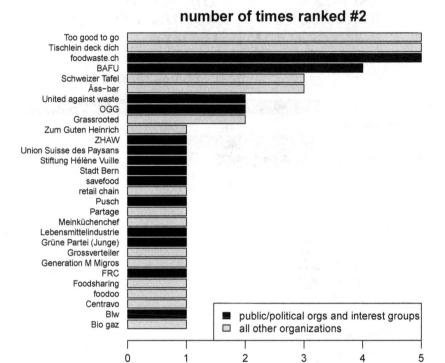

Fig. A2.   Number of Times an Organization Is Ranked as Second Most Important.

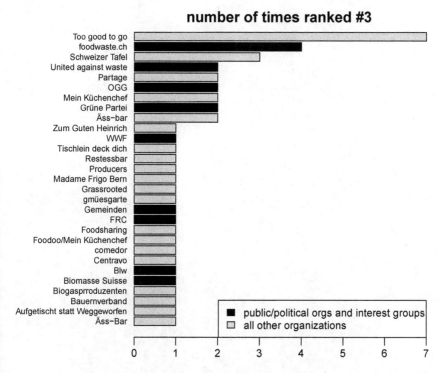

Fig. A3. Number of Times an Organization Is Ranked as Third Most Important.

ORGANIZATIONS AS CARRIERS OF STATUS AND CLASS DYNAMICS: A HISTORICAL ETHNOGRAPHY OF THE EMERGENCE OF BORDEAUX'S CORK ARISTOCRACY

Grégoire Croidieu[a] and Walter W. Powell[b]

[a]emlyon Business School, France
[b]Stanford University, USA

ABSTRACT

This paper seeks to understand how a new elite, known as the cork aristocracy, emerged in the Bordeaux wine field, France, between 1850 and 1929 as wine merchants replaced aristocrats. Classic class and status perspectives, and their distinctive social closure dynamics, are mobilized to illuminate the individual and organizational transformations that affected elite wineries grouped in an emerging classification of the Bordeaux best wines. We build on a wealth of archives and historical ethnography techniques to surface complex status and organizational dynamics that reveal how financiers and industrialists intermediated this transition and how organizations are deeply interwoven into social change.

Keywords: Research paper; class; status; social closure; historical ethnography; Bordeaux wine

Sociological Thinking in Contemporary Organizational Scholarship
Research in the Sociology of Organizations, Volume 90, 141–173

ISSN: 0733-558X/doi:10.1108/S0733-558X20240000090006

INTRODUCTION

The origins of any institution are often contingent. They reflect not only the social context at the time of emergence but also struggles among parties with different degrees of power and status.

A central feature of institutional persistence is that these historically contingent origins become obscured; those who are on the winning side are often able to erase the alternative arrangements that were once considered possible (Stinchcombe, 1968). Our work seeks to undercover how and why this process occurred in the context of Bordeaux, France, by studying the formation of a new elite, known as the cork aristocracy,[1] that subsequently played a critical role in the maintenance of a wine classification system that became frozen in time (Croidieu et al., 2018).

Today, Bordeaux holds a commanding position as one of the world's most venerated wine regions, if not the most sacrosanct, famous for its red wines and châteaux, with its coveted veneer of aristocracy and history (Coates, 2004; Robinson & Harding, 2015). This unique position owes certainly much to the prestige of Bordeaux' most renowned wines, whose ranking originated in 1855. The second universal exhibition held in Paris that year provided an opportunity to draw a temporary list of the best Bordeaux wines, which eventually became the best-known wine classification globally and came to define the Bordeaux social order. None of the classified wine owners, largely landed aristocrats (60%), were asked if they wanted to be on the list.[2] Yet, 75 years later, the classification persisted, unchanged, baked in a seemingly immutable aristocratic tradition and drawing a consequential line between those on and off the list. A provisional ranking drawn by just four men became an entrenched status hierarchy, even though ownership turned over dramatically (90%).

Underneath the seeming stability of the Bordeaux wine hierarchy were massive social changes and power struggles. Aristocratic families, once dominant landowners, were uprooted by wine merchants, bankers, industrialists, and politicians. These new owners, however, celebrated rather than tore down the aristocratic legacy, embracing aristocratic paraphernalia, constructing grandiose *châteaux* (e.g., castles, the traditional aristocratic home[3]), and ennobling existing buildings. This remarkable transformation raises several empirical puzzles: how did aristocrats as a social group fall while their social status and tradition remained exalted? How do seemingly lower status owners, merchants, and others, move in without diluting the 1855 classification's prestige, while embracing a tradition that excluded them? In this paper, our goal is to understand how power struggles over 1855 estates ownership led to the formation of the cork aristocrats, who participated in the later persistence[4] of the 1855 list.

Classical sociology offers competing insights into this question. Class and status notably provide two distinctive lenses to understand how power struggles lead to elite formation (Weber, 1978). Ownership change is first a material transformation, in which social classes struggle to control the means of production (Marx, 1867). From this perspective, this competition over property reflects the age of capital arriving in Bordeaux, with its old feudal order in a losing battle with a rising capitalist class. These societal forces not only swept England and its industries but also France and other nations (Hobsbawm, 1975/2010). Ownership shifts also have a social meaning, as new owners join a community and develop social relations (Weber, 1978). From this perspective, owning an 1855 estate is a symbolic token that conveys the owner's social standing and honor. Once a status hierarchy is developed, these associations become consequential, and status frequently co-occurs with differences in property and power (Arnold & Foureault, 2024, this volume; Ridgeway, 2019; Sauder et al., 2012). Ownership change is then interpreted through the politics of association that status competition triggers. Thus, class and status offer rival material and symbolic accounts of the power struggle shaping elite formation, a core social stratification process with deep consequences for resource distribution and institutional persistence, which shapes who is included or excluded and how (Khan, 2012; Mills, 1956). These lenses also differ in how they understand organizations as either nested in hierarchical social systems or embedded in place-based communities (see Laryea & Brandtner, 2024, this volume).

Both class and status dynamics rely on a process of social closure. Closure refers to the drawing of social and symbolic boundaries, which results in the appropriation of economic or social rewards by an insider group that excludes others, accruing its power and bounding a group (Weber, 1978). A Marxian perspective on closure emphasizes exploitation. A usually well-connected elite controls valuable resources, such as the means of production, from which they derive rewards, excluding others from the value they contribute to (Grusky & Sørensen, 1998; Tilly, 1998, pp. 86–91). Exploitation typically unfolds in labor relations, yet also applies to inheritance or succession. A Weberian account, in contrast, highlights opportunity hoarding, where elite or non-elite groups close off opportunities to outsiders, which weakens competition, eases the harvest of rewards, and hence increases insiders' power (Parkin, 1979; Tilly, 1998. pp. 91–95).

We study these competing accounts by analyzing a host of primary and secondary archives as a historical ethnography. We first gathered authoritative directories of Bordeaux wine estates and documented the social identities of all the 1855 owners we found, including social class, status, occupations, families, or location, by combining materials from multiple other archives. We completed this dataset by collecting additional archives on the buildings located on the 1855 estates. By assembling this information in a panel dataset between 1850 and 1929, we systematically documented changes in ownership, for example, who entered and who exited, when, which families, but also social closure dynamics, for instance, who bought from whom or where in the classification. We then connected these changes to the changes in owners' social identities and their building practices. We deepened the analysis of aggregated patterns by studying individual cases, often collecting new archives, and interpreted the results iteratively with the lenses of class, status, and closure. Last, we consulted a broader set of sources to embed our interpretation in the tumultuous context of this study. This immersion in the archives afforded us deep insights about the obscured power struggle at the apex of Bordeaux wine. Our study is thus an ethnography in the archives (Merry, 2002), in which we "elicit structure and culture from the documents created" (Vaughan, 2004, p. 321).

Our historical ethnography retraces the transition from a landed aristocracy to a cork aristocracy by contrasting a class with a status perspective. First, unlike preexisting accounts of the change in power in Bordeaux (e.g., Butel, 2008; Faith, 2005; Ulin, 1996), our findings underscore that the merchants did not wrest power from the hands of aristocrats or single-handedly build an aristocratic wine tradition: financiers and industrialists cushioned this transition. With the arrival of different kinds of capitalist owners, Bordeaux underwent a massive material transformation, yet the formation of a cork aristocracy is only partially explained by a class-based account. Second, we show that complex and unforeseeable status and organizational dynamics account for the formation of this new elite. Merchants did not buy out aristocrats but, rather, sought to join them by purchasing 1855 estates from non-aristocratic owners, for the arbitrary classification mattered initially as high-status aristocrats populated its ranks. As a status competition started and raged, aristocrats, elites from the industrial revolution, and merchants, among other owners, participated in the ennoblement of Bordeaux wines, a symbolic race merchants finished on top in the 1920s. In this ennobling process, an aristocratic tradition switched camp, values were transposed from an Old Regime enclave to a modern wine world, and the 1855 list persisted. As a consequence, an 1855 estate bestowed high status to its owner and became a membership card into the new cork aristocracy. Third, with its fixed number of seats, 1855 has always been about closure. In a patrimonial wine economy, one could expect closure to unfold through successions within families, as dynasties. Surprisingly, only four families retained their property throughout the period. Instead, status closure prevailed as owners kept changing and competed over lifestyles.

We contribute to this volume by (re)connecting organization studies with core themes in sociology. We reintroduce classic concerns with status, class, and social closure to organizational analysis in two ways. First, the status feedback loop we uncovered, from landed aristocrats to estates and then from estates to new owners (the cork aristocrats), offers an opportunity to analyze how organizational dynamics intersect with social stratification processes and elite formation. On the one hand, organizational scholars have showed how organizations are both sites and drivers of social actions as they interact with their environment (Barley, 2010; Powell & Brandtner, 2016; Stinchcombe, 1965). On the other hand, social scientists have shown how institutional persistence, such as in the case of the Nigerian constitution or the German vocational training system, relied on classifications and individual-level elite structures (Laitin, 1986; Thelen, 2004). The feedback loop our case unravels links these separate multilevel dynamics. These complex status and organizational processes suggest that organizations are more deeply interwoven into the social fabric than previously thought. Organizations carry and alter social processes, in addition to sheltering or triggering social actions (Perrow, 2002). Second, our cork aristocracy case differs from the typical social closure process, where the old elite maintains the status quo. In this view, closure fosters institutional persistence through elite reproduction and value maintenance (Stinchcombe, 1998; Tilly, 1998). As in many wine regions, one would have expected the aristocratic class to maintain power through family succession, with dynasties retaining elite wine in the realm of an aristocratic world. Our findings unravel obscured status and organizational dynamics where those initially excluded by a tradition came to espouse and glorify its values and maintain, rather than tear down, the 1855 status order. Ownership of an 1855 estate allowed merchants and others to become an aristocratic-like elite with no bloodline, with the privilege of a wine estate supporting their social influence. Our case links closure with persistence through elite change and value transposition. In so doing, we contribute to closure and boundary studies as the porosity of symbolic boundaries resulted in the tightening of new social boundaries (Grodal, 2018; Lamont & Molnar, 2002). Lastly, we take advantage of this paper to describe and explain how we used historical ethnography. This method, pioneered by organizational scholars such as Diane Vaughan (1996), allowed us to combine the study of biographies with organizational and group formation dynamics, a multilevel analysis that unraveled obscured processes that shed new light on elite formation. We hope these insights will inspire others interested in archival work and interpretive methods.

A HISTORICAL ETHNOGRAPHY: CONTEXT, DATA, AND METHODS

Context

This study is part of a series of papers on the persistence of the 1855 classification and focuses on the power struggles among classified estate owners in the first 75 years of this list. The Bordeaux Chamber of Commerce proposed this classification to present its "best" wines to the universal exhibition held in Paris that year. The exhibition was organized under the imperial patronage of Napoleon III to showcase France's industrial and agricultural achievements. This list ranked estates producing red wines into five ordered categories, the first being the best. This ordering was unusual because most prior classifications listed four tiers. At that time, wines from the Médoc subregion (oddly with one estate from the Graves sub-area, Haut-Brion), on the left bank of the Gironde River, were regarded as constituting the elite. The ranking was a pedagogical device to guide attention at the exhibition. Although historians are unsure how exactly the four Bordeaux wine brokers who drew the list proceeded, we know they were at least partly guided by market prices (Markham, 1998). As best as we can tell, there was little outcry among those left off this list. Several estates showed their wines independently at the exhibition, and many received prizes.

Wine production has been both remarkably constant and altered since 1855. In terms of work organization, wine estates differ from many organizations we know today, in the sense that contracts were – and still are – not the primary means to manage tasks, relationships, and boundaries (Powell, 1990). The smaller estates were run within the family, with limited external labor involved (e.g., Féret, 1898, p. 53). Medium-sized estates were run by the owner, who typically cultivated his land with owned or rented horses, while supervising servants or prix-faîteurs, who were farm workers paid for tasks such as plowing, manure, or pruning (but not the harvest) on an annual basis. Larger estates combined employed servants and prix-faîteurs with different layers of intermediary staff, such as régisseur, maître de chai, or maître de culture, who supervised the whole estate, the winemaking, or the viticulture. These managerial occupations within the estate typically passed from fathers to sons. Temporary workers joined most of these estates during the harvest. The larger estates were also more vertically integrated; some had schools like the one shared by Lafite- and Mouton-Rothschild or a hospital for Mouton (Pijassou, 1980). The post-1890s witnessed social unrest and the emergence of unions in the commune of St-Estèphe. Nevertheless, jobs in these leading wine estates were envied as these owners provided pensions for their key staff and covered medical expenses for all the workers, years before these social advances became mandatory (Pijassou, 1980). Even though the legal footing of wineries has changed since the 19th century, many of these work arrangements survive until today in Bordeaux, California, and elsewhere.

If the division of labor of wineries remained stable, Bordeaux' wines experienced a quiet revolution between 1850 and 1929, and the Médoc area was at its forefront. With three bouts of pestilence devastating its vineyards, Bordeaux' winegrowers welcomed newly minted chemists in their fields. Their many innovations often provided a relief and contributed to the doubling of vineyard yields (Roudié, 1988). In the case of phylloxera, botanists succeeded where chemists failed because only grafting American roots suppressed the aphid's destructive appetite. As many vines died between the early 1850s powdery mildew crisis and the 1880s when both the downy mildew and phylloxera plights culminated, owners sought new grape varieties to replant. During that period, Médoc shifted from predominantly mixing white grape varieties, cultivated "en foule," without trellis, to red grape varieties trained and pruned along posts. Cabernet sauvignon replaced malbec as the dominant red, while varieties like camerouge, chalosse, graput, folle, or boutignon lost ground. Scientific progress also remade winemaking as fermentation came to be understood and controlled, while countless experiments tested the most suitable wood type to age wine (Pijassou, 1980; Roudié, 1988). These changes not only altered the rich variety of viticultural and winemaking practices in Médoc, they also standardized them. For instance, the Bordeaux barrique came to be strictly defined as a 225-liter container, while the nonlocal syrah grape was expelled to the benefit of merlot and petit verdot, which are now part of the typical Médoc grape varieties. Similarly, estate-bottling became a widespread, and later compulsory, norm, which replaced the merchants' practice to mix estate wines in their cellars and sell theses "assemblages" in barriques (Croidieu et al., 2018). This uniformization foreshadowed the Appellation Contrôlée legal system that emerged from the 1910s onward and codified typical local uses. Over 80 years, these combined changes resulted in a complete metamorphosis of the taste of Médoc wines, while the new owners facilitated, if not funded, the implementation and diffusion of these changes.

Even though the 1855 list was supposed to be temporary, and wine production, markets, and the soil have changed dramatically, the classification has persisted until today, with only one change[5] (Croidieu et al., 2018). The grip of the classification on the world of wine may be somewhat less firm today than it was throughout the 20th century, as upstart Chinese and other foreign owners have barged in, but its importance cannot be understated. As our analysis focuses on the shift in power from aristocrats to new owners, we attend to a specific slice of our data: ownership changes between 1850 and 1929, a period of ferment during which the once arbitrary and temporary 1855 list became established as a taken-for-granted institution embodying elite wineries.

Data Sources

To document the ownership of the classified estates, we relied on the Féret wine directories as our primary archive. Féret is a leading publishing house in Bordeaux, and its local wine directories have been equally used by professionals and historians (Pijassou, 1980; Roudié, 1988). These directories have been irregularly published since 1850, and until 1929, Féret published nine editions, in 1850, 1868, 1874, 1881, 1893, 1898, 1908, 1922, and 1929. To space the panels as regularly[6] as possible, we focused on six editions published in 1850, 1868, 1881, 1898, 1908, and 1929 that will constitute our panels. We use the other editions as complementary sources. The directories allow us to obtain consistent information on the names of the growths,[7] their location, the name of the owner(s), aristocratic titles, or the size of the estate. They often provide additional information, including pictures of the estate building, owner's occupation, historical information on the estate, or the family of the owners, and events such as participations in exhibitions, awards, and new buildings. This first analysis notably revealed the number of 1855 estates, though fixed, keeps changing as the organizations split, merge, cease, or resurge. The 1855 list initially comprised 57 organizations and, in total, we identified 62 distinctive classified organizations until 1929. We also learned that 81% of the classified estates had a single owner, though a few had as many as four. Only one organization was listed as an owner, a bank, for only one Féret panel. All the other owners were individuals, investing their own money.

For every Féret panel, we listed the owners and their social identities. We extracted the relevant information available in Féret, complementing it with another primary source – the Bordeaux directories of merchants, which describe the name and address of all the wine merchants and brokers in Bordeaux. We focused on the 1850, 1870, 1880, 1890, 1900, 1910, 1920, and 1930 editions for our analyses and coding. These two primary sources were matched with a host of other sources, which we use to triangulate and further document these identities (Mayrl & Wilson, 2020). Our archival efforts relied on many public and private archives in France (Bordeaux, Paris) and abroad (USA, England), as well as online archival sources such as Gallica.

With these primary archives, we constructed an unbalanced panel dataset to track changes in ownership across estates and over time. The 6 panels and 62 organizations resulted in 357 observations. Only a single organization is present but once, the Dubignon estate in 1868. This classified growth ceased existence in the early 1870s; the name was never claimed, and the vineyard sold to multiple owners. We excluded from the 1855 sample one first growth, Haut-Brion, as it was geographically not in the same area as the other classified growths. All the figures and tables we present are extracted from this panel dataset.

Coding and Measurement

To track class, status, and closure dynamics at the individual and organizational levels, we coded several indicators based on ownership, occupations, aristocracy, and different markers of honor. To measure ownership, ownership change, and family change, we relied on the six Féret panels described above. Every time we noticed the name of a new owner or the addition of one, we coded a change in ownership. To capture family changes, we relied on ownership changes, and every time a surname changed, we looked for family ties through different sources. If the names changed because of a marriage (for instance, properties owned by wives were often declared as their husband's estates), we coded no family change. When there was no family relationship, then we coded family change. When in-laws took over, we coded a family change. When the *Caisse Hypothécaire* bank took over the Palmer estate, we coded a family change.

We track class dynamics by looking into the occupations of the owner(s). The coding of occupations relies on multiple sources that changed from one case to the other. The Bordeaux merchant directories are our primary source. For the other occupations, we turned to additional sources. First, Féret expanded its directories from the 1880s onward by adding a lot of text and images that provide occupational information for new owners. We also use a series of Bordeaux year-books, such as the *Annuaire du tout Sud-Ouest*. We consulted several editions published at the turn of the 19th century, which give biographical notes for owners. Historians (and geographers) have also written extensive organizational histories of some 1855 estates or biographies of owners that proved useful to glean additional information. For instance, Pijassou (1980) dug into the Latour archives, while Paul Butel (2008) portrayed dynasties in Bordeaux. We cross-checked and triangulated many similar secondary sources to collect this information. Digitally, the abcduvin website (www.abcduvin.com), run by Sylvain Torchet,[8] proved to be well and thoughtfully documented, though sources are not systematically listed.

We were able to collect occupational information for all owners, often gathering information about family ties and location in the process. One problem we faced was the variety of occupations: genealogist, king's prosecutor, painter, lawyer, liquorist, medical doctor, perfumer, retired military, etc. There is no standard classification of 19th-century occupations; in contrast, the Bordeaux wine trade has become organized between wine merchants (*négociants*), brokers (*courtiers*), and owners (*propriétaires*). We recoded our list of occupations to both reduce the number and preserve some granularity to make the analyses tractable and meaningful.

As we sorted the occupational data, we tried several codings, settling for a four-category scheme distinguishing merchants, financiers and industrialists, law professionals and politicians, and owners. In the merchant category, we included all the Bordeaux merchants and brokers systematically identified through the directories, as well as the shipowners (*armateurs*). We also coded as merchants all those not from Bordeaux who distributed wines, whether in Paris, the United Kingdom, the Netherlands, or Germany (they mostly entered the dataset in the early 20th century). This group is largely understood as the trade in the wine world. We coded all the financiers (mostly bankers) and industrialists (across many industries) together as they are, with one exception, not from Bordeaux and reflect the growing economic class spearheading the French industrial revolution. Law professionals and politicians (either members of parliament (MPs) or mayors) who have no other occupations were grouped together. In his "Class, Status, Party" chapter, Weber distinguishes social and economic power from political power. For this reason, we kept this category "pure" and separate. For instance, merchants, like Pierre-François Guestier, mayor of Saint-Julien, or brokers like Armand Lalande, who held positions as mayor of Bordeaux, MP, and president of the Chamber of Commerce, typically occupied political positions while remaining active in the wine world. We coded them as merchants and not politicians.

Our last occupational category is owner, literally someone whose sole or main occupation is owning an 1855 estate. Owner is not a well-bounded occupation, unlike merchants and brokers, who are registered professionals at the Chamber of Commerce. Only the title deed defines the owner occupation. It is hence the category sheltering the highest diversity of occupations. Owner, for instance, includes all owners with an aristocratic name and no clear occupation (a minority, like the de Bethmann family, are, for instance, merchants: they were coded both merchant and aristocrat). This subgroup represents 88% of the owners in 1850, declining to 25% in 1929. The genealogist, painter, retired military, or medical doctor occupations also fall in this owner category as their occupations do not clearly intersect with the power struggle at the top of Bordeaux. To our understanding, they only participate in this contestation as 1855 owners.

Two subgroups of owners, however, possess multiple ties with the Bordeaux wine world, which go beyond the sole ownership of an 1855 estate. First, several estates have an administrator, who runs the daily operations (*régisseur*). Few of these administrators managed to become 1855 owners like Théodore Skawinski or Armand Feuillerat. Second, some individuals, and then families, came to own several estates, including one or more 1855 growths. The Castéja is one of these families. These new owners with vested interests in the Bordeaux wine world largely emerged at the turn of the 19th century. We note their increasing presence, yet we are not able to identify clear patterns, for instance, whether they came to wine first and then to 1855 or the contrary.

Aristocracy is not an occupation, however, it relates to both class and status, and, as a result, its coding is subject to debate. For Max Weber, aristocracy is an inherited source of honor and social standing, whereas from a Marxian perspective, aristocrats in Bordeaux were primarily landowners controlling the means of wine production. Aristocracy is widely understood as a remnant of a feudal order, which was overturned with the French Revolution. Yet, the extent to which the fall of the Bastille reshuffled the social order is open to much discussion (Tocqueville, 1859). Social scientists nevertheless agree that the prevalence of aristocrats in the French economy and society sharply declined after World War I (Coulmont, 2019; Daumard, 1988). Thus, most of our case falls during the historical period where measuring and interpreting the role of aristocracy is contested.

The history of French aristocracy is even more confusing than its social theory and determining who is from aristocratic ascent is also controversial. Until 1789, aristocrats were a separate legal category of "citizens," whereas aristocratic distinctions became purely honorific from 1814 onward when the title was restored. As the legal category disappeared, many aristocrats added to their name a nobiliary particle (*de* such as in Eric de Bethmann), in a logic of social distinction.[9] This signaling spread as a widely understood sign of aristocratic ascent (Beaumaine, 1953, Bordeaux, 1861). A particle is, however, not proof of nobility; it only implies someone is seemingly aristocratic (Beaumaine, 1953; Coulmont, 2019; Daumard, 1988). Signifying a particle originated in a controversial pre-revolutionary practice when nobles expanded their family names by adding the name of the place where they came from, as if the authors of this paper added "de Lyon" or "de Palo Alto" to their family names. Of course, with the legal blurring of this category and the honorary benefits that it suggested, usurpation spread. The practice was decriminalized in 1832, and more joined in, contributing to the growth of the purportedly aristocratic social group in the first half of the 19th century (Tudesq, 1988). This expansion was also enabled by marriages and novel ennoblements, as France morphed into different kinds of empires and royalties before settling into a république. This expansion stopped in 1858 when usurpation became sanctioned and aristocratic membership was codified (Bordeaux, 1861).

This pre-1850s growth of the aristocracy contributed to its lasting influence up until WWI. There is, however, little doubt that the meaning of nobility changed during this period, and that 1780 and 1890 noblemen had a different ethos and practices (Daumard, 1988). For instance, historians narrate how noblemen left Paris and went back to the countryside from the 1830s onward, while managing their patrimony in bourgeois terms, as the fragmentation of land that Napoleonic primogeniture laws triggered put pressure on their revenues. Many also entered the job market at that time. Different kinds of nobility also started competing, as a lower status yet moneyed nobility emerged, such as the Rothschild bankers. Partly for these economic reasons, intermarriage, a rare practice restricted to Paris before the 1850s, spread nationally. Daumard (1988) sums up this transformation by pointing out that nobility became less about social origins and more about who claims the honor. Consequently, aristocracy is more than a class in our analysis as noblemen entered a status competition with laymen like merchants.

Given this history, we code for aristocracy using the *de* particle in the owner's family name as an indicator. We regard the particle as an appropriate status marker because this symbol was widely understood and patrolled during most of our observation window, and it is easily observable. Looking at names is also a reliable source as many of the landowners indicate their titles, like "marquis" or "baron," providing a second cue of aristocratic membership. Féret is our main source, triangulated with many others.

We track status through multiple other indicators, following Weber's (1978) guidelines. In addition to hereditary prestige (aristocratic surnames and titles), we look at lifestyle (buildings construction and enhancements), associations (Sauder et al., 2012), position in a cultural and status hierarchy (Gould, 2002; Ridgeway, 2019), and status competition (Podolny, 2005). Buildings and estate enhancements are tracked through Féret, which published some images between 1850 and 1881, then was quite systematic from 1898 until 1929. This source was completed by the work from contemporaries and historians (e.g., Boyé, 2001; Danflou, 1867; Déthier et al., 1989; Galard, 1823–1825; Guillon, 1866–1869; Lorbac, 1868; Ribadieu, 1856). Associations, hierarchies, and status competition are derived from comparing the behaviors of each social group we identified, the ties they created or not, or the practices they emulated or not.

Closure can also be appreciated with different measures. Occupation, professions, property inheritance, bloodline, or dynastic succession are conducive carriers of exclusionary dynamics and can facilitate closure in the context of ownership change (Parkin, 1979; Stinchcombe, 1998; Weber, 1978). Following Parkin (1979), we also distinguish the exclusionary practices from insiders barring others to join from the usurpatory practices from outsiders attempting to join.

Analysis and Interpretation

We analyze our data as a historical ethnography. Historical ethnography is a method used by sociologists, anthropologists, and organizational scholars (e.g., Merry, 2002; Vaughan, 1996, 2004; Zipp, 2021) that allows the study of systems of representations of past societies and cultures (Comaroff & Comaroff, 1992). The core assumption is that distance in time is akin to distance in space, generating a comparable experience of otherness. As the past is a foreign country, the historian and the ethnographer share the same methodological concerns of analyzing estranged symbolic practices (Lévi-Strauss, 1963, pp. 16–17). In our case, we seek to understand how 19th-century aristocrats wielded power to retain their control over their wineries, while new owners gained a foothold, which interrogate what these estates meant and afforded.

The texts that survived time and that ended in the archives are the only medium to access this past. Historical ethnography is hence essentially an ethnography of the archives (Merry, 2002), where the researcher immerses him- or herself in documents to grasp past systems of representations. Historical ethnographers have, for instance, used legal texts to study marginalized groups, who tend to leave little textual footprints along their trail (Merry, 2002) or procedures and meeting notes that are constitutive of decision-making or safety processes in many organizations (Vaughan, 1996, 2021). Historical ethnographers recommend constructing your own archives that espouse the specifics of the phenomenon a researcher studies, within, across, and beyond official sources or archival funds one can get access to. Tabulating systematically the numerous and diverse sources of information is also key to navigate the archives and iterate, "passing from text to context and back again, until [one] has cleared a way through a foreign mental world" (Vaughan, 1996, p. 61).

Historical ethnography differs from other methods using texts as sources, such as case studies, content analysis, or the archival work historians do. Historical ethnographies are systematic yet interpretive analyses of the corpus of texts available. They are not thematic analyses that focus on the content of the text as the unit of analysis. They also analyze multiple archives, primary or secondary, rather than dig one or two primary archives with secondary sources in the background.[10] Historical ethnography also differs from ethnography, where participant observation is central to the method (e.g., Dumont, 2022). An immersion in the archives cannot grasp what the observation of small group interactions would. Yet, the diversity of archives affords to track and straddle multiple levels of analyses, between individuals, social groups, organizations, and their environments (Vaughan, 2021), which is central to the analysis we conduct. Historical ethnography is a method of choice to study biographies and how they relate to the formation of new groups and collective identities (Comaroff & Comaroff, 1992).

This method is also fitting for our study as we can only interpret the power struggle and varied meanings 1855 estates owners held over time. This historical ethnography of ownership is the outcome of this analytical journey, "a social history that reveals how participants interpreted actions and events" (Vaughan, 1996, p. 282). As we build on a large, heterogenous body of archives, we faced concerns about how to draw inferences. There are several ways of using archival data, and of course, researchers sometimes combine approaches (Mayrl & Wilson, 2020; Ventresca & Mohr, 2002). One strategy is to analyze a defined set of materials, perhaps all annual reports over a fixed amount of time, and search for patterns. This has the benefit of comparability and can be easily replicated by another researcher, even as it leaves valuable sources of information untapped. An alternative is to collect as many kinds of archival data as can be found, which affords the possibility for a researcher to get much closer to the phenomena. This approach, however, leaves open the questions about the author's interpretation and can make replication difficult. Our analysis combines these two approaches, yet ultimately rests on our interpretations of the archives we pieced together.

Our ethnographic interpretations are also both enabled and constrained by our theoretical question on how power struggles lead to elite formation. We use the class, status, and closure concepts to enlighten but also discipline our analysis (Vaughan, 2004). Yet, other avenues could have been pursued. For example, we do not interrogate the roles gender may have played in this transition.[11] We also have some evidence that marriage, political, and religious affiliations mattered, as many of the rising merchants investing in 1855 held political mandates (MPs, mayors, etc.) and/or lived in the Bordeaux Protestant community. Further studies should address these limitations.

FINDINGS: THE FORMATION OF A CORK ARISTOCRACY

Our historical ethnography investigates the struggle over the ownership of the 1855 estates and the rise of a cork aristocracy as a result, during the first 80 years of the classification's imprint. If, on the surface, 1855 looks immutable and Bordeaux's aristocratic veneer smooth and pristine, our analysis uncovers a decline of aristocratic owners beneath this apparent continuity and the ascendance of a cork aristocracy. How did aristocrats fall while their status remained, and how did lower status merchants and owners move in and acquire 1855 estates without diluting the classification's prestige?

A Material Transformation: The Fall of the Old Regime and the Ascendance of the New

The analysis of Féret directories reveals a constant, profound churning of 1855 owners, both in terms of individuals and families. Ownership change between 1850 and 1929 occurred inevitably through a demographic process. Our 79-year observation window approximates three generations, borrowing from sociologist Karl Mannheim (1952), who argued that a generation once lasted 25 years. We counted 196 ownership changes within the 62 different entities we track, an average of 3.16 individual owners per estate, which is a slightly higher, yet not significantly different from the number of generations. The x-axis of Fig. 1 captures the frequency of ownership change, which varies between 0, the case of Dubignon, who ceased early in the 1870s, and 5. The distribution is close to normal, and our data reflect this natural demographic transition. This turnover, however, is an undercount of the true number of changes, because of our non-continuous measures, suggesting this churning is greater than a natural demographic change.

We next looked at family changes, reported on the y-axis of Fig. 1. Wine estates have often harnessed the power of family to create a tapestry that builds on the legacy of their predecessors. A wine connoisseur might expect that old families and dynasties hold onto estates for generations. We nonetheless counted 111 family changes, which point to the impressive amount of churning in Fig. 1.[12] Excluding Dubignon, only four families, Barton at Langoa-Barton, Castéja at Duhart-Milon, Duroy de Suiduraut at Grand-Puy Ducasse, and Pichon de Longueville at Biron-Pichon, remain the sole owners throughout this period, while Latour remained in the hands of the same families. These exceptions aside, there is a 90% change in family ownership. This is quite striking as winegrowing

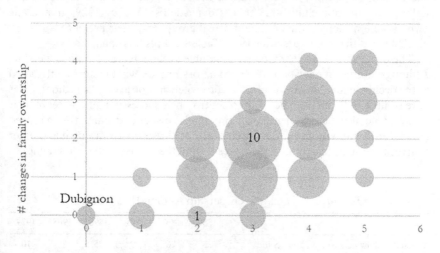

Fig. 1.   1855 Ownership and Family Changes, 1850–1929.
Source: Féret directories, 1850–1929, joint distribution.
Note: The size of the bubbles varies from 1 to 10 estates.

and winemaking has long been a family business. Yet, here in the most acclaimed wine region in the world, we find family has a modest pull. Even though organizational membership in the 1855 classification became fixed and enduring on the surface, beneath its ownership was neither monolithic nor invariant.

What is driving this change and how could it happen? If Bordeaux has an image of continuity, this silent churning implies the status quo was disrupted, vested interests upset, pressures escalated, and, potentially, the grip of institutions unfastened. How did an apparently conservative community change and allow new people in? We start by inquiring who the old owners were, what these estates and 1855 meant for these families, and how they lost control.

Wine ownership in 1850 Bordeaux is remarkably akin to the image one has of the Old Regime landed gentry. Aristocratic ownership had been a feature of the Bordeaux wine trade since the 18th century (Forster, 1961; Pijassou, 1980). By the 19th century, this social group owned land throughout Bordeaux and Médoc (Figeac, 1996). Our analysis of detailed 1838 data from *Le Producteur*, a journal dedicated to the struggle of owners against the trade revealed aristocrats represented 12% of all the owners in the Médoc region, while accounting for 24% of the volume and a higher fraction of the sales value (in *francs*). In 1850, aristocrats owned 60% of the future 1855 estates (Féret data), adding evidence of mid-century aristocratic entrenchment among elite wineries. By 1929, only 16% of the 1855 estate owners had an aristocratic surname or a title. This trend parallels the declining presence of nobles within French society's elite positions, whether among MPs, magistrates, entrepreneurs, or clergy (Coulmont, 2019). This transformation unfolded somewhat more slowly in Bordeaux, as respectively 48% and 42% of the owners were still aristocratic in 1881 and 1898. Their decline accelerates after 1908 (35%). Thus, for most of the 1850–1929 period, 1855 was essentially an aristocratic club rather than a dynastic list. Yet, by 1929, aristocratic owners were no longer the dominant social group, and their presence was marginal, a trend that continues after 1929. Table 1 details this change.

The ownership data clearly depict a notable decline in aristocratic ownership. Although this decline in status occurred across France, what factors contributed to the declining fortunes of the aristocratic owners in Bordeaux? Why did families have so little pull and were not able to control their succession and preserve their estates? One of the most scientifically progressive owners, Armand d'Armailhacq (1855, 1867), has written a revealing chronicle of this era. We draw on it and other sources to provide insight into the forces behind the demise of the old regime.

Table 1.   Aristocratic Ownership Among 1855 Estates.

	1850	1868	1881	1898	1908	1929
# estates with owners with an aristocratic surname	33	26	29	25	21	10
Total # estates	55	61	60	60	60	61
%	60	43	48	42	35	16

Source: Féret directories, 1850–1929.

Aristocratic owners invested massively in vineyards from the early 18th century onward (Pijassou, 1980), which led to the creation of countless new estates. For instance, in the commune of Pauillac, three aristocratic entrepreneurs, Pontet, Brane, and d'Armailhacq, bought land in the 1720s from the powerful Ségur family in the neighboring hamlets of Canet, Poulayet, and Mouton. These three owners founded three new estates, Pontet-Canet, Brane-Mouton, and Mouton d'Armailhacq, adding their family names to the name of the place where their estate was located. These properties were then handed over from generation to generation until a new family moved in or the estate was disbanded. Many families built homes on these estates, especially after the 1830s when aristocrats moved out of cities to live in rural areas (Figeac, 1996).

Four main factors altered this situation and weakened the grip of aristocratic families on their estates. First, if the 18th century was the golden age of wine investment, the first half of the 19th century was far less amenable and the commercial situation of the Médoc was dire until the late 1850s. The Napoleonic wars triggered bans and prohibiting tariffs, which stalled exports, a traditional outlet for Bordeaux wine for decades. Thanks to the newly arrived train,[13] Paris and the rest of France became more accessible, yet high transportation costs, city tariffs, and lower prices than on international markets slashed margins. In these conditions, winegrowing was a "ruinous" activity, weakening the grip of families over estates (d'Armailhacq, 1855, pp. ix–xii). Mouton d'Armailhacq, for instance, went bankrupt in 1843, and the family had to sell 10 hectares of renown vineyards to its direct neighbor to keep the property.

Second, vineyards required increasing investments during these years, which further burdened the estates. Scientific progress changed the way vines were grown, requiring new vineyard structures. Progress in chemistry yielded effective yet costly vine treatments, and some owners started investing in higher quality varietals, such as cabernet sauvignon. Cabernet was easier-to-grow than existing reds and gave a distinctive and seductive *sève* and *velours* (sap and velvet) texture to the wines (d'Armailhacq, 1855; Saint-Amant, 1855). The Bordeaux wine community struggled between 1852 and 1858 with the "horrible" powdery mildew disease that "devours the vines," halts production, and "spreads desolation" (Saint-Amant, 1855, pp. 99–100). Two other vine diseases, the phylloxera and the (downy) mildew, further afflicted Bordeaux before 1929, a period also marked by the 1890 great depression and WWI (Roudié, 1988). Estates spent fortunes to fight these plagues, at a time they also had to finance the construction of homes and face unruly markets.

Third, another factor that eroded aristocratic presence was the end of primogeniture laws and the rise of the Napoleonic code, which ensured all children equally inherited from their parents' estate. Many vineyards had to be sold to allow such an equal split. Of course, families were also the theaters of personal drama that affected their wineries. For instance, Pichon Longueville split into Pichon Comtesse and Pichon Baron when the Pichon son and daughter feuded irreparably about the inheritance of the family estate. As the daughter kept the existing building, the son built a brand-new château for his newly created estate Pichon Baron, facing his sister's residence across the road. Fourth, the boom in wine and then in estate prices during most of the 1855–1890 period, what the late historian Philippe Roudié (1988) called *une pluie d'or* (a shower of gold), also whetted the appetite of neighbors and newcomers, who made offers many owners could not refuse.

Most aristocratic owners resisted change. For instance, Armand d'Armailhacq (1855) pioneered many techniques to run his estate at a lower cost and sought grants and prizes to fund his discoveries and property. The owner of Mouton d'Armailhacq also fought with his new and deeper-pocketed neighbor, the Baron de Rothschild, who claimed the exclusive rights over the Mouton name[14] (d'Armailhacq, 1867). When Armand passed away in 1868 without any heir, his sister convinced her husband, the Comte de Ferrand, to buy the family property. Later, their son launched a wine trade business to further finance the estate, an unusual activity for an owner. To grow his activity, he partnered with the Baron de Rothschild's heirs. Yet, this effort was not sufficient and, in 1933, the Baron de Rothschild took over Mouton d'Armailhac, later named château d'Armailhac.[15] Technological innovations, external funding, marriage, legal contestation, new venture creation, or partnership were some of the solutions owners employed to resist change. Much ingenuity went into keeping endeared family estates, controlling succession, and maintaining closure.

Yet, despite this resistance, the arrival of new owners is dramatic, with the merchants' ascent into 1855's ranks perhaps the most striking aspect. As a seaport, Bordeaux developed an extensive trade community in the 18th century following the granting of royal privileges to the city (Pariset & Higounet, 1968). The merchants' economic success led them to acquire wine estates, and by 1850, they were the second-largest group of (future) 1855 owners with 33% of the classified estates. By 1929, merchants increased their presence to 41%, becoming the leading ownership group (Table 2).

While their increased presence is notable, merchant dominance is reflected more in how they climbed the status order. In 1850, 9 of the 18 estates owned were ones that were designated in 1855 as the fifth category, 5 were in the third category, and 2 in the fourth and second classes (Table 3). The first category was 100% owned by aristocrats. By 1929, one shipbuilder owned a first growth,[16] Margaux, and 10 of the 25 estates owned by merchants belonged to the second

Table 2.   Occupation and Ownership Among 1855 Estates.

	1850	1868	1881	1898	1908	1929
Owners	32	26	27	31	30	24
Merchants	18	23	21	17	17	25
Financiers and Industrialists	4	10	10	9	9	9
Law and Politicians	1	2	2	3	4	3
Owners %	58	43	45	52	50	39
Merchants %	33	38	35	28	28	41
Financiers and Industrialists %	7	16	17	15	15	15
Law and Politicians %	2	3	3	5	7	5

Source: Occupational dataset.

Table 3. Merchant ownership among 1855 Estates.

Merchant ownership among 1855 estates	1850	1898	1929
1st rank	0	0	1
2nd rank	2	6	10
3rd rank	5	4	6
4th rank	2	1	4
5th rank	9	6	4
Total	18	17	25

Source: Merchant and Féret directories.

category. Merchants also owned six estates in the third, and "only" four in the fourth and fifth categories. The rise of merchants from the bottom to the top of the classification signals their accrued economic power, and the climb clearly signals a marked status gain.

Other non-aristocratic owners also joined. First, financiers and industrialists invested in 1855 estates (and throughout the Médoc). There were only four in 1850; they more than doubled by 1929 with nine estate owners. These financiers and industrialists were outsiders who were attracted to invest in Médoc during the boom period between 1850 and 1890, rather than in Champagne even though it was closer to Paris. They included famous, powerful bankers including the two branches of the Rothschild family, the Péreire brothers, and the Comte d'Erlanger, the governor of the *Banque de France*. These newcomers were some of the wealthiest people in France. Yet they were of a lower social standing than aristocrats, even if they were ennobled like the Rothschild family or the Comte d'Erlanger. They were considered money aristocracy, not proper aristocracy (e.g., Daumard, 1988). Second, the industrialists were also nonlocal and included prominent figures like Gustave Roy, the founder of Haute Ecole Commerciale (HEC) business school, and Jean-Baptiste Rigaud, a famous Parisian perfumer. These *arrivistes* move to Bordeaux, and their uneasy fit with both merchants and aristocrats could be the stuff of many novels. As far as we know, most of the financiers and industrialists did not live in Bordeaux or on their estates. They usually appointed a *régisseur* to manage the estate, be it a merchant, an owner, or a professional. To the locals, they embodied the new industrial elite.

Lastly, two other groups expanded their ownership position between 1850 and 1929. First, several new owners held political positions, as mayor of a Médoc commune, as a Bordeaux city council member, or in a few cases as MP. Some held positions at the Chamber of Commerce and later at the 1855 union, created in 1905. These political roles were, in most cases, combined with other occupations, while a subgroup was composed of law professionals.

Second, there is also a group of owners for whom we could not identify a specific occupation beyond being an owner, and, for most cases, being a manager of the estate. Armand d'Armailhacq is one of these "owners" listed in Table 2, which are known locally and in the wine sector as *la propriété* (*Le Producteur*, 1838). This occupational group includes both aristocratic landowners and non-aristocratic owners. We listed 32 of these "owners" in 1850, which will decline by a quarter by

1929. Yet, 28 of these 32 owners in 1850 had aristocratic surnames (88%), while only 6 had such a family name in 1929 (25%). The non-aristocratic "owners" include many figures that became well known in Bordeaux, such as Théodore Skawinski, Léonce Récapet, or Armand Feuillerat. These local figures almost exclusively bought estates listed in 1855 in the early 20th century. Some of these new owners already owned some estates in Bordeaux. Others had ties with estate suppliers like Skawinski, who was *régisseur* at Léoville-Las-Cases, a second growth, while his brother ran a business providing sulfur and other chemical vine treatments. Still others, like Récapet, had commercial ties with the wine world as a liquorist.

In sum, in 1850, the hamlet of Poulayet and its surroundings were a typical aristocratic neighborhood among many in Bordeaux. By 1929, all the neighbors of the descendants of Armand d'Armailhacq's in-laws had departed and new owners arrived: the Lafite vineyard on the west was now owned by one branch of the Rothschild family, on the north, stood Mouton-Rothschild (another branch), and in the south Pontet-Canet was now the property of the powerful Cruse merchant family. New capitalist elites took over Poulayet, and a similar transformation prevailed throughout the Médoc. Even though d'Armailhacq and his aristocratic in-laws preserved their estate until 1933, most aristocratic families did not. The social composition of 1855 owners changed drastically over these 80 years. The owners with new occupations were no longer tied to the Old Regime social structures, and place and land were far removed from their identities and inheritance. Their wealth, earned through trade and industry, helped unlock the doors of these châteaux. Money and prestige replaced land and locale.

To a large extent, this transition from an aristocratic-dominated community to a capitalist-dominated group looks like a class struggle. This struggle has deep roots in the Bordeaux wine trade. Given their position in the supply chain, estate owners and merchants (*la propriété et le négoce*) compete over prices and wine allocation, which led to stark oppositions over time between the two groups. For instance, the journal *Le Producteur*, run by Lecoultre de Beauvais, an aristocrat, between 1838 and 1841, was created to foster awareness and collective action to defend the owners' interests against the merchants. Another example comes from the early 1900s with the rise of the cooperative movement and peasant revolts, in the wake of murderous events in Champagne and Languedoc regions, to provide either an alternative or a counterweight to the merchants. In addition, back then even the leading estates rarely bottled their wines. Merchants oversaw these operations; many used a merchant label instead of an estate one. In the process, wines were often adulterated with other wines. As a result, estate bottling of 1855 wines turned into a bitter fight between owners and merchants that was only resolved in the 1920s (Croidieu et al., 2018).

Yet, despite the aristocratic resistance and closure, the new capitalist elite gained dominance, introducing many changes. With their wealth, they invested massively in their estates, renewing and extending the vineyards and the buildings. The Rothschild family for instance built a brand-new château on their Mouton property in 1880. They changed the estate names and they also harnessed ongoing technical progress in winemaking like the barrel, while improving viticultural techniques to fight disease and grow production.

In summary, the material[17] transformation of ownership between 1850 and 1929 led to an almost complete replacement of the original families by new classes of owners. Aristocrats declined from the dominant group to a marginal one. Wealthy, but lower status, owners moved in, buying the aristocrats out. The newcomers included both old and new merchant families, elite French capitalists from Paris, rising local bourgeois politicians and lawyers, and other non-aristocratic owners. Looking at these transformations through a material lens is fundamental to document the path through which 1855 evolved, as it sheds light on how the struggles among groups with different degrees of power shaped the renewal of the Bordeaux wine elite.

A Symbolic Transformation: The Transposition of Aristocratic Codes into the Wine World

A material perspective, however, falls short in explaining how aristocrats retained their prestige as they exited as owners, and why the 1855 classification rose so markedly in prestige as lower status owners became associated with it. This demise of aristocratic owners was curiously combined with a cultural celebration of aristocracy, as the new entrants both adopted and created lavish symbols and lifestyles. By 1929, all but one 1855 of the estates was named with the "château" (castle) prefix, a direct reference to the traditional housing of old regime nobles. The previous geographic convention for naming estates after place gave way to ostensible grandeur as names were changed and labels greatly embellished (Croidieu et al., 2018). In addition, between 1850 and 1929, new owners built nine new château-like buildings, with grandiose towers, parks, and elaborate dining halls. Meanwhile, countless château-like enhancements were fitted to existing buildings (Lorbac, 1868). While aristocratic owners declined, the status of their estates remained, as the 1855 growths were renewed by owners who appropriated aristocratic codes. The new arrivals' growing stature in the life of Bordeaux led them to be nicknamed the cork aristocrats.

Even though merchants grew in dominance rather late in the process, they did not create a mercantile world. They absorbed the aristocratic lifestyle, and once in, they protected it. Like so many new victors, they could have flipped it, and yet they acted as custodians. A class analysis of ownership does not account for this transposition of values. Also, the aristocratic wine tradition resulted from uncoordinated actions of different kinds of owners. This cultural invention is not the sole product of a dominant class, be it aristocrats, bankers, or merchants. We argue an alternative symbolic lens, grounded in status dynamics (Weber, 1978), is needed to understand the meanings that guided these actions. Reading this archival material as a class-based power struggle illuminates as much as it obscures deeper motivations and forces at play in the rise of the cork aristocracy.

Since 1855 was initially an aristocratic club, we suggest that the increasing involvement of merchants and financiers is motivated by their desire to mingle with aristocrats. When these new owners bought 1855 estates, they did not want to kick aristocrats out, they wanted to stand next to them and elevate their own social status. Merchants are wealthy and powerful individuals, living locally, with longstanding reputations in Bordeaux. Across wine regions and historical periods, merchants have shown little interest in producing wines; their trade is to sell wine. Owning an 1855 estate became then a means to look like peers with the revered aristocrats, very much like participating in horse racing allowed merchants to sit in the same grandstand as aristocrats. By joining 1855, merchants became neighbors and members of the same club; the politics of association is what mattered to them then.

Status is a cultural schema for organizing social relations. High-status actors receive deference and honor from lower status ones. As merchants aspired to climb the social ladder and close the status gap with aristocrats, they not only bought into the 1855 aristocratic club but also mimicked and emulated the lifestyle, often in lavish ways. The purpose of this cultural appropriation was not to buy out aristocrats and steal their clothes but rather to join their club and blend in. Whether unintendedly or not, this mimicry helped preserve aristocratic social standing. To claim social esteem (Weber, 1978, p. 305), merchants ennobled the buildings located on their 1855 properties. First, they fitted grand, noble, or château-like enhancements to existing buildings, the château embodying the aristocratic house. For instance, Nathaniel Johnston (IV), a prominent Bordeaux wine merchant, who became an MP, and who owned a stud-farm and pioneered horse racing in Gironde (Faith, 2005, p. 115), actively imitated aristocratic housing codes. The Johnston family owned the Dauzac estate before it became classified in 1855 as a fifth growth. Nathaniel Johnston acquired the second growth Ducru-Beaucaillou in 1866 through his first wife, Lucie Dassier. While Dauzac had an elegant *chartreuse*[18] building on its property (built prior to 1850), Ducru-Beaucaillou's building was a neglected *château*, close to dereliction. Instead of investing in his family-owned Dauzac's estate and enhancing Dauzac's building, Johnston spent a small fortune to renovate the newly acquired Ducru-Beaucaillou and turn it into a grandiose *château* (Féret, 1898, p. 197, see Fig. 2).

| 1874 – first enhancements | 1881 – two towers added in 1878 |

Fig. 2.   The Enhancement of *Château* Ducru-Beaucaillou, Saint-Julien, Médoc.

As we coded the images of 1855 buildings, we found that merchants, at a minimum, made 31 major costly enhancements to their estate buildings, between 3 and 7 enhancements during each panel. In contrast, financiers and industrialists made only eight such enhancements. Not surprisingly, those lesser in status, and with less money, played the symbolic card more strongly. Second, merchants also built noble, grand, or *château*-like buildings like Alphonse Delor for Durfort-Vivens (a second growth), or Armand Lalande at Brown-Cantenac, a third growth. Our coding revealed five new grand buildings between 1868 and 1929. Merchants went a long way to emulate aristocrats.

Of course, merchants' claims of social esteem went beyond their 1855 estates, as Johnston, Eschenauer, and Guestier competed in various sports and shared memberships in different clubs and salons (Faith, 2005, p. 114), akin to conspicuous consumption (Veblen, 1899). After the premature death of his first wife, Nathaniel Johnston married Marie Caradja, princess of Constantinople. An unintended effect of these status-claiming behaviors is that merchants participated in the construction of a symbolic order, where 1855 became ennobled in an Old-Regime aristocratic fashion. From then on, *châteaux* and *château*-like buildings mushroomed in Médoc.

As merchants acquired higher status, aristocrats competed with them and, even though outnumbered, matched their efforts to upgrade estates. As part of this competition, aristocrats made 37 grand or *château*-like enhancements to their preexisting 1855 estates. These efforts were concentrated in the 1850–1898 period and subsequently declined. They also built five new *châteaux* during that period. This aristocratic "reclaiming" fueled a status competition, which declined in the 20th century as merchants ascended to dominance.

This status competition was heightened because the 1855 list has a fixed, limited number of seats, without mobility within the classification. A place in the 1855 classification was a positional good, creating a zero-sum social order. This feature is consequential in many ways, notably with closure strategies attempted by aristocrats. First, aristocrats rarely co-own 1855 growths with non-aristocrats. If prior research showed business partnership mattered in transitioning from one regime to the other (Padgett & Powell, 2012), it was hardly the case in Bordeaux. Out of the 68 cases of multiple owners, 53 (78%) were exclusively between aristocrats or non-aristocrats. The 15 remaining cases of co-ownership across this divide are split among seven estates, which mean these associations are both limited and temporary. Second, sales of estates across the status divide were rare. Out of the 111 family changes, only 8 transactions went from aristocrats to merchants (7%), the two dominant social groups (Margaux, Durfort, Lascombes, Comtesse, Giscours, St-Pierre, Cantemerle, and Alesme), and a mere 5 transactions flowed from merchants to aristocrats (Camensac, Lynch Bages, Pédesclaux, Haut-Bages Liberal and Alesme).

Third, the two groups seldom overlap. Very few aristocrats were merchants, the de Bethmann and de Sarget families being two notable exceptions. Also, merchants could be ennobled, such as Pierre-François Guestier, yet they were rare cases. Only four transactions occurred between these "hybrid" owners and either aristocrats or merchants. Although five estates remain aristocratic throughout the period (Lafite, Latour, Pichon Baron, d'Armailhacq, and Grand-Puy Ducasse) and only one remained merchant owned (Langoa-Barton), the transition from aristocracy to merchant occurred largely through financiers, industrialists, and new owners. These new owners were the middlemen between these two groups, as aristocrats preferred selling their family estate to nonlocal strangers rather than handing over to familiar local merchants. In sum, aristocrats were cautious not to be associated directly with merchants and carefully maintained their distance, aiming at drawing and tightening a boundary between these two groups and excluding merchants.

Though stringent, these aristocratic closure practices did not prevent the new owners from buying in and joining 1855 and its aristocratic assembly. The new owners, however, had to go a long way to overcome these growing barriers, and they achieved their goals through different means. We briefly list examples of these usurpatory strategies new owners employed to enter the well-guarded 1855 club. First, money was a necessary ingredient. The inflation in the 1850–1890 estate and wine prices reflect the rising costs of joining the aristocratic club (Roudié, 1988). Second, as Nathaniel Johnston's case showed, marriage was central to ascent into these circles, as it gave access to a broader network of opportunities. Third, relationships between merchants and aristocratic owners were multiplex. For instance, if the aristocrats reluctantly sold their estates to merchants, they, however, gladly sold them their wine. And merchants negotiated fiercely to ensure the supply of the best wines. The *abonnement* practice, where the price of a leading estate, like Lafite, is kept constant over a decade or so in exchange for an exclusive predefined volume and price for wine, is an example of these complex ties, where economic transactions become relations. In these occasions, merchants were able to turn tables as gatekeepers of market access and hence could apply pressure on owners. Differently, some merchants also took managerial, *régisseur*, positions in leading estates to help new owners, which gave them valuable information about these estates and their neighbors. Fourth, there is also evidence of scams and lawsuits, as some new owners crossed legal lines to acquire estates. Fifth, merchants were not only competing for the best wines, but some also organized themselves collectively to improve their position. We have found evidence in our data, the literature, and our interviews with a late broker, of a Protestant merchant cluster of marriages within this group (e.g., Faith, 2005; Pacteau de Luze, 1999). For example, Herman Cruse, the owner of Pontet-Canet, married his two sons to Sophie Lawton (a broker's daughter) and Suzanne Baour (a merchant's daughter). Finally, playing with names and joining the political network were also certainly parts of the strategies new owners deployed to reach their goal of ownership and respond to the tighter closure imposed by aristocrats.

Our review of these closure strategies reveals that merchants did not simply buy out aristocrats and replace them. Aristocrats instead lost their prominence through complex organizational and status dynamics, as they embellished their homes, fought the entry of merchants, and partnered with new types of owners to forestall their eventual exit. An unintended consequence is the formation of a new symbolic order, which associated wine with aristocracy. Unlike other cases of symbolic transposition where resources were converted into new political power or the creation of new industries (Clemens, 1997; Padgett & Powell, 2012), the transposition of aristocratic trappings into the wine world initially served no practical purpose other than making status claims under the disguise of mimicry. This emulation created a symbolic order that, as it spread, acquired a high-status patina as the status competition raged. Put differently, the declining aristocrats had little leverage to resist the economic changes, but they accepted them in a manner that normalized the shift in power. The transformation preserved the positive identity of 1855 estates. We have shown elsewhere how owning 1855 estates became prized (Croidieu et al., 2018). For example, in subsequent wine competitions at international fairs, the 1855 designation did not initially translate into prizes. Non-classified wines that were exhibited in 1855 and 1862 performed equally well. But by the 1890s, every wine from the 1855 classification received awards. In this sense, status became translated into economic clout.

This competition eventually solidified the elevation of 1855 at the pinnacle of Bordeaux, creating a status hierarchy both within and outside of Bordeaux that wine growers worldwide aspired to climb. If we borrow from Balzac, in 1929, "there is no nobility anymore" in the 1855 classification, "there is only an aristocracy left," and it was a cork aristocracy.

DISCUSSION

The 1855 classification is a fascinating case of persistence, in which an idiosyncratic ranking remained unchanged for more than 160 years and grew in importance 40–50 years after its creation and came to assume worldwide veneration. This list came to define an elite in the wine world, which, beneath this apparent stability, transitioned from a landed aristocracy to a cork aristocracy between 1850 and 1929. By examining the dramatic yet obscured ownership changes that occurred, this case of elite formation offers an opportunity to ask how power struggles led to the rise of a new collective stamped with a new identity. Our analysis of this tumultuous period, with three bouts of pestilence, two wars, and a major economic depression, reveals a remarkable transformation, where an old regime of aristocratic families, rooted in place and land, declined and came to be supplanted by merchants, with new families erecting grandiose buildings. These newcomers built the past in the present, adding invented layers to the region's history.

We first presented occupation and ownership data that capture an economic struggle between these two contenders, umpired by new capitalist elites who rose with the industrial revolution, and were freshly arrived in Bordeaux. Although this class perspective illuminates and reinforces the profound material transformation that historians of Bordeaux have documented (Pijassou, 1980; Roudié, 1988), we also uncovered a notable symbolic shift as we considered 1855 as a status community and analyzed organizational dynamics within 1855 estates. Instead of purging Bordeaux of its aristocratic past, the new entrants surprisingly adopted and celebrated the trappings of nobility. These new owners created a new version of Bordeaux, with transposition, cultural appropriation, and invention of symbols and buildings. In terms of social closure, this new status community became even more tightly policed than was the old. A cork aristocracy was born out of a landed aristocracy.

Consequently, our account of the remarkable transformation that the Bordeaux wine world underwent rests on an analysis of status dynamics. The 1855 classification initially was an aristocratic club and remained so until the turn of the century. Within this club, the individual status of aristocrats spilled over to the newly formed 1855 estates. Merchants and other capitalists were drawn to it as they aspired to belong to this "noble" club. Decades later, as 1855 became a status hierarchy, new owners were drawn to it as a closed, prestigious club. Owning an 1855 estate granted exalted status to individuals. These two distinctive forces help explain both the formation of a new elite and the transposition of the tradition of the old elite into the new elite world, even though this tradition initially excluded them. Our analysis reinforces Stinchcombe's (1968) point that the rise of a new elite often obscures prior arrangements.

For someone familiar with Bordeaux, the transition from aristocrats to merchants is not surprising. Bordeaux as a wine region has been extensively commented upon since the 18th century, and the bibliography of work is immense (e.g., Gabler, 2003).[19] Regarding the transformation we describe, it is widely acknowledged that aristocrats invested in Bordeaux vineyards in the 18th century and controlled its production, whereas by the 1930s, the merchants had become the leading figures of the wine trade. The 18th-century Bordeaux merchants were often foreigners and largely lived together in one district by the river, *les Chartrons*, that was originally outside the city walls. Aristocrats and merchants were socially and spatially segregated in a heavily stratified Old Regime city. After the French Revolution, these boundaries persisted, and the two groups hardly overlapped; nevertheless, aristocrats' revenues declined as the new century unfolded. The dominant interpretation in the Bordeaux literature is that merchants took over, or even seized power, thanks to growing trade revenues, that allowed them to buy out and replace aristocratic landowners as proprietors of leading estates (e.g., Brook & Latham, 2001; Butel, 2008; Coates, 2004; Faith, 2005; Penning-Rowsell, 1967; Réjalot, 2007; Ulin, 1996; Unwin, 1991).

Although this extant account captures the main storyline, we revisit it for several reasons. First, the accepted account is not systematic. Only a few authors acknowledge the role of bankers, industrialists, or even politicians in this transition. Second, these analyses insufficiently connect changes in ownership to changes within the properties. The existing literature assumes a continuity of 1855 estates, in terms of their names, labels, location, and buildings. Apart from the description of the diffusion of the *château* label by Philippe Roudié (1988, 2000), we are not aware of any systematic study that examines the transposition of aristocratic codes into the wine world. In contrast, we observe the creation of an invented tradition (Hobsbawm & Ranger, 1983) that massively transforms these properties, what they looked like, what they meant, and what they offered. We think these organizational transformations are key to understanding ownership change. In our view, the strength of historical ethnography is to analyze changes at multiple levels (Vaughan, 2021) and how new owners' biographies relate to the rise of a new collective identity. Specifically, the transposition and borrowing of an aristocratic lifestyle by the bourgeois merchants lead us to go beyond the material struggle that prior work highlights and attend to complementary status dynamics. Third, we think the temporality of these co-occurring processes is essential to interpret this change, even though it has received little attention. The 1855 classification evolved sharply, and the reasons to join 1855 differed over time and across actors. Although we learned from and build upon the abundant literature on Bordeaux, our work is a sociological exposé, where "the sociologist [...] looks beneath the obvious surface that preoccupies the other social sciences" (Perrow, 1986, p. 177).

As the 1855 list came to embody first an aristocratic club forged by ascription, and later a cork aristocracy, our case is akin to the Ivy league, which persisted, seemingly unchanged on the surface, first a sports club about class, then as an academic club about educational achievement, both equally marked by excellence and social reproduction albeit through different mechanisms (e.g., Cappello, 2012; Goldstein, 1996). Similarly, the 1855 list persisted during that period under different disguises, not through elite reproduction and value maintenance, but through elite renewal and cultural invention, which usually predict institutional change (Stinchcombe, 1998; Tilly, 1998).

To account for this unusual path to persistence, one needs to look more closely at closure. We showed how the 1855 list triggered early on closure as the aristocrats that composed the list kept new owners at bay; when the classification became consequential, closure dynamics changed (e.g., Bowker & Star, 2000). Categories have received considerable attention in organizational research, emphasizing how audiences patrol boundaries and discipline behaviors (e.g., Grodal, 2018; Lamont & Molnar, 2002; Rao et al., 2003; Zuckerman, 1999). Closure processes, however, largely remain in the background of these conversations, whereas they play a complementary disciplinary role, central to the formation of the cork aristocracy category. Interestingly, our case reveals how symbolic boundaries proved to be incredibly porous as the status competition led to the transposition of the aristocratic tradition, while this process resulted in a new collective, the cork aristocracy, with tighter social boundaries.

As 1855 shifted from an aristocratic club to a cork aristocracy, the classification gained force through social closure that first prevented the merchants from buying in and gaining power over aristocrats but instead attracted them to the old regime. Because of closure, merchants aspired to join aristocrats, not kick them out. These same dynamics of closure meant aristocrats were loath to sell to Bordeaux merchants, even when their backs were against the wall. They instead favored strangers, Parisian financiers, or French industrialists, and let them in their family homes to own the places that bore their names. We do not know whether these strangers were perceived as more "honorable" than merchants, or if aristocrats were reluctant to sell to merchants, but sales to rich outsiders were regarded as less of a status degradation. Once these new owners were admitted into these social circles, closure triggered transposition and imitation. The merchants did not bulldoze the aristocratic heritage, unlike so many winners in history, they gladly elevated, and expanded it.

If these first new owners bought their way in an aristocratic club, they most likely did not know it would become something larger than a club, a status community, that would take on a life of its own. In terms of status dynamics, the entry of lower status members into a high-status club should have diluted the prestige of 1855. Yet, 1855 rose in status, attracting more new members, who then kept imitating and expanding ongoing practices. The rise of the 1855 listing in status was certainly unexpected. In that sense, buying an 1855 estate in the 1870s, instead of its non-1855 neighbor, was akin to a lottery. Even though phylloxera and other plagues brought enormous uncertainty, owners most likely had a sense of which were the good estates. Yet, which estate would become enshrined was most likely undecipherable until later. Our data on all the classifications of the best (Médoc) wines (not presented here) clearly show membership and ranks kept changing until the late 1800s, while exhibition data show 1855 estates only became consecrated at a similar time. By the turn of the century, 1855 was taken for granted and widely understood as Bordeaux' pinnacle. External audiences certainly had a hand in shaping the cork aristocracy, yet status closure completed this process by ordering the category early and, later, amplifying the audience's consecration.

Closure is not the only classical sociology concept we combine with our organizational analysis. Status and class trace back to the founders of sociology as a discipline, notably Karl Marx and Max Weber. Both continue to be crucial touchstones in contemporary sociology but have often been elided in more recent organizational research. To be sure, status has been treated as a signal or marker that organizes markets in economic sociology (Podolny, 2005), but organizations themselves are seldom seen as the embodiment of status, and aside from work on elites, social class rarely falls within the scope of organizational analysis (Khan, 2011).

Our findings on the status feedback loop, from aristocrats to estates and then from estates to cork aristocrats, notably informs a growing line of work on how inequalities and organization intersect (Amis et al., 2018, 2020; Powell & Brandtner, 2016). We suggest the study of inequalities and organizations could be advanced by building on earlier work on social structures and organizations (Stinchcombe, 1965) and unpacking how they are enmeshed. The unanticipated complex status and organizational dynamics that our historical ethnography uncovered link individual mobility with societal change through changing organizations, which durably shaped the Bordeaux economy. Our case shows organizations not only sheltered or triggered social actions but also altered them as they carried complex social processes. Sewell (1996) argued that events are consequential when they transform social structures. The power struggle at the top of Bordeaux wine cascaded into the redrawing of class and status, which marginalized the pre-revolutionary agrarian political economy and resulted in the formation of a cork aristocracy headed by ennobled merchants. The 62 wine estates were pivotal in this process.

We could speculate that had the merchants not prevailed, Bordeaux would have certainly looked much more like Burgundy, a vast wine territory fragmented into tiny estates that melt away over time, like a *peau de chagrin*, as families pursue their desires to maintain control over their estates yet cannot afford to do so. Merchants were key in building Bordeaux as we know it today, by opening international markets and preserving most of the value created locally. Our historical ethnography suggests they assumed a pivotal role in funding the elite estates, preserving and ennobling large-scale properties, inventing a tradition, and elevating and maintaining 1855. As the classification rose, merchants become the new power holders in Bordeaux (Croidieu et al., 2018). Bordeaux became a merchant world, rather than a winemaker world. Today, you know a Bordeaux wine by the name of the estate, whereas in many other wine regions, the winemaker is more central.

But unlike some historical accounts (Faith, 2005), 1855 is not a merchant coup. Vested interests to champion 1855 were limited; indeed, the 1855 union emerged only in 1905, and we have shown how different merchant dynasties competed over the 80 years we studied. Only the Bartons survived this churning, and merchant coordination occurred much later (Croidieu et al., 2018). That said, Marxian scholars could argue that our status account is in fact a beautiful illustration of a mystification process, where a dominant elite manipulates the past to disguise their interests and legitimize their ascendency. Merchants bought their way in by inventing a wine tradition, culturally appealing to the then powerful aristocrats, creating an aspiration for others. The 1855 classification is clearly an invented tradition, as defined by Hobsbawm and Ranger (1983). Yet, this appealing mystification account falls short in accounting for the politics of association that fueled the remarkable transformation we described. If merchants were 1855 champions and custodians, the invented tradition also starts before the merchants assume power, in a distributed manner. This mystification account also fails to explain how the complex status dynamics we depicted were tightly intertwined with multigenerational organizational changes within the estates.

Classical sociologists could also object that what we describe as a failed merchant coup, in the sense merchant dynasties keep changing, is oblivious to "invisible" reproductive mechanisms we fail to report. To a large extent, the merchant class does not survive on 1855 ownership. Merchants maintained power through trade alliances between merchant families, the transmission of trade businesses within merchant families, and the formation of endogamous marriages across merchant families, knowing the same families met on Sundays at the horse track after attending the mass at the temple together – dynamics for which we have only tangential evidence (e.g., Butel, 2008; Faith, 2005). From a Bourdieusian perspective (1984, 1986), merchants achieve social distinction by converting economic capital, accumulated in commerce, into symbolic (e.g., cork aristocrats), social (e.g., marrying a princess), and even political capital (e.g., becoming a MP). In that sense, 1855's persistence would be a nouveau riche story, with a rising elite buying its way in, thanks to favorable conditions, and smartly converting its new money in different capitals as it sought to transmit its power. From this lens, owning an 1855 estate could even be understood as a fluid economic capital. Which family owns them is irrelevant as long as the merchant class maintains its grip.

This powerful account falls short, however, in accounting for the whole transformation. Some merchant dynasties certainly grew throughout the period, yet these dynasties were largely renewed, and the dense merchant familial network we noted is rather a product than an antecedent of this transition. Similarly, the 1855 ranking looks at its beginning like a translation of the social order, with the aristocrats owning the top estates, then the financiers, and then the merchants, yet this ordering is reshuffled dramatically while the tradition emerges later. The aristocratic wine tradition is a symbolic transposition, not a social translation. Also, the merchant habitus would predict they overturned the aristocratic codes, whereas they emulated them. Merchants acted as owners when building and ennobling expansive homes. Likewise, financiers and other new owners largely broker this transition between aristocrats and merchants, yet fail to imprint their codes: many such as the Rothschilds settled and blend in. The rise of the cork aristocracy results from complex status and organizational dynamics that social reproduction can only partially account for.

There is a thriving current literature in organization studies that chronicles how firms in a number of sectors (wine and spirits, fine art, mechanical watches, etc.) have creatively reinterpreted their history or even re-imagined their past to create a new contemporary brand (Delmestri & Greenwood, 2016; Khaire & Wadhwani, 2010; Kroezen & Heugens, 2019; Raffaelli, 2019). We also see new brands in the food products field attempt to tie themselves to an older, purer agrarian tradition (Weber et al., 2008). Even in the wine trade, contemporary enthusiasm for natural wines is an illustration of this category purity process by tying one's products to the past. In our view, these are excellent cases of brand categorization processes, where status is invoked strategically. The persistence of the 1855 classification is not such a market niche strategy but rather a social and economic upheaval, in which wine estates became the vehicles for changing the class structure of Bordeaux. Elite control of Bordeaux wine was the product of this struggle.

We have argued, following Sewell (1996), that events resonate in history when they create ruptures in (elite) social structures, be they class or status. The persistence of 1855 is the consequence of the transformation of status orders in Bordeaux. Our account more quietly highlights the pivotal role organizations played in this process. As 1855 emerged, capitalism arrived in Bordeaux, and this societal transformation influenced the Bordeaux community, which, as a place, gained a new identity. As the Western world became capitalist and market economies rose, Bordeaux, the port dominated by aristocrats, adapted, and found its place in this new world by becoming the world's leading wine region; at its head were merchants navigating new markets. This story is not only about the individuals and the winds of class and status change. Our historical case reveals that organizations, the wine estates, carried much of the status dynamics so central in our story. The chateaux, the wine, and their trappings became the cultural materials that merchants, financiers, and politicians used to claim their control. Organizations scholars have long argued that society is shaped by its organizations (Perrow, 2002). We extend this perspective by showing that organizations are also the carriers of status and class dynamics, a major cog in the wheel of societal change.

NOTES

1. Cork aristocracy is an expression *François Mauriac*, a laureate of the Nobel Prize in literature from Bordeaux, coined in a 1924 novel, whose main characters navigate the boundaries of the Bordeaux merchant world. The expression spread widely afterward.

2. We interchangeably use 1855 classification, list, ranking, or status hierarchy to refer to the focal institution of our study.

3. The word *château* is a physical building but also came to signify a wine estate in Bordeaux as the label diffused widely (Croidieu et al., 2018; Roudié, 1988). Also, many 1855 estates, but not all, have a chateau-like physical building on their property, which adds to the confusion. We use château with both meanings in this manuscript and insert markers to signal whether we refer to the building or the estate.

4. We define institutional persistence as the temporal continuity of an institution, where prior characteristics of any social system affect its long-term state. If the 1855 list is the institution we focus on, the wine estates classified in this list are the organizations owners struggle over.

5. The sole exception was the promotion of Mouton-Rothschild from the second to the first tier in 1973, more than a century later.

6. Regularity in panel spacing facilitates comparisons over time, especially as we study individuals and generations of owners, whose life events affect the estates. See Blossfeld et al. (2019) and Wooldridge (2002) for a discussion of panel data structures, spacing, and the underlying random sampling assumption.

7. Wineries in Bordeaux were historically called crûs, translated as growths, which has remained, despite the growing use of the château label (Roudié, 1988, 2000). We use estates, growths, or organizations interchangeably to refer to these wineries.

8. Sylvain Torchet is a French postman, whose passion and dedication to cataloging wine knowledge gained him recognition in the wine community, very much like amateur historians, scientists, or artists (e.g., Croidieu & Kim, 2018).

9. The French "de" is distinctive from the Spanish "de," which denotes to whom one got married.

10. See, for instance, Ventresca and Mohr (2002) for a discussion of different kinds of archivalism.

11. The owners in our sample were mainly male (81%), yet wives, widows, sisters, daughters, or mothers, all hidden under owner change but no family change, often played an important role in the transformations we tracked. For instance, the powerful merchant Johnston was able to buy Ducru-Beaucaillou thanks to his wife's family network. Armand d'Armailhacq's mother recapitalized the family estate of her husband when it went bankrupt, while we will discuss later the pivotal role his sister played in preserving the estate.

12. Fig. 1 plots the joint frequency of family and ownership change. As with turnover in owners, family changes are close to normally distributed. On average, an 1855 estate shifted hands almost twice during that period (average = 1.79), and a few changed as many as four times (Malescot, Kirwan, and Cos d'Estournel).

13. The rail spread throughout France in multiple steps (Dobbin, 1994): the first train circulated in 1827, while the full Bordeaux-Paris line was completed in 1853.

14. Brane-Mouton became Mouton-Rothschild when acquired in 1853.

15. The orthograph of d'Armailhacq varies greatly over time.

16. Until today, the sale of 1855 first growths is a very rare event. A tentative explanation would be that these world famous organizations, some much larger than other classified estates, are less sensitive to market changes as they remain exclusive with higher prices and hence benefit from a greater economic stability. Haut-Brion is also excluded from our sample.

17. By material, we refer to class-based economic power as a source of change, as in Weber (1978), such as newly moneyed elite buying estates from old families. Although buildings, place, and physicality matter in our case (see also our multimodal analysis in Croidieu et al. (2018), we do not mean material as materiality and, instead, show that the material buildings are indicators of a lifestyle and status dynamics.

18. A chartreuse is a typical one-storey building you find in the Bordeaux countryside.

19. Our bibliography lists more than 200 books by academics, critics, trade professionals, enthusiasts, etc. In addition, there is a large academic literature (e.g., Fourcade, 2012; Malter, 2014; Ody-Brasier & Vermeulen, 2014) and (wine) press publications.

ACKNOWLEDGMENTS

The authors thank Oliver Alexy, Miriam Bird, Christof Brandtner, Bruce Carruthers, Stewart Clegg, Guillaume Dumont, Michael Grothe-Hammer, Joachim Henkel, Brayden King, John Padgett, Madeleine Rauch, Kathia Serrano-Velarde, Diane Vaughan, and an anonymous reviewer, as well as the participants in the 2022 EGOS subtheme on Doing Sociology in Organization Studies in Vienna and in a Technical University of Munich seminar for their insights and supportive comments. Usual caveats apply.

REFERENCES

Amis, J. M., Mair, J., & Munir, K. A. (2020). The organizational reproduction of inequality. *Academy of Management Annals*, *14*(1), 195–230.

Amis, J. M., Munir, K. A., Lawrence, T. B., Hirsch, P., & McGahan, A. (2018). Inequality, institutions and organizations. *Organization Studies*, *39*(9), 1131–1152.

d'Armailhacq, A. (1855). *De la culture des vignes de la vinification et les vins dans le Médoc avec un état des vignobles d'après leur réputation*. P. Chaumas.

d'Armailhacq, A. (1867). *De la culture des vignes de la vinification et les vins dans le Médoc avec un état des vignobles d'après leur réputation* (Deuxième édition). P. Chaumas.

Arnold, N., & Foureault, F. (2024). Status in socio-environmental fields: Relationships, evaluations, and otherhood. In S. Clegg, M. Grothe-Hammer, & K. Serrano Velarde (Eds.), *Sociological thinking in contemporary organizational scholarship* (Research in the Sociology of Organizations, Vol. 90, pp. 109–140). Emerald Publishing.

Barley, S. R. (2010). Building an institutional field to corral a government. *Organization Studies*, *31*(6), 777–805.

Beaumaine, F. (1953). Exposé historique et juridique de la particule DE comme preuve de noblesse. *Revue Internationale D'onomastique*, *5*(1), 31–44.

Blossfeld, H. P., Rohwer, G., & Schneider, T. (2019). *Event history analysis with stata*. Routledge.

Bordeaux, R. (1861). Review of Code de la noblesse française, ou Précis de la législation sur les titres, épithètes, noms, particules nobiliaires et honoritiques, les armoiries, etc. *Deuxième édition*. *Revue Historique de Droit Français et Étranger (1855–1869)*, *7*, 193–202.

Bourdieu, P. (1977). Distinction: A social critique of the judgement of taste.

Bourdieu, P. (1986). The forms of capital. In J. Richardson (Ed.), *Handbook of theory and research for the sociology of education* (pp. 46–58). Greenwood.

Bowker, G. C., & Star, S. L. (2000). *Sorting things out: Classification and its consequences*. MIT Press.

Boyé, M. (Ed.). (2001). *Le patrimoine des communes de la Gironde*. Flohic.

Brook, S., & Latham, G. (2001). *Bordeaux: People, power, and politics*. M. Beazley.

Butel, P. (2008). *Les dynasties bordelaises: Splendeur, déclin et renouveau* (Éd. réactualisée). Perrin.

Cappello, D. (2012). *The Ivy league*. Assouline Publishing.

Clemens, E. S. (1997). *The people's lobby: Organizational innovation and the rise of interest group politics in the United States, 1890–1925*. University of Chicago Press.

Coates, C. (2004). *The wines of Bordeaux: 1952–2003*. University of California Press.

Comaroff, J. L., & Comaroff, J. (1992). *Ethnography and the historical imagination*. Westview Press.

Coulmont, B. (2019). Dupont n'est pas du Pont: Sociographie de la noblesse d'apparence. *Histoire & Mesure*, *XXXIV*(2), 153–192.

Croidieu, G., & Kim, P. H. (2018). Labor of love: Amateurs and lay-expertise legitimation in the early U.S. radio field. *Administrative Science Quarterly*, *63*(1), 1–42.

Croidieu, G., Soppe, B., & Powell, W. W. (2018). CRU, GLUE, and status: How wine labels helped ennoble Bordeaux. In M. A. Höllerer, T. Daudigeos, & D. Jancsary (Eds.), *Multimodality, meaning, and institutions* (Vol. 54B, pp. 37–69). Emerald Publishing Limited.

Danflou, A. (1867). *Les grands crus bordelais: monographies et photographies des châteaux et vignobles.* Librairie Goudin.

Daumard, A. (1988). Noblesse et aristocratie en France au XIXe siècle. *Publications de l'École Française de Rome*, *107*(1), 81–104.

Delmestri, G., & Greenwood, R. (2016). How Cinderella became a queen: Theorizing radical status change. *Administrative Science Quarterly*, *61*(4), 507–550.

Déthier, J., Melvin, A., & Centre Georges Pompidou. (1989). *Chateaux Bordeaux*. Mitchell Beazley.

Dobbin, F. (1994). *Forging industrial policy: The United States, Britain, and France in the railway age.* Cambridge University Press.

Dumont, G. (2022). Immersion in organizational ethnography: Four methodological requirements to immerse oneself in the field. *Organizational Research Methods*, *26*(3), 441–458.

Faith, N. (2005). *The winemasters of Bordeaux*. Carlton Books.

Féret, E. (1898). *Bordeaux et ses Vins Classés par Ordre de Mérite* (7ème édition). Editions Féret.

Figeac, M. (1996). *Destins de la noblesse bordelaise, 1770–1830*. Éditions Mimésis.

Forster, R. (1961). The noble wine producers of the Bordelais in the eighteenth century. *Economic History Review*, *14*(1), 18.

Fourcade, M. (2012). The vile and the noble: On the relation between natural and social classifications in the French wine world. *The Sociological Quarterly*, *53*(4), 524–545.

Gabler, J. M. (2003). *Wine into words: A history and bibliography of wine books in the English language* (2nd ed.). Bacchus Press Limited.

Galard, G. de. (1823–1825). *Album bordelais, ou Caprices*. M. de Galard.

Goldstein, R. (1996). *Ivy League autumns: an illustrated history of college football's grand old rivalries.* St. Martin's Press.

Gould, R. V. (2002). The origins of status hierarchies: A formal theory and empirical test. *American Journal of Sociology*, *107*(5), 1143–1178.

Grodal, S. (2018). Field expansion and contraction: How communities shape social and symbolic boundaries. *Administrative Science Quarterly*, *63*(4), 783–818.

Grusky, D. B., & Sørensen, J. B. (1998). Can class analysis be salvaged? *American Journal of Sociology*, *103*(5), 1187–1234.

Guillon, J. M. (1866–1869). Les grands vins de bordeaux. Société de l' "Annuaire de la Gironde," Delmas, Bordeaux.

Hobsbawm, E. J. (1975/2010). *Age of capital: 1848–1875*. Orion.

Hobsbawm, E. J., & Ranger, T. (1983). *The invention of tradition*. Cambridge University Press.

Khaire, M., & Wadhwani, R. D. (2010). Changing landscapes: The construction of meaning and value in a new market category – Modern Indian art. *Academy of Management Journal*, *53*(6), 1281–1304.

Khan, S. (2011). *Privilege: The making of an adolescent elite at St. Paul's school*. Princeton University Press.

Khan, S. (2012). The sociology of elites. *Annual Review of Sociology*, *38*, 361–377.

Kroezen, J. J., & Heugens, P. P. M. A. R. (2019). What is dead may never die: Institutional regeneration through logic reemergence in Dutch beer brewing. *Administrative Science Quarterly*, *64*(4), 976–1019.

Laitin, D. D. (1986). *Hegemony and culture: Politics and religious change among the Yoruba*. University of Chicago Press.

Lamont, M., & Molnar, V. (2002). The study of symbolic boundaries. *Annual Review of Sociology*, *28*, 167–195.

Laryea, C., & Brandtner C. (2024). Organizations as drivers of social and systemic integration: Contradiction and reconciliation through loose demographic coupling and community anchoring. In S. Clegg, M. Grothe-Hammer, & K. Serrano Velarde (Eds.), *Sociological thinking in contemporary organizational scholarship* (Research in the Sociology of Organizations, Vol. 90, pp. 175–200). Emerald Publishing.

Le Producteur. (1838). Journal des intérêts spéciaux de la propriété vignoble du département de la Gironde (1838–1841). Bordeaux.

Lévi-Strauss, C. (1963). *Structural anthropology*. Basic Books Inc.

Lorbac, C. de. (1868). *Les richesses gastronomiques de la France les vins de Bordeaux*. Illustré par C. Lallemand.

Malter, D. (2014). On the causality and cause of returns to organizational status: Evidence from the Grands Crus Classés of the Médoc. *Administrative Science Quarterly*, *59*(2), 271–300.

Mannheim, K. (1952). The problem of generations. In P. Kecskemeti (Ed.), *Essays on the sociology of knowledge. Collected works of Karl Mannheim* (Vol. 5, pp. 276–322). Routledge.

Markham, D. (1998). *1855: A history of the Bordeaux classification*. Wiley.

Marx, K. (1867). *Capital: A critique of political economy*. History of Economic Thought Books.

Mauriac, F. (1924). *Préséances*. Flammarion.

Mayrl, D., & Wilson, N. H. (2020). What do historical sociologists do all day? Analytic architectures in historical sociology. *American Journal of Sociology*, *125*(5), 1345–1394.

Merry, S. E. (2002). Ethnography in the archives. In J. Starr & M. Goodale (Eds.), *Practicing ethnography in law* (pp. 128–142). Palgrave Macmillan.

Mills, C. W. (1956). *The power elite*. Oxford University Press.

Ody-Brasier, A., & Vermeulen, F. (2014). The price you pay: Price-setting as a response to norm violations in the market for champagne grapes. *Administrative Science Quarterly*, *59*(1), 109–144.

Pacteau de Luze, S. (1999). *Les Protestants de Bordeaux*. Mollat.

Padgett, J. F., & Powell, W. W. (2012). *The emergence of organizations and markets*. Princeton University Press.

Pariset, F.-G., & Higounet, C. (1968). *Bordeaux au XVIIIe siècle*. Féd. Historique du Sud-Ouest.

Parkin, F. (1979). *Marxism and class theory*. Columbia University Press.

Penning-Rowsell, E. (1967). *The wines of Bordeaux* (3rd revised ed.). Penguin.

Perrow, C. (1986). *Complex organizations: A critical essay* (3rd ed.). Scott-Forbes.

Perrow, C. (2002). *Organizing America: Wealth, power, and the origins of corporate capitalism*. Princeton University Press.

Pijassou, R. (1980). *Un grand vignoble de qualité: le Médoc*. Jules Tallandier.

Podolny, J. M. (2005). *Status signals*. Princeton University Press.

Powell, W. W. (1990). Neither market nor hierarchy: Network forms of organization. *Research in Organizational Behavior*, *12*, 295–336.

Powell, W. W., & Brandtner, C. (2016). Organizations as sites and drivers of social action. In S. Abrutyn (Ed.), *Handbook of contemporary sociological theory* (pp. 269–291). Springer International Publishing.

Raffaelli, R. (2019). Technology reemergence: Creating new value for old technologies in Swiss mechanical watchmaking, 1970–2008. *Administrative Science Quarterly*, *64*(3), 576–618.

Rao, H., Monin, P., & Durand, R. (2003). Institutional change in Toque Ville: Nouvelle cuisine as an identity movement in French gastronomy. *American Journal of Sociology*, *108*(4), 795–843.

Réjalot, M. (2007). *Les logiques du château: filière et modèle viti-vinicole à Bordeaux, 1980–2003*. Presses Universitaires de Bordeaux.

Ribadieu, H. (1856). *Les châteaux de la Gironde*. Justin Dupuy et Comp.

Ridgeway, C. L. (2019). *Status: Why is it everywhere? Why does it matter?* Russell Sage Foundation.

Robinson, J., & Harding, J. (2015). *The Oxford companion to wine*. Oxford University Press.

Roudié, P. (1988). *Vignobles et Vignerons du Bordelais*. Presses Universitaires de Bordeaux.

Roudié, P. (2000). Vous avez dit «château»? Essai sur le succès sémantique d'un modèle viticole venu du Bordelais. *Annales de Géographie*, *109*(614), 415–425.

Saint-Amant, S.-A. (1855). *Le vin de bordeaux: promenade en médoc 1855*. Chaumas.

Sauder, M., Lynn, F., & Podolny, J. M. (2012). Status: Insights from organizational sociology. *Annual Review of Sociology*, *38*(1), 267–283.

Sewell, W. H. (1996). Historical events as transformations of structures: Inventing revolution at the Bastille. *Theory and Society*, *25*(6), 841–881.

Stinchcombe, A. L. (1965). Social structure and organizations. In J. G. March. (Ed.), *Handbook of organizations* (pp. 142–193). Rand McNally.

Stinchcombe, A. L. (1968). *Constructing social theories*. University of Chicago Press.

Stinchcombe, A. L. (1998). Monopolistic competition as a mechanism. Corporations, universities, and nation-states in competitive fields. In P. Hedstrom & R. Swedberg (Eds.), *Social mechanisms* (pp. 267–305). Oxford University Press.

Thelen, K. (2004). *How institutions evolve: The political economy of skills in Germany, Britain, the United States, and Japan.* Cambridge University Press.

Tilly, C. (1998). *Durable inequality.* University of California Press.

Tocqueville, A. de. (1856). *L'Ancien Régime et la Révolution.* Michel-Lévy frères.

Tudesq, A.-J. (1988). L'élargissement de la noblesse en France dans la première moitié du XIXe siècle. *Publications de l'École Française de Rome, 107*(1), 121–135.

Ulin, R. C. (1996). *Vintages and traditions: an ethnohistory of southwest French wine cooperatives.* Smithsonian Institution Press.

Unwin, T. (1991). *Wine and the vine: An historical geography of viticulture and the wine trade.* Routledge.

Vaughan, D. (1996). *The challenger launch decision.* University of Chicago Press.

Vaughan, D. (2004). Theorizing disaster: Analogy, historical ethnography, and the challenger accident. *Ethnography, 5*(3), 315–347.

Vaughan, D. (2021). *Dead reckoning: Air traffic control, system effects, and risk.* University of Chicago Press.

Veblen, T. (1899). *The theory of the leisure class.* MacMillan.

Ventresca, M. J., & Mohr, J. W. (2002). Archival research methods. In J. A. C. Baum (Ed.), *The Blackwell companion to organizations* (pp. 805–828). Blackwell Publishing Ltd.

Weber, K., Heinze, K. L., & DeSoucey, M. (2008). Forage for thought: Mobilizing codes in the movement for grass-fed meat and dairy products. *Administrative Science Quarterly, 53*(3), 529–567.

Weber, M. (1978). *Economy and society* (G. Roth & K. Wittich, Eds.). University of California Press.

Wooldridge, J. M. (2002). *Econometric analysis of cross section and panel data.* MIT Press.

Zipp, D. Y. (2021). Chinatowns lost? The birth and death of urban neighborhoods in an American city. *City & Community, 20*(4), 326–345.

Zuckerman, E. W. (1999). The categorical imperative: Securities analysts and the illegitimacy discount. *American Journal of Sociology, 104*(5), 1398–1438.

Society within Organizations:
Organizational Perspectives on Social
Integration and Marginalization

ORGANIZATIONS AS DRIVERS OF SOCIAL AND SYSTEMIC INTEGRATION: CONTRADICTION AND RECONCILIATION THROUGH LOOSE DEMOGRAPHIC COUPLING AND COMMUNITY ANCHORING

Krystal Laryea[a] and Christof Brandtner[b]

[a]Stanford University, USA
[b]EM Lyon Business School, France

ABSTRACT

Sociologists have long thought of the integration of people in communities – social integration – and hierarchical social systems – systemic integration – as contradictory goals. What strategies allow organizations to reconcile social and systemic integration? We examine this question through 40 in-depth, longitudinal interviews with leaders of nonprofit organizations that engage in the dual pursuit of social and systemic integration. Two processes reveal how the internal structure of organizations often mirrors the ways in which organizations are embedded in their local environments. When organizations engage in loose demographic coupling, *relegating those who "match" the community to the work of social integration, they produce internal inequalities and justify them by claiming community building as sacred work. When engaging in com-munity anchoring, organizations challenge internal and external inequalities*

Sociological Thinking in Contemporary Organizational Scholarship
Research in the Sociology of Organizations, Volume 90, 177–200
ISSN: 0733-558X/doi:10.1108/S0733-558X20240000090007

simultaneously, but this process comes with costs. Our findings contribute to a constructivist understanding of community, the mechanisms by which organizations produce inequalities, and a place-based conception of organizations as embedded in community.

Keywords: Sociology of organizations; community; social and systemic integration; goal conflicts; organizational inequality; race; nonprofits

INTRODUCTION

Since Tönnies' (1887) famous distinction between *Gemeinschaft* and *Gesellschaft*, sociologists have studied whether and how people can be integrated into *community* – interpersonal relationships of trust and mutual support – and *society* – complex systems such as healthcare, education, law, and the economy. Although both are essential for equitable development, scant research has investigated how organizations navigate the potential trade-offs of engaging in the production of social and systemic integration, respectively (Brandtner & Laryea, 2022; Marwell & McQuarrie, 2013). Understanding the processes by which people are simultaneously integrated into community and society is critical for addressing the persistent social and economic inequalities we face in contemporary societies. This tension is especially pronounced in global cities, which are often sites of extreme inequality but also sites that create unique social and economic opportunities.

Organizations play a crucial role in facilitating people's integration into community and society in cities, as sites and drivers of social action (Powell & Brandtner, 2016; see King, 2024, this volume). Nonprofit organizations, in particular, are often stylized as relieving the urban poor through the knitting of networks among community members and subsidized service provision (Marwell, 2007). Nonprofits and associational organizations such as churches, social service agencies, and recreational clubs have indeed long played a critical role in fostering community and connecting individuals to complex societal systems (Brandtner, 2022; Brandtner & Dunning, 2020; Small, 2009b). While nonprofits are traditionally theorized as complements or competitors to collective good provision through corporations in the public sector, there is increasing recognition that they play a unique role in driving community cohesion by fostering "institutional completeness" through informal social norms (Marwell & Morrissey, 2020; Sampson, 2012) and acting as "third places" and "social infrastructures" in which people commune together (Klinenberg, 2015; Oldenburg & Brissett, 1982; Brandtner, Douglas et al., 2023).

In this paper, we explore how urban nonprofit organizations strive to produce social *and* systemic integration for their members. Classic modernity theory assumes inherent tensions between community and society: as complex bureaucratic and technological systems have been built out to address individuals' basic needs, intimate, spatially proximate communities where resources are shared between friends and neighbors have attenuated (Giddens, 1991; see Schirmer, 2024, this volume; Wellman, 1979). These tensions shape day-to-day life in modern organizations. For example, pressures on nonprofits to extend their work beyond community building and focus on tractable, systemic impact introduces persistent paradox to the field (Clegg et al., 2002; Smith & Lewis, 2011). These pressures have emanated from institutional funders, including foundations and government agencies, that encourage nonprofits to articulate a formal theory of change; push toward measuring performance and impact on society; and suggest how to develop new, "integrated" sources of market income that allow nonprofit models to be scale beyond the local level (Mair et al., 2016; Mair & Seelos, 2017).

Yet we have limited knowledge of how organizations practically navigate the tensions between producing social and systemic integration, nor how the different practices they adopt may have complex consequences for the (re)production of inequalities (Amis et al., 2020; Marwell & Morrissey, 2020). On one hand, when nonprofits are run by and for the community, for instance, by pursuing collectivist-democratic goals, they may lack access to institutional resources that extend beyond the local community (Baggetta, 2016; Chen & Chen, 2021; Rothschild-Whitt, 1979). On the other hand, when nonprofits become more professionalized, expert knowledge and its highly credentialed carriers are often found outside of the communities that organizations serve (Eyal, 2013; Hwang & Powell, 2009; Suárez, 2010). The result may be a widening gap between the "white-washed" expertise of leaders and the "local" expertise of frontline workers (Kang et al., 2016). This gap highlights the importance of understanding how different and unequal professional groups relate to each other within organizations and when cross-occupational collaboration is most successful (Anteby et al., 2016; DiBenigno, 2018; DiBenigno & Kellogg, 2014).[1]

We focus on how the complex internal structures of organizations mirror the multiple ways in which organizations are embedded in their environments. Investigating organizations' inner workings is indispensable for understanding their integrative potential (Marquis & Battilana, 2009). This approach requires organization-level data on internal structures and practices as well as data on organizations' relationships to their urban environments. We collected such data through a survey and interviews with a representative sample of over 200 nonprofit organizations in the San Francisco Bay Area, an urban context marked by extreme economic inequality, due to limited government support (Laryea et al., 2022; Manduca, 2019), as well as extreme social inequality, given the long-standing racialized structures of American society (Bonilla-Silva, 2006). We first quantitatively identified organizations that display different levels of social and systemic integration. We then conducted and analyzed in-depth interviews with 40 leaders from 20 of these organizations to examine the relationship between the organization's internal personnel structures and the practices the organization pursues to achieve social and systemic integration.

Our analysis reveals that many organizations *do* simultaneously pursue social and systemic ends. However, they vary in how they go about reconciling these two orientations. In-depth interviews with leaders demonstrate that this association is often due to a process that we call *loose demographic coupling*: some members of the staff (often women and people of color) are relegated to community work, while the leadership team (often men and White) manage systemic goals. This strategy is problematic, because organizations reproduce inequalities within their organizations to challenge inequalities in their urban environments. A subset of organizations pursued a different strategy, challenging the assumed value of professional expertise and pushing for a *re-anchoring* in local communities and elevating community stakeholders above or alongside experts (Haß & Serrano-Velarde, 2015). These two orientations look similar in terms of organizational outcomes but are very different inside organizations in terms of who has power and voice. We describe both approaches using modal case examples in our findings.

Our paper makes three contributions. First, we contribute to a sociological understanding of a community, which is pregnant with meaning (Collins, 2010) and frequently racialized (Levine, 2017). Second, our paper furthers understanding of organizations as racialized entities that may reproduce inequality internally even as they aim to reduce inequality in their urban environments. Finally, we provide insights on how locally embedded organizations have the potential to both hinder and advance social and systemic integration in cities and communities (Marquis & Battilana, 2009).

THEORETICAL FRAMEWORK
Tensions Between Pursuing Social and Systemic Integration

The question of integration is a core concern in sociology: how are shared social worlds built across lines of difference? Tönnies (1887) first introduced the question in *Gemeinschaft and Gesellschaft* where he distinguishes community, which has "real organic life," from society, a "purely mechanical construction" (p. 17). Our conception of community is informed by communitarian theorists (Etzioni, 1996; Sandel, 1998; Taylor, 1989) who view people as communal beings and are skeptical of the modern liberal focus on individualism. As such, communitarian theorists have long understood community as "a goal to be achieved and a moral state to which we can aspire" (Levine, 2021, p. 17). Communal bonds bounded by such spaces as neighborhoods and cities afford social organization and are, resultantly, a resource for community members (Sampson, 2012). At the same time, Levine (2021) argues, community is a social construct with symbolic boundaries that can become the subject of political contestation (Collins, 2010). Our conception of society, on the other hand, aligns with a Weberian view that modern nation-states and cities are marked by complex bureaucratic, institutional systems that are often agnostic about interpersonal aspects of well-being. While we share the communitarian aim in finding ways to protect and promote valued forms of communities of place, memory, identity, and interest (Bell, 2006), such an aim is not mutually exclusive with a well-functioning society. Complex institutions often systemically disadvantage the poor and marginalized (Lara-Millan, 2021) and tend to foster bureaucratic mazes that are extremely difficult for individuals to navigate (Paik, 2021). But society can be (re)formed in ways that enable its institutions to advance equity, provide crucial resources, and ensure social order. Without systemic stability and rules of fairness, the community can devolve into despotic conditions or favoritism.

These conceptions align with Marwell and McQuarrie's (2013) distinction between organizations that primarily produce *social* integration and those that produce *systemic* integration by connecting communities to the complex system of society. *Social integration* is the work of fostering community. It is often based on face-to-face interaction and occurs in small group settings. Social integration can alleviate but also deepen, existing inequalities by fostering social capital, networks of social support and trust, and collective efficacy (Sampson, 2012; Small, 2004). At a basic level, organizations contribute to social integration by acting as holding spaces for individuals with shared interests or identities to come together. *Systemic integration* refers to "relations that connect people to one another through formal organizations, representative systems, information flows, economic production, or markets" (Marwell & McQuarrie, 2013, p. 130). According to Tönnies (1887), society consists of "separate *individuals* who *en masse* work on behalf of society in general, while appearing to work for themselves, and who are working for themselves while appearing to work for society" (p. 57). Organizations contribute to systemic integration by connecting their constituents to resources and complex systems – including social services, healthcare, education, politics, housing, and the economy.

We do not suggest that the integration into one, community or society, should take precedence over the other. Rather, we argue that a crucial aspect of addressing inequality in cities is ensuring that all people can experience both forms of integration. Organizations play a crucial role in producing both social and systemic integration (Marwell & McQuarrie, 2013). While many organizations may focus exclusively on one form of integration or the other, the capacity to produce both forms of integration may be especially valuable for serving marginalized populations and mitigating inequality through integration. Fig. 1 summarizes the potential of a single organization to generate either form or both forms of integration.

While many organizations do strive to foster hybrid forms of integration for their members and communities, developing the organizational capacity to simultaneously produce social and systemic integration is challenging, because these two forms of integration are linked to different organizational goals, practices, and forms of expertise (Brandtner & Laryea, 2022). Our analysis thus focuses on the upper right quadrant of Fig. 1. The purpose of our analysis is to examine how this dual pursuit is achieved. But first, we outline existing work that addresses how contradictory aims are pursued in organizational contexts and discuss how contradictory aims can foster the reproduction of internal inequalities among organizational members.

Conflicting Goals and the Production of Inequality Within Organizations

A large body of scholarship has considered how organizations manage conflicting goals (Cyert & March, 1963; DiBenigno, 2018; March & Simon, 1993; Pache & Santos, 2013). This work highlights that integration *within* organizations is an ongoing achievement (Bechky, 2011). As noted above, there is often a gap between

Fig. 1. Conceptual Framework of Dual Pursuit of Social and Systemic Integration.
Source: Adapted from Brandtner and Laryea (2022).

the expertise of leaders, who have training in management and social networks that connect them to other leaders in business, politics and philanthropy, and the expertise of frontline workers, who have deep knowledge of the local community and social networks that connect them to beneficiaries, volunteers, and community members (Brandtner & Laryea, 2022).

The divergence between these groups is not power-neutral. A large body of work in organizational sociology highlights the fact that organizations reproduce inequalities, both through their internal structures and through their effects on the broader institutional and geographic environments they are embedded within (Amis et al., 2020). Stainback et al. (2010, p. 226) argue that "organizations are the *primary* site of the production and allocation of inequality in modern societies" (emphasis ours).

A wide body of research documents how gender, race, and class differences are maintained and strengthened within organizations through macro-level inequality regimes, interlinked organizing processes that produce patterns of complex inequalities (Acker, 2006). She identifies the organizational practices, structures, and logics that contribute to gender inequality in the workplace (Acker, 1990; Correll et al., 2020; Ridgeway, 2011; see Piggott et al., 2024, this volume). Empirical research on race likewise highlights ongoing racial disparities (Carton & Rosette, 2011; Kang et al., 2016; Mithani & Mooney Murphy, 2017). Ray (2019, p. 27) argues that organizations are fundamentally racialized structures that "reproduce (and challenge) racialization processes." Finally, a large body of work demonstrates that class differences shape recruitment (Rivera & Tilcsik, 2016), hiring (Rivera, 2012, 2017), promotion (Bull & Scharff, 2017; Kish-Gephart & Campbell, 2015), and levels of compensation (Cobb, 2016).

Relative to these advances in understanding how macro-sociological inequalities are justified and reproduced in organizations, we know less about the meso-level processes that challenge inequalities and promote equity within organizations. Nonprofits are a particularly generative context to study these dynamics because they often aim to challenge and combat inequalities in their broader environment, but they are not immune to inequality regimes and racialization processes within their midst (Baggetta, 2016).

Recent work, for example, highlights the uneasy tensions of addressing inequalities in nonprofits and social movements. For example, Radoynovska (2018) theorizes discretion work as a mechanism that explains how service workers justify providing beneficiaries with unequal resources. Likewise, Reinecke (2018) examines the relationships between activists and homeless people in Occupy London, showing how "macrolevel inequalities that protestors set out to fight resurfaced in the day-to-day living of the camp itself." Finally, Levine (2017, 2021) highlights how the term "community" is often invoked by those with power (such as local politicians), which enables them to retain ultimate authority while seeming to empower neighborhood residents.

Contributing to this line of work, we argue that one of the meso-level mechanisms that reproduces social inequality in organizations is the management of conflicting goals, which often occurs through assigning divergent goals to organizational members with different forms of expertise. Recent theoretical progress has been made in understanding how goal conflicts are transcended: through superordinate identification with an overarching goal or identity (Besharov, 2014; Dutton et al., 1994), anchored personalization practices (DiBenigno, 2018), and dyadic toolkits that promote shared meanings and emotional scripts (DiBenigno & Kellogg, 2014). But these processes are often assumed to be race, gender, or class neutral, not attending to what identities gain the status of superordination identification, what practices are prioritized, and whose meanings are buried in the creation of dyadic toolkits (Ray, 2019). Moreover, such practices may reduce conflict but entrench inequality within organizations, leading to a thin celebration of collaboration across differences in ways that devalue discussions of continuing inequality (Douds, 2021).

We therefore suggest that the dual pursuit of social and systemic integration may come at the cost of internal *dis*-integration. Drawing on our empirical cases, we identify two processes through which the dual pursuit of social and systemic integration is achieved. The first is *loose demographic coupling,* which we define as a bifurcation within a staff team wherein frontline workers (who "match" beneficiaries in terms of demographic characteristics) are responsible for the work of social integration, while executive leaders (who "match" powerful systemic actors in terms of demographic characteristics) are responsible for the work of systemic integration. This seemingly neutral process reproduces internal racial and gender inequalities when there are significant differences in salary and decision-making power between these two groups, and especially when executive leaders benefit from the work of social integration that frontline workers carry out, while limiting opportunities for their advancement to positions of power and leadership.

This raises the question: how can organizations resist loose demographic coupling while still pursuing social and systemic goals? As Ray (2019) notes, organizations not only reproduce racialization processes – they also can challenge these processes. Yet little is known about how such challenging works in practice. Our empirical findings reveal a second approach that we call *community anchoring*, which we define as elevating leaders with street-level, community-based expertise to positions of authority that are equal to (or above) leaders with suite-level professional expertise (Laryea & Brandtner, 2022). We expect that this process is not without costs, in terms of how organizations are perceived in their broader environment (which is also racialized) as well as ongoing tensions within organizations that are not marked by a rigid decision-making hierarchy. Yet, these costs may be essential to bear if organizations are deeply committed to challenging social inequalities, which entails challenging inequalities in urban environments as well as among organizational members. In the findings to follow, we further unpack these two approaches to the dual pursuit of integration.

METHODS

Our data stem from a longitudinal research project that examines a representative sample of nonprofits in the San Francisco Bay Area in 2019 (completed in 2020 before the onset of the Covid-19 pandemic) to understand the organizational dimension of civic life in cities (Laryea et al., 2022). The project involves a comprehensive survey[2] and selected interviews with nonprofit leaders – typically executive directors or board presidents if the organization had no manager. The goal was to examine the practices and people involved in nonprofit organizations and their relationship to the places where they are located relative to other cities (Brandtner & Powell, 2022) and relative to research conducted in the same area using similar methods in 2004 and 2014 (Brandtner, Powell, et al., 2024; Hwang & Powell, 2009). To understand how organizations navigate the challenge of simultaneously pursuing social and systemic integration and how this plays out in day-to-day organizational life, the in-depth qualitative interviews with leaders were essential. Drawing on rich survey and interview data for 254 organizations, we engaged in theoretical sampling (Small, 2009b) to choose a set of organizational cases with whom we conducted firsthand interviews focused on how they relate to their communities and the organizational practices they utilize to pursue and produce integration.

We first developed quantitative measures for the pursuit of social and systemic integration, using an exploratory factor analysis, which allowed us to locate each organization in a two-dimensional space in terms of their social and systemic integration practices, respectively. The indicator is based on the extent to which the organization has adopted practices aimed to further community building, such as by strategically building trust among constituents, putting on recreational events, and interacting with constituents on a personal level, or to further individuals in the system, such as through informational events, formal advocacy, or collaborations with other organizations. We describe the measurement and validation of the qualitative indicators of social and systemic integration using survey data in detail in Brandtner and Laryea (2022). Based on these measures, Fig. 2 shows each organization's location on the two-dimensional space of social and systemic integration, with great variation with respect to two crucial organizational properties highlighted as the size and shade of the data point: the organization's size indicated by the total annual expenditures and the racial composition of its staff; we will return to these aspects later.

Based on the extent such practices were present in organizations, we then chose a subset of organizations to interview based on their pursuit of social integration, systemic integration, or both. For this paper, our emphasis lies on the latter category of organizations that combine practices related to social and systemic integration – our particular attention is again the top right quadrant of Fig. 2, identified as dual integration in Fig. 1. We sought to identify matched pairs, cases where organizations were doing similar kinds of work but diverged in terms of internal structures and practices, so we could assess variation in organizational approaches to pursuing both forms of integration without confounding differences in the types of programs they offer or clients they serve. Overall, we conducted 22 interviews with leaders of 20 organizations in 2020 (in a few cases, we interviewed more than one leader). For most organizations, previous team members had interviewed their leaders in 2004, and for a few, our team conducted intermediary interviews in 2014. While we focus on the interviews, we conducted

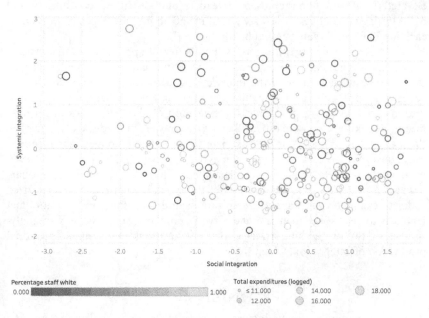

Fig. 2. Systemic and Social Integration by Racial Profile of Organization's Staff. *Source*: Authors.

firsthand in 2020 in the findings, the longitudinal dataset (40 interviews in total) enabled us to understand how these 20 organizations evolved over time.

Before conducting each interview, we read through the organization's 2019 surveys, their former 2004/2014 interviews, and researched information available through their website and other public sources. We used a general interview guide in all interviews but added additional contextual questions for each organization based on past interviews and survey data. The interviews were semi-structured, open-ended, and lasted between 60 and 90 minutes. All interviews were recorded and transcribed verbatim. In total, 22 interviews were conducted by either or both authors (primarily via Zoom), while the remaining 18 interviews were conducted by research team members in prior years.

Our analytic method was abductive in nature (Timmermans & Tavory, 2012, p. 169), which is a "a qualitative data analysis approach aimed at theory construction" that is gaining traction among qualitative sociologists due to its theory-generating capacity. Abductive analysis is a process of double-fitting data and theory by focusing on puzzles that arise in the data and pragmatic challenges that people face. In this case, we focused our analytic gaze on the practical challenge of pursuing social and systemic integration simultaneously and, specifically, on how leaders think about this challenge in relation to the structure and management of their staff teams. As we began interviewing leaders, it became clear that they had very different approaches to managing the tensions they experienced that came with the dual production of social and systemic integration. While some organizations clearly had racialized practices and approaches, others elevated local and underrepresented leaders and distrusted consultants and MBA-trained executives. A few sought to include both ideal types of workers at each level of their organizational hierarchy.

After categorizing organizations by these different approaches (and considering organizational change in approaches over time as staff and leaders turned over), we went back through the interviews to develop first- and second-order codes (e.g., axial coding) that highlighted the different internal processes organizations used as well as the leaders' justification of their processes (a form of meaning-making). We were especially attuned to when and how leaders invoked the idea of "community" as well as their efforts to build connections to politicians, business leaders, and philanthropies (e.g., "society"). The first author developed a coding scheme which was implemented with the help of an undergraduate research assistant (to ensure interrater reliability) and organized and categorized codes to examine trends across organizations and over time. Both authors met regularly to discuss key themes that emerged from the coding process. Our analysis revealed two overarching strategies that organizations used to manage the dual production of integration, which we outline below.

FINDINGS

Pursuing social and systemic integration simultaneously is challenging because it requires divergent strategies, relational networks, and expertise. We identify two processes by which this dual pursuit is carried out, which we term *loose demographic coupling* and *community anchoring*. We highlight how each approach works, as well as its implications for the relationship between social inequalities internal and external to the organization, by focusing on a subset of empirical cases that are representative of the trends we identified in our broader interview sample. As noted in the methods, all quotes come from interviews conducted in 2020 by the two authors, but our understanding of these cases is informed by our longitudinal analysis of each case.

Loose Demographic Coupling

In this section, we draw on two organizations that combine social and systemic integration to highlight the process of loose demographic coupling, wherein women and minorities are assigned to pursue social goals while leaders (who are typically male and White or Asian) focus on systemic goals. We also consider the implications of this process for reproducing and challenging inequalities.

Lonnie, an Asian American man, leads the Jones Center, an organization that provides for the needs of low-income families through early education and child-care, workforce development, and family support services. Their goals are primarily systemic – to support and empower poor families by offering critical resources at a reduced price. But given that a substantial portion of their work focuses on early childhood development, their work has an inherently social aspect, not unlike the daycare centers Small (2009a) studied. When we asked Lonnie about the demographics and backgrounds of his staff, he replied:

> I'd say that most people, probably 85% of our staff are women of color, maybe half immigrant. This may be the highest they're going to go, in some ways. The handful of professionals that we have – many have master's, so the 10% of people that are professionals here, we can have a little better living. But the staff, they are of the community or newer immigrants. This is not necessarily their perfect career, but some people have been with me for 30 plus years.

Lonnie suggests that for his frontline staff, the vast majority of whom are women of color, "this is the highest they are going to go." The comments are notable because, as the executive director, Lonnie makes decisions about career ladders. It is not given that his staff are "stuck" career wise, but rather the result of lack of internal pathways for frontline staff to become leaders, which is within Lonnie's power to develop and implement as the executive director.

He went on to say:

> I wouldn't recommend this to my daughter, the career that they have, because there's not necessarily a ladder up. We're the poorest cousin of the education system, K-12, college, unionized, better benefits, more time off. We are asked to do the most with the least amount of resources, especially in early childhood education.

Lonnie justifies the lack of a "ladder up" by highlighting their center's lower-tier position in the broader system that they are embedded within. Early childhood education may be an institutional field with limited resources in the United States, but the bifurcation between "professionals," who have master's degrees, and the staff, who he described as "of the community" is not a given. He did not explain why "professionals" deserved a higher wage than those who have been in the organization for 30 years.

Frontline staff play an essential role in fostering social integration. Lonnie described one of their childcare sites where:

> Sometimes we have grandmothers working for us, the mother's a teacher, and the child comes, maybe the great-grandchild comes to us now. It's the place to go because we're close, we're good, and we know people there. So that is kind of a community.

In short, the Jones Center's ability to produce social integration is not due to Lonnie or the executive team living in the neighborhoods they serve or connecting with neighbors, yet their work relies on these relationships being built. Ultimately, it is the (underpaid) mothers and grandmothers who are responsible for cultivating deep community relationships. While this fact will not surprise those who have long argued for a view of organizations as gendered and racialized entities, the justification that Lonnie offers is noteworthy: the staff are "of the community," and they themselves form "kind of a community" with beneficiaries. Community is lauded as an end that is valuable in itself. This aligns with Hill Collins' (2010, p. 7) argument that community "constitutes an elastic political construct that holds a variety of contradictory meanings" which we discuss more below.

The second case we highlight is an organization that runs after-school programs for disadvantaged youth ("Kids Club"). We spoke with their CEO, a former business executive who had been hired to expand the systemic dimension of the organization, primarily through cultivating new funding streams and attracting high net worth donors. Sam (White man) was explicit in his commentary on how he believes the dual pursuit of social and systemic integration depends on the bifurcation of two levels of staff:

> The executive team, myself and others, as we go out and try to raise funds and do things, I don't want to ever let the team that's focused on serving the youth, the team that's focused on actually interacting with young people speaking into their lives, helping them with their studies, helping them develop as leaders, all of our different priorities as an org, I don't want those people to focus on anything other than their work.

He went on to say, regarding the frontline staff:

> That's what they're gifted at. That's their role. They're trained in that. They're qualified for that. The kids connect with them. I don't think we should broaden their scope of expectations to where they're more worried about a pitch to Amazon to get a new grant than they are about Albert that's sitting in front of them who they need to mentor, right?

Sam frames this separation as positive; he doesn't want to burden the youth-focused team with anything other than "their work." Of course, most organizations are marked by a division of roles and responsibilities based on position. But what is notable about this division is that frontline staff do not get to participate in broader decision-making processes.

Further, this distinction aligns with racial and class differences. Sam said, in comparing on-the-ground staff to the executive team:

> You'd find that [staff in the clubs] have very different backgrounds, very different levels of proficiency in English or bilingual capabilities, very different education backgrounds, very different socioeconomic status, culture, ethnicities, everything.

Just as Lonnie was, Sam is explicit about the demographic division of the staff team, which has clear consequences for representation and voice in the organization. When we asked Sam how he thinks about issues of representation, he quickly replied: "Very humbly, especially as a privileged White male," but was unable to elaborate on any concrete ways that this recognition shaped the opportunities he created for staff to move into positions of power or any efforts to address internal inequalities within the organization.

In both these cases, leaders indicated surface-level awareness of positionality differences and the ways that their organizations are gendered and racialized. But they justified these divisions as essential for connecting with "the community." The divisions between frontline staff and leaders were not only positional, but they were also spatial. In both organizations, leadership teams worked at an office headquarters while frontline staff worked at community-based sites. This physical segregation of staff (and of leaders from beneficiaries) is a further indicator of demographic coupling in organizations that has implications for how different organizational members and stakeholders interact and form ties with one another (Small & Adler, 2019).

As Levine (2017, 2021) notes, those in power often evoke the notion of "community" as an abstract ideal, thus retaining ultimate authority while seeming to empower neighborhood residents. The two cases presented here highlight a parallel process wherein frontline staff are assumed to have an esteemed, even sacred role, of community building which justifies "protecting" them from the burden of participating in broader organizational decisions or taking on more lucrative positions that are reserved for professionals. Ultimately, loose demographic coupling is not solely attributable to executive directors. Another leader at Kids Club, who also applied to the CEO role, discussed with us how the board of directors chose Sam over him because of his fundraising potential and relational network, which included local politicians and the executives of large-tech firms.

Overall, these cases reveal how loose demographic coupling works and its consequences. The work of social integration is treated as separate from the work of systemic integration, which is manifest most clearly in the division of organizational members who are responsible for each form of integration. Frontline staff are responsible for the morally valorized work of community building and are seen as uniquely capable of carrying out this work because they "match" beneficiaries in terms of demographic characteristics. But frontline staff have less power, make less money, and have fewer opportunities for professional growth. When community building is kept distinct from systemic work, this produces professional precarity and internal social inequalities (Dunning, 2022), even as organizations see themselves as challenging inequality in their urban environments.

Community Anchoring

A subset of organizations in our sample developed an alternative approach to loose demographic coupling. What distinguished these organizations was their commitment to diversity in demographics and expertise *across* the organizational hierarchy. These organizations prioritized street-level expertise and rejected a division between frontline staff and leaders. For example, Greg, a White man leading a nonprofit that provides shelter and programs for homeless people, told us:

> This one of those organizations where you can crawl in through the front door on your hands and knees drunk and then retire 30 years later as the executive director. It's kind of an amazing, weird thing.

John, the Asian leader of a community center, discussed the importance of demographic diversity at all levels: "N2N is not led by Asian folks, it is mainly Brown and Black leadership." Micah, the director of a program for underrepresented college students and the only White person on staff, told us: "we don't hire anybody from the outside." When Micah retired in 2021, he chose David, a Black man on his staff team and first-generation college student, to be his successor.

Across organizations that adopted the community anchoring approach, there was strong resistance to bifurcating social and systemic goals. Staff at all levels of the organization were involved in both forms of integration: leaders fostered relationships with beneficiaries' alongside frontline staff, and frontline staff played a role in organizational decision-making. To highlight how this approach works, we focus primarily on two organizational cases: Hope Arts (a dance school in a historically Black, gentrifying neighborhood) and College4All (a nonprofit focused on educational equity and college access in a historically Latinx, gentrifying neighborhood).

Salome, a Black woman and the artistic director and former executive director of Hope Arts, explained to us how her organization has always prioritized being embedded in their local neighborhood:

> The school had been in the neighborhood for a long time .... It's *embedded*. And what our founder was good at was engaging the folks that were in the immediate neighborhood .... So her community spirit laid the ground for the way we could do this, and she never made it about money. Which – when she left after being there for nine years I was like, well, we've got to make it about money *somewhat*, because it must be financially sustainable for the people who are teaching.

In order to "make it about the money somewhat," Salome explained how she eventually gave the executive director position to her White development director, Rina, in order to be the artistic director. This change was not without challenges:

> When me and Rina flipped and she was my boss, I'm not going to lie, there were difficult moments about that. Our office, we were in a bullpen basically, with no dividers and no privacy. And she'd be going "oh my God, these files," and I would be like "can you come here for a second. Let's have a conversation." Violence prevention and conflict resolution, right? I was like "Do you see me sitting right here? I don't need all that. I know that I didn't do everything perfectly, but you need to just calm down." She was like, "oh, yeah, I feel you. I'm sorry."

This quote highlights that transcending loose demographic coupling requires significant relational work and distinct organizational practices, including spatial proximity of staff and an openness to conflict and tensions. Further, it shows that while Salome gave up the position of Executive Director, she did not lose her authority in the organization. At Hope Arts, the executive and artistic director positions both have equal authority as senior leadership roles but different responsibilities.

In short, Hope Arts has never had a predominantly White or male leadership team overseeing a multiracial team of (mostly women) dance teachers. Further, both social and systemic integration efforts and expertise are seen as essential to the organization. As Salome noted, "we've got to make it about money somewhat" – to pay teachers well. Rina had the fundraising skills and social network that allowed Hope to expand and grow. The ability to acquire resources – which, for nonprofits, involves building relationships with donors, philanthropies, and corporations – depends on cultural and social capital that is distinct from the kind of cultural and social capital needed to build trust in urban neighborhoods.

But even though there was clear recognition that Hope's organizational members have different forms of expertise that shape their roles, all members were spatially and relationally proximate. On the former, Salome said: "the secret sauce of an intimate organization is – all the admin team were in one office. The hard part was overhearing everybody's conversations. But the *great* part was overhearing everybody's conversations." When they moved to a larger building with separate offices, they worked hard to mitigate the risk of bifurcation: "we were proactive about creating systems, developing protocols of cc'ing each other on email. We meditate with each other. We check in before handling business in each meeting." Even when everyone does not in a single room, the leaders prioritized organizational practices that enabled open communication between organizational members with different roles, identities, and expertise.

A second organization, College4All, showed similar patterns in their efforts to integrate socially and systemically oriented staff. The organization's director Greg, a White man, told us:

> It's an intentional thought on our part to seem professional so that we can partner with individuals and corporations that we think can help support our community. But most of our students or our parents have different [online] portals. I feel like it's our job to do the code switching. We want to make sure that young people and parents are getting support, and so we want to make it as easy as possible to get people in to make that happen. And so we're going to help translate and be that go-between.

Likewise, in terms of staff dynamics, he said:

> There's a push and pull in terms of the professional or corporate culture, and what that looks like, as opposed to people doing this work because they're focused on the values and the social justice aspect of our work. That's one of our growing pains.

This tension, though, arose within each team, including the leadership team: "there's a couple of us that ran, and tend to be more grassroots, and then we've got people that are from corporate culture that are helping us to build our infrastructure so that we can continue to scale." As with Hope Arts, College4All has distinct "cultural strains," but these differences cut across the organizational hierarchy rather than aligning with organizational positions.

Community anchoring, like loose demographic coupling, has important implications. For example, Micah told us that his organization serving underrepresented college students "operates under the radar" where they are neither "a threat to the university" nor do they get "much recognition." He sees this as a strength, because they do not have to deal with "the shit and the politics." But operating under the radar may limit their ability to help marginalized student populations integrate into broader systems of university resources, networks, and opportunities.

Overall, our interviews suggest that community anchoring has positive effects on the organizational capacity to produce social integration and mixed effects on the organizational capacity to produce systemic integration. John, the director of Neighbor2Neighbor, explained that their community anchoring approach means that county officials turn to them as a trustworthy organization for the distribution of resources. During the pandemic, for example,

> The county said, "We need organizations that are good at distributing food to those who most need it, we don't want this to be the regular, 'we give millions of dollars, and then we get complaints from the community'. We *need* people not hungry."

But on the other hand, John also discussed his frustrations with the dominant practices associated with systemic integration and accruing resources from funders. On evaluation, he said:

> For us the most powerful thing – even though folks are getting more into results-based accountability – but for us, the most powerful way to share our work is through stories and anecdotes. And I just wish that folks would - instead of wanting aggregated numbers of the impact that we made, based on these surveys ... I'm not – I get research methods and all that, but it's just, I see the surveys after surveys, and I am just like, wow, you know, because that's not very trusting. Anyway, so I feel like stories you can, they're powerful, they're not only reliable, but they're also powerful.

In part because N2N resists professional practices and networking (which John associates with "networking"), they operate on a relatively small budget. Achieving scale often requires formal expertise and social connections to powerful actors in business, government, and philanthropy. Community anchoring is an approach that puts the local community first, not only in terms of the organization's priorities but also its internal structure. This approach can be costly, especially in terms of gaining external support and organizational growth but may be essential for holistically challenging inequalities – both in the broader urban environment and within an organization's own operations. A community anchoring approach typically involves embracing tensions as a fundamental aspect of organizational life and prioritized physical proximity of the entire team. Both practices can lead to inefficiencies that a more rigid division of labor could reduce. But organizational leaders saw this as a small price to pay compared to the benefits of cultivating more socially and economically integrated organizations.

By contrast, the organizations that adopted a demographic loose coupling approach prioritized organizational efficiency and productivity and typically kept leaders and frontline workers spatially as well as divisionally separated. This approach had benefits: organizations that adopted this approach tended to grow more quickly and accrue more resources to funnel into their programs, potentially enabling them to produce more social and systemic integration in their urban environments. But this comes at a high cost: the maintenance and reproduction of internal inequalities are justified by the pursuit of greater integration, especially systemic integration, in relation to broader urban environments.

Of course, these two processes are ideal types, and many organizations adopt approaches that combine elements of community anchoring and loose demographic coupling. As such, the two processes can be viewed as a continuum rather than a duality. That said, they are opposing in that they prioritize different values and goals: community anchoring prioritizes local community participation, representation, and internal integration and equity, while loose demographic coupling prioritizes expert participation, efficiency, productivity, and measurable impact. These distinct orientations and processes may be relevant in a wider array of organizational contexts, which we address in the discussion and avenues for future research.

DISCUSSION

Our primary goal in this paper has been to answer the question: how do organizations simultaneously pursue social and systemic integration? Through the production of social and systemic integration, organizations can challenge and counteract inequalities, especially in urban environments. But a key part of doing sociology in organizational studies is recognizing the ways that inequality in terms of macro-sociological categories such as race, gender, or class can simultaneously be produced *and* challenged in the day-to-day life of organizations (Amis et al., 2020; Baron & Bielby, 1980; Powell & Brandtner, 2016). Our findings suggest that organizational structures and processes, particularly in terms of how staff are tasked with managing conflicting goals, are one of the central ways in which organizations may reproduce inequalities – even as they seek to counteract them.

Our paper identifies two meso-level processes by which organizations dually pursue social and systemic integration, with different implications for how inequalities are reproduced or counteracted. Although organizations *do* manage to pursue contradictory integration goals, the resulting tensions underscore the long-standing sociological insight that organizations are racialized, gendered, and classed (Hirschman & Garbes, 2021; Ray, 2019; Ridgeway, 2014; Wooten, 2006). Our analysis sheds light on the complex, multifaceted ways through which demographics come into play within organizations that specifically aim to reduce inequality in their cities through the production of social and systemic integration. Internal inequalities can be legitimized by the external pursuit of equality. Further understanding when this happens in different kinds of organizations and institutional contexts is a critical avenue for future research.

We theorize one process that may be especially relevant in nonprofit and social movement contexts: *loose demographic coupling,* wherein organizational members who "match" beneficiaries are relegated to the work of social integration ("community building") and receive less compensation and are given less decision-making power. By contrast, those who "match" donors and powerful city actors are given positions on the executive team that are better compensated and come with more decision-making power. This process both underscores and extends Rivera's (2012) finding that cultural matching is one of the ways in which inequalities are reproduced in hiring processes. Boards of directors often chose leaders based on their cultural match with local elites – which often entails choosing leaders who are White and/or men with prestigious credentials but little to no understanding of the communities that their organizations serve. To be clear, loose demographic coupling did sometimes enable significant organizational growth and impact, highlighting the fact that individual organizations always operate in broader institutional fields that are themselves marked by persistent inequalities (Ray, 2019). Future work therefore ought to consider how changes among various field actors may shape pressures to pursue loose demographic coupling. For example, Barrett Cox (2021) examines how a philanthropic foundation sought to transfer grant-making decisions to a community-based board, theorizing the interactional practices they used to do so. More broadly, changes in who has grant-making decision power can have ripple effects on local organizations, disincentivizing loose demographic coupling. A broader consideration of how our argument links to theorizing on the (re)distribution of power in organizations is a promising area for future work. Finally, we note that loose demographic coupling is evident in organizations broadly, as the highest-paying positions of leadership in firms, schools, hospitals, and other fields are consistently held by men and Whites. That said, the justifications for these divisions will vary across institutional contexts. Notions of "community" and "meaningful work" are valorized in the nonprofit sector; understanding the "accounts" for loose demographic coupling across other organizational contexts is a crucial avenue for future research (Scott & Lyman, 1968).

We also theorize a second process that supports the dual pursuit of social and systemic integration, which we call *community anchoring*. Organizations that adopted this process intentionally resisted loose demographic coupling and placed leaders with community expertise at the top of the organizational hierarchy – typically alongside leaders with systemic expertise. This approach strives to foster interactions across the organizational hierarchy by prioritizing physical office layouts where staff members at all levels work together in the same building (Kellogg, 2009; Kornberger & Clegg, 2004) and often led to tensions within teams (such as the leadership team) where team members had different priorities and identities. Rather than seeing conflict as something to be avoided, a community anchoring approach typically involved embracing disagreement as a fundamental aspect of organizational life (DiBenigno, 2018). The implications of community anchoring were complex: acquiring systemic resources was more difficult but deep community relationships often led to a high degree of trust with local government officials, as the Neighbor2Neighbor case revealed. Theorizing community anchoring is a significant contribution of our paper, given that most existing work focuses on how inequalities are reproduced, rather than how they are challenged in contemporary organizations. An important avenue of future research is to understand why some organizations are able to pursue community anchoring and to better understand the potentially ambivalent implications this process has in terms of an organization's overall capacity to produce social and systemic integration. The presence of community anchoring in our nonprofit sample also suggests that there may be a broader cultural turn away from professional expertise, at least in some aspects of the nonprofit sector, which aligns with a broader turn toward self-styled experts (Sheehan, 2022) and resistance to elite institutions and knowledge (DeCoteau, 2021). More work is needed to determine whether community anchoring approaches will grow in prominence or remain a niche within overall professionalized spheres. But if we consider other trends, whether the rise of self-help expertise (Sheehan, 2022) or local parent groups that challenge broader medical institutions (DeCoteau, 2021), it seems plausible that we may see a shift away from professionalized nonprofits that resemble modern organizations (Bromley & Meyer, 2015) toward those that are more profoundly anchored in the community.

Our data on the racial composition of organizations' staff do not allow us to directly quantify and analyze what determines strategies for dual integration. Fig. 2 indicated that organizations in the mid-range of racial heterogeneity (indicating diverse staff) run the gamut in terms of their integrative strategies. Future work may compare different levels of management more directly to examine the effects of alignment or mismatch of social and systemic integration. Furthermore, we imagine that demographic characteristics of the neighborhood and city context in which organizations interact with their constituents would influence the extent to which these practices translate into desirable outcomes for organizations and their communities. Our paper offers a theoretical framework and some language for how to investigate the nexus of community affiliations within and outside of organizations, which we hope will lead to greater cross-over between organizational sociology and the sociology of social inequality, gender, and race.

We make two additional contributions. First, we contribute to a scholarship that examines "community" as a political construct (Collins, 2010). Levine (2017, 2021) highlights how the term "community" is invoked to obscure who has power in local contexts, where politicians often claim they are working on "behalf of the community" to advance their own interests. In our case, community is invoked in a different sense. Professional leaders of nonprofits, like Lonnie and Sam, told us how their (underpaid) frontline workers were engaged in the sacred, priceless work of engaging with the community, which was used to justify their lack of participation in broader organizational processes and decision-making. As Sam put it, "I don't want those people to focus on anything other than their work." Community is a multivocal term (Collins, 2010; Padgett & Ansel, 1993) – and participation in and the cultivation of local communities is often seen as deeply meaningful (Vaisey, 2007). But when marginalized organizational members are the ones relegated to community building and social integration, "community" proves thin, acting as a veneer for justifying the reproduction of inequality rather than a genuine pursuit to connect people across lines of difference. How notions of community are mobilized toward diverse (and potentially contradictory) ends is a process worthy of further analysis. In-depth ethnographic observations within organizations have the potential to provide much deeper insights on how this process works.

Finally, our examination of the dual pursuit of integration also contributes to a place-based view of organizations as embedded in their local community (Brandtner & Powell, 2022; Kim, 2021; Kim & Kim, 2021; Lawrence & Dover, 2015; Schneiberg et al., 2023). Organizational scholarship has long recognized that organizations have the potential to contribute to the integration of cities and communities, without distinguishing between different forms of integration

(Marquis & Battilana, 2009; Marwell & McQuarrie, 2013; McQuarrie & Marwell, 2009). Integration is, in fact, a pathway through which imaginative organizations are contributing to more democratic, collectivist futures (Chen & Chen, 2021). Our paper shows that many organizations strive to contribute to both social and systemic integration but not at the same rate. Further, internal dynamics highlight how social and systemic efforts are often bifurcated within organizations, which limit organizations' ability to advance the integration of those who are marginalized in relation to community and society. Loose demographic coupling can turn nonprofits into sources of new precarity for those low in the organizational status hierarchy (see Arnold & Foureault, 2024, this volume; Croidieu & Powell, 2024, this volume). Community anchoring can serve as a countermeasure against such status-based divisions. Our findings show how internal organizational structures can create new divisions if there is dissonance between these structures and the organizations' efforts to embed in their environment. But our findings also highlight the pragmatic and creative ways through which some organizations strive to produce internal and external integration and equity. Overall, our study underscores how social categories seep into organizations – both in terms of their personnel and structure – and shapes how organizations relate to their institutional environments and their ability to foster more equitable communities *and* societies.

NOTES

1. Scholars have noted this general trend. Dunning (2022) argues that the nonprofit workforce is bifurcated between service workers and knowledge workers, with little opportunity for the former to become the latter. While the sector aims to *address* inequality, it can also *produce* inequality. Understanding when and how nonprofits do and do not exacerbate existing inequalities in cities is the puzzle we aim to address.

2. Survey data collection occurred in 2018 and 2019, while follow-up interviews with leaders took place in 2020 and 2021. Typically, the executive director filled out the survey, though in some organizations another leader or the board president filled out the survey. The survey required approximately 25 minutes to fill out and included questions on staff, management and technological practices, finances, relationship to the community, collaborations and partnerships, advocacy, and other topics.

ACKNOWLEDGMENTS

We thank our colleagues at the Stanford Civic Life of Cities Lab for their fruitful collaboration and acknowledge generous research support by the Stanford Center on Philanthropy and Civil Society. We also thank the participants of the 2022 EGOS track on *Doing Sociology in Organization Studies*, the editors, and an anonymous reviewer for their helpful feedback. We gratefully acknowledge financial support from the CIFAR Azrieli Global Scholars program to make this volume openly accessible.

REFERENCES

Acker, J. (1990). Hierarchies, jobs, bodies: A theory of gendered organizations. *Gender & Society*, *4*(2), 139–158.

Acker, J. (2006). Inequality regimes: Gender, class, and race in organizations. *Gender & Society*, *20*(4), 441–464.

Amis, J. M., Mair, J., & Munir, K. A. (2020). The organizational reproduction of inequality. *Academy of Management Annals*, *14*(1), 195–230.

Anteby, M., Chan, C. K., & DiBenigno, J. (2016). Three lenses on occupations and professions in organizations: Becoming, doing, and relating. *Academy of Management Annals*, *1*, 183–244.

Arnold, N., & Foureault, F. (2024). Status in socio-environmental fields: relationships, evaluations, and otherhood. In S. Clegg, M. Grothe-Hammer, & K. Serrano Velarde (Eds.), *Sociological thinking in contemporary organizational scholarship* (Research in the Sociology of Organizations, Vol. 90, pp. 109–140). Emerald Publishing.

Baggetta, M. (2016). Representative bridging: Voluntary associations' potential for creating bridging ties in demographically diverse urban areas. *Nonprofit and Voluntary Sector Quarterly*, *45*(1S), 72S–94S.

Baron, J. N., & Bielby, W. T. (1980). Bringing the firms back in: Stratification, segmentation, and the organization of work. *American Sociological Review*, *45*(5), 737.

Barrett Cox, A. (2021). Powered down: The microfoundations of organizational attempts to redistribute power. *American Journal of Sociology*, *127*(2), 285–336.

Bechky, B. A. (2011). Making organizational theory work: Institutions, occupations, and negotiated orders. *Organization Science*, *22*(5), 1157–1167.

Bell, D. (Ed.). (2006). *Memory, trauma and world politics: Reflections on the relationship between past and present*. Springer.

Besharov, M. L. (2014). The relational ecology of identification: How organizational identification emerges when individuals hold divergent values. *Academy of Management Journal*, *57*(5), 1485–1512.

Bonilla-Silva, E. (2006). *Racism without racists: Color-blind racism and the persistence of racial inequality in the United States*. Rowman & Littlefield Publishers.

Brandtner, C. (2022). Green American city: Civic capacity and the distributed adoption of urban innovations. *American Journal of Sociology*, *128*(3), 627–679.

Brandtner, C., & Laryea, K. (2022). *Street smarts and org charts: Professional expertise and the pursuit of urban integration*. [Working Paper on SocArXiv]. https://osf.io/preprints/socarxiv/ve85b

Brandtner, C., Douglas, G. C., & Kornberger, M. (2023). Where relational commons take place: The city and its social infrastructure as sites of commoning. *Journal of Business Ethics*, *184*(4), 917–932.

Brandtner, C., & Dunning, C. (2020). *Nonprofits as urban infrastructure* (W. W. Powell & P. Bromley, Eds.). Stanford University Press.

Brandtner, C., & Laryea, K. (2022). *Street smarts and org charts: Professional expertise and the production of urban integration*. https://osf.io/preprints/socarxiv/ve85b/

Brandtner, C., & Powell, W. W. (2022). *Capturing the civic lives of cities: An organizational, place-based perspective on civil society in global cities*. Global Perspectives.

Brandtner, C., Powell, W. W., & Horvath, A. (2024). From iron cage to glass house: Repurposing of bureaucratic management and the turn to openness. *Organization Studies*, *45*(2), 193–221 .

Bromley, P., & Meyer, J. W. (2015). *Hyper-organization: Global organizational expansion*. Oxford University Press.

Bull, A., & Scharff, C. (2017). 'McDonald's Music' versus 'Serious Music': How production and consumption practices help to reproduce class inequality in the classical music profession. *Cultural Sociology*, *11*(3), 283–301.

Carton, A. M., & Rosette, A. S. (2011). Explaining bias against black leaders: Integrating theory on information processing and goal-based stereotyping. *Academy of Management Journal*, *54*(6), 1141–1158.

Chen, K. K., & Chen, V. (2021). (Vol. 72). *Organizational imaginaries: Tempering capitalism and tending to communities through cooperatives and collectivist democracy*. Emerald Group Publishing.

Clegg, S. R., Cunha, J. V., & Cunha, P. M. (2002). Management paradoxes: A relational view. *Human Relations*, *55*(5), 483–503.

Cobb, J. A. (2016). How firms shape income inequality: Stakeholder power, executive decision making, and the structuring of employment relationships. *Academy of Management Review*, *41*(2), 324–348.

Collins, P. H. (2010). The new politics of community. *American Sociological Review*, *75*(1), 7–30.

Correll, S. J., Weisshaar, K. R., Wynn, A. T., & Wehner, J. D. (2020). Inside the black box of organizational life: The gendered language of performance assessment. *American Sociological Review*, *85*(6), 1022–1050.

Croidieu, G., & Powell, W. W. (2024). Organizations as carriers of status and class dynamics: A historical ethnography of the emergence of Bordeaux's cork aristocracy. In S. Clegg, M. Grothe-Hammer, & K. Serrano Velarde (Eds.), *Sociological thinking in contemporary organizational scholarship* (Research in the Sociology of Organizations, Vol. 90, pp. 141–174). Emerald Publishing.

Cyert, R. M., & March, J. G. (1963). *Behavioral theory of the firm*. Wiley-Blackwell.

Decoteau, C. L. (2021). *The western disease: Contesting autism in the Somali diaspora*. University of Chicago Press.

DiBenigno, J. (2018). Anchored personalization in managing goal conflict between professional groups: The case of US Army mental health care. *Administrative Science Quarterly*, *63*(3), 526–569.

DiBenigno, J., & Kellogg, K. C. (2014). Beyond occupational differences: The importance of cross-cutting demographics and dyadic toolkits for collaboration in a U.S. hospital. *Administrative Science Quarterly*, *59*(3), 375–408.

Douds, K. W. (2021). The diversity contract: Constructing racial harmony in a diverse American suburb. *American Journal of Sociology*, *126*(6), 1347–1388.

Dunning, C. (2022). *Nonprofit neighborhoods: An urban history of inequality and the American state*. University of Chicago Press.

Dutton, J. E., Dukerich, J. M., & Harquail, C. V. (1994). Organizational images and member identification. *Administrative Science Quarterly*, *39*, 239–263.

Etzioni, A. (1996). A moderate communitarian proposal. *Political Theory*, *24*(2), 155–171.

Eyal, G. (2013). For a sociology of expertise: The social origins of the autism epidemic. *American Journal of Sociology*, *118*(4), 863–907.

Giddens, A. (1991). *Modernity and self-identity: Self and society in the late modern age*. Stanford University Press.

Haß, R., & Serrano-Velarde, K. (2015). When doing good becomes a state affair: Voluntary service in Germany. *VOLUNTAS: International Journal of Voluntary and Nonprofit Organizations*, *26*(5), 1718–1738.

Hirschman, D., & Garbes, L. (2021). Toward an economic sociology of race. *Socio-Economic Review*, *19*(3), 1171–1199.

Hwang, H., & Powell, W. W. (2009). The rationalization of charity: The influences of professionalism in the nonprofit sector. *Administrative Science Quarterly*, *54*(2), 268–298.

Kang, S. K., DeCelles, K. A., Tilcsik, A., & Jun, S. (2016). Whitened résumés: Race and self-presentation in the labor market. *Administrative Science Quarterly*, *61*(3), 469–502.

Kellogg, K. C. (2009). Operating room: Relational spaces and microinstitutional change in surgery. *American Journal of Sociology*, *115*(3), 657–711.

Kim, S. (2021). Frame restructuration: The making of an alternative business incubator amid Detroit's crisis. *Administrative Science Quarterly*, *66*(3), 753–805.

Kim, S., & Kim, A. (2021). Going viral or growing like an oak tree? Towards sustainable local development through entrepreneurship. *Academy of Management Journal*, *65*(5), 1709–1746.

King, B. G. (2024). Revitalizing organizational theory through a problem-oriented sociology. In S. Clegg, M. Grothe-Hammer, & K. Serrano Velarde (Eds.), *Sociological thinking in contemporary organizational scholarship* (Research in the Sociology of Organizations, Vol. 90, pp. 17–54). Emerald Publishing.

Kish-Gephart, J. J., & Campbell, J. T. (2015). You don't forget your roots: The influence of CEO social class background on strategic risk taking. *Academy of Management Journal*, *58*(6), 1614–1636.

Klinenberg, E. (2015). *Heat wave: A social autopsy of disaster in Chicago*. University of Chicago Press.

Kornberger, M., & Clegg, S. R. (2004). Bringing space back in: Organizing the generative building. *Organization Studies*, *25*(7), 1095–1114.

Lara-Millán, A. (2021). *Redistributing the poor: Jails, hospitals, and the crisis of law and fiscal austerity*. Oxford University Press.

Laryea, K., Zhao, Y., & Powell, W. W. (2022). San Francisco Bay area: A left Coast Metropolis Grapples with technocracy and inequality. *Global Perspectives*, *3*(1), 36212. https://doi.org/10.1525/gp.2022.36212.

Lawrence, T. B., & Dover, G. (2015). Place and institutional work: Creating housing for the hard-to-house. *Administrative Science Quarterly*, *60*(3), 371–410.

Levine, J. R. (2017). The paradox of community power: Cultural processes and elite authority in participatory governance. *Social Forces*, *95*(3), 1155–1179.

Levine, J. R. (2021). *Constructing community: Urban governance, development, and inequality in Boston.* Princeton University Press.

Mair, J., & Seelos, C. (2017). *Innovation and scaling for impact: How effective social enterprises do it.* Stanford University Press.

Mair, J., Wolf, M., & Seelos, C. (2016). Scaffolding: A process of transforming patterns of inequality in small-scale societies. *Academy of Management Journal*, *59*(6), 2021–2044.

Manduca, R. A. (2019). The contribution of national income inequality to regional economic divergence. *Social Forces*, *98*(2), 622–648.

March, J. G., & Simon, H. A. (1993). *Organizations*. John Wiley & Sons.

Marquis, C., & Battilana, J. (2009). Acting globally but thinking locally? The enduring influence of local communities on organizations. *Research in Organizational Behavior*, *29*, 283–302.

Marwell, N. P. (2007). *Bargaining for Brooklyn: Community organizations in the entrepreneurial city.* University of Chicago Press.

Marwell, N. P., & McQuarrie, M. (2013). People, place, and system: Organizations and the renewal of urban social theory. *The Annals of the American Academy of Political and Social Science*, *647*(1), 126–143.

Marwell, N. P., & Morrissey, S. L. (2020). Organizations and the governance of urban poverty. *Annual Review of Sociology*, *46*, 233–250.

McQuarrie, M., & Marwell, N. P. (2009). The missing organizational dimension in urban sociology. *City & Community*, *8*(3), 247–268.

Mithani, M. A., & Murphy, A. M. (2017). *It's not so Black and White after all: Black first name bias persists regardless of race and rank* (Vol. 2017, p. 16637). Academy of Management Briarcliff Manor.

Oldenburg, R., & Brissett, D. (1982). The third place. *Qualitative Sociology*, *5*(4), 265–284.

Pache, A.-C., & Santos, F. (2013). Inside the hybrid organization: Selective coupling as a response to competing institutional logics. *Academy of Management Journal*, *56*(4), 972–1001.

Padgett, J. F., & Ansell, C. K. (1993). Robust action and the rise of the medici, 1400-1434. *American Journal of Sociology*, *98*(6), 1259–1319.

Paik, L. (2021). *Trapped in a maze: How social control institutions drive family poverty and inequality.* University of California Press.

Piggott, L. V., Hovden, J., & Knoppers, A. (2024). Why organization studies should care more about gender exclusion and inclusion in sport organizations. In S. Clegg, M. Grothe-Hammer, & K. Serrano Velarde (Eds.), *Sociological thinking in contemporary organizational scholarship* (Research in the Sociology of Organizations, Vol. 90, pp. 271–286). Emerald Publishing.

Powell, W. W., & Brandtner, C. (2016). Organizations as sites and drivers of social action. In S. Abrutyn (Ed.), *Handbook of contemporary sociological theory* (pp. 269–291). Springer.

Radoynovska, N. M. (2018). Working within discretionary boundaries: Allocative rules, exceptions, and the micro-foundations of inequ(al)ity. *Organization Studies*, *39*(9), 1277–1298.

Ray, V. (2019). A theory of racialized organizations. *American Sociological Review*, *1*, 26–53.

Reinecke, J. (2018). Social movements and prefigurative organizing: Confronting entrenched inequalities in Occupy London. *Organization Studies*, *39*(9), 1299–1321.

Ridgeway, C. L. (2011). *Framed by gender: How gender inequality persists in the modern world.* Oxford University Press.

Ridgeway, C. L. (2014). Why status matters for inequality. *American Sociological Review*, *79*(1), 1–16.

Rivera, L. A. (2012). Hiring as cultural matching: The case of elite professional service firms. *American Sociological Review*, *77*(6), 999–1022.

Rivera, L. A. (2017). When two bodies are (not) a problem: Gender and relationship status discrimination in academic hiring. *American Sociological Review*, *82*(6), 1111–1138.

Rivera, L. A., & Tilcsik, A. (2016). Class advantage, commitment penalty: The gendered effect of social class signals in an elite labor market. *American Sociological Review*, *81*(6), 1097–1131.

Rothschild-Whitt, J. (1979). The collectivist organization: An alternative to rational-bureaucratic models. *American Sociological Review*, *44*(4), 509–527.

Sampson, R. J. (2012). *Great American city: Chicago and the enduring neighborhood effect*. University of Chicago Press.

Sandel, M. (1998). *Liberalism and the limits of justice*. Cambridge University Press.

Schirmer, W. (2024). Organization systems and their social environments: The role of functionally differentiated society and face-to-face interaction rituals. In S. Clegg, M. Grothe-Hammer, & K. Serrano Velarde (Eds.), *Sociological thinking in contemporary organizational scholarship* (Research in the Sociology of Organizations, Vol. 90, pp. 287–308). Emerald Publishing.

Schneiberg, M., Goldstein, A., & Kraatz, M. S. (2023). Embracing market liberalism? Community structure, embeddedness, and mutual savings and loan conversions to stock corporations. *American Sociological Review, 88*(1), 53–85.

Scott, M. B., & Lyman, S. M. (1968). Accounts. *American Sociological Review, 33*(1), 46–62.

Sheehan, P. (2022). The paradox of self-help expertise: How unemployed workers become professional career coaches. *American Journal of Sociology, 127*(4), 1151–1182.

Small, M. L. (2004). *Villa Victoria: The transformation of social capital in a Boston barrio*. University of Chicago Press.

Small, M. L. (2009a). How many cases do I need?' On science and the logic of case selection in field-based research. *Ethnography, 10*(1), 5–38.

Small, M. L. (2009b). *Unanticipated gains: Origins of network inequality in everyday life*. Oxford University Press.

Small, M. L., & Adler, L. (2019). The role of space in the formation of social ties. *Annual Review of Sociology, 45*, 111–132.

Smith, W. K., & Lewis, M. W. (2011). Toward a theory of paradox: A dynamic equilibrium model of organizing. *Academy of Management Review, 36*(2), 381–403.

Stainback, K., Tomaskovic-Devey, D., & Skaggs, S. (2010). Organizational approaches to inequality: Inertia, relative power, and environments. *Annual Review of Sociology, 36*, 225–247.

Suárez, D. F. (2010). Street credentials and management backgrounds: Careers of nonprofit executives in an evolving sector. *Nonprofit and Voluntary Sector Quarterly, 39*(4), 696–716.

Taylor, V. (1989). Social movement continuity: The women's movement in abeyance. *American Sociological Review, 54*(5), 761–775.

Timmermans, S., & Tavory, I. (2012). Theory construction in qualitative research: From grounded theory to abductive analysis. *Sociological Theory, 30*(3), 167–186.

Tönnies, F. (1887). *Gemeinschaft Und Gesellschaft: Abhandlung Des Communismus Und Des Socialismus Als Empirischer Culturformen*. Fues.

Vaisey, S. (2007). Structure, culture, and community: The search for belonging in 50 urban communes. *American Sociological Review, 72*(6), 851–873.

Wellman, B. (1979). The community question: The intimate networks of East Yorkers. *American Journal of Sociology, 84*(5), 1201–1231.

Wooten, M. E. (2006). Soapbox: Race and strategic organization. *Strategic Organization, 4*(2), 191–199.

WHY ORGANIZATION STUDIES SHOULD CARE MORE ABOUT GENDER EXCLUSION AND INCLUSION IN SPORT ORGANIZATIONS

Lucy V. Piggott[a], Jorid Hovden[a] and Annelies Knoppers[b]

[a]Norwegian University of Science and Technology, Norway
[b]Utrecht University, The Netherlands

ABSTRACT

Sport organizations hold substantial ideological power to showcase and reinforce dominant cultural ideas about gender. The organization and portrayal of sporting events and spaces continue to promote and reinforce a hierarchical gender binary where heroic forms of masculinity are both desired and privileged. Such publicly visible gender hierarchies contribute to the doing of gender beyond sport itself, extending to influence gender power relations within sport and non-sport organizations. Yet, there has been a relative absence of scholarship on sport organizations within the organizational sociology field. In this paper, we review findings of studies that look at how formal and informal organizational dimensions influence the doing and undoing of gender in sport organizations. Subsequently, we call for scholars to pay more attention to sport itself as a source of gendered organizational practices within both sport and

Sociological Thinking in Contemporary Organizational Scholarship
Research in the Sociology of Organizations, Volume 90, 201–226
ISSN: 0733-558X/doi:10.1108/S0733-558X20240000090008

non-sport organizations. We end with suggestions for research that empirically explores this linkage by focusing on innovative theoretical perspectives that could provide new insights on gender inclusion in organizations.

Keywords: Sport organizations; doing and undoing gender; gender binary; formal and informal organizational dimensions; conceptual paper

INTRODUCTION

The influence and power of modern sport organizations in Western societies are both multifaceted and complex, and sport organizations hold the potential to create social transformations beyond the sporting sphere (Bergsgaard, 2005; Coakley & Pike, 2014; Elling et al., 2019). Such potential stems from their immense geographical and social dissemination, which globally bonds together nations, regions, and local societies across divides of class, gender, sexuality, and race. Sport organizations reflect and showcase dominant societal values, cultures, and imageries that are publicly celebrated and contested (Bairner & Han, 2022). Thus, sporting events can act as symbols of, and models for, dominant cultural ideas about gender, such as the "true nature" of men and women (Adjepong, 2019). Resultantly, sport organizations possess ideological power to influence how gender is "done," "undone," and "redone" both within sport and wider society (Rahbari et al., 2019). For example, the history of sport organizations as male-dominated spaces has led to the resistance and exclusion of women from sport participation, politics, and governance (Coakley & Pike, 2014; Elling et al., 2019; Hargreaves, 1994). Despite advances in gender inclusion among athletes (48% of the athletes that competed at Tokyo 2020 were women; IOC, 2019), women are still grossly underrepresented in sport leadership and governance positions at all levels and across all corners of the globe (Adriaanse, 2019; Matthews & Piggott, 2021). Specifically, globally, men continue to form a significant majority of coaches, athletic/club directors, sport managers, board members, and the like. There remains a persistent trend: the higher the level, the fewer women.

The existing feminist body of research on sport organizations, as reviewed by Burton (2015) and Evans and Pfister (2021), has explored how many men continue to be privileged within male-dominated leadership structures. Theories frequently used to explain the underrepresentation and undervaluing of women include those that focus on human capital, agency, gender difference/essentialism, patriarchy, positional power, critical mass, and organizational structure (Burton, 2015; Evans & Pfister, 2021; Kanter, 1977; Reddy & Jadhav, 2019). Acker (1990), in her theory on gender and organizations, has argued that the primary (formal and informal) activities of an organization shape how gender is done within that organization. Resultantly, a distinct stream of research has developed on both sport and non-sport organizations that has sought to understand how organizational factors shape board gender composition (Evans & Pfister, 2021; Kirsch, 2018). In doing so, scholars (e.g., Bridges et al., 2022; Bridges et al., 2020; Sogn, 2023) have argued that gender is done, undone, and redone through an association between organizational activities and dominant practices associated with (hetero-sexual) masculinities. We describe and explain some of these practices throughout this paper.

Since sport occurs in mediated and public spaces, the visibility of women ath-letes, especially on the world stage, has contributed to undoing a long-held gen-dered belief that women are physically weak (Hargreaves, 1994). Simultaneously, the organization and portrayal of this public space continues to promote and rein-force a hierarchical gendered binary where heroic forms of masculinity are both desired and privileged. Women athletes may be seen as competent and strong, but men are constructed as *more* competent and *stronger* (Ryan & Dickson, 2018). This public visibility, moreover, contributes to the doing of gender beyond sport itself and underlines the need to pay attention to how gendered public discourse in sport and the resources devoted to it, influence the gendering of both sport and non-sport organizations.

In this paper, we attempt to address this in several ways. We first use a socio-logical lens to review findings of studies that look at how formal and informal organizational dimensions influence the doing and undoing of gender in sport organizations. Subsequently, based on the increasing global significance of institu-tionalized sport, we call for scholars to pay more attention to sport itself as a source of gendered organizational practices within both sport and non-sport organiza-tions. For example, we argue that the linkage between sport and constructions of desirable masculinity may also infiltrate conceptualizations of desirable leaders in non-sport organizations and shape gender ratios in positions of leadership in these organizations. This goes some way in answering calls within organizational scholarship to shift attention away from the most common theoretical paradigms and instead focus on more innovative perspectives that could provide new insights on gender inclusion in organizations (Joshi et al., 2015; Rao & Donaldson, 2015; Warren et al., 2019). We end with suggestions for research that empirically explores this linkage.

We contribute to the aim of this volume to explore the new boundaries of organizational sociology in several ways. First, there has been a relative absence of scholarship on sport organizations within the organizational sociology field, despite the powerful social influence of sport organizations on societal practices, as previously indicated. We therefore deem our paper to be an important con-tribution to limited scholarship on this topic within the field of organizational studies. Second, despite other papers having an inclusion or secondary gender focus (e.g., see Papers 6 and 9, this volume), our paper is the only contribution within this volume with a central gender focus. We believe that any organizational sociology issue or scholarly volume should minimally include several contribu-tions that centralize gender since much of the gender inequity that exists in indus-trial societies is created and reproduced within organizational settings through the daily activities of working and organizing work (Acker, 2006). Finally, while conceptual papers and literature reviews already exist on gender inclusion within sport organizations, few of these contributions have a central focus on the role of social theory and on the implications for non-sport organizations. Therefore, in this paper, we hope to contribute to deepening understanding within this sub-field by bringing a novel contribution to a growing body of (sport) organizational research, and the ways gender is done, undone, and at times redone, in organizations (Knoppers & Spaaij, 2021; Pape, 2020; Piggott, 2021).

DOING AND UNDOING GENDER

The conceptualization of gender as something that is "fluid, dynamic and as something that has to be done" has increasingly gained popularity within organizational research (Kelan, 2010, p. 174). "Doing gender" is a term developed by West and Zimmerman (1987) to conceptualize gender as a social product of doing, as an activity or practice that is part of interactions, rather than as a set of traits or roles. Butler (1990) further posits that "gender is always a doing" (p. 25). Organizations are particularly potent sites for doing gender as organizational practices can produce and reproduce gender in a way that positions men as "naturally" more competent and suitable for status roles, such as managerial, sport leadership, or coaching positions (Claringbould & Knoppers, 2012; Kvande, 2007). Additionally, occupations constructed as masculine are perceived to require skills and qualities that men supposedly possess and women supposedly lack (Ely & Meyerson, 2010). This essentialist masculine occupational identity is further reinforced by the numerical dominance of men within these occupations. The invisible nature of such gendered status hierarchies can often mask the mechanisms that reinforce and sustain them (Claringbould & Knoppers, 2012).

"Undoing gender" is a concept that was introduced by Butler (2004) and developed by Deutsch (2007) out of dissatisfaction with the one-dimensional nature of doing gender. It refers to social practices and interactions that reduce gender differences and produce change toward gender inclusion. An increasing body of work is exploring how undoing gendered practices within organizations can help to move toward greater gender equity (e.g., Benshop & Verloo, 2011; Claringbould & Knoppers, 2008; Ely & Meyerson, 2010; Kelan, 2018). A further body of work also points to ways that gender can be undone and subsequently redone. For example, Claringbould and Van Liere (2019) revealed how sport boards of governance that had actively recruited women to balance the gender ratio no longer engaged in this policy once the presence of an equal number of women and men indicated gender had been undone. When women left these boards, they tended to be replaced by a male, and thus gender was redone. Messner and Bozada-Deas (2009) also found that gender was undone when both women and men were encouraged and recruited to be leaders in youth sport organizations. Gender was redone, however, because women were implicitly found to be most suitable for supportive roles while men ended up being most of the coaches. Thus, although both women and men volunteered to be leaders, occupational segregation still occurred along traditional gendered lines.

Gender is done, undone, and redone within all organizations across both formal and informal organizational dimensions. Korvajärvi (2002) provides a helpful distinction between the two. First, formal dimensions include ways of organizing work, formal job requirements, job descriptions, and organizational structures and hierarchies. An important element of formal dimensions is that they can always be documented or textualized, such as written rules, organograms, job titles, and statistics, as well as logos or uniforms (Korvajärvi, 2002). Conversely, informal organizational dimensions are more nuanced and include interactions, symbols, and attitudes. Such practices are not easily documented and often lack visibility (Korvajärvi, 2002). Within the next section, we draw on the concepts of doing and undoing gender across formal and informal organizational dimensions to provide a deeper understanding of how organizational practices and processes contribute to (a lack of) gender inclusion in sport organizations.

DOING AND UNDOING GENDER IN SPORT ORGANIZATIONS

Formal Organizational Dimensions and Doing Gender

Formal organizational dimensions contribute to doing gender by organizational rules and actions privileging men and masculinity within internal organizational structures, such as leadership and governance hierarchies. A structural dimension that is both a *symptom* and *cause* of doing gender is vertical gender segregation. A common finding across sport organizations (as well as non-sport organizations) is that the more senior or influential the role or space within an organization, the fewer the women (e.g., Adriaanse, 2019; Cabrera-Fernández et al., 2015; Clayton-Hathway, 2022; Halliday et al., 2021; Kirsch, 2018; Litchfield, 2015; Melton & Bryant, 2017; Preston & Velija, 2022; Simpkins et al., 2022; Wilson et al., 2017). This works to do gender by reproducing perceptions that men belong in (sport) leadership roles, while the presence of women is positioned as the exception rather than the norm (Deutsch, 2007). This vertical gender segregation within sport organizations has been conceptualized in different ways. For example, Wilson et al. (2017) drew on Low and Iverson's (2016) work on socially just public spaces to position the lack of women in decision-making spaces within Australian rules football organizations as a form of procedural injustice. Procedural justice is concerned with "the ways in which decisions about public spaces are made" and the extent to which such spaces are "the object of genuinely democratic and inclusive public debate" (Low & Iverson, 2016, p. 21). Wilson et al. (2017) argue that the exclusion of women/women's agendas from Australian Football League decision-making spaces can result in women being "'locked out' of decision making that goes on behind closed doors" (p. 1710). This results in unjust processes that do gender by contributing to a wider climate of unjust organizational politics of gender exclusion both inside and outside of the boardroom (Low & Iverson, 2016).

Adriaanse (2019) analyzed such politics of exclusion by drawing on Kanter's (1977) critical mass theory to discuss how uneven gender ratios across the boards of European national sport federations (NSFs) shape organizational conditions. She argued that the lack of a critical mass (30%) of women across boards indicates that sport organizational cultures will remain male dominated and that prospects for women to undo gender via cultural change are limited. Research continues to find that a critical mass of women is needed on boards for women to influence the culture of an organization, both within and beyond sport (e.g., Hovden, 2016; Joecks et al., 2013; Konrad et al., 2008; Kramer et al., 2006). Yet, critical mass theory has also received critique within the wider organizational literature for its lack of insight on whether an increased proportion of women leaders works to undo gender by disrupting dominant board culture and positively influencing change toward greater gender equity within organizations (Childs & Krook, 2008). Board members may, for example, be selected on the basis of perceived fit with the dominant board culture. Thus, a critical mass of women on a board may not necessarily mean a change in gendered policies or that women members will be supportive of each other.

The lack of opportunity to undo gender by changing board culture as a result of compositional change is further reflected in Preston and Velija's (2022) study. They drew on Rao et al.'s (1999) concept of exclusionary power to discuss how men overwhelmingly hold "positional power" within the English Football Association (The FA) by dominating decision-making positions. The minority of women who did hold positional power felt fearful of having their knowledge and competence questioned due to their hypervisibility as isolated women leaders. Preston and Velija concluded that, within such gender imbalanced organizational structures, positional power among women leaders often fails to translate into having a voice or power to make decisions. This finding highlights how it is not only the gender composition of organizational roles that does gender but also that gendered status hierarchies within organizational decision-making bodies continue to empower men more than women as decision-makers. This was further discussed by Hedenborg and Norberg (2019), who drew on Acker's (1992) work on gendered institutions. They conceptualize the underrepresentation of women leaders on Swedish sport boards as a gendered production of power in favor of men that results from the production of gender division. That is, gendered perceptions, symbols, and images result in notions about leadership that lack gender neutrality and justify (consciously or subconsciously) gender divisions that continue to privilege many men (Acker, 1992).

An increasing number of scholars have addressed vertical gender segregation from an intersectional lens, highlighting how marginalizing practices in sport organizations have a more profound impact on some women over others depending on their intersecting identities. That is, doing gender has different meanings for different people across different organizational situations and contexts. This aligns with a growing body of non-sport scholarship that considers "the various ways in which multiple social categories intersect to shape outcomes for women in the workplace" (Rosette et al., 2018, p. 1). Yet, academic discussions on the opportunities and experiences of women sport leaders have overwhelmingly been framed around the experiences of White women doing gender within sport organizations. For example, women have been traditionally portrayed as docile, communal, and supportive, which often ignores the experiences of Black women doing gender within sport organizations that are also defined by racial ideology and accompanying stereotypes, such as that Black women are loud, aggressive, and independent (Simpkins et al., 2022).

Both Simpkins et al. (2022) and Melton and Bryant (2017) found that there is a severe underrepresentation of Black women within US sport organizations. Melton and Bryant (2017) revealed that there were just two women of color that held the position of president or CEO of teams in the Women's National Basketball Association at the time of writing, despite women of color making up a large proportion of players in the league. Additionally, Simpkins et al. (2022) applied the Sport Intersecting Model of Power (SIMP; Simpkins, 2019) to examine how a person's positionality can play a critical role in the amount and type of access that an individual has to power and privilege. These scholars found that vertical racialized gender segregation resulted in Black women sport leaders experiencing "outsider within status" (Hill Collins, 1986). That is, although the women themselves occupied leadership positions, and so were "inside" the top rung of the organizational hierarchy, they were constantly aware of being Black because they were often the only Black women present in these organizational spaces. Resultantly, their outsider status was even more visible compared to their White female counterparts, and so the doing of gender (and Whiteness) within sport organizations resulted in both men and White women being positioned as "naturally" more competent for positions of authority. Research on managers/leaders in non-sport organizations shows similar results (e.g., Bloch et al., 2021). Ironically, the notable presence of women of color in elite sport means that a pool of knowledgeable women is available for work in sport organizations. This pool does not, however, translate into more women of color occupying positions of leadership in sport organizations compared to non-sport organizations (Bernard et al., 2021; Dadswell et al., 2022; Miller, 2021).

A range of formal organizational dimensions have been found to *contribute* to continued vertical (racialized) gender segregation within sport organizations and ultimately to the doing of gender. For example, Karacam and Koca (2019) discussed the gendered influence of formal rules within Turkish sport governance. One such rule was that presidential candidates of NSFs were required to make a non-refundable donation of €40,000 to the NSF prior to an election. Drawing on Bourdieu's concept of economic capital, they argued that such institutional practices disproportionly benefit a small number of highly privileged men who have access to considerable amounts of economic capital. Due to gender unequal economic conditions within wider Turkish society, these formal organizational practices have resulted in the vast majority of presidency and board positions of Turkish NSFs being occupied by businessmen whose suitability has become normalized within sport leadership roles. Similarly, Piggott and Matthews (2021) drew on Bourdieu's concepts of capital, habitus, and field to discuss how formal processes within English national governing bodies (NGBs) of sport contribute to doing and undoing gender. They found that formal processes acted as conservation strategies to maintain male dominance in organizational leadership and governance hierarchies in terms of both representation and recognition. This included a gendered election rule that guaranteed more elected men than women on the board, and a merger between a men's and a women's NGB that resulted in women becoming peripheralized and lacking autonomy in the newly merged organization. These examples are specific to the formal policies and structures of individual sport organizations but are also symptomatic of a wider critique of how the traditional governance structures and rules of sport organizations make them particularly susceptible to poor practice, corruption, and unethical leadership (Tomlinson, 2014).

Scholars have also discussed the challenge of the *lack* of formal action or policy that attempts to undo gender. For example, Litchfield (2015) found that no policy existed across Australian recreational hockey clubs to ensure that men and women were afforded the same opportunities to engage in decision-making practices. This meant that even when women at the clubs recognized unequal practices, no complaint procedure was available to express concerns. Drawing on Connell and Messerschmidt's (2005) theory of gender relations, Litchfield (2015) argued that this lack of policy, combined with other factors, produces organizational cultures where women are systematically disenfranchised from power structures. Additionally, Norman et al. (2018) discussed the lack of strategic leadership within The FA to identify and provide opportunities for career progression for underrepresented women football coaches and coach developers. Drawing on Schein's theory of organizational culture, the authors identified a disconnect between espoused (championed) values within the FA and actual practice on the ground. This led informants to feel that they were on the "cliff edge" after gaining tutoring qualifications due to fewer job opportunities compared to men. The existence of glass ceilings that need to be shattered or glass cliffs that occur when women are hired for precarious positions is common for women managers in both sport and non-sport organizations (Ahn & Cunningham, 2020; Groeneveld et al., 2020).

A range of scholars have explored formal *implications* of gendered power structures, beyond vertical gender segregation, because of formal organizational dimensions doing gender. For example, Preston and Velija (2022) discussed how a lack of "positional power" among women in The FA resulted in men dominating "agenda setting power." This led to agenda items in decision-making spaces (e.g., board or leadership meetings) often being dominated by matters related to the men's game. This demonstrates how male-dominated leadership can influence the doing of gender within other areas of the organization outside of leadership spaces and matters. Furthermore, Velija (2022) developed a sociological analysis of the gender pay gap in UK sport organizations, finding that male dominance across many sport organizations resulted in men being paid more, on average, than women. The highest disparity in gender pay was across organizations where professional sport is commercialized relating to male performance (with an average gender pay gap of 59.1% in 2018–2019 across such organizations). Drawing on figurational theory, Velija discussed how gender pay gap reporting highlights differences in power relations between groups but also develops higher levels of mutual understanding as organizations are, at least to some extent, forced to consider how the gender pay gap affects female employees. Velija argued that, while the reporting of gender pay gap data may reflect a process of equalization (undoing gender), the results highlight ongoing inequalities that continue to exist despite an expectation that the gender pay gap should be reduced. This demonstrates how doing gender is most strongly reinforced within organizations most aligned with competitive male sport and in turn heroic masculinity.

Formal Organizational Dimensions and Undoing Gender

As well as formal organizational dimensions contributing to doing gender, they also have the potential to undo gender when organizations are committed to increasing the representation, remuneration, and valuing of women leaders. Such structural changes work to undo gender by "promot[ing] changes at the interactional level by undermining the perception that women are less competent in the domains that matter" (Deutsch, 2007, p. 118). Within sport organizations, this includes the implementation of structural strategies and actions such as the use of gender quotas, targets, and gender pay gap reporting (Fasting & Sisjord, 2019; Hovden, 2016; Jakubowska, 2019; Piggott, 2022; Velija, 2022) and more cultural means such as diversity steering groups and action plans (Clayton-Hathway, 2022), equity training (Norman, 2016), and formal mentoring schemes (Clayton-Hathway, 2022; Norman et al., 2018). The implementation of such formal organizational strategies and actions largely reflects those that have been introduced within non-sport organizations, which have led organizational scholars to dedicate "massive efforts towards understanding ... the appropriate actions and policies to advance women's equality" (Belingheri et al., 2021, p. 2; Cabrera-Fernández et al., 2015).

Within the sporting context, drawing on Schein's theory of organizational culture, Norman et al. (2018) discussed how the development of quality workplace relations through formal mentoring schemes at The FA went beyond an "espoused philosophy" toward practices that are undoing gender through women experiencing a sense of belonging and being valued within the workplace. Additionally, Velija (2022) drew on figurational analyses of shame and embarrassment to highlight the potential of gender pay gap reporting as a form of social control over sport organizations to challenge ongoing gender inequalities. That is, the interactive and social dimension of shame as a collective phenomenon can influence those not following gender equity expectations to commit to more equal labor patterns and, in turn, positively influence gender inclusion.

A commitment to undoing gender via more equal labor patterns was also discussed by Clayton-Hathway (2022), who drew on an institutional theory perspective to highlight the important role of the British Horse Racing Authority in establishing norms of valuing inclusion and diversity across the entire horse-racing industry. Such norms were established through the implementation of formal top-down rules and practices. This included the development of a Diversity in Racing Steering Group and a Diversity in Racing Action Plan that incorporated a 30% minimum target for female representation on horse-racing boards. Clayton-Hathway (2022) argued that the legitimization of gender inclusion as a serious issue for horse racing "positively reinforces cultural and ethical expectations, supporting 'institutional isomorphism' [in] encouraging other organizations to assess and adopt shared goals and processes" (p. 171). Similarly, Piggott (2022) drew on Bourdieu's concepts of field, habitus, and capital to discuss how the implementation of top-down regulations in English sport governance has changed the rules of the field to encourage NGBs of sport to reform their internal governance rules and structures to be more gender equitable. Here, the implementation of "A Code for Sports Governance" by UK Sport and Sport England in 2016, which included a 30% minimum gender target on the boards of sport organizations in receipt of public funding, resulted in a significant increase in female representation on sport boards. Fifty-five out of 58 NGBs hit the 30% target by the end of 2017 and average female representation on NGB boards was at 40% by 2019 (Piggott, 2022). Several other studies, both in sport and non-sport organizations, have also argued that gender quotas as a structural fast track strategy have led to fast-paced and substantial increases in the representation of women in male-dominated boards (Dahlerup & Freidenvall, 2005; Fasting & Sisjord, 2019; Hovden, 2012; Terjesen et al., 2015). For example, the quota law in Norwegian sport organizations, approved in 1991, resulted in the highest percentage of women board members among national sports federation globally (Adriaanse, 2019).

While positive impacts have resulted from formal actions aiming to make sport leadership and governance more gender inclusive, some scholars have critiqued the extent to which such practices genuinely contribute to undoing gender (and in some cases result in the redoing of gender). For example, Piggott (2022) found that, while the majority of English NGBs complied with the formal requirements of "A Code for Sport Governance," the principles and values of the code were not internalized. A clear indicator of this was the lack of change in gender ratios among leadership positions not regulated by the governance code (e.g., executive leadership positions). This suggests that the code did not go far enough in transforming the deep-rooted organizational culture of NGBs. A similar conclusion was made by Jakubowska (2019), who drew on Nancy Fraser's (2007, 2013) concept of social justice to argue that the implementation of gender quotas for sport governance positions is an example of affirmation, with an increased recognition of women but without undoing gender by changing the underlying culture-value structure. Likewise, Norman (2016) drew on a critical feminist framework to argue that interventions being implemented by The FA, such as equity training for coaches, attempt to change structures that produce inequality without implementing corresponding interventions addressing the beliefs that legitimate this inequality. The contribution of formal organizational dimensions to undoing gender is, therefore, complex and can vary depending on the type of organization and the political context within which it is located. Within organizational research, *informal* institutions and practices have been important research topics in helping scholars to understand this gap between espoused formal institutional practice or change and actual outcomes (Waylen, 2013). This is where we now turn our attention.

Informal Organizational Dimensions and Doing Gender

Informal practices influence doing gender within sport organizations by positioning men and masculinity as synonymous with leadership and decision-making roles and in turn positioning women and femininity as synonymous with supporting or peripheral roles. For example, Piggott and Pike (2020) drew on Bourdieu's concepts of field, habitus, and capital to explore how informal organizational practices within two English NGBs of sport impacted upon gender representation and equity within their leadership and governance. Such informal practices included gendered dress codes (e.g., awarding all board members with a blazer and tie on election), gendered language (e.g., sexist humor and the use of gendered terms like "Chairman"), informal gender segregation (e.g., women sitting with women and men sitting with men within board meetings), and informal expectations for leaders to work long and unsociable hours. The influence of socially embedded gendered processes, and particularly those relating to appointment processes and social networks, has similarly been a key focus in the non-sport literature (Kirsch, 2018). Piggott and Pike (2020) highlighted how such informal practices can result in gendered disparities in capital accumulation and align sport leadership to the dominant male habitus. For example, informal gender segregation in the boardroom can work to reinforce gender stereotypes and strengthen "old boys' clubs" that are continually found to benefit the accumulation and value of social capital for men over women (Hotham et al., 2021; Karacam & Koca, 2019). Additionally, long and unsociable working hours in sport and non-sport organizations are mostly incompatible with the cultural habitus of motherhood that continues to normalize the position of women as the primary caregivers of children (Claringbould & Van Liere, 2019; Piggott & Pike, 2020). These authors argue that increased organizational consciousness of such informal practices and their implications is needed as a first step in creating organizational change that undoes gender.

Informal organizational cultures that privilege men and masculinity also influence the individual experiences of women leaders. For example, Hotham et al. (2021) found that, compared to men, women working in Australian male team sports felt underestimated, patronized, and lacking respect in relation to their experience, knowledge, and skills. Drawing on a third-wave feminist lens, the authors discussed how this was the result of hegemonic masculinity and male privilege, which led to a disparate level of power between men and women. Resultantly, women often feel as though they must work harder or have superior skills compared to men to be valued in the same way within sport organizations (e.g., Hotham et al., 2021; Hovden, 2013; Melton & Bryant, 2017). This is not a new finding, with 20-year-old organizational scholarship similarly reporting that women have higher standards imposed on them (Eagly et al., 2003). Such gendered power disparities have led to some women leaders feeling unwelcome, marginalized, and othered within organizational spaces.

As aforementioned, researchers are increasingly exploring how experiences of otherness can be heightened for some women over others because of diverse experiences of gender being done. For example, Rankin-Wright et al. (2019) drew on a critical race theory approach that engaged insights from Black feminist thought to explore the experiences of Black men and women coaches in the United Kingdom. One woman within their study explained how she felt detached from the "ideal image" of a traditional coach in her sport because her "Pakistani female body was immediately marked as 'different" to the "unmarked normative positions of Whiteness and masculinity dominant in this sport" (Rankin-Wright et al., 2019, pp. 609–610). Other women felt like intruders within spaces that have typically privileged White men. Rankin-Wright et al. (2019) discussed how such experiences of marginalization are underpinned by racialized and gendered occupational stereotypes that lead to conscious or subconscious assumptions that Black women are more suited to assistant positions and less suited to leadership positions. Such gendered and racialized stereotypes are reproduced by "the cultures of sport organizations [that] often have a line of entitlement and privilege running through them such that whiteness and maleness are celebrated in leadership positions" (Simpkins et al., 2022, p. 47). Puwar (2004) has revealed how this feeling of being a space invader in a male-dominated organizational culture also occurs among those holding positions in parliamentary bodies in government.

In response to racialized and gendered meritocratic ideals, Melton and Bryant (2017) discussed how women leaders with multiple marginal identities in US sport organizations adopt techniques and strategies to fit in or connect with the dominant group within their organization. This includes using various techniques to downplay parts of their identity, such as their sexuality or gender. One identity management technique that has been commonly discussed within the sport leadership literature is women sport leaders and coaches adopting masculine leadership styles to be accepted and respected within male-dominated organizational spaces (Hotham et al., 2021; Preston & Velija, 2022; Tjønndal, 2019). However, Hotham et al. (2021) found that women sport leaders faced negative backlash if they adopted more agentic or masculine behaviors due to a perceived incongruency between styles associated with masculinity and their biological gender. This demonstrates the "double bind" that women leaders often face in both sport and non-sport organizations. If they behave like men, they risk having their femininity, and in turn womanhood, called into question. However, if they behave like women, they appear incapable and unfit for the job (Bourdieu, 2001; Shaw & Hoeber, 2003).

Preston and Velija (2022) drew on Rao et al.'s (1999) concept of hidden power to discuss *how* informal gendered practices and outcomes continue to be reproduced within sport organizations to reinforce the doing of gender. Hidden power refers to forms of power that are exercised to the detriment of others without their knowledge. It is a similar notion to other theoretical ideas that conceptualize invisible or consensual forms of power, such as Bourdieu's (1991, 1992, 2000) symbolic violence and Gramsci's (1971) theory of hegemony. In the context of The FA, hidden power was seen to play out through female employees changing their behaviors upon joining the organization and accepting this as "normal" or "just football" (Preston & Velija, 2022). Additionally, some female employees seemed to accept that male employees had a greater likelihood of promotion or career progression than their female counterparts. Preston and Velija (2022) discussed how this was likely due to hidden power relations normalizing cultural assumptions that men have more right to be promoted within the organization. In doing so, "the dominance of men and the valued forms of masculinity [will continue to be] … considered synonymous with dominant forms of leadership" (Preston & Velija, 2022, p. 160). This demonstrates the often-invisible workings of doing gender that mask the very mechanisms that reinforce and sustain gendered status hierarchies (Claringbould & Knoppers, 2012). While scholarship on non-sport organizations has discussed how all institutions are "substantively gendered through numerous mechanisms that result in gender bias" (Waylen, 2013, p. 215), these hidden power dynamics are particularly prominent within sport organizations when "images and discourses associated with management and leadership in sport are infused with masculine traits and characteristics such as toughness, sport playing experience, and instrumentality" (Schull et al., 2013, p. 59).

Informal Organizational Dimensions and Undoing Gender

In addition to doing gender, informal organizational dimensions also have the power to undo gender by reducing perceptions of gender differences within sport organizations and in turn developing more inclusive and equitable practices. However, unlike proactive, strategic, and intentional formal actions and strategies, informal dimensions tend to work subconsciously, accidentally, or indirectly to undo gender. Waylen (2013) argued that "informal norms and rules can play an important part in the extent to which new formal rules take root, often with complex and contradictory outcomes not intended by institutional designers, and this varies in different contexts" (p. 221). Yet, organizational scholarship has been critiqued for being too rigid and deterministic in understanding and theorizing (a lack of) institutional change, adopting concepts like path dependence and critical junctures to explore externally driven change (Clegg, 1990; Waylen, 2013). This means that less focus has been given to how informal, internal institutional rules, norms, and practices uphold, surpass, or subvert the formal in achieving certain organizational aims, including undoing gender.

A handful of studies have explored examples of informal organizational dimensions that contribute to undoing gender within the sporting context. For example, Spaaij et al. (2018) drew on Ahmed's critical analytical lens for investigating diversity practices in institutional contexts to examine diversity work in Australian community sport organizations. Their findings indicated that diversity work within these organizations was "mostly haphazard or accidental" (Spaaij et al., 2018, p. 292). In particular, they discussed how the emergence of informal "diversity champions" within sport clubs (those who "exhibit extra-role behaviors aimed at ensuring the success of diversity initiatives") tended to happen by chance (Spaaij et al., 2018, p. 292). This is because the development of these positions tended to be the result of an individual club member with an existing formal position (e.g., committee member) being committed to diversity rather than it being strategically initiated at the club level. The authors discuss how such informal strategies are important in developing more welcoming and inclusive organizational environments, as well as ensuring that equality, diversity, and inclusion issues do not fall off the clubs' agendas. However, they also highlight how such informal roles tend to lack systematic embedment within sport organizations and so can be unsustainable and insufficient in achieving organizational change. A key element of this is the lack of accountability associated with informal strategies to undo gender. Whereas the success of formal roles or strategies are (ideally) subject to appraisal or review processes, informal roles and strategies are not monitored or evaluated in the same way. Spaaij et al. (2018) argue for the need for informal diversity work to become more formalized and systematically integrated into organizational life to be effective.

The formalization of informal organizational dimensions has not always been found to be effective in supporting the undoing of gender within sport organizations, however. For example, Sisjord (2019) drew on perspectives of doing and undoing gender to support her understanding of the dynamic aspects of women's agency within the Norwegian Snowboard Federation (NSF). She found that the development of an informal snowboard network was influential in undoing gender through a high engagement of women in political activity, resulting in the undoing of stereotypical notions of gender in sport governance. However, she also found that the replacement of this network with a more formal performance-focused project anchored in the national snowboard federation pushed the doing of gender more in line with "traditional" sport. This problematically resulted in a smaller pool of strong female candidates for board positions and acts as an example of redoing gender, where gender has been undone via an informal activity and subsequently redone by the formalization of this activity.

Other scholars have also observed informal networks being effective in undoing gender in sport organizations. For example, Hotham et al. (2021) found that support and being empowered by men and other women was important for women while working in male Australian team sports clubs. This contributed to the development and maintenance of confidence in their own ability. Drawing on a third-wave feminist lens, Hotham et al. (2021) discussed how some participants who felt such empowerment were "understood to be claiming pockets of ownership within a male dominated sporting space and exerting confidence whilst doing so" (p. 408). Similarly, Norman et al. (2018) found that positive horizontal relationships across the coaching workforce of The FA were facilitative for coach development. Many coaches had maintained informal relationships with fellow coaches following participation on formal coaching courses, which led to frequent, day-to-day supportive interactions among these individuals. Drawing on Schein's theory of organizational culture, the authors highlight how the quality, consistency, and meaningfulness of relationships in the workplace are a key tenet of organizational culture in supporting the progression of women as football coaches and tutors. Norman et al. (2018) discuss how the nurturing of personal relations is rarely a formal focus of organizations, despite low social integration often correlating with occupational burnout. Therefore, they call for increased attention to be paid by organizations to the socio-relational elements of women's working conditions in sporting contexts. This is an example of interaction as a site of change, with interactions between individuals having the potential to change normative conceptions of gender (Deutsch, 2007).

In addition to the workings of informal actions and processes, some researchers have found that simply having female representation within certain organizational positions can positively influence the undoing of gender in sporting contexts. For example, drawing on Haavind's theory of gender as a cultural code, Tjønndal (2019) discussed how the representation of women as boxing coaches is "challenging the general perceptions of what a boxing coach is" (p. 93). This aligned with research within non-sport literature that has found that an increase of women's representation among positions of organizational power is gradually leading to a normalization of women in roles and positions formerly possessed by men (Benshop & Verloo, 2011; Stainback et al., 2016). Similarly, drawing on Rao et al.'s (1999) concept of exclusionary power, Preston and Velija (2022) found that women holding senior positions within The FA continue to push for change and, in doing so, often challenge traditional mindsets within the organization. This challenging of mindsets did not come without resistance, however, with some women being viewed as a nuisance and some men within the organization being displeased by women holding leadership positions (Preston & Velija, 2022).

Within this section, we have shown how a wide range of theoretical perspectives have been used to aid an understanding of how organizations do and undo gender through both formal and informal organizational dimensions. However, in engaging with this existing literature, we have also identified a notable theoretical gap. That is, there has been a lack of focus on how binary orders in and through sport may influence structures and the doing of gender within (sport) organizations. We will now discuss how a future focus on sport as a source of (formal and informal) gendered organizational practices could be a fruitful approach in further developing scholarship within the organizational sociology field.

THE REPRODUCTION OF BINARY ORDERS IN AND THROUGH SPORT

A notable omission in the use of theoretical perspectives to explain how gender is done within sport organizations is the absence of grounding explanations in the unique way sport is organized and in the enactment of gender binaries within competitive sport. This is in line with Ahmed's (2006) argument for the need to explore the history of objects and how historical constructions have shaped understandings of what bodies can do (in sport). Since the beginning of the formal organization of sport, sport participation has been based on hierarchical gendered binary classifications that are assumed to be fixed. Much of formal sport is organized into women's sport and men's sport. This binary classification has always been justified with the use of an essentialized differentiation between women and men's bodies (Pape, 2020). This binary, however, is based on a gendered hierarchy that assumes a male body has a superior capacity to that of a woman's in terms of qualities such as size, musculature, speed, and aggression.

Although leadership positions in sport are purportedly not based on the ability to execute sport skills, qualifications for positions of leadership often require the candidates to have a sport history (Knoppers et al., 2021). Most sport careers begin in childhood, a time when children not only learn sport skills and strategies but also begin to understand the gender hierarchy that constitutes the structure and culture of sport (Larneby, 2016; Lütkewitte, 2023; Persson, 2022). Importantly, the residual effect of the sporting history of (potential) sport leaders may leak into ideas about who is best suited to be a leader, whether it be in sport or other organizations. Ryan and Dickson (2018) have argued that "the intersection of sport, leadership and gender provides an otherwise unavailable insight into what is normalized, men and the masculine subtext of leadership" (p. 329).

Attention, therefore, needs to be paid to the extent to which the gendered sport binary may shape managerial practices in both sport and non-sport organizations. Few scholars have looked at the role that images of, and ideas about, athletic masculinities play in managerial practices in non-sport organizations. Knoppers (2011) found that male senior managers working in various non-profit organizations in sport, in public safety (military and police), in health care, and in service organizations attributed their team and leadership skills, toughness, and ability to persevere to their athletic history. They also asserted that they preferred to hire those who had a sport history, preferably in team sports. Furthermore, Agarwal et al. (2016) highlighted the importance of women playing golf – a historically male preserve (Hargreaves, 1994) – as a social networking tool for board access. No available research has explored how a sport history in women's team sports may contribute to women's ascension through the managerial ranks. These relatively few findings not only suggest more research is needed but also that the hierarchical gendered sport structure and culture may indirectly contribute to gendered managerial practices, including recruitment and selection in non-sport organizations.

The link between male athletic history and managerialism could also be embedded in practices of heteronormative masculinity that may shape organizational culture and leadership conceptualizations in both sport and non-sport contexts (Hovden, 2000; Staunæs & Søndergaard, 2006; Sørhaug, 2004). Practices associated with the male sporting body in elite sport, and with heroic or desirable masculinity, have become the norm for coaching behaviors, values, and attitudes (e.g., Gearity, 2014; Kamphoff, 2010; Thomas et al., 2021). Few have explored how this norm is enacted at the leadership level and acts as a filter for exclusion of women administrators/managers/leaders in organizations. This goes beyond the social capital men may build through their sport participation (Darcy et al., 2014; Piggott & Pike, 2020) and extends to an essentialized perception that men "naturally" embody sport and, therefore, are deemed to be best suited to enact leadership regardless of the organization (although it seems most visible in sport organizations). Research on football coaching, for example, suggests that men who have never played women's football are assumed to be more qualified to coach women than women who have played the sport (Knoppers et al., 2022). Women are routinely rejected for coaching positions in men's football due to their supposed lack of knowledge and experience in men's football. In other words, women's bodies in sport organizations are, and continue to represent, abject bodies (Mavin & Grandy, 2016). This finding suggests that theorizing about the relative lack of women in positions of (sport) leadership may need to focus on possible linkages between the seemingly fixed binary structure of competitive sport and how this notion infiltrates and facilitates thinking about the enactment and embodiment of leadership in general. In turn, this may shape the numerical dominance of men in (sport) leadership positions.

We suggest that the gender binary, the hierarchy that is linked to it at the athlete level, and its possible influence on (sport) management, need to be queered. We understand queering as a verb reflecting theoretical frameworks that challenge and possibly disrupt a seemingly fixed social order (Moulin de Souza & Parker, 2022). An institutional queering of bodies as they are embedded in the management of organizations, including coaching, would, therefore, require problematizing the standardization of gender categories at the competitive sport or sport participation level (Knoppers et al., 2022). This would inform an exploration of how constructions of gender at the athlete level subtly may infiltrate the gendering of (sport) leadership. The current binary structure of competitive sport has meant that many boys/men have developed a male-oriented sport habitus as part of their sport history. For them, sport has become a primary site for the development of male bonding (Messner, 1990, 1995). Holgersson (2013) has suggested that male homosociality plays a large role in the tendency of men to hire men as managers of organizations. This male homosocial desire may be even greater in organizations associated with sport and/or among men who have been active in team sports. To date, no research has explored this phenomenon.

Similarly, little scholarly attention has been paid to how practices at the leadership/administration level are shaped by heteronormativity and fears of femininity. These practices of masculinity that pervade the sport setting are visibly and audibly shaped by homonegativity, grounded in fear of being seen as feminine, and dominate many sporting contexts (Allison & Knoester, 2021; Amstutz et al., 2021; Denison et al., 2020; Rollè et al., 2022; Smits & Knoppers, 2020). Yet, few scholars have focused on how misogyny – that is, a disdain for an enactment of stereotypes associated with femininity – may exclude many women as well as men from becoming (sport) administrators/leaders. Practices that have become the norm in elite male-dominated sport, therefore, need to be queered to expand understandings of how women may be kept out of not only sport administration/ leadership but leadership of non-sport organizations as well.

Queer theory has already heavily influenced scholarship on the participation of trans athletes in sport. Their presence challenges the rigid gender binaries that exist at the participatory level; trans athletes undo gender in ways that cannot be reduced to fixed gender binaries and often require a response from sport organizations in the form of policy (re)creation (Moulin de Souza & Parker, 2022; Piggott, 2020). The ways they disrupt the binary can be seen as a form of activism and as undoing gender. Relatively little is known, however, about the experiences of nonbinary and trans people who work in and for organizations, especially those in sport (Piggott, 2020; Sawyer et al., 2016). The impact that various policies of exclusion of male-to-female transgender individuals in women's sport may have on the inclusion of transgender individuals in positions of leadership is unknown (Bekker et al., 2022; Posbergh, 2022). If transgender women are excluded from women's sports due to their perceived association with masculinity, are they then seen as more suited for positions of leadership than cisgender women? This question suggests that if the focus of research on exclusion in sport leadership is widened to include those who do not conform to cisgender norms, a better understanding of practices of desirable masculinities embodied by and enacted in leaders may emerge.

CONCLUSION

Within this paper, we have shown how gendered practices work to do and undo gender across both formal and informal dimensions of sport organizations. First, we presented evidence from the literature that demonstrates how formal organizational dimensions contribute to doing gender by privileging men and desirable masculinity within organizational leadership and governance hierarchies. We discussed how gender and sport leadership researchers have drawn on a range of social theories to analyze how (a lack of) formal rules and structures have worked to exclude and lock women out of formal decision-making structures and agendas within sport organizations. This has led to a lack of female influence, procedural justice, and positional power within sport organizations, as well as an increase in gender divisions and gender pay gaps. This reinforces the doing of gender by normalizing the belonging of (dominant) men and exclusion of women, and especially minority women, in sport leadership. Subsequently, perceptions of gender differences in the leadership capabilities of men and women are maintained or increased. When women do access formal leadership structures, it tends to be the most privileged (White, able-bodied, heterosexual) women who influence decision-making, demonstrating that doing gender within (sport) organizations influences women differently. Additionally, when women do hold positions within formal sport leadership structures, they can experience a lack of empowerment due to their hypervisibility as "the other" within organizations where the physical and cultural presence of men is normalized and legitimized.

Much less scholarly attention has been paid to the ways in which formal organizational dimensions undo gender in sport organizations. We discussed within the paper how formal practices are proactive, strategic, and intentional, such as gender quotas and targets, action plans, training, and mentoring schemes. Despite some of these actions, particularly gender quotas, having documented positive impacts on female representation and recognition in decision-making structures, scholars have drawn on diverse social theories to discuss how gender equity strategies can also lack internalization, neglect to change the underlying culture-value structure, and fail to address beliefs that legitimate inequality. Subsequently, the extent to which formal strategies are effective in undoing gender through creating long-term and sustainable change can be variable.

We also drew on literature to show how informal organizational dimensions have considerable influence on doing gender by positioning men and desired masculinity as synonymous with leadership and decision-making. Informal practices and structures provide men with increased opportunity to accumulate and convert valuable forms of power and align (sport) leadership with the dominant male culture. This results in disparate levels of power between men and women, and women leaders feeling unwelcome, marginalized, and othered within (sport) organizational spaces. Problematically, women often consent to or reinforce such informal practices without knowledge of the wider problematic implications. This demonstrates how both men and women may contribute to doing gender within (sport) organizations. Both majority and minority women adopt identity management techniques to attempt to fit in and connect with the dominant and most powerful groups within their organizations, yet this can often be ineffective due to the doing of gender within sport organizations creating a perceived incongruency between dominant and normalized leadership styles and the (assumed) racial and/or gender roles.

Finally, we analyzed how sport scholars have used social theory to examine the role of informal dimensions in undoing gender in sport organizations. Overall, it has been found that informal organizational dimensions tend to work subconsciously, accidentally, or haphazardly to undo gender by reducing gender differences and developing more inclusive and equitable practices. This includes the implementation of strategies such as informal diversity champions, informal social networks, and simply having female representation within decision-making positions. While some have argued that the lack of formalization or embedment of informal practices within organizations can lead to a lack of influence, others have found that the very informal nature of dimensions can be empowering and develop new opportunities for the inclusion of women outside of traditional, male-dominated (sport) organizational structures. This demonstrates the non-linearity of processes of undoing gender within sport organizations.

Overall, our findings demonstrate how sport organizations are characteristic of "extremely gendered" organizations due to male dominance existing in both practice and numbers and because the doing of gender is often legitimized and normalized (Sasson-Levy, 2011). In this sense, scholarly analyses of sport and other extremely gendered organizations, such as the military, can complement each other and provide needed contemporary insights. Furthermore, the diverse, layered, and at times contradictory nature of empirical and theoretical contributions on gender inclusion and exclusion in sport organizations demonstrates the complexity of the issue. Yet, despite theoretically informed scholarship providing new insights on the causes and symptoms of gender inequity in sport organizations, there continues to be a lack of representation and recognition of women leaders. Throughout the paper, we have identified how findings regarding the lack of representation and recognition of women in sport organizations mostly reflect findings in the wider organizational literature, albeit with some variations in conditions for women across different sectors. However, within our paper, we have also identified an opportunity to extend theoretical knowledge in both the sport and non-sport fields by grounding analyses in the unique ways that sport is organized according to gender binaries. In doing so, we advocate the application of queer theory to make visible, challenge, and possibly disrupt the seemingly fixed binary social order of sport. This would enable a greater understanding of how constructions of gender at the athlete level may subtly infiltrate the gendering of (sport) leadership. For example, how homosocial and homonegative practices can benefit men and disadvantage women within (sport) coaching, administration, and leadership teams.

As we pointed out in the beginning of this paper, the global visibility of sport can contribute to ways gender is done and leadership is defined in non-sport organizations. The sport history of many men may shape informal interactions and male bonding within non-sport organizations as well as their perceptions of desirable leadership. Yet, few scholars have explored the ways in which athletic masculinities influence managerial practices in either sport or non-sport organizations. Furthermore, most literature in the field (both sport- and non-sport-focused) seem to lack an understanding of feminist-based activism, despite an exploration of this activism having the potential to enrich theoretical perspectives. Bell et al. (2019) have argued that feminist theory needs to be intertwined with activism because both play an important role in understanding practices that exclude.

In sum, although much work has been done to uncover dynamics resulting in the relatively low number of women in (sport) leadership positions, the picture is incomplete, requiring different theoretical approaches than those that have been used. We suggest that critically and queerly examining the unique context of the historic binary structuring of competitive sport may offer a good starting point for future theoretical developments in organizational research, both within sociology of sport and wider organizational sociology.

REFERENCES

Acker, J. (1990). Hierarchies, jobs, bodies: A theory of gendered organizations. *Gender & Society*, *4*(2), 139–158. https://doi.org/10.1177/089124390004002002

Acker, J. (1992). From sex roles to gendered institutions. *Contemporary Sociology: A Journal of Reviews*, *21*(5), 565–569. https://doi.org/10.2307/2075528

Acker, J. (2006). Inequality regimes: Gender, class, and race in organizations. *Gender and Society*, *20*(4), 441–464. https://doi.org/10.1177/0891243206289499

Adjepong, A. (2019). Are you a footballer?: The radical potential of women's football at the national level. In S. Neck (Ed.), *Routledge handbook of queer African studies* (pp. 76–89). Routledge.

Adriaanse, J. (2019). Europe in world perspective: The Sydney Scoreboard global index for women in sport leadership. In A. Elling, J. Hovden, & A. Knoppers (Eds.), *Gender diversity in European sport governance* (pp. 11–20). Routledge.

Agarwal, S., Qian, W., Reeb, D. M., & Sing, T. F. (2016). Playing the boys game: Golf buddies and board diversity. *American Economic Review*, *106*(5), 272–276. https://doi.org/10.1257/aer.p20161033

Ahmed, S. (2006). *Queer phenomenology*. Duke University Press.

Ahn, N. Y., & Cunningham, G. B. (2020). Standing on a glass cliff? A case study of FIFA's gender initiatives. *Managing Sport and Leisure*, *25*(1–2), 114–137. https://doi.org/10.1080/23750472.2020.1727357

Allison, R., & Knoester, C. (2021). Gender, sexual, and sports fan identities. *Sociology of Sport Journal*, *38*(3), 310–321. https://doi.org/10.1123/ssj.2020-0036

Amstutz, N., Nussbaumer, M., & Vöhringer, H. (2021). Disciplined discourses: The logic of appropriateness in discourses on organizational gender equality policies. *Gender, Work & Organization*, *28*(1), 215–230. https://doi.org/10.1111/gwao.12541

Bairner, A., & Han, P. (2022). Sport, nationalism, and national identities. In L. A. Wenner (Ed.), *The Oxford handbook of sport and society* (pp. 86–103). Oxford University Press.

Bekker, S., Storr, R., & Posbergh, A. (2022). Inclusion, fairness and non-discrimination in sport: A wider lens. *British Journal of Sports Medicine*, *56*(19), 1064–1065. https://doi.org/10.1136/bjsports-2022-105926

Belingheri, P., Chiarello, F., Fronzetti Colladon, A., & Rovelli, P. (2021). Twenty years of gender equality research: A scoping review based on a new semantic indicator. *PLoS ONE*, *16*(9), e0256474. https://doi.org/10.1371/journal.pone.0256474

Bell, E., Merilainen, S., Taylor, S., & Tienari, J. (2019). Time's up! Feminist theory and activism meets organization studies. *Human Relations*, *72*(1), 4–22. https://doi.org/10.1177/0018726718790067

Benshop, Y., & Verloo, M. (2011). Gender change, organizational change and gender equality strategies In E. Jeanes, D. Knights, & P. Y. Martin (Eds.), *Handbook of gender, work and organization* (pp. 277–291). Wiley-Blackwell.

Bergsgaard, N. A. (2005). *Idrettspolitikkens maktspill. Endring og stabilitet i den idrettspolitiske styringsmodellen* [*The power play of sports politics. Change and stability in the governing model of sports politics*] [Doctoral thesis, University of Oslo, Oslo].

Bernard, W. T., Sangster, S., & Hay, A. M. (2021). Concrete ceilings: African Canadian women and the pursuit of leadership in the public sector. *Intersectionalities: A Global Journal of Social Work Analysis, Research, Polity, and Practice, 8*(1), 98–116.

Bloch, K. R., Taylor, T., Church, J., & Buck, A. (2021). An intersectional approach to the glass ceiling: Gender, race and share of middle and senior management in us workplaces. *Sex Roles, 84,* 312–325. htpps://doi.org/10.1007/s11199-020-01168-4

Bourdieu, P. (1991). *Language and symbolic power.* Polity Press.

Bourdieu, P. (1992). *The logic of practice* (R. Nice, Trans.). Polity Press.

Bourdieu, P. (2000). *Pascalian meditations.* Polity Press.

Bourdieu, P. (2001). *Masculine domination.* Polity Press.

Bridges, D., Bamberry, L., Wulff, E., & Krivokapic-Skoko, B. (2022). "A trade of one's own": The role of social and cultural capital in the success of women in male-dominated occupations. *Gender, Work & Organization, 29*(2), 371–387. htpps://doi.org/10.1111/gwao.12764

Bridges, D., Wulff, E., Bamberry, L., Krivokapic-Skoko, B., & Jenkins, S. (2020). Negotiating gender in the male-dominated skilled trades: A systematic literature review. *Construction Management and Economics, 38*(10), 894–916. htpps://doi.org/10.1080/01446193.2020.1762906

Burton, L. (2015). Underrepresentation of women in sport leadership: A review of research. *Sport Management Review, 18*(2), 155–165. htpps://doi.org/10.1016/j.smr.2014.02.004

Butler, J. (1990). *Gender trouble: Feminism and the subversion of identity.* Routledge.

Butler, J. (2004). *Undoing gender.* Routledge.

Cabrera-Fernández, A. I., Martínez-Jiménez, R., & Hernández-Ortiz, M. J. (2015). Women's participation on boards of directors: A review of the literature. *International Journal of Gender and Entrepreneurship, 8*(1), 69–89. htpps://doi.org/10.1108/ijge-02-2015-0008

Childs, S., & Krook, M. L. (2008). Critical mass theory and women's political representation. *Political Studies, 56*(3), 725–736. htpps://doi.org/10.1111/j.1467-9248.2007.00712.x

Claringbould, I., & Knoppers, A. (2008). Doing and undoing gender in sport governance. *Sex Roles, 58*(1–2), 81–92. htpps://doi.org/10.1007/s11199-007-9351-9

Claringbould, I., & Knoppers, A. (2012). Paradoxical practices of gender in sport-related organizations. *Journal of Sport Management, 26*(5), 404–416. htpps://doi.org/10.1123/jsm.26.5.404

Claringbould, I., & Van Liere, M. (2019). The Netherlands: Transformations but still a great deal to be done. In A. Elling, J. Hovden, & A. Knoppers (Eds.), *Gender diversity in European sport governance* (pp. 94–104). Routledge.

Clayton-Hathway, K. (2022). Governance and leadership in British horseracing: A gender perspective. In P. Velija & L. Piggott (Eds.), *Gender equity in UK sport leadership and governance* (pp. 163–178). Emerald.

Clegg, S. (1990). *Modern organizations: Organization studies in the postmodern world.* Sage.

Coakley, J., & Pike, E. (2014). *Sports in society: Issues and controversies.* McGraw-Hill Education.

Connell, R. W., & Messerschmidt, J. W. (2005). Hegemonic masculinity: Rethinking the concept. *Gender & Society, 19*(6), 829–859. htpps://doi.org/10.1177/0891243205278639

Dadswell, K., Mandicos, M., Flowers, E. P., & Hanlon, C. (2022). Women from culturally diverse backgrounds in sport leadership: A scoping review of facilitators and barriers. *Journal of Sport and Social Issues, 47*(6), 535–564. htpps://doi.org/10.1177/019372352211346

Dahlerup, D., & Freidenvall, L. (2005). Quotas as 'fast track' to equal representation for women. *International Feminist Journal of Politics, 7,* 26–48. htpps://doi.org/10.1080/1461674042000324673

Darcy, S., Maxwell, H., Edwards, M., Onyx, J., & Sherker, S. (2014). More than a sport and volunteer organisation: Investigating social capital development in a sporting organisation. *Sport Management Review, 17*(4), 395–406. htpps://doi.org/10.1016/j.smr.2014.01.003

Denison, E., Bevan, N., & Jeanes, R. (2020). Reviewing evidence of LGBTQ+ discrimination and exclusion in sport. *Sport Management Review, 24*(2), 389–409. htpps://doi.org/10.1016/j.smr.2020.09.003

Deutsch, F. M. (2007). Undoing gender. *Gender & Society, 21*(1), 106–127. htpps://doi.org/10.1177/0891243206293577

Eagly, A., Johannesen-Schmidt, M., & van Engen, M. (2003). Transformational, transactional, and laissez-faire leadership styles: A meta-analysis comparing women and men. *Psychological Bulletin*, *129*(4), 569–591. htpps://doi.org/10.1037/0033-2909.129.4.569

Elling, A., Hovden, J., & Knoppers, A. (Eds.). (2019). *Gender diversity in European sport governance*. Routledge.

Ely, R., & Meyerson, D. (2010). An organizational approach to undoing gender: The unlikely case of offshore oil platforms. *Research in Organizational Behavior*, *30*, 3–34. htpps://doi.org/10.1016/j.riob.2010.09.002

Evans, A., & Pfister, G. (2021). Women in sports leadership: A systematic narrative review. *International Review for the Sociology of Sport*, *56*(3), 317–342. htpps://doi.org/10.1177/1012690220911842

Fasting, K., & Sisjord, M. (2019). Norway: Gender, governance and the impact of quota regulations. In A. Elling, J. Hovden, & A. Knoppers (Eds.), *Gender diversity in European sport governance* (pp. 131–140). Routledge.

Fraser, N. (2007). Feminist politics in the age on recognition: A two-dimensional approach to gender justice. *Studies in Social Justice*, *1*(1), 23–35.

Fraser, N. (2013). *Fortunes of feminism. From state-managed capitalism to neo-liberal crisis*. Verso.

Gearity, B. T. (2014). Learning like the men: Collegiate female strength and conditioning coaches' knowledge development. *Research Quarterly for Exercise and Sport*, *85*(S1), A165–A166.

Gramsci, A. (1971). *Selections from the prison notebooks* (Q. Hoare & G. Nowell Smith, Eds.). International Publishers.

Groeneveld, S., Bakker, V., & Schmidt, E. (2020). Breaking the glass ceiling, but facing a glass cliff? The role of organizational decline in women's representation in leadership positions in Dutch civil service organizations. *Public Administration*, *98*(2), 441–464. htpps://doi.org/10.1111/padm.12632

Halliday, C. S., Paustian-Underdahl, S. C., & Fainshmidt, S. (2021). Women on boards of directors: A meta-analytic examination of the roles of organizational leadership and national context for gender equality. *Journal of Business and Psychology*, *36*, 173–191. htpps://doi.org/10.1007/s10869-019-09679-y

Hargreaves, J. (1994). *Sporting females: Critical issues in the history and sociology of women's sports*. Routledge.

Hedenborg, S., & Norberg, J. (2019). Sweden: A gender perspective on sport governance. In A. Elling, J. Hovden, & A. Knoppers (Eds.), *Gender diversity in European sport governance* (pp. 141–151). Routledge.

Hill Collins, P. (1986). Learning from the outsider within: The sociological significance of black feminist thought. *Social Problems*, *33*(6), 14–32. htpps://doi.org/10.1525/sp.1986.33.6.03a00020

Holgersson, C. (2013). Recruiting managing directors: Doing homosociality. *Gender, Work & Organization*, *20*(4), 454–466. htpps://doi.org/10.1111/j.1468-0432.2012.00595.x

Hotham, G., Litchfield, C., & Osborne, J. (2021). Going on a 'witch hunt': Investigating the lived experiences of women working in male teamsports in regional Australia. *Sport in Society*, *24*(3), 396–411. htpps://doi.org/10.1080/17430437.2019.1672156

Hovden, J. (2000). "Heavyweight" men and younger women? The gendering of selection processes in Norwegian sport organizations. *NORA: Nordic Journal of Women's Studies*, *8*(1), 17–32. htpps://doi.org/10.1080/080387400408035

Hovden, J. (2012). Discourses and strategies for the inclusion of women in sport – The case of Norway. *Sport in Society*, *15*(3), 287–301. htpps://doi.org/10.1080/17430437.2012.653201

Hovden, J. (2013). Gender, sport and power: Women as leaders and coaches. In G. Pfister & M. K. Sisjord (Eds.), *Gender and sport: Changes and challenges* (pp. 33–50). Waxmann.

Hovden, J. (2016). The "fast track" as a future strategy for achieving gender equality and democracy in sport organizations. In Y. Auweele, E. Cook, & J. Parry (Eds.), *Ethics and governance in sport. The future of sport imagined* (pp. 35–43). Routledge.

IOC. (2019). Promotion of gender equality in sport: Statistics. https://www.olympic.org/women-in-sport/background/statistics

Jakubowska, H. (2019). Poland: Underrepresentation and misrecognition of women in sport leadership. In A. Elling, J. Hovden, & A. Knoppers (Eds.), *Gender diversity in European sport governance* (pp. 59–69). Routledge.

Joecks, J., Pull, K., & Vetter, K. (2013). Gender diversity in the boardroom and firm performance: What exactly constitutes a 'critical mass'? *Journal of Business Ethics, 118*(1), 61–72. htpps://doi. org/10.1007/s10551-012-1553-6

Joshi, A., Neely, B., Emrich, C., Griffiths, D., & George, G. (2015). Gender research in AMJ: An overview of five decades of empirical research and calls to action. *Academy of Management Journal, 58*, 1459–1475. htpps://doi.org/10.5465/amj.2015.4011

Kamphoff, C. S. (2010). Bargaining with patriarchy: Former female coaches' experiences and their decision to leave collegiate coaching. *Research Quarterly for Exercise and Sport, 81*(3), 360–372. htpps://doi.org/10.5641/027013610x13088600028851

Kanter, R. (1977). Some effects of proportions in group life: Skewed sex ratios and responses to token women. *American Journal of Sociology, 82*(5), 965–990. htpps://doi.org/10.1086/226425

Karacam, M., & Koca, C. (2019). Turkey: Men's resistance to gender equality in sport governance. In A. Elling, J. Hovden, & A. Knoppers (Eds.), *Gender diversity in European sport governance* (pp. 25–35). Routledge.

Kelan, E. K. (2010). Gender logic and (un)doing gender at work. *Gender, Work & Organization, 17*(2), 174–194. htpps://doi.org/10.1111/j.1468-0432.2009.00459.x

Kelan, E. K. (2018). Men doing and undoing gender at work: A review and research agenda. *International Journal of Management Review, 20*, 544–558. htpps://doi.org/10.1111/ijmr.12146

Kirsch, A. (2018). The gender composition of corporate boards: A review and research agenda. *The Leadership Quarterly, 29*, 346–364. htpps://doi.org/10.1016/j.leaqua.2017.06.001

Knoppers, A. (2011). Giving meaning to sport involvement in managerial work. *Gender, Work & Organization, 18*(s1), e1–e22. htpps://doi.org/10.1111/j.1468-0432.2009.00467.x

Knoppers, A., de Haan, D., Norman, L., & LaVoi, N. M. (2022). Elite women coaches negotiating and resisting power in football. *Gender, Work and Organization, 29*(3), 880–896. htpps://doi. org/10.1111/gwao.12790

Knoppers, A., & Spaaij, R. (2021). The politics of positions of leadership in sport: The subtexts of women's exclusion. In G. Molnar & R. Bullingham (Eds.), *Routledge handbook of gender politics in sport and physical activity* (pp. 38–46). Taylor and Francis.

Knoppers, A., Spaaij, R., & Claringbould, I. (2021). Discursive resistance to gender diversity in sport governance: Sport as a unique field? *International Journal of Sport Policy and Politics, 13*(3), 517–529. htpps://doi.org/10.1080/19406940.2021.1915848

Konrad, A. M., Kramer, V., & Erkut, S. (2008). Critical mass: The impact of three or more women on corporate boards. *Organizational Dynamics, 37*(2), 145–164. htpps://doi.org/10.1016/j.org-dyn.2008.02.005

Korvajärvi, P. (2002). Locating gender neutrality in formal and informal aspects of organizational cultures. *Culture and Organization, 8*(2), 101–115. htpps://doi.org/10.1080/14759550212838

Kramer, V., Konrad, A., & Hooper, M. (2006). *Critical mass on corporate boards: Why three or more women enhance governance.* Wellesley Centers for Women.

Kvande, E. (2007). *Doing gender in flexible organizations.* Fagbokforlaget.

Larneby, M. (2016). Transcending gender hierarchies? Young people and floorball in Swedish school sport. *Sport in Society, 19*(8–9), 1202–1213. htpps://doi.org/10.4324/9781315228662-7

Litchfield, C. (2015). Gender and leadership positions in recreational hockey clubs. *Sport in Society, 18*(1), 61–79. htpps://doi.org/10.1080/17430437.2014.919262

Low, S., & Iverson, K. (2016). Propositions for more just urban public spaces. *City, 20*(1), 10–31. htpps://doi.org/10.1080/13604813.2015.1128679

Lütkewitte, S. (2023). Sports participation and beliefs about male dominance: A cross-national analysis of sexist gender ideologies. *Social Sciences, 12*(4), 207–248. htpps://doi.org/10.3390/socsci12040207

Matthews, J. J. K., & Piggott, L. V. (2021). *Is gender on the international agenda? Female representation and policy in international sport governance.* https://www.uksport.gov.uk/-/media/files/international-relations/research-final-report.ashx

Mavin, S., & Grandy, G. (2016). A theory of abject appearance: Women elite leaders' intra-gender 'management' of bodies and appearance. *Human Relations, 69*(5), 1095–1120. htpps://doi.org/10.1177/0018726715609107

Melton, E. N., & Bryant, M. J. (2017). Intersectionality: The impact of negotiating multiple identities for women in sport leadership. In L. Burton & S. Leberman (Eds.), *Women in sport leadership: Research and practice for change* (pp. 62–82). Routledge.

Messner, M. (1990). Boyhood, organized sports, and the construction of masculinities. *Journal of Contemporary Ethnography, 18*(4), 416–444.

Messner, M. (1995). *Power at play: Sports and the problem of masculinity.* Beacon Press.

Messner, M., & Bozada-Deas, S. (2009). Separating the men from the moms: The making of adult gender segregation in youth sports. *Gender & Society, 23*(1), 49–71. htpps://doi.org/10.1177/0891243208327363

Miller, D. A. (2021). Black British female managers – The silent catastrophe. *Gender, Work & Organization, 28*(4), 1665–1682. https://doi.org/10.1111/gwao.12688

Moulin de Souza, E., & Parker, M. (2022). Practices of freedom and the disruption of binary genders: Thinking with trans. *Organization, 29*(1), 67–82. https://doi.org/10.1177/1350508420935602

Norman, L. (2016). The impact of an "equal opportunities" ideological framework on coaches' knowledge and practice. *International Review for the Sociology of Sport, 51*(8), 975–1004. htpps://doi.org/10.1177/1012690214565377

Norman, L., Rankin-Wright, A. J., & Allison, W. (2018). "It's a concrete ceiling; it's not even glass": Understanding tenets of organizational culture that support the progression of women as coaches and coach developers. *Journal of Sport and Social Issues, 42*(5), 393–414. htpps://doi.org/10.1177/0193723518790086

Pape, M. (2020). Gender segregation and trajectories of organisational change: The underrepresentation of women in sports leadership. *Gender & Society, 34*(1), 81–105. htpps://doi.org/10.1177/0891243219867914

Persson, M. (2022). Playing without goals: Gendered practices in recreational youth football. *Journal of Youth Studies, 26*(5), 577–592. htpps://doi.org/10.1080/13676261.2021.2022641

Piggott, L. (2020). *Transgender, intersex and non-binary people in sport and physical activity: A review of research and policy.* https://www.sportandrecreation.org.uk/pages/transgender-intersex-and-non-binary

Piggott, L. (2021). Gender and social inequity in and through sport leadership. In E. Pike (Ed.), *Research handbook on sports and society* (pp. 159–173). Edward Elgar.

Piggott, L. (2022). Past, present, future: Policy and gender equity in English sport leadership and governance. In P. Velija & L. Piggott (Eds.), *Gender equity in UK sport leadership and governance* (pp. 71–86). Emerald Publishing Limited.

Piggott, L., & Matthews, J. (2021). Gender, leadership, and governance in English national governing bodies of sport: Formal structures, rules, and processes. *Journal of Sport Management, 35*(4), 338–351. https://doi.org/10.1123/jsm.2020-0173

Piggott, L., & Pike, E. (2020). 'Ceo equals man': Gender and informal organisational practices in English sport governance. *International Review for the Sociology of Sport, 55*(7), 1009–1025. htpps://doi.org/10.1177/1012690219865980

Posbergh, A. (2022). Defining 'woman': A governmentality analysis of how protective policies are created in elite women's sport. *International Review for the Sociology of Sport, 57*(8), 1350–1370. https://doi.org/10.1177/10126902211072765

Preston, R., & Velija, P. (2022). Exclusionary power and women's experiences of working at The Football Association. In P. Velija & L. Piggott (Eds.), *Gender equity in UK sport leadership and governance* (pp. 149–163). Emerald.

Puwar, N. (2004). *Space invaders: Race, gender and bodies out of place.* Berg Publisher.

Rahbari, L., Longman, C., & Coene, G. (2019). The female body as the bearer of national identity in Iran: A critical discourse analysis of the representation of women's bodies in official online outlets. *Gender, Place & Culture, 26*(10), 1417–1437. https://doi.org/10.1080/0966369x.2018.1555147

Rankin-Wright, A. J., Hylton, K., & Norman, L. (2019). Negotiating the coaching landscape: Experiences of Black men and women coaches in the United Kingdom. *International Review for the Sociology of Sport, 54*(5), 603–621. htpps://doi.org/10.1177/1012690217724879

Rao, A., Stuart, R., & Kelleher, D. (1999). *Gender at work: Organizational change for equality.* Kumarian Press.

Rao, M. A., & Donaldson, S. I. (2015). Expanding opportunities for diversity in positive psychology: An examination of gender, race, and ethnicity. *Canadian Psychology/Psychologie Canadienne*, 56, 271–282. htpps://doi.org/10.1037/cap0000036

Reddy, S., & Jadhav, A. M. (2019). Gender diversity in boardrooms – A literature review. *Cogent Economics & Finance*, 7(1), 1644703. htpps://doi.org/10.1080/23322039.2019.1644703

Rollè, L., Cazzini, E., Santoniccolo, F., & Trombetta, T. (2022). Homonegativity and sport: A systematic review of the literature. *Journal of Gay & Lesbian Social Services*, 34(1), 86–111. htpps://doi.org/10.1080/10538720.2021.1927927

Rosette, A. S., Ponce de Leon, R., Zhou Koval, C., & Harrison, D. A. (2018). Intersectionality: Connecting experiences of gender with race at work. *Research in Organizational Behavior*, 38, 1–22. htpps://doi.org/10.1016/j.riob.2018.12.002

Ryan, I., & Dickson, G. (2018). The invisible norm: An exploration of the intersections of sport, gender and leadership. *Leadership*, 14(3), 329–346. htpps://doi.org/10.1177/1742715016674864

Sasson-Levy, O. (2011). The military in a globalized environment: Perpetuating an "extremely gendered" organization. In E. Jeanes, D. Knights, & P. Yancey Martin (Eds.), *Handbook of gender, work and organization* (pp. 391–411). Yancey Martin.

Sawyer, K., Thoroughgood, C., & Webster, J. (2016). Queering the gender binary: Understanding transgender workplace experiences. In T. Köllen (Ed.), *Sexual orientation and transgender issues in organizations: Global perspectives on LGBT workforce diversity* (pp. 21–42). Springer. htpps://doi.org/10.1007/978-3-319-29623-4_2

Schull, V., Shaw, S., & Kihl, L. A. (2013). If a woman came in… she would have been eaten up alive: Analyzing gendered political processes in the search for an athletic director. *Gender & Society*, 27(1), 56–81. htpps://doi.org/10.1177/0891243212466289

Shaw, S., & Hoeber, L. (2003). "A strong man is direct and a direct woman is a bitch": Analyzing discourses of masculinity and femininity and their impact on employment roles in sport organizations. *Journal of Sport Management*, 17(4), 347–376. htpps://doi.org/10.1123/jsm.17.4.347

Simpkins, E. (2019). *Black women in sport leadership: An exploration of the sport intersectional model of power (SIMP)*. Unpublished doctoral thesis, University of Michigan.

Simpkins, E., Velija, P., & Piggott, L. (2022). The sport intersectional model of power (SIMP) as a tool for understanding intersectionality in sport governance and leadership. In P. Velija & L. Piggott (Eds.), *Gender equity in UK sport leadership and governance* (pp. 37–50). Emerald Publishing Limited.

Sisjord, M. (2019). Snowboarding: Women's agency from outsiders to insiders in the organisation. In A. Elling, J. Hovden, & A. Knoppers (Eds.), *Gender diversity in European Sport Governance* (pp. 165–176). Routledge.

Smits, F., & Knoppers, A. (2020). The way we roll: The use of longboards and cameras by girls to roll through the urban outdoors. *Annals of Leisure Research*, 25(4), 491–507. htpps://doi.org/10.1080/11745398.2020.1836664

Sogn, H. (2023). *Spillets gang: En institusjonell etnografisk undersøkelse om kjønn, makt og styring i idrettsorganisasjonen i Norge* [*The course of the game: An institutional ethnographic study of gender, power and governance in sports organisations in Norway*]. (Doktorgradsavhandling). Norges Idrettshøgskole, Oslo.

Spaaij, R., Magee, J., Farquharson, K., Gorman, S., Jeanes, R., Lusher, D., & Storr, R. (2018). Diversity work in community sport organizations: Commitment, resistance and institutional change. *International Review for the Sociology of Sport*, 53(3), 278–295. htpps://doi.org/10.1177/1012690216654296

Stainback, K., Kleiner, S., & Skaggs, S. (2016). Women in power: Undoing or redoing the gendered organization? *Gender & Society*, 30(1), 109–135. htpps://doi.org/10.1177/0891243215602906

Staunæs, D., & Søndergaard, D. (2006). Corporate fictions. *Tidsskrift for Kjønnsforskning*, 3, 69–87.

Sørhaug, T. (2004). *Managementalitet og autoritetens forvandling [Managerialism and the transformation of authority]*. Fagbokforlaget.

Terjesen, S., Aguilera, R. V., & Lorenz, R. (2015). Legislating a woman's seat on the board: Institutional factors driving gender quotas for boards of directors. *Journal of Business Ethics*, 128(2), 233–251. htpps://doi.org/10.1007/s10551-014-2083-1

Thomas, G., Guinan, J., & Molnar, G. (2021). "It's not particularly PC, you know...": Women coaches' performing gender in strength and conditioning. *Women in Sport and Physical Activity Journal*, *29*(2), 106–116. htpps://doi.org/10.1123/wspaj.2020-0049

Tjønndal, A. (2019). "Girls are not made of glass!": Barriers experienced by women in Norwegian Olympic boxing. *Sociology of Sport Journal*, *36*(1), 87–96. htpps://doi.org/10.1123/ssj.2017-0130

Tomlinson, A. (2014). The supreme leader sails on: Leadership, ethics and governance in FIFA. *Sport in Society*, *17*(9), 1155–1169. htpps://doi.org/10.1080/17430437.2013.856590

Velija, P. (2022). A sociological analysis of the gender pay gap data in UK sport organisations. In P. Velija & L. Piggott (Eds.), *Gender equity in UK sport leadership and governance* (pp. 197–216). Emerald Publishing.

Warren, M. A., Donaldson, S., I., Lee, J. Y., & Donaldson, S. I. (2019). Reinvigorating research on gender in the workplace using a positive work and organizations perspective. *International Journal of Management Reviews*, *21*, 498–518. htpps://doi.org/10.1111/ijmr.12206

Waylen, G. (2013). Informal institutions, institutional change, and gender equality. *Political Research Quarterly*, *67*(1), 212–223. htpps://doi.org/10.1177/1065912913510360

West, C., & Zimmerman, D. (1987). Doing gender. *Gender and Society*, *1*(2), 125–151. htpps://doi.org/10.1177/0891243287001002002

Wilson, M., Tye, M., Gorman, S., Ely-Harper, K., Creagh, R., Leaver, T., Magladry, M., & Efthimiou, O. (2017). Framing the women's AFL: Contested spaces and emerging narratives of hope and opportunity for women in sport. *Sport in Society*, *21*(11), 1704–1720. htpps://doi.org/10.1080/17430437.2017.1409727

PART 3

REDISCOVERING SOCIOLOGICAL CLASSICS FOR ORGANIZATION STUDIES

Reflexivity and Control

NARRATING THE DISJUNCTIONS PRODUCED BY THE SOCIOLOGICAL CONCEPT OF EMOTIONAL REFLEXIVITY IN ORGANIZATION STUDIES

Bruno Luiz Americo[a], Stewart Clegg[b] and Fagner Carniel[c]

[a]Pontificia Universidad Católica del Perú, Peru
[b]The University of Sydney, Australia
[c]State University of Maringá, Brazil

ABSTRACT

Despite being conjointly stronger in their synergies in the past, there is still a significant gap between management and organization studies and sociology. The temporal lag is also, on occasion, a substantive lag. The emergent sociological concept of emotional reflexivity has recently been used in organizational studies. The question that animates this contribution concerns the nature of this translation, reception, and extension; thus, we ask how organization studies have been using the sociological concept of emotional reflexivity? We will examine recent seminal sociological studies on emotional reflexivity to answer this inquiry and consider some organizational studies citing these. We describe the reception of sociological ideas of emotional reflexivity in management and organization studies literature. By analyzing the differences and disconnections

Sociological Thinking in Contemporary Organizational Scholarship
Research in the Sociology of Organizations, Volume 90, 229–251

ISSN: 0733-558X/doi:10.1108/S0733-558X20240000090009

produced within this discourse, it will be possible to understand that emotional reflexivity is rarely addressed in emotional encounters between people and other modes of being in modern organizations. We introduce narrative fiction as a method; the narrative focuses on the relationships between humans and other beings in the workplace dynamics of a vocational school. The story tells how Charlie, a deaf student, changed his life after entering the vocational school and becoming involved with different pedagogical teaching-learning strategies. Adopting two deaf dogs, which had both suffered from past unsuccessful adoption experiences, produced life-enhancing emotional reflexivity. We conclude with a research agenda scoping further directions.

Keywords: Management and organization studies; sociology; emotional reflexivity; narrative fiction; organizational esthetics; esthetically theorizing

INTRODUCTION

Reflections on social transformations in affective dynamics have always been present in the texts constituting the Western sociological tradition. For instance, Georg Simmel and Émile Durkheim present classic examples. In 1903, Simmel wrote an essay titled "The Metropolis and Mental Life," in which he defended the idea that the blasé attitude, a mixture of reserve, coldness, and indifference, one that could potentially lead to hatred, would result from the psychic demands imposed by the intense flow of urban life with its heterogeneous sensory overload. Durkheim, in turn, elaborated a sophisticated theory of solidarity in *The Division of Labor in Society*, initially published in 1893, from which he sought to answer how social cohesion could be maintained in the face of a lack of affective intensity produced by social differentiation in modern societies.

The boundedness of sociology as a discipline is loose. It relates easily to and spills over into related fields such as anthropology and organization studies. Indeed, Durkheim was as much an anthropologist as a sociologist theorist, while Simmel was as much an urban theorist or social psychologist as a sociologist. The lines were not sharply drawn. That this was the case is hardly surprising; at the dawn of disciplines, before the institutionalization of professionalizing missions, borders yet to be constructed were easily crossed. Their contributions, along with many other reflections on emotions in the social sciences, remained marginal to explanations of the practices and processes of rationalizing social life during much of the 20th century. For instance, that living a work life of legal-rational order might indeed be a strongly emotional vocation for public servants, a message articulated clearly in Weber's (1946) "Politics as a Vocation," was a message that seemed to be lost in translating his ideas into dimensions of bureaucracy (see Clegg, 1990). Indeed, rationality won out over emotionality in the discussion of organizations until the tide turned as a result of the work of sociologists such as Hochschild (1979, 1983) and Albrow (1997). With these contributions, how organizations both induce emotional work and are themselves emotional vessels filtered into the lexicon of management and organization studies. As the work of Werner Schirmer published in this issue demonstrates, emotional aspects are increasingly relevant to organizational life nowadays.

Organization studies, in many ways the orphaned offspring of the sociology of organizations, has recently begun to explore emotional reflexivity. How organization studies use and might use the emergent sociological concept of emotional reflexivity is the research question that we address. We examine recent seminal sociological studies on emotional reflexivity and consider some organizational studies citing these. Then, we describe the disjunctions – the transformations and disconnections produced through the incorporation of emotional reflexivity in organization studies leading to theoretical advances (Hibbert et al., 2014; Strathern, 1987) – produced in management and organization studies' use of emotional reflexivity and elaborate on remaining lacunae. One of these is a residual humanism that marginalizes the consideration of other beings (as well as non-beings) as objects of emotional attachment. To contribute to organizational discussions about organizational reflexivity, we introduce narrative fiction about emotional reflexivity as part of the relationships between humans and other beings in the workplace dynamics of a bilingual vocational school (Portuguese and Libras) and conclude with a research agenda.

LITERATURE REVIEW

Recently, organizational research has extended sociological concepts of emotional reflexivity by decentering the idea of authorial rationality (e.g., Hibbert et al., 2019; Koning & Ooi, 2013) to overcome individualistic and cognitive conceptions of reflexivity (e.g., Cunliffe, 2003; Duncan & Elias, 2021; Hibbert et al., 2014; Weick, 2002). We will consider recent seminal sociological research on emotional reflexivity (e.g., Blackman, 2007; Burkitt, 1997, 2012; Holmes, 2015; Holmes et al., 2021; King, 2006) and citations of them by organization studies. The sociology of emotions is a vast field, and our interest herein lies in its intersection with classic debates on reflexivity. We will consider the shifts produced through the incorporation of emotional reflexivity as a trope from social theory used in organization studies and anthropological scholarship (Hibbert et al., 2014; Strathern, 1987).

In recent years, there has been an increasing consideration of the emotions engaged by relationships between researchers and their subjects, especially regarding research practices, methods, and theories (cf. Cassell et al., 2020; Duncan & Elias, 2021; Gilmore & Kenny, 2015; Hibbert et al., 2014; Munkejord, 2009). Reflexive practice increasingly accommodates the consideration of both researchers' and subjects' agendas and emotions (Cassell et al., 2020; Ruebottom & Auster, 2018). Emotions influence social interactions (e.g., Blakely, 2007; Campbell, 2001; Gilbert, 2001; Harris & Huntington, 2001; Whiteman, 2010). Practices of field-based data collection and analysis of the materials collected are social interactions (Cassell et al., 2020; Munkejord, 2009; Whiteman et al., 2009). Reflection on emotions involved in social interactions is an analytical tool enabling the production of "emotional reflexivity" (Cassell et al., 2020; Munkejord, 2009; Ruebottom &

Auster, 2018; Whiteman et al., 2009). Investigations interpreting how reflexivity is facilitated by emotions (Hibbert et al., 2021) within productive, transformative, and enabling relationships and interactions are increasingly common (Hibbert et al., 2021; Ruebottom & Auster, 2018). Consideration of emotions is an analytical foci for change through learning (Hibbert et al., 2019); emotions illuminate hidden aspects of research practice (Koning & Ooi, 2013), and reflexivity is required if they are to be apprehended as intersubjective processes (Duncan & Elias, 2021). The sociological concept of emotional reflexivity can address emotions at and in work, using emotional reflexivity to take them seriously. Doing so combats the often emotionless protocols of academia (Campbell, 2001; Ellis, 2007; Mohrman, 2010; Mumby & Putnam, 1992; Whiteman et al., 2009, p. 49, 2010). Researchers recognizing the emotionality of their research subjects become emotionally reflexive in making these connections.

In conceptualizing emotional reflexivity as an intersubjective process (e.g., Burkitt, 2012; Cunliffe, 2003; Duncan & Elias, 2021; Hibbert et al., 2014; Holmes, 2015), sociologically influenced scholarship largely addresses relationships between researchers and research subjects through conversational means (cf. Hibbert et al., 2014). Conversation, as an ongoing form of sensemaking and repairing of breaches in the process of achieving understanding, generates confrontation of the performatively projected and looking-glass selves (Cooley, 1902). When it does so, it facilitates reflexive practice (Hibbert et al., 2019, 2021; Ruebottom & Auster, 2018).

Sociologically inclined studies of organizations primarily admit emotional reflexivity as a part of the interactive human condition without considering that other modes of being can enact intersubjective emotions. Multiple realities are continuously being constructed, linking the different worlds of human beings and other modes of being in the world (Kohn, 2015). Human beings enjoy intense emotional relationships with diverse actants that often enter the workplace in emotional discursivity. These can be as diverse as their nation, sovereign, football team, possessions, houses, and devices. As topics and as actants, these can be extremely strong objects of emotional attachment, often leading to interesting and sometimes emotionally charged conversations.

Peoples' emotional attachment can also be with their animals, some of whom enter workplaces not only discursively but also physically, guide dogs, for instance, or as pets. Hence, emotional reflexivity concerning other forms of being than the human should be admitted as part of all the embodied heterogeneous relationships that might occur while working in organizations (Burkitt, 1997, 2012; Castro, 2014; Holbraad & Pedersen, 2017; Holmes, 2010, 2015; Kohn, 2013; Latour, 2005). As far as relationships between people and animals are concerned, recent work on the topic problematizes many taken-for-granted assumptions (Jammaers, 2023). Agonistic and symbiotic relationships between human beings and other animal beings (cf. Cunha et al., 2019; Dashper, 2019; Hamilton & McCabe, 2016; Knights & Clarke, 2018) may or may not be part of the core business of the organizations researched by sociological inquiries (cf. O'Doherty, 2017; Wilkin et al., 2016). Sociological thinking about animals is gaining importance (Kruse, 2002) even as it remains somewhat under-utilized by applied sociology in business and management schools. Hence, the organizational significance of investigation into what Donna Haraway terms human and more-than-human companion species' emotional relationships (Cunha et al., 2019; Labatut et al., 2016).

PROBLEMATIZING THE EMOTIONALIZATION OF REFLEXIVITY IN CONTEMPORARY SOCIOLOGY

Illouz (1997) observed that a focus on objective regularities, patterns of behavior, and institutionalization processes may well be related to a particular fear that the study of subjective, invisible, and personal phenomena (e.g., affections) might undermine the sociological vocation. Fortunately, this scenario has changed (McCarthy, 1994). Emotions are not considered merely as psychological entities but also as cultural and social facts that are historically and hierarchically organized in terms of embodied and socio-cultural moral qualities within relationships (Burkitt, 1997). As a perspective on the importance of emotions in studying embodied relationships, this has become routinized in several fields of social theory, including those dedicated to theorizing reflexivity.

Over the last decade, King (2006) provided a foundational theoretical framework for studies interested in the sociological concept of emotional reflexivity. The concept has developed in critical dialogue with Touraine's (1995, p. 207) theory of subjectivation. King (2006) recognizes the central role that social movements play in producing social changes in late modernity but warns of the need to investigate affective dynamics in the formation of what Touraine called the will to act and be recognized as an actor. King (2006, p. 876) mobilizes the concept of emotional reflexivity to signify a set of "practices of co-counselling" by social activists that would "enable them to both sustain their activism and act creatively in producing society." Holmes (2010), building on this antecedent, developed an approach that was more comprehensive than King's (2006), suggesting that emotions are vital for understanding all forms of sociability. He challenges the lack of attention to emotions in contemporary theories of reflexivity centered on "detraditionalization" (Giddens, 1990) and "risk" (Beck, 1992).

Holmes (2010) was influenced by Mead's (1962) symbolic interactionism. According to Holmes (2010, p. 140), reflexivity should be considered "an emotional, embodied and cognitive process" through which anyone can experience their presence in a world that depends on heterogeneous others. The idea that social theories need to emotionalize reflexivity to build relational and socially embedded models of explanation of human relationships was further advanced by Burkitt (2012). Using Mayrhofer's (2011) study on non-suicidal self-injury, Burkitt (2012, p. 467) argues that "the 'I' that thinks and reflects on itself and the world is based on feelings about its own self that are connected to the relational social world of interaction, in which it is always situated." From this point of view, the debate should focus on how emotions as modes of communication within relationships are monitored or controlled by social habitus and power relations as well as how they inform and motivate reflective thinking (Burkitt, 1997).

There is a lack of emotional reflexivity (Holmes, 2015) in notions that only individualize and objectify affective dynamics in terms of inner processes and practices (Burkitt, 1997), such as emotional intelligence (Goleman, 1996) and emotional work (Hochschild, 1983). There is an analytical distinction between feelings (vague and nebulous) and emotions (articulated and nameable). When we ponder our feelings, they can become categorically assigned among the range of emotions within relationships occurring in social contexts. The categorical device that names the emotion is attached to patterns of interaction in specific situational social contexts (Sacks, 1972). Emotions stem from members' categorization devices in use in relationships, rather than from some individual ability to identify and regulate one's emotions and understand the emotions of others. These categorization devices, as they are experienced, become embrained and embodied (Castells, 2010). By the latter, we mean that the identification of emotions within relationships becomes fused into our ways of thinking, neurologically, as well as our ways of reacting in "emotional" situations, as they are enacted by embodied techniques learned in complex and heterogeneous social contexts (Burkitt, 1997; Holmes, 2015; Latour, 2005). These techniques can range, for instance, from the coldest kind of cool to the most heated form of hot in the emotional register.

Holmes (2015) problematized two research strategies commonly used in the sociology of emotions to investigate intersubjective practices of interpreting feelings: textual analysis and interviewing. After reporting her exploratory study on the profusion of tips on good manners in the use of the social network, Facebook, Holmes (2015, p. 64) concluded that the textual analysis of what people "say" offers essential information about emotional norms but is limited because they cannot convey bodily cues about how they "feel." Holmes (2015, p. 65) further reflects on interviews she conducted with couples in long-distance relationships in the United Kingdom to demonstrate that when multiple interactions occur in a joint interview, we can perceive that "emotional reflexivity is a capacity not just of researchers, but of participants." Emotional reflexivity is relational.

The construction of a sociological concept of emotional reflexivity positions emotions within heterogeneous relationships as central to understanding reflexivity rather than something that can be avoided in reflexive practice (Mills & Kleinman, 1988) or a barrier to doing good research (cf. Blackman, 2007; Burkitt, 2012). Understanding how emotional reflexivity is constituted within relationships sheds sociological light on affective life's intersubjectively embodied and embrained character. It helps to consider "hidden" aspects of social investigations by addressing how emotions are accomplished and theory about these subsequently enacted (Blackman, 2007). As Holmes (2015) wrote, interviewing the members of social relations individually rather than as couples misses the emotional reflexivity that creates the construction of emotional affect.

BECOMING EMOTIONALLY REFLEXIVE IN RESEARCH

Different sociological approaches to the concept of emotional reflexivity (cf. Blackman, 2007; Burkitt, 2012; Holmes, 2010; 2015; Holmes et al., 2021; King, 2006) have been translated into the field of organizations in different ways (cf. Duncan & Elias, 2021; Hibbert et al., 2019, 2021; Koning & Ooi, 2013; Munkejord, 2009; Ruebottom & Auster, 2018). A dialogue began in the 2000s when Munkejord (2009) researched a department of a Fortune 500 company and outlined the idea of "methodological emotional reflexivity," inspired by the concept of "emotional reflexivity" proposed by King (2006). Researchers could be seen to be as emotional as any other craftspeople.

The implications of researchers' emotional involvement when doing fieldwork are multifaceted. They range from a concern with being faithful to those theoretical traditions to which one defers (Clegg & Hardy, 2006). They can include somewhat solipsistic renderings of self-reflection (Shalin, 1986) as well as intersubjective understanding (Tomkins & Eatough, 2010). Munkejord (2009) included the emotions, values, and political agendas of researchers and subjects in academic research, using terms also suggested by Mohrman (2010). Methodological innovations were produced that addressed complex and ambiguous organizational issues (e.g., the changing nature of organizations and ecological crises). Munkejord (2009, p. 151) explored his emotions, using grounded theory to reflect on "emotional labour (Hochschild, 1983), emotional intelligence, moods in organizations, and affective events." The focus was not only on how emotion registers in the daily life of organizations but also on how emotions impact research practices. The idea of "methodological emotional reflexivity," suggested by Munkejord (2009), includes emotional awareness, empathic understanding, and emotions in decision-making. Recording these can be part of memoing in grounded theory.

Blee (1998) notes that once emotions are addressed as "relational expressions" beyond "individual emotional experiences," they can be seen to play a more significant part in the research process. What is required is attention to the researcher's emotions and the emotional relationship that is built between the researcher and researched (cf. Blackman, 2007). Researchers are often encouraged to be detached, objective, impartial, and disinterested in their subjects (Bird, 2020). Whiteman et al. (2009, p. 49), considering what they called the "emotion-less culture of academia" (cf. Campbell, 2001; Ellis, 2007; Mohrman, 2010; Mumby & Putnam, 1992; Whiteman, 2010), examined how emotional experiences from qualitative research add to management studies. The authors re-wrote past research as reflexive examples, contributing to scholarship integrating the emotions of fieldwork in research practice (cf. Mumby & Putnam, 1992; Weick, 2002).

Using emotional experiences is different from identifying and labeling emotions through "cognitive reflexivity" and deciding how to show emotions through "reflexive agency" in the research process. Whiteman et al. (2009) concentrate on emotions as analytic tools to develop new questions, concepts, and analytical insights (cf. Blakely, 2007; Campbell, 2001; Gilbert, 2001; Harris & Huntington, 2001; Whiteman, 2010). They warn that emotions and their attributed meanings should not be separated from cognition, feelings, and interpretations carried out in fieldwork (cf. Campbell, 2001; Gilbert, 2001; Lofland et al., 2006). Whiteman et al. (2009) indicate that it is necessary to understand the disjunctions produced in the process of the emotional culture of researching, creating methodologies, and modeling relations, stressing the importance of mapping the extent to which emotions lead to new questions, concepts, and theories (cf. Blakely, 2007; Weick, 2002). The sociological concept of emotional reflexivity has become a central analytic tool influencing social interaction and how data are collected and analyzed (Munkejord, 2009; Whiteman et al., 2009).

Koning and Ooi (2013) also address the concept of emotional reflexivity (cf. Blackman, 2007; Burkitt, 2012) to present "awkward" ethnographic encounters in the field. The researcher's rationality is usually privileged in the practice of research at the expense of emotions produced between the researcher and researched in the field (cf. Burkitt, 2012). Koning and Ooi (2013, p. 17) favor an "inclusive reflexivity" that allows researchers to highlight hidden aspects of organizational ethnography to improve our understanding of organizational reality. From this perspective, research reports should be "inclusive of the dimensions we all hesitate to explicitly reveal (e.g., fear, heartbreak, alienation, embarrassment), and inclusive of the research participants and their anxieties and agendas."

Ruebottom and Auster (2018) explored the emotional landscape of reflexivity (cf. Burkitt, 2012; King, 2006) from the vantage afforded by institutional theory, demonstrating how reflexivity is produced through emotional dynamics that (dis) embed actors. The authors show that institutional work demands reflexivity, exploring how it can enact an understanding of the social world. For Ruebottom and Auster (2018, p. 4), interactions such as dialogue (cf. Cunliffe, 2002) and storytelling (Gorli et al., 2015) between people of different social positions are central to reflective practice and thinking. In line with Burkitt (2012) and Holmes (2010), they argue that reflexivity demands cognitive and emotional disembedding of entangling emotions. These are "defined as the fleeting sensations and reactions to experience, moods, and the longer-term affective attachments that bond people to each other (p. 3). Reflexivity should be used for "understanding the recursive influence between social structure and emotions, whereby emotions can also alter understandings and facilitate new structural arrangements" (p. 2). To this end, they investigated We Day stadium-hosted youth days as an interstitial event bringing together different perspectives (cf. Cunliffe, 2002) to produce a community of "change-makers." The research findings suggest that such events reflexively disembed actors from given attachments and embed them within new social bonds through (1) personal narratives of injustice/action and (2) individual–collective empowering, challenging actors' conceptions of self/others and changing their way of thinking (also see Biggart, 1989, on the affective relations produced by the embedding processes of "charismatic capitalism" on direct sellers of commodities, such as Avon cosmetics. The emotional reflexivity induced was life-changing).

Dealing with social change but from a different theoretical perspective, Hibbert et al. (2019) contend that while several texts recognize reflexivity as a *driver* for change (cf. Alvesson et al., 2008; Gorli et al., 2015), few regard it as the source of energy for change, an *engine* of change. Hibbert et al. (2019) address how researchers as agents within organizations (Gorli et al., 2015) use reflexive practices, deployed by emotions, rationality, and relationships (Whiteman, 2010; Whiteman et al., 2009), to avoid engaging in changing their self (self-reflexivity/

inward orientation) and/or context (critical reflexivity/outward orientation) (cf. Cunliffe, 2003; Hibbert et al., 2014). Responsibility is at issue (cf. Hibbert & Cunliffe, 2015; Paulsen, 2015). A team of researchers employ "a relationally reflexive approach" in which they "assumed the roles of both researchers and practitioners" (Hibbert et al., 2019, p. 1). Hibbert et al. (2019) map the existence of four styles of reflexive practice by individuals (resigning, relocating, resisting, and reconfiguring). The authors were able to show the extent to which these reflexive practices involve rationality and emotions (cf. Burkitt, 2012; Davies, 2012; Holmes, 2010), noting that emotions, together with reflexive practices, act as motors of change (cf. Burkitt, 2012).

Cassell et al. (2020) claim that emotional experiences generate reflexivity as part of a dialogic and emotional process between researchers and research interlocutors (cf. Burkitt, 2012; Hibbert et al., 2019). These emotional experiences are related to participant reflexivity. Cassell et al. (2020) consider that authorial reflexivity has been privileged to such an extent that little has been written about participant reflexivity. Hence, they recognize the importance of detailing relational and methodological issues that allow the engagement of the research interlocutor in reflexive practice. Specifically, Cassell et al. (2020) identify participant reflexivity produced from a photo-elicitation study of work-life balance and conflict. The types of internal dialogue conveyed when research interlocutors engage in self-reflexivity are outlined, detailing how it is possible to access participant reflexivity methodologically through emotions (cf. Gatrell, 2009).

Hibbert et al. (2021) consider how reflexive practices allow learning from negative emotional experiences, leading to self-change (cf. Hibbert et al., 2019). They investigate experiences in academic organizations through a relationally reflexive (cf. Hibbert et al., 2014) and autoethnographic (cf. Boncori & Smith, 2019) method. The authors address how organization members use reflexive practices of attending, dialoguing, and realigning to learn from negative emotions. For Hibbert et al. (2021), individuals' focus on how containing the pain of traumatic experiences obstructs learning; according to the authors, overcoming such barriers requires resilience from the researchers and research interlocutors. Rather than avoiding trauma, they must seek to engage with emotional experiences that can lead to learning with others (Hibbert et al., 2019). Consequently, there can be a change of understanding about emotional experiences and beliefs (cf. Ogden & Fisher, 2014; Ramsey, 2008) and how future practice proceeds (cf. Hibbert & Cunliffe, 2015). In this context, emotion can be seen as a facilitator of reflexivity (e.g., Burkitt, 2012; Gilmore & Kenny, 2015; Holmes, 2010; King, 2006), especially when dialoguing and interacting with the experience, vocabulary, and expressions of others is possible (e.g., Burkitt, 2012; Gilmore & Kenny, 2015; Holmes, 2010).

Duncan and Elias (2021) also draw insights from the sociological concept of emotional reflexivity, linking up with countertransference to inquire into the unconscious dimensions of field experiences that foster radical reflexivity. They develop a method of writing and analyzing field notes that includes observing, capturing the story, articulating countertransference, and developing interpretations that foreground unconscious dimensions of experience. In making their field notes visible, the authors show how researchers can account for inter-subjective processes, uniting conscious and unconscious dimensions of experi-ence, and producing a shared understanding of organizational dynamics. Duncan and Elias (2021) challenge earlier discourses on reflexivity (e.g., Burkitt, 2012) by defining it as an intersubjective process (e.g., Holmes, 2015) and examining how reflexivity is enacted from the (un)conscious and relational dynamics in research processes between two collaborators.

THE IMPACT OF THE CONCEPT OF EMOTIONAL REFLEXIVITY

The sociological concept of emotional reflexivity led to theoretical and methodo-logical innovations (cf. Hibbert et al., 2014; Strathern, 1987). Overly individualis-tic and cognitive conceptions of reflexivity (e.g., Cunliffe, 2003; Duncan & Elias, 2021; Hibbert et al., 2014, 2019; Koning & Ooi, 2013; Weick, 2002) were overcome by addressing the emotional relationship built between researcher and researched (Munkejord, 2009). The researcher's rationality is decentered by prioritizing the emotions of researchers and subjects in research practices involving accessing each parties' emotional reflexivity (Cassell et al., 2020; Duncan & Elias, 2021; Gilmore & Kenny, 2015; Hibbert et al., 2014; Munkejord, 2009). Emotions are central analytic tools with a reciprocal impact on social interaction (e.g., Blakely, 2007; Campbell, 2001; Gilbert, 2001; Harris & Huntington, 2001; Whiteman, 2010), including data collection and analysis (Munkejord, 2009; Whiteman et al., 2009). In addition, reflexive practice is now taken to include researchers' agendas and their positive and negative emotions toward these agendas as well as those of their interlocutors (Cassell et al., 2020; Ruebottom & Auster, 2018). Instead of being hidden from the final result of the research (Koning & Ooi, 2013) or exposed only in highly emotional contexts (Bennett, 2004; Holmes, 2015), emotions have started to be considered possible engines of change and learning (Hibbert et al., 2019, 2021; Ruebottom & Auster, 2018).

In conceptualizing emotional reflexivity as an intersubjective process, investi-gations primarily address relationships between human subjects in organizations. For instance, sociologically influenced scholarship recognizes the constitutive role of "conversations" between scholars and participants, theory and practice sparked by organizational encounters (Hibbert et al., 2014). In accounting for the role of emotions in facilitating reflexive practices, radically reflexive research-ers understand interactions between people as shared and naturalized, construct-ing intersubjectively the realities being studied (Cunliffe, 2003; Hibbert et al., 2021). The focus has been on how interactions between people of different social classes, producing self-confrontation, can generate reflexive practice (Hibbert et al., 2019, 2021; Holmes, 2010; Ruebottom & Auster, 2018). Emotional reflexivity is admitted as a part of the interactive human condition. Emotional reflexivity is necessary as "relations with others become more diverse and less well-defined, and social conditions more complex" (Holmes, 2015, p. 461). In this sense, it is important to note that social-movement studies; science and technology studies; ethnicity, gender, and class studies; as well as animal studies are examples of transdisciplinary fields of study that allow sociology to be inclusive of human–animal–more-than-human relationships (Kruse, 2002). Sociological understanding grasps the extent to which complex sociality and heterogeneous others jointly are (re)produced (cf. Holmes et al., 2021). Can emotional reflexivity be part of the conditional relationships between human beings and other forms of being? This is the question that we address next in a move to broaden the humanistic scope of the discussion thus far.

A METHODOLOGICAL PROLEGOMENON
Case and Methodology

How does one begin to investigate the emotional relationships between a discursive and non-discursive being? Cases that problematize the discursive privileges of "normal" human beings are one way to proceed. We contribute to discussions about emotional reflexivity through an exercise in theorizing that arises from our research and work experiences with disability, animal welfare, and deafness. We introduce a narrative fiction that addresses emotional reflexivity as part of the embodied relationships between humans and non-human beings in the workplace dynamics of a vocational school.

The descriptive power of narrative fiction can bring singular organizational phenomena into relief as an elaborated version of the methodology of ideal types, as pioneered by Weber (1949; also see Aspalter, 2020). Rather than create a static ideal type as an artificial representation of characteristics accentuated for analytical purposes, we use narrative fiction based on fieldwork to analytically highlight processes in their emotionality. We follow in the steps of earlier pioneers (cf. Jermier, 1985; Phillips, 1995; Whiteman & Phillips, 2008) who were able to "tell us something about the world" encountered (Hansen et al., 2007, p. 113), making valuable contributions to knowledge. Stories, written as qualitative data narratives, can create compelling accounts and raise provocative questions that see the world differently, questioning the previously tacitly taken for granted, to make social reality as it appears to be, "problematic" (Blum, 1971). Through capturing scenes from everyday lives, recording them in detail, and attending to naturally occurring conversations, encounters, and the mundane materiality of daily life, is not easily captured in a traditional ideal type; hence narrative fiction (Américo et al., 2022). Narrative fiction allows us to position the seemingly ordinary processes of emotional reflexivity within a more expansive consideration of ontological matters that can account for other modes of existence (Kohn, 2013; Latour, 2005; O'Doherty, 2017).

To contribute to organizational discussions that deal with discussions about emotional reflexivity, we have produced a narrative fiction based on data drawn from an actual case. People organizing disabled people's education that worked with deaf students initially introduced us to the case, doing so during a lunch break at the Federal Institute of Santa Catarina, bilingual campus (Portuguese and Libras). The narrative was subsequently written after meeting and working with deaf people and consulting sociological narratives about deafness. Our methodological and authorial responsibility to the researched subjects and readers (Hansen et al., 2007, p. 123; Rhodes & Brown, 2005; Strathern, 1987), as authors without the disabilities under consideration, is to move "the reader toward direct participation in knowledge building" (Hansen et al., 2007, p. 113; see also Ng & Cock, 2002). We cannot write from the position of the subjects but strive to capture some of the emotional resonances we encountered.

We produced a narrative fiction to encapsulate the case so that we could theorize about emotional reflexivity as part of the embodied relationships existing between humans and other modes of being in the workplace dynamics of a vocational school. After the narrative fiction is described, we present conclusions, proposing a research agenda to explore how emotional reflexivity can be seen within a more expansive consideration of ontological matters concerning heterogeneous workplaces and organizational relationships. We consider how theoretical sociological research can build an understanding of organizations able to address emotions within increasingly complex social relationships. Before this, we must introduce our narrative and its characters.

The narrative is based on actual people, situations, data, and experiences, as stated. We used fieldwork notes on the management learning of deaf students as well as interview transcripts of interviews and discussions. These were conducted with other educational professionals working with them, as well as with a deaf person who adopted two deaf dogs and an employee working in an Animal Welfare Board of Santa Catarina, Brazil. The protagonist of the narration is Charlie, a deaf student whose life changed when he entered the vocational school and became involved with innovative pedagogical teaching-learning strategies. The vocational school uses dogs for educational purposes. Every Wednesday, the fire department takes two rescue dogs to interact with deaf students to help in the teaching-learning process. Over time, Charlie adopted two dogs that had suffered from unsuccessful adoption experiences, largely because they were also deaf. Thus, the narrative fiction draws attention to how, in a vocational school that calls on deaf people to give meaning to their social experience through heterogeneous pedagogical actions, emotional reflexivity between humans and other modes of existence is produced.

DEAFNESS, DOGS, AND LEARNING

The Narrative

Time was one of the last things I had that late afternoon in December 2018. The selection process for a vacancy as a substitute professor at the Federal Institute of Santa Catarina had been long and tiring. Finally, I was in the last stage: the interview. While waiting for my turn, I walked through the institute's internal courtyards, thinking about the heavy traffic I would face when returning from there, on the mainland, to the capital, on the island of Florianópolis, where I live.

What would it be like to walk this path daily? The best thing was not to think about it too much. I just needed that job.

There was a group of young people playing football with others around the court cheering, dating, or just talking. I sat next to the students, watching the match to rest, distracting myself a little. Summer vacation had already started, yet the school seemed full. After a few moments, I realized that all the students around me were deaf; they were users of Brazilian sign language, and that is how I could tell. I knew that this was a bilingual school. I just did not think it was exclusive to deaf people. I felt butterflies in my stomach as I realized how difficult that language seemed to me at the time. Even more so when one of them, Charlie, came to talk to me. I did not understand what he was trying to tell me, and as soon as he understood the situation, he turned away and went back to his group.

Half an hour later, during the interview, the examining board explained that the bilingual campus was initially conceived as a vocational and technological education unit for primary and higher education primarily aimed at the sign language user community. However, over the years, that group, composed chiefly of hearing teachers who were sign language users, understood that there would not be enough demand to fill all the vacancies. In addition, there was also an insufficiency of teachers proficient in sign language for all curricular units. Therefore, the institute's pedagogical project was changed to integrate deaf and hearing students into a bilingual modality. Without any previous contact with the language, teachers like me would be invited to take courses offered by the institute and would have the support of interpreters in classes with deaf students.

A few weeks later, I received the approval notice. It was a mixture of joy and grief. Despite the possibility of learning many new things when working in a bilingual school, I started to worry about the pedagogical difficulties involved in that work. How would I teach the content if I could not communicate properly with my students? Would it always depend on the mediation of interpreters? How would this affect the dynamics of my classes? Should I organize more expository classes? What type of resources would be more accessible? Should I write on the board or favor slides with images? Could I use subtitled movies? Would I have to evaluate them in Portuguese or sign language?

Learning about Oliver Sacks' (1990) perspectives on Gallaudet University in Washington, DC, and the social history of deafness in American culture in the second half of the 20th century, did not alleviate the anxiety of not knowing what could happen in the classroom. Moreover, the online introductory course to Brazilian sign language that I took did not help much either. After all, I simply did not have any pedagogical training to deal with the tensions involved in navigating the regimes of deafness and hearing, regimes that traditionally expelled deaf people from the hearing world of education.

With the feeling of having to start from "zero," the school year effectively started in February 2019. I would be teaching the subject of entrepreneurship in four high school technical vocational education classes, one of them very small, composed of only seven deaf students, the first class I engaged. Upon entering, Charlie greeted me with a surprised expression, followed by a warm smile. I said,

"Hi," and I went to the teacher's desk to organize the slides to start; that was pretty much all I knew how to signal. He observed me while his classmates chatted absently and signed something. Pedro, the interpreter who had just entered the room at that moment, told me what this was, right after class, while laughing a lot. "Another teacher who cannot talk? At least he is cute!" "Excuse me," he said. "I did not mean to be disrespectful, but it is nice to see how Charlie has matured over the last few years." "How so?" I asked.

It is just that Charlie has been with us since elementary school, and we follow all of his personal development. However, you know, he is the only child of a rigorous Catholic family, of family farmers, without much schooling. And seeing him express his sexuality in front of the class so naturally makes us emotional.

Curious, I wanted to know more details about my new student's story: "So, it was not just at home that Charlie struggled to come out with his sexuality but at school itself, right?" "Yes, Charlie was a very withdrawn boy," explained Pedro,

He signalled badly because his parents never learned sign language, and his classmates made fun of him a lot. So, I think it took him a long time to make friends and expose himself a little more at school. When everyone found out he was gay, it was a general surprise.

"And didn't people handle it well at the time?" I asked. "No, it was complicated for him," he told me, "A year ago, he fought almost every day, his classmates did not like him, the teachers complained about his behaviour, and the parents even wanted to take Charlie out of school."

"But how did things change?" I asked again. He answered, "It was neither one nor another particular thing. Do you know when different beings and parts come together simultaneously?" "Especially after Jessica and Flávia, who are also deaf students, started dating. Yes, I think that was decisive for Charlie and his colleagues to understand that this was a normal situation." After a few moments, Pedro added:

It also was aided by the development of communication. Charlie got a cell phone, went on social media, and started posting intimate things about his feelings. These days, he even has a popular YouTube channel among them. Comedy, can you believe it? He posts all the work done for the technical course in Visual Communication here at the Institute; he loves posting behind-the-scenes stories. It was a way for him to express himself and his feelings to the school and rebuild his image, you know? Moreover, with boosted communication, he can express himself and experience a new world that has opened up to him.

Pedro went on to say:

When Charlie was already on the upswing, he started participating in an educational project hosted by IFSC together with the local fire department, which brings two rescue dogs on Wednesday afternoons to help with the anxiety of deaf students who enter the institution and are in the process of learning Libras. From arrival to departure of the local fire department, Charlie did not let go of these dogs.

Thoughtfully, he said:

That is when he went he looked at the animal welfare board on Instagram and decided to adopt a deaf dog. And then another. Surely, this was a central turning point in his life. The dogs he adopted suffered from chronic stress, as they had lived, discouraged, for years in the shelter, running from house to house as the tutors who adopted them ended up returning them, not accepting their deafness, which was seen as different from the normal.

The teacher responded by saying that: "Adopting a dog is, in fact, a complex experience; it involves many feelings and sensations, negative but mostly positive, that affect us. Pets have beneficial effects on us just by being in the room."
The interpreter agreed with the teacher:

> It sounds a cliché, but having a puppy helps reduce the owner's stress, anxiety, and depression. I noticed that Charlie even started to exercise and entertain more because he likes walking the dogs in the vicinity of the school, throwing sticks in the park, and taking walks in the street for the animal's needs.

As I stored the computer in the bag, I asked: "what made him adopt the deaf dog?"

> "First, Charlie was touched by Huggies' story."

Charlie met Huggies and his story through Instagram and decided he would adopt that deaf dog, who had already been adopted and returned to the shelter numerous times. He told me that when he arrived at the shelter, Huggies put both paws on the chair where he was sitting and put his head on his leg. Charlie looked at that white-haired being and burst into tears. The dog also cried a lot, communicating and connecting with Charlie. Deep down, Charlie knew that, from that moment on, he could not fail him because it would depend on him forever, recalls the interpreter. "The experience was so gratifying that a few months later, he learned of the arrival of another deaf dog at the shelter and adopted the puppy." At the door, Pedro said:

> These two deaf dogs are like Charlie's children. They play and walk together every day. He takes them to day-care too. He perfected his sign by teaching them daily new commands (signs in Libras). They learned the meanings of the signs so fast and make Charlie feel loved! His life was never the same after he adopted Huggies and Angel. For Charlie, he and the dogs feel the same since they are deaf, and one produces a change in the other's behaviour. They are very attached since they are deaf. The most amazing thing, according to Charlie, is that they love to receive visits from deaf people "like us," do you believe it?

He then observed:

> This shows how we can constantly be relearning through different bodies, whether our own, those of colleagues, or our companion animals. This brings us back to our initial conversation; it is a pity that we do not have many people who can work with gender and sexuality in this class. Last year, they had a teacher who worked a lot with theatre and tried to bring this discussion to the classes, but I think the students were not as mature as they are now.

Listening carefully to the story, I asked, "Do you think I should try to incorporate issues of gender and sexuality into my classes more directly?" Pedro replied: "Wow, if you could do that, I am sure it would be something very significant for this group." "I could research some cases of companies that work with the inclusion of trans people to exemplify the content that I intend to address throughout the bimester or organizations that had to deal with gender conflicts publicly," I pondered. "I had already imagined doing this but concerning quotas for people with disabilities in the labor market. Perhaps both – I can present a more general idea of inclusion that encompasses sexual diversity. What do you think?"

Enthusiastically, Pedro retorted, "That is exactly what I feel they need." Then, he expanded on this declaration.

You know, the teachers who arrive here are always very good-willed. They want to help deaf people by bringing the classes closer to their reality. Nevertheless, they often do not realize that deaf people are not just their deafness. You know they have ideas, dreams, desires; they have colours, pets, styles, beliefs, you know? They are as plural and contradictory as anyone else.

I must have looked surprised, judging from Pedro's expression, a reaction that made him smile discreetly, encouraging him to launch one last provocation:

A few years ago, a business professor came by and did an amazing thing. She abandoned the test and the traditional classes, organizing and recording a theatre, which was later uploaded to Charlie's YouTube channel. I think she called it business games: is that it, professor? Students loved this possibility to embody a character, immerse themselves in an imagined environment, and express themselves through performance. Maybe you will come up with something like that too!

DISCUSSION: TOWARD A CONCLUSION AND A RESEARCH AGENDA

What can we learn from this narrative? Charlie and his dogs were not unusual; while they were all deaf, so are many animals. What was unusual was that, despite lacking the discursivity to categorize emotions, deafness did not preclude the formation of emotional reflexivity. Positioning emotions within relationships as primarily discursive omits all that precedes discourse or exists outside its domain, including emotional reflexivity that is non-discursive and that incorporates more than human beings. Charlie does not discourse conventionally any more than do his two deaf dogs. While he learns to speak by signing so that he can communicate with the dogs in this way, as well as with people who have the facility to sign, it is evident from the story that there are essential parts of his emotions within relationships that were maturing before discourse was available to him.

Charlie's being in the world was not defined by his rural background, his largely illiterate parents, or the simple Christianity that shaped all their lives in the country. There is an emotional reflexivity to Charlie's relationships that allows for conversations with others about the nature of his sexuality and the formation of intimate relations with his two companions. The embodied and corporeal aspects of his emotions as communication are not a phenomenon of inner discursive positioning, but one that is enacted by his body within relationships in a social context premised on power relations (cf. Burkitt, 1997). As Charlie matured, his sexuality emerged. While Charlie is objectively deaf and always has been, he is much more than the "objective features" (cf. Illouz, 1997) of his innate deafness and his recognition of his sexuality suggests.

Charlie, a poor boy of an impoverished family in rural Brazil, raised without sign language and living in a silent world riddled with Catholic orthodoxies, discovers his sexuality, despite its stigmatization in his local environment. Later, as he matures at the institute, learning to sign, he gains confidence with different pedagogical strategies, including using dogs to improve teaching-learning practices. From the example of other students, Charlie begins to communicate through social media, often through comedy. On social media, Instagram, he seeks and encounters animal welfare and discovers that they have a dog, Huggie, a dog that is deaf as he is. Another deaf dog turns up. Both had been spurned by other potential owners and keepers, who could not communicate with the dogs. Charlie can. He forges an intense emotional relationship with these dogs. Charlie's emotional reflexivity is not bounded by intersubjective relations with human beings but is bolstered by his emotional attachment with companion species.

It is an emotionally powerful narrative. It has a purpose. To recapitulate, we used narrative fiction to position the seemingly ordinary substances of emotional reflexivity involved in managing and organizing. The story places emotional reflexivity within a more expansive and flat consideration of ontological matters in which different modes of existence can be accommodated (Kohn, 2013; Latour, 2005; O'Doherty, 2017). Dogs are an exemplar of a creature with whom emotional reflexivity is shared. Humans do not circumscribe the limits of emotional reflexivity; as Cunha et al. (2019) note, dogs in organizations are not an anomaly. Neither is emotional reflexivity in relating to them. Nor are emotions within relationships wholly discursively formed. Emotions are a privileged form of communication in themselves (Burkitt, 1997). If that were not so, how could Charlie have come to be who he came to be?

The narrative demonstrates that emotions and emotional reflexivity do not reside within people but arise within relationships. The narrative builds what Burkitt (2012) and Holmes (2010) call a relational and socially embedded explanation of relationships. If reflexivity can be considered an emotional, embodied, and cognitive practice, it is possible to experience our existence in a world that depends on heterogeneous others (Holmes, 2010, p. 140). After all, researchers think and reflect about themselves and research phenomena based on their feelings in situated relations with others, whether these others be human or not (Burkitt, 2012).

Emotional reflexivity, as an analytic tool, influences social interaction and how data are collected and analyzed (Munkejord, 2009; Whiteman et al., 2009), uniting emotions and their attributed meanings to categorizations, cognitions, feelings, and interpretations enacted in fieldwork (see Campbell, 2001; Gilbert, 2001; Lofland et al., 2006). Emotional reflexivity materializes in everyday social and organizational life interactions not only through the interiorization of discourse or cognition but also through the body. Understanding this allows emotions within relationships to become central analytic tools (Harris & Huntington, 2001) for decentering the author's rationality and reflexivity (e.g., Cunliffe, 2003; Duncan & Elias, 2021; Gilmore & Kenny, 2015; Hibbert et al., 2014, 2019; Koning & Ooi, 2013; Weick, 2002). The concept of emotional reflexivity offers organization studies a tool for understanding the role of emotions in producing research findings, subjects, and contexts (Whiteman et al., 2009). Being open to diverse bodily emotions within organizational work would benefit from addressing relations more encompassing and embodied than conventional discourse.

We live in an increasingly complex organizational world, with many sources of dissonance and affect, in which emotions influence how we work and express ourselves. People are constantly asked how they are feeling. It is a common media trope. Whether asked of competitors in the Olympics, Wimbledon, or at the end of any sporting event that is televised (Emmison, 1987), competitors are often asked, "how do you feel about X." In fact, this is one of the most asked questions by interlocutors, whether professionally in the media or everyday life. Emotions are routinely called for. Social catastrophes, environmental crises, and other challenging events seem to encourage analysis of different emotional contexts and relationships. When people answer such queries, they may think that they are referring to something they feel; we would argue that they are, indeed, really feeling something emotional, but they do so not by addressing some inner state of being so much as by making use of members' categories available in public language.

Not all emotional expressions are constituted categorically. The embrainment of a repertoire of emotions is corporeal as well as discursive. The lesson is not that the researcher (or the research subject) needs to be emotionally reflexive to register phenomena but that emotional reflexivity arises within relationships for which categories are available for use in accounts. That is, emotional reflexivity can only be produced within relationships. In the case under consideration, it was produced in relationships between researchers, research subjects, and other modes of existence. It is not that the researchers became emotionally reflexive to register emotional phenomena; it was the relationship established with former co-workers at the Instituto Federal de Santa Catarina (IFSC) and, later, with Charlie and his dogs that allowed emotional reflexivity to emerge as a topic, decentering our (the authors') rationality and individual/cognitive conceptions of reflexivity. Charlie's emotional reflexivity in his relations with his two deaf dogs was pre-discursive and only subsequently expressed through signing. Signing assigned categories but before there were categories, there was an emotional relationship. Organizational studies are most comfortable studying relationships between humans in the workplace. So, just as traditional sociology is being rethought considering developments in the social sciences, such as animal studies, we claim that organizational studies also need to be rethought considering current theoretical and methodological developments in sociology.

Considering the relevance of the sociological concept of emotional reflexivity for management and organization life, our theorizing has relevance for several specific kinds of theorizing, such as the sociology of management learning, reflexivity, sustainability, emotional work, emotional intelligence as well as critical management studies. The implications for theorizing are the need to acknowledge and use emotions in relationships in the workplace theoretically, including relations built by researchers to study events, beings, and subjects in question (Strathern, 2014). Realize also that emotional relations and reflexivity are not just a feature of relations between human beings; they can include more than human beings (Stengers, 2015), other beings that are non-human actants. Future research may well also extend emotional reflexivity to relations with technological and material actants, such as digital devices. As Fisogni (2023) suggests, the "onlife" world, where the real and the digital are conjoined, provides an environment that makes possible the existence of an enlarged sensitivity on the part of relationships between humans and devices.

We propose a research agenda building on sociologically inspired research into emotional reflexivity (e.g., Duncan & Elias, 2021; Hibbert et al., 2019, 2021; Koning & Ooi, 2013; Munkejord, 2009; Ruebottom & Auster, 2018). First, we question how emotional reflexivity can be seen within a more expansive consideration of ontology in which emotions are a mode of communication with embodied and social-cultural aspects that can only emerge within relationships (Burkitt, 1997). If emotions experienced within relationships are a form of communication, then the sociology of organizations can extend emotional reflexivity to relations between people and other modes of existence that nowadays permeate modern organizations (cf. O'Doherty & Neyland, 2019). The investigation of emotional reflexivity should focus on the multiple interpretive and relational situations of researchers, research subjects, other modes of existence, and the kinds of communications established in carrying out joint initiatives. What efforts are made to recognize and address emotions in complex organizational interactions and relationships? Discourse on the page cannot easily capture the essential emotionality of inflection, embodiment, glances, and shifts. Videography can but the camera should not point only at the research subjects. It needs to capture what emotions arise from the relationship between researchers, research subjects, as well as between humans and other modes of existence in the organization.

Second, Cunha et al. (2019) note that the field of sociologically oriented organization studies has been largely impermeable to the influence of the new discipline of human–animal studies (DeMello, 2012; Hosey & Melfi, 2014; Shapiro & DeMello, 2010). Even though, more recently, critical research has begun to address the relationships enacted between humans and animals in organizations (Jammaers, 2023), sociological thinking about animals has been under-utilized by applied organizational sociology (cf. Kruse, 2002). Much more can be said about the emotions within relationships between researchers, workers, and other modes of existence in organizations (Cunha et al., 2019; Labatut et al., 2016). Organizations are primarily thought of as exclusively human preserves in which other forms of life, as well as non-vital actant, events, and artifacts, have not been granted a significant role (Michel, 2014). Sociologically, they should be, if only because social interaction or the resolution of intersubjective controversies can occur through unconscious meanings attached to everyday objects, kinds of being, and events (Kohn, 2013; Latour, 1996). As science increasingly produces evidence of the catastrophic effects of human activity on Earth (Heikkurinen et al., 2021; Stengers, 2015), relationships between humans and natures are changing in different, increasingly emotional, organizational contexts. Thus, investigations of emotional reflexivity should concentrate on the emotions within relationships between employees and other modes of existence, other natures, especially in terms of the organizationally anthropocentric effects of practices on nature in general.

Third, sociologically, the primacy of researchers' rationality is being decentered by incorporating the emotions of both researchers and research subjects through research practices, methods, and theories allowing access to their joint emotional reflexivity (Cassell et al., 2020; Duncan & Elias, 2021; Gilmore & Kenny, 2015; Hibbert et al., 2014; Munkejord, 2009). However, cognitive and human-centered conceptions still largely frame the rationality of the researcher. Scholarship would benefit from sociological research embracing social contexts as complex and heterogeneous constructions (Burkitt, 1997; Holmes, 2015; Latour, 2005) to expand the emotionalization of reflexivity.

The boundaries between subjectivity and objectivity, nature, and culture were blurred in Charlie's story and are becoming hazier in sociological approaches to areas such as ecological social movements, science and technology studies, as well as animal studies (Kruse, 2002). Other beings and entities comprise significant parts of the social scene in relationships with humans in all of these arenas. Beings other than humans (Kohn, 2013; O'Doherty, 2017), as well as objects and events (Latour, 1996, 2005), enact emotions within relationships in changing times (Holmes, 2015). Other kinds of beings, even deaf dogs, see and represent us, and their relations with us matter meaningfully (cf. Castro, 2014; Kohn, 2007, 2013). Even seemingly voluntary total institutions (Sundberg, 2024, this volume), which deaf schools might be thought to be, as both institutional schools and institutional spaces of silence, contain relationships and beings that articulate and create an emotional register of the "sounds of silence." Similarly, as Kohn (2013) maintains,

we can know something of how red might be experienced by a blind person, what it might be like to be a bat, or what those dogs might have been thinking moments before they were attacked, however mediated, provisional, fallible, and tenuous these understandings may be. (p. 89)

Sociologically, we cannot limit ourselves only to questioning people about their interpretation of the world, using what they say to explain what they do (Latour & Woolgar, 1986), limiting understanding of what is "distinctively human by means of that which is distinctive to humans" (Kohn, 2013, p. 6). We need to consider how other modes of existence treat us as selves rather than regard their relations with us as a subsidiary, secondary, of less consequence. Developing this sociological and emotional reflexivity will be an increasingly important part of a post-humanist agenda for a truly sociological analysis of organizing and organizations, its materials, affordances, and emotionality, whether in relation to various forms of life or other phenomena.

REFERENCES

Albrow, M. (1997). *Do organizations have feelings?* Routledge.
Alvesson, M., Hardy, C., & Harley, B. (2008). Reflecting on reflexivity: Reflexive textual practices in organization and management theory. *Journal of Management Studies, 45*, 480–501.
Américo, B., Clegg, S. R., & Tureta, S. (2022) *Qualitative management research in context: Data collection, interpretation and narrative.* Routledge.
Aspalter, C. (Ed.). (2020). Back to the origins: The ideal-type methodology in social sciences as developed by Max Weber. In *Ideal types in comparative social policy* (pp. 90–104). Routledge.
Beck, U. (1992). *Risk society.* Sage.
Bennett, K. (2004). Emotionally intelligent research. *Area, 36*(4), 414–422.
Biggart, N. W. (1989). *Charismatic capitalism: Direct selling organizations in America.* University of Chicago Press.
Bird, F. (2020). A defense of objectivity in the social sciences, rightly understood. *Sustainability: Science, Practice and Policy, 16*(1), 83–98.
Blackman, S. J. (2007). Hidden ethnography: Crossing emotional borders in qualitative accounts of young people's lives. *Sociology, 41*(4), 699–716.
Blakely, K. (2007). Reflections on the role of emotion in feminist research. *International Journal of Qualitative Methods, 6*(2), 59–68.
Blee, K. M. (1998). White-knuckle research: Emotional dynamics in fieldwork with racist activists. *Qualitative Sociology, 21*(4), 381–399.

Blum, A. F. (1971). Theorizing. In J. D. Douglas (Ed.), *Understanding everyday life: Towards the reconstruction of sociological knowledge* (pp. 301–331). Routledge & Keagan Paul.

Boncori, I., & Smith, C. (2019). I lost my baby today: Embodied writing and learning in organizations. *Management Learning, 50*, 74–86.

Burkitt, I. (1997). Social relationships and emotions. *Sociology, 31*(1), 37–55.

Burkitt, I. (2012). Emotional reflexivity: Feeling, emotion and imagination in reflexive dialogues. *Sociology, 46*(3), 458–472.

Campbell, R. (2001). *Emotionally involved: The impact of researching rape*. Routledge.

Cassell, C., Radcliffe, L., & Malik, F. (2020). Participant reflexivity in organizational research design. *Organizational Research Methods, 23*(4), 750–773.

Castells, M. (2010). *Communication power*. Oxford University Press.

Castro, E. (2014). *Cannibal metaphysics*. University of Minnesota Press.

Clegg, S. R. (1990) *Modern organizations: Organization studies in the postmodern world*. Sage.

Clegg, S. R., & Hardy, C. (2006). Representation and reflexivity. In S. R. Clegg, C. Hardy, W. Nord, & T. Lawrence (Eds.), *Handbook of organization studies* (new, completely rev. 2nd ed., pp. 423–444). Sage.

Cooley, C. H. (1902). *Human nature and the social order*. Scribner.

Cunha, M. P. E., Rego, A., & Munro, I. (2019). Dogs in organizations. *Human Relations, 72*(4), 778–800.

Cunliffe, A. L. (2002). Reflexive dialogical practice in management learning. *Management Learning, 33*, 35–61.

Cunliffe, A. L. (2003). Reflexive inquiry in organizational research: Questions and possibilities. *Human Relations, 56*(8), 983–1003.

Dashper, K. (2019). Challenging the gendered rhetoric of success? The limitations of women-only mentoring for tackling gender inequality in the workplace. *Gender, Work & Organization, 26*(4), 541–557.

Davies, P. (2012). 'Me', 'me', 'me': The use of the first person in academic writing and some reflections on subjective analyses of personal experiences. *Sociology, 46*, 744–752.

DeMello, M. (2012). *Animals and society: An introduction to human-animal studies*. Columbia University Press.

Duncan, C. M., & Elias, S. R. (2021). (Inter) subjectivity in the research pair: Countertransference and radical reflexivity in organizational research. *Organization, 28*(4), 662–684.

Ellis, C. (2007). The emotional life: Honoring Ronald J. Pelias. In N. K. Denzin (Ed.), *Studies in symbolic interaction* (pp. 9–15). Oxford University Press.

Emmison, J. M. (1987). Victors and vanquished: The social organization of ceremonial congratulations and commiserations. *Language & Communication, 7*(2), 93–110.

Fisogni, P. (2023). Machine learning and emotions. In D. Phung, G. I. Webb, & C. Sammu (Eds.), *Encyclopedia of data science and machine learning* (pp. 961–970). Springer.

Gatrell, C. (2009). Safeguarding subjects? A reflexive appraisal of researcher accountability in qualitative interviews. *Qualitative Research in Organizations and Management: An International Journal, 4*(2), 110–122.

Giddens, A. (1990). *The consequences of modernity*. Stanford University Press.

Gilbert, K. (2001). *The emotional nature of qualitative research*. CRC Press.

Gilmore, S., & Kenny, K. (2015). Work-worlds colliding: Self-reflexivity, power and emotion in organizational ethnography. *Human Relations, 68*(1), 55–78.

Goleman, D. (1996). *Emotional intelligence: Why it can matter more than IQ*. Bloomsbury.

Gorli, M., Nicolini, D., & Scaratti, G. (2015). Reflexivity in practice: Tools and conditions for developing organizational authorship. *Human Relations, 68*, 1347–1375.

Hamilton, L., & McCabe, D. (2016). 'It's just a job': Understanding emotion work, de-animalization and the compartmentalization of organized animal slaughter. *Organization, 23*(3), 330–350.

Hansen, H., Barry, D., Boje, D. M., & Hatch, M. J. (2007). Truth or consequences: An improvised collective story construction. *Journal of Management Inquiry, 16*(2), 112–126.

Harris, J., & Huntington, A. (2001). Emotions as analytic tools: Qualitative research, feelings, and psychotherapeutic insight. In K. Gilbert (Ed.), *The emotional nature of qualitative research* (pp. 129–146). CRC Press.

Heikkurinen, P., Clegg, S., Pinnington, A. H., Nicolopoulou, K., & Alcaraz, J. M. (2021). Managing the Anthropocene: Relational agency and power to respect planetary boundaries. *Organization & Environment, 34*(2), 267–286.

Hibbert, P., Beech, N., Callagher, L., & Siedlok, F. (2021). After the pain: Reflexive practice, emotion work and learning. *Organization Studies, 43*(5), 797–817.

Hibbert, P., Callagher, L., Siedlok, F., Windahl, C., & Kim, H. S. (2019). (Engaging or avoiding) Change through reflexive practices. *Journal of Management Inquiry, 28*(2), 187–203.

Hibbert, P., & Cunliffe, A. (2015). Responsible management: Engaging moral reflexive practice through threshold concepts. *Journal of Business Ethics, 127*(1), 177–188.

Hibbert, P., Sillince, J., Diefenbach, T., & Cunliffe, A. L. (2014). Relationally reflexive practice: A generative approach to theory development in qualitative research. *Organizational Research Methods, 17*(3), 278–298.

Hochschild, A. R. (1979). Emotion work, feeling rules, and social-structure. *American Journal of Sociology, 85,* 551–575.

Hochschild, A. R. (1983). *The managed heart: Commercialization of human feeling.* University of California Press.

Holbraad, M., & Pedersen, M. A. (2017). *The ontological turn: An anthropological exposition.* Cambridge University Press.

Holmes, M. (2010). The emotionalization of reflexivity. *Sociology, 44*(1), 139–154.

Holmes, M. (2015). Researching emotional reflexivity. *Emotion Review, 7*(1), 61–66.

Holmes, M., Jamieson, L., & Natalier, K. (2021). Future building and emotional reflexivity: Gendered or queered navigations of agency in non-normative relationships? *Sociology, 55*(4), 734–750.

Hosey, G., & Melfi, V. (2014). Human animal interactions, relationships and bonds: A review and analysis of the literature. *International Journal of Comparative Psychology, 27*(1), 117–142.

Illouz, E. (1997). *Consuming the romantic utopia.* University of California Press.

Jammaers, E. (2023). On ableism and anthropocentrism: A canine perspective on the workplace inclusion of disabled people. *Human Relations, 76*(2), 233–257.

Jermier, J. M. (1985). "When the sleeper wakes": A short story extending themes in radical organization theory. *Journal of Management, 11*(2), 67–80.

King, D. S. (2006). Activists and emotional reflexivity: Towards Touraine's subject as social movement. *Sociology, 40*(5), 873–91.

Knights, D., & Clarke, C. (2018). Living on the edge? Professional anxieties at work in academia and veterinary practice. *Culture and Organization, 24*(2), 134–153.

Kohn, E. (2007). How dogs dream: Amazonian natures and the politics of transspecies engagement. *American Ethnologist, 34*(1), 3–24.

Kohn, E. (2013). *How forests think.* University of California Press.

Kohn, E. (2015). Anthropology of ontologies. *Annual Review of Anthropology, 44*(1), 311–327.

Koning, J., & Ooi, C. S. (2013). Awkward encounters and ethnography. *Qualitative Research in Organizations and Management: An International Journal, 8*(1), 16–32.

Kruse, C. (2002). Social animals: Animal studies and sociology. *Society & Animals, 10*(4), 375–379.

Labatut, J., Munro, I., & Desmond, J. (2016). Animals and organizations. *Organization, 23*(3), 315–329.

Latour, B. (1996). On interobjectivity. *Mind, Culture, and Activity, 3*(4), 228–245.

Latour, B. (2005). *Reassembling the social: An introduction to actor-network-theory.* Clarendon.

Latour, B., & Woolgar, S. (1986). Laboratory life. Sage.

Lofland, J., Snow, D. A., Anderson, L., & Lofland, L. H. (2006). *Analyzing social settings: A guide to qualitative observation and analysis* (4th ed.). Wardsworth.

Mayrhofer, A. (2011). *The practice of non-suicidal self-injury: A sociological enquiry.* Peter Lang GmbH.

McCarthy, D. E. (1994). The social construction of emotions: New directions from culture theory. *Social Perspectives on Emotion, 2,* 267–279.

Mead, G. H. (1962). *Mind, self, and society: From the standpoint of a social behaviourist.* University of Chicago Press.

Michel, A. (2014). The mutual constitution of persons and organizations: An ontological perspective on organizational change. *Organization Science, 25*(4), 1082–1110.

Mills, T., & Kleinman, S. (1988). Emotions, reflexivity, and action: An interactionist analysis. *Social Forces, 66,* 1009–1027.

Mohrman, S. A. (2010). Emotions, values, and methodology: Contributing to the nature of the world we live in whether we intend to or not. *Journal of Management Inquiry, 19*(4), 345–347.

Mumby, D. K., & Putnam, L. L. (1992). The politics of emotion: A feminist reading of bounded rationality. *Academy of Management Review, 17,* 465–486.

Munkejord, K. (2009). Methodological emotional reflexivity: The role of researcher emotions in grounded theory research. *Qualitative Research in Organizations and Management: An International Journal, 4*(2), 151–167.

Ng, W., & Cock, C. D. (2002). Battle in the boardroom: A discursive perspective. *Journal of Management Studies, 39*(1), 23–49.

O'Doherty, D. P. (2017). *Reconstructing organization: The loungification of society*. Palgrave Macmillan.

O'Doherty, D., & Neyland, D. (2019). The developments in ethnographic studies of organizing: Towards objects of ignorance and objects of concern. *Organization, 26*(4), 449–469.

Ogden, P., & Fisher, J. (2014). *Sensorimotor psychotherapy: Interventions for trauma and attachment*. Norton.

Paulsen, R. (2015). Non-work at work: Resistance or what? *Organization, 22*, 351–367.

Phillips, N. (1995). Telling organizational tales: On the role of narrative fiction in the study of organizations. *Organization Studies, 16*(4), 625–649.

Ramsey, C. M. (2008). Managing to learn: The social poetics of a polyphonic classroom. *Organization Studies, 24*, 543–558.

Rhodes, C. H. & Brown, A. D. (2005). Writing responsibly: Narrative fiction and organization studies. *Organization, 12*(4), 467–491.

Ruebottom, T., & Auster, E. R. (2018). Reflexive dis/embedding: Personal narratives, empowerment and the emotional dynamics of interstitial events. *Organization Studies, 39*(4), 467–490.

Sacks, H. (1972). An initial investigation of the usability of conversational data for doing sociology. In D. Sudnow (Ed.), *Studies in social interaction* (pp. 31–73). The Free Press.

Sacks, O. (1990). *Seeing voices: Journey into the deaf world*. University of California Press.

Shalin, D. N. (1986). Pragmatism and social interactionism. *American Sociological Review, 51*(2), 9–29.

Shapiro, K., & DeMello, M. (2010). The state of human–animal studies. *Society & Animals, 18*(3), 307–318.

Stengers, I. (2015). *In catastrophic times: Resisting the coming barbarism*. Open Humanities Press.

Strathern, M. (1987). Out of context. *Current Anthropology, 28*(3), 251–281.

Strathern, M. (2014). Reading relations backwards. *Journal of the Royal Anthropological Institute, 20*(1), 3–19.

Sundberg, M. (2024). The promise of total institutions in the sociology of organizations: Implications of regimental and monastic obedience for Underlife. In S. Clegg, M. Grothe-Hammer, & K. Serrano Velarde (Eds.), *Sociological thinking in contemporary organizational scholarship: research in the sociology of organizations* (Research in the Sociology of Organizations, Vol. 90, pp. 253–270). Emerald Publishing.

Tomkins, L., & Eatough, V. (2010). Towards an integrative reflexivity in organisational research. *Qualitative Research in Organizations and Management: An International Journal, 5*(2), 162–181.

Touraine, A. (1995) *Critique of modernity*. Basil Blackwell.

Weber, M. (1946). *From Max Weber* (H. H. Gerth & C. W. Mills, Eds.). Oxford University Press.

Weber, M. (1949). Objectivity in social science and social policy. In E. A. Shils & H. A. Finch (Eds.), *The methodology of the social sciences* (pp. 49–112). Free Press.

Weick, K. E. (2002). Essai: Real-time reflexivity: Prods to reflection. *Organization Studies, 23*(6), 893–898.

Whiteman, G. (2010). Management studies that break your heart. *Journal of Management Inquiry, 19*(4), 328–337.

Whiteman, G., Müller, T., & Johnson, J. M. (2009). Strong emotions at work. *Qualitative Research in Organizations and Management: An International Journal, 4*(1), 46–61.

Whiteman, G., & Phillips, N. (2008, December). *The role of narrative fiction and semi-fiction in organizational studies*. ERIM Report Series Research in Management.

Wilkin, C. L., Fairlie, P., & Ezzedeen, S. R. (2016). Who let the dogs in? A look at pet-friendly workplaces. *International Journal of Workplace Health Management, 9*(1), 96–109.

THE PROMISE OF TOTAL INSTITUTIONS IN THE SOCIOLOGY OF ORGANIZATIONS: IMPLICATIONS OF REGIMENTAL AND MONASTIC OBEDIENCE FOR UNDERLIFE

Mikaela Sundberg[a,b]

[a]Department of Sociology, Stockholm University, Sweden
[b]SCORE, Stockholm University, Sweden

ABSTRACT

Goffman's (1961) work on total institutions has been relatively neglected in the fields of organizational research. This paper compares the conceptions of obedience to authority in two different types of voluntary total institutions and how such conceptions affect interaction contrary to the aims of the organizations. Consequently, by addressing how conceptions of authority and constructions of the obedient self shape conditions for underlife, the analysis provides knowledge about the variety of ways in which total institutional authority works and contributes to the understanding of the mechanisms of organizational underlife.

Keywords: Total institutions; authority; obedience; research paper; underlife

Sociological Thinking in Contemporary Organizational Scholarship
Research in the Sociology of Organizations, Volume 90, 253–269
ISSN: 0733-558X/doi:10.1108/S0733-558X20240000090010

INTRODUCTION

Sociologists of organization have studied all kinds of organizing and organizations, from many different perspectives. Erving Goffman's (1961) work on total institutions has been relatively "neglected" (Clegg, 2006b) however, and inspired few studies and discussions within the fields of organizational research (for exceptions, see, e.g., Clegg et al., 2012; Sundberg, 2015a). This is a pity because of the insights into authority his perspective offers. Because the total institution is a "social hybrid, part residential community, part formal organization" (Goffman, 1961, p. 12), it challenges the boundary between organizational life and private life that studies of organizations often maintain (at least implicitly). As walled-in-units where people work, eat, and sleep, they break down the barriers typical of modern Western society. Containing the totality of the lives of those living there implies exercising a great deal of authority over them: "The handling of many human needs by the bureaucratic organization of whole blocks of people (...) is the key fact of total institutions," Goffman (1961, p. 6) says. This has led some scholars to view total institutions as showing the "dark" side of organization (Clegg, 2006a). Manning (2008, p. 683) claims that Goffman's (1961) analysis is "premised on the notion that a formal organization that denies what might be called humanity (...) cannot function" and Clegg's (2006b) discussion on the neglect of Goffman (1961) focuses primarily on its usefulness for understanding crimes against humanity. The scope of authority of total institutions is indeed extremely encompassing compared to most other types of organizations. Yet does this necessarily mean that total institutions only offer us a closer inspection of the malfunctioning and negative consequences of organization?

In this paper, I draw inspiration from Goffman's (1961) concept but take a neutral stance relative to the authority of total institutions. More specifically, I shift focus from the shaping of selves that sociological studies of total institutions often engage in, to analyze conceptions of obedience to authority and how such conceptions affect interaction contrary to the aims of the organizations. By comparing two different types of voluntary total institutions, this paper provides more detailed knowledge about the variations in how total institutional authority works.

THE CONCEPT OF THE TOTAL INSTITUTION

Goffman (1961) introduced the concept of the total institution in *Asylums*, a collection of four essays based on the ethnography of a psychiatric hospital in Washington, DC, where the vivid description of life in that specific context served as a case study of a significant phenomenon under extreme circumstances. The psychiatric ward is but one *example* among a whole set of different types of total institutions, all of which are characterized by closed residency, detailed regulation of everyday living, and a goal to change its inhabitants. These three characteristics may be present in various degrees, in other words, total institutions can be *more or less* closed, regulated, and focused on identity change. More specifically, Goffman

(1961, p. xiii) defined a total institution as "a place of residence and work where a large number of like-situated individuals cut off from the wider society for an appreciable period of time together lead an enclosed formally administered round of life." Based on their different functions, Goffman (1961, pp. 4–5) sketched five different types of total institutions. Care for the incapable, who are unintentionally harmful, includes psychiatric hospitals or, historically, homes for those with an infectious disease. Protection from the harmful and dangerous, who appear as intentionally threatening, is a second type, represented by institutions such as prisons and prison camps. The third type, care for the harmless, disabled, and incapable, includes homes for the elderly and orphanages. Monasteries are prime examples of the fourth type: sanctuaries for those who voluntarily retreat from society. The final type is those institutions that enable the collective pursuit of an educational or work task, such as boarding schools and military camps.

In subsequent work, scholars have applied Goffman's concept of the total institution to studies of prisons (e.g., Crewe et al., 2014; McCorkel, 1998), residential youth care (e.g., Wästerfors, 2012), extermination camps (Clegg et al., 2012), homes for the elderly (e.g., Bennett, 1963; Gubrium, 1997), army/garrison life (e.g., Kirke, 2010; Sundberg, 2015a), and monasteries (e.g., Clot-Garrell, 2022; Sundberg, 2022). Studies have also extended the concept to types not mentioned by Goffman, like the kibbutz system (Goldenberg & Wekerle, 1972), folk high schools (Fürst, 2022), and different types of ships (e.g., Reyes, 2018; Tracy, 2000; Zurcher, 1965). Shenkar (1996) even reflected on the total institutional characteristics of firms.[1] Such expansions can be fruitful but must pay attention to the defining characteristics of total institutions as social hybrids of both residency and work to not lose track of what is distinctive about them.

As a place of residence, life in total institutions differs from both a family household and solitary living not only by being a form of batch living but also by its rigid regulation and by the scheduling of all areas of life. Total institutions limit access to valued resources, including material possessions, time, personal space, control over one's daily routines, personal contact with outsiders, and sometimes also with insiders. Entering total institutions generally involves having to ask for permission to do things adults are normally entitled to do. In doing so, total institutional residence entails the renunciation of individual sovereignty by giving up a significant amount of the autonomy that an adult typically has, at least relative to matters outside work life. The detail of regulations makes total institutional life distinctive: "[A]uthority of total institutions is directed to a multitude of items of conduct (…) that constantly occur and constantly come up for judgment" (Goffman, 1961, p. 41). Yet *who* is making those judgments depends on the characteristics of total institutions as workplaces. Total institutions exhibit different social differentiation and dynamics when it comes to the positions and roles of the people who frequent them. In the case of, for example, prisons, youth care, and homes for the elderly, staff work with inmates, and the division between these categories is sharp and definitive. Within the army, the division between enlisted men and officers often corresponds to a "staff–inmate" relationship. In monasteries, the division between staff and inmates is inexistent. I return to the implications of this for authority below.

THE TRADITIONAL FOCUS: SHAPING NEW SELVES

Goffman (1961) addresses the extensive authority and restrictions in terms of the effect on inmate identity. Restrictions form an essential part of the "mortification process" (Goffman, 1961, pp. 14–48) of total institutions ultimately aiming to form a new inmate self.[2] Because total institutional arrangements are intense and all-encompassing, one would expect them to be effective at resocializing, but total institutional "programs" do not always succeed. In the context of the psychiatric hospital in Goffman's (1961) study, patients did not necessarily identify with the label as "mentally ill," nor did they transform the way the staff's "work" on them intended. Goffman (1961) also noted self-respecting tendencies, serving to distance actors from the roles ascribed to them by the institution and maintain a sense of their previous identity. More specifically, Goffman (1961, pp. 54–60, 188–207) distinguished between primary and secondary adjustments. Primary adjustment refers to how members who have learned the official rules act by following organizational expectations, whereas secondary adjustment refers to the tactics and strategies through which members use unauthorized means to achieve authorized goals, or vice versa. Consequently, these are two different ways in which socialized members deal with organizational expectations. What constitutes primary and secondary adjustments depend on the institutional arrangement, but both forms exist across all types of organizational life. Adjustments are not exclusively individual affairs, however. In their more collective versions, secondary adjustments in the psychiatric hospital (and elsewhere) constitute what Goffman refers to as the institutional *underlife*. As a distinctive interaction context with its own socialization and mechanisms of informal social control, it is a context of central concern in Goffman's (1961) analysis of the psychiatric hospital.

How members resist, adapt, or internalize the identity imposed upon them is a common theme in subsequent studies of total institutions. For example, how residents' self-conceptions change because of their interaction with staff and the restrictions (Bennett, 1963) or in contrast, how residents manage to enact imagined identities against rigid structures and work-related categories of the staff (Paterniti, 2000). The spatial organization of a total institution can shape the inmates' behaviors and secondary adjustments often depend to some extent on "free space" where to perform them (cf. Goffman, 1961, pp. 230, 305). Different total institutions vary significantly concerning the existence of such spaces. Some studies reveal almost inescapable expectations, on emotional expression for example (Tracy, 2000), or control in "double" total institutions, such as drug treatment programs for incarcerated offenders (e.g., McCorkel, 1998).

A common misunderstanding is to see repressive power and forced change – "killing" the old self against the inmates' will, as it were – as intrinsic to total institutions (see also Mouzelis, 1971, p. 114). Goffman's (1961) introductory and at times inconsistent discussion certainly provides some support for such reasoning. For example, referring to total institutions as "forcing houses for changing people," Goffman (1961, p. 12) implies that involuntary re-socialization is a central aspect of total institutions. This is also the empirical focus in *Asylums*. At the same time, Goffman (1961, pp. 46–48) mentions that the meaning of "mortification" procedures is radically different depending on the institution in which they take place and also suggests the degree of self-regulated change and a spirit of entry as some of the ways in which total institutions differ (see Goffman, 1961, pp. 113–123). Although the distinction is not always clear-cut empirically, analytically distinguishing between *coercive* and *voluntary* total institutions is important. For example, the adaptation, conception, and experience of authority among those who are affected by it must differ depending on if they have been forced, perhaps even locked in, into such places or whether they have willingly entered to submit. An active underlife is also likely to be less common and less significant in a voluntary total institution composed of, presumably, like-minded members who share the aim to transform their identity (Scott, 2011). Assuming that total institutions are "dark" is problematic concerning the latter cases, in part because it implies that the members of voluntary total institutions are "cultural dopes," not understanding their own best (cf. Scott, 2011).

A NEW FOCUS: AUTHORITY AND OBEDIENCE IN VOLUNTARY TOTAL INSTITUTIONS

I suggest that voluntary total institutions offer research sites for studies of more or less total forms of authority. Authority implies that members have agreed in principle to adhere to decisions made (Ahrne, 2021, p. 67). In one of the classic contributions to organization studies, Barnard (1968) suggested that a "zone of indifference," within which subordinates accept without discussion the decision of superiors, is a precondition for authority in organizations (see Lodrup-Hjorth & du Gay, 2024, this volume, for extensive discussion of other features of Barnard's (1968) work). According to Barnard (1968, p. 169),

> there are a number [of directives] which are clearly unacceptable, that is which will certainly not be obeyed, there is another group somewhat more or less on ... neutral lines .... And a third group unquestionably acceptable. This last group lies within "the zone of indifference." The person affected will accept orders lying within this zone and is relatively indifferent to what the order is.

Because total institutional authority extends into what is commonly thought of as personal and private decisions, many directives of total institutions would in other organizations be regarded as unacceptable. In other words, the "zone" is, presumably, expected to be large among those who frequent voluntary total institutions. Given that the "functions" (goals, activities, etc.) of total institutions differ, it is relevant to reflect upon potential differences in the meaning of "indifference" however. Courpasson and Dany (2003) remark that the term zone of indifference seems to imply mindless, blind, and uncritical support of orders but argue that moral pillars must legitimize and sustain obedience. According to Courpasson and Dany (2003, p. 1241), obedience to authority is a social process where orders will be obeyed because subordinates share certain beliefs about the validity of the order (and about the person of their superior), related to the content of the zone of indifference. This view implies that obedience is connected to the moral support of behavioral compliance. This discussion seems to focus primarily on how individual members relate to authority, but what are the implications for interaction?

If members of voluntary total institutions are more inclined to pursue interaction in line with the aim of the organization compared to coercive total institutions, this means that there is a limited underlife (see also Scott, 2011). Discussing the implications of Goffman (1961) for organization studies, Manning (2008, p. 685) claims that "[e]very organization has an underlife – the modes of interacting in place and times that are contrary to the stated instrumental aim of the organization." The presence (and importance) of such interaction contexts points to one of the general ways in which Goffman's (1961) work is relevant for the sociology of organizations. It is, furthermore, evident that the underlife is made up of different concrete modes of interaction and activities depending on the organization. Previous research points to the implications of "spaces" for engaging in them, as mentioned above. In the present paper, I contribute to the understanding of the mechanisms of organizational underlife by addressing how *conceptions* of authority and obedience shape *conditions* for underlife. Even if the zone of indifference is located in individual subordinates, the conceptions of obedience affect social interaction among those subordinates.

COMPARING VOLUNTARY TOTAL INSTITUTIONS: METHOD AND MATERIAL

My exploration of authority is based on comparing cases of two specific types of voluntary total institutions. How do the conceptions of obedience to authority in a professional military unit differ from monastic obedience and what are the implications for underlife? The comparison draws material from two multi-sited, qualitative case studies. The first study dealt with everyday life within regiments of the Foreign Legion (see Sundberg, 2015a, for more details). At present, the force comprises around 9,000 men, based at 11 regiments, most of them located in southern France and 2 abroad. I conducted interviews, observations, and participant observations at the main administrative regiment, the education regiment, the cavalry regiment, and the parachute regiment. These regiments were chosen to create as much variation as possible regarding location and specialty. At all regiments except for the last, each visit lasted for about a week, and I visited one of the combat regiments twice.

I observed activities such as control of guard duties, office work, shooting exercises, language classes, etc., with a particular focus on vertical and horizontal social interaction. I also participated in informal gatherings such as lunch breaks and after-work beer at company clubs, and this involved many informal conversations with members of various nationalities and formal ranks. My 10 shorter visits to the main administrative regiment were mostly related to interviews and meetings regarding the other regimental visits because these visits required permission from the general in command. All visits and conversations were recorded in field notes. Importantly, spending time at regiments was crucial for observing everyday life but also for selecting, getting in contact with, and gaining the confidence of my interviewees. I conducted interviews with 6 volunteer recruits (the term for the new members during their first five weeks), 27 enlisted members, 13 non-commissioned officers (henceforth NCOs), and 9 former members. To generate maximum richness, I have strived for as much variation as possible regarding formal rank and nationality. I have also interviewed 11 officers, 2 regimental social assistants, and 1 regimental priest. In total, my interviewees include 63 persons. Most interviews were conducted in French, 10 in Swedish, and 5 in English. Thirty-nine interviews were recorded, and I took field notes for the rest. The length of the interviews varied greatly. Most of the interviews at regiments lasted for about 30–60 minutes. A few interviews with officers and NCOs lasted around 1.5 hours. Whereas three of the interviews with former members in the retirement home for legionnaires were very short (15 minutes), an interview with another former member lasted for almost 6 hours in total. Interview guides for officers were tailored to their specific position, whereas most interviews with enlisted men and NCOs focused on different aspects of everyday life at the regiment, including working duties, experiences of rules and punishments, atmosphere, and social relations with superiors and other members of different and the same ranks.

The second study explored social relations in monastic communities of the Cistercian Order of Strict Observance (henceforth OCSO) in France (see Sundberg, 2022, for details).[3] To become acquainted with the monastic setting and tailor an adequate research design, I visited two monasteries in France. I stayed about one week each in the guest houses of one monk monastery within the Cistercian Order of Common Observance and one OCSO monastery for nuns, respectively, and interviewed two monks and one nun in these monasteries. I also interviewed a monk in a different community within the Cistercian Order of Common Observance and one former member of this community. Based on this preparatory work, I decided to concentrate on OCSO in France exclusively, because France is the country with the largest population of OCSO communities.[4] Focusing on one country facilitated selection and access because members, especially superiors, can share useful information and offer helpful recommendations regarding other communities. The choice of France maximized available options along this principle.

In selecting communities to contact for the main study, I aimed for variation concerning gender, size, and strictness. I visited one large nun monastery four times and one average-sized nun monastery and two average-sized monk monasteries once. I stayed almost a week in each guesthouse and focused primarily on interviewing. Interviews include 20 nuns between 35 and 87 years old, with 8–68 years of experience of Cistercian monastic life, and 15 monks, between 39 and 78 years old, and with 9–51 years of experience of Cistercian monastic life. The members held various positions and were involved in various types of work. The interviews typically lasted for about an hour and a half (ranging from 45 minutes to 2 hours), and they were recorded and transcribed verbatim, except for the first, three early interviews when I took notes. All interviews were semi-structured, including questions on the entrance to monastic life, work, decision-making, relations and contact with other members, including the superior, and contact with outsiders. I also adjusted questions to incorporate emerging insights in subsequent interviews.

During one of the visits to a nun monastery, I stayed four days within the community and joined the community in all its daily activities (offices, meals, work, meetings, etc.). Although the silent atmosphere of monasteries significantly reduces opportunities for the informal chats that are typical ingredients of ethnographic research, staying at monastic guesthouses allowed me to talk to other guests. This provided information and "gossip" about the communities that helped in the selection of communities to visit. In addition, I studied regulatory documents including the Rule of Saint Benedict and the Constitutions of the order, books on Cistercian spirituality, and webpages of the order and individual communities.

The types of voluntary total institutions included in these two studies share a great and explicit emphasis on obedience, but their "functions" differ. Contemplative monasteries are sanctuaries for religious men and women who voluntarily retreat from society. Professional military units like the French Foreign Legion enroll soldiers for them to collectively pursue the task of training and being prepared for armed defense. By comparing these cases, we gain a deeper understanding of how authority and obedience in voluntary total institutions differ. While taking the classification of such different sites as total institutions as a departure point, it must be pointed out that my analysis is not entirely "Goffmanesque," in other words, focusing on situational interaction. Not only is this due to the material as interview based rather than observation based, but primarily because I concentrate on *conceptions* of obedience and *conditions* for underlife. This also means that the analysis is static rather than processual and not considering the socialization process of members and the methods and measures used for that (cf. Alvesson & Willmott, 2002; van Maanen, 1978).[5]

THE MEANING OF OBEDIENCE TO AUTHORITY

The Foreign Legion enrolls men from all over the world and has a reputation as one of the world's most notorious fighting forces. The Foreign Legion is formally part of the French Army and deployed to the same kinds of missions, but it is a distinct unit, with specific regiments, a separate recruitment process, and certain special rules of service for its members. To join the Foreign Legion, legionnaires sign a contract for five years, whereas subsequent times of service may differ in length, from days to several years. Armed forces exist to be able to fight, protect, or in some way help out in situations of crisis. The idea that soldiers will eventually participate in such a mission is important for motivating soldiers and proving the importance of obedience for performing the collective, coordinated actions necessary for completing such missions successfully. Yet as with most armed forces of the world, the men of the Foreign Legion spend most of the time training (and waiting) rather than fighting. Even if these activities are related, I address the total institutional conditions of everyday *regimental* life specifically. What is the understanding of obedience here?

Submission to authority is constitutive of military life. In practice, it is based on a detailed rank structure and execution of orders. An order is a communicative directive from a superior, telling a subordinate what to do.[6] In the Foreign Legion, orders should be executed, without questions or hesitations. One captain explained[7]:

> For me, the legionnaire is a man who doesn't think. That's the strength. If tomorrow the colonel says "Faros, tomorrow the company is going to meet at that place," Captain Faros says "All right, sir." I don't think about it. I can't say "yes, but well, tomorrow at 10 ...." No. If the colonel has said at 10, everybody is there, because the colonel has said so, you understand? We don't ask questions. Why, how, why?

This captain (referring to himself in the third person) prized legionnaires' supposed lack of reflection. Especially among superiors in the Foreign Legion, it is commonly stated that legionnaires are more obedient than other soldiers. This is a source of pride, presented as something positive, in line with the appreciation of obedience in the military, in general, and during combat, in particular. The conception of, or perhaps rhetoric of, obedience is not exclusive to those of high ranks, like Captain Faros. Legionnaires share the understanding that Foreign Legion has a traditional "shut-up-and-do-what-you're-told" culture where subordinates should not "talk back" – perhaps more so than in many other Western armed forces (see Sundberg, 2015b). For example, Oleg, a corporal at the instruction regiment tried to explain what the Foreign Legion was like by saying that questions are not allowed and one should not hesitate to "reflect" or think twice about an order: If a superior says $1 + 1$ is 3, then that is the way it is. Importantly, however, superiors only expect subordinates to execute orders promptly. Whether subordinates have second thoughts or feelings about them is less relevant (Sundberg, 2015a, 198f.).

The Order of Cistercians of the strict observance is a contemplative, cloistered order. Within the Cistercian tradition, the primary purpose of monastic membership is to deepen the relationship with Christ, within the context of a monastic community. Entering a monastery is supposed to be the starting point of a journey of conversion, meant to involve a growing out of a life centered on the own ego, to a life centered on Christ – but loving the other sisters/brothers in the monastery is also a significant aspect of this (Sundberg, 2022). Membership in a monastic order is based on an active choice to seek out this style of living, and the profession to become a Cistercian monk or nun involves three promises (see, e.g., OCSO, 2018), casting the sacrifices, and "mortification," they imply in a positive and desirable light. The vow of stability is a promise to live the rest of one's life with one monastic community – it is a permanent engagement, in contrast to legionnaires' temporary submission to military authority. The vow of conversion of manners is the promise to live the monastic life, in all its parts, as described by the Rule of Saint Benedict and the Constitutions of the Order, signifying a voluntary commitment to change. The vow of obedience is a promise to obey the superior (the abbot or abbess) and put one's own will aside. Monastic obedience refers to external behavior but also to an inner state. In monasteries, "[o]bedience must be given gladly"; it is unacceptable to obey "grudgingly" or to grumble, "not only aloud but also in his heart" (Rule of Saint Benedict, Chapter 5, see also Merton, 2009, p. 121).[8]

The monastic conception of obedience is different from the behavioral focus in the Foreign Legion but also because it is justified by a blending of social and divine authority. According to Catholic catechism, obedience to God is unlimited and Catholicism prepares monastic members for the more encompassing and concrete submission subscribed by the Rule of Saint Benedict, comprising critical moral pillars that members have chosen to follow by entering a monastery. Abbots and abbesses serve under God and the Rule of Saint Benedict, but as superiors, they both represent the divine authority (Christ) a formal, social authority (cf. the Rule of Saint Benedict, Chapter 2). Obedience to a monastic superior is therefore connected to faith.

Besides meeting about seven times a day in church, sharing meals in the refectory, and meeting in the chapter room, OCSO members devote approximately five hours a day, six days a week to some form of work. Cistercian monasteries typically fabricate, pack, and sell some food products. All monasteries have a guesthouse and a shop. Much work also derives from the fact that the community is a place of residence. Members take care of gardening, laundry, sewing, and maintenance and rotate to help out with household chores (and church services). There is someone responsible for every, more or less extensive, sector of the monastery, whether it is production, packaging, or sales. This often includes the supervision of one or several members assisting in subordinate roles. The expectations regarding obedience apply to all sorts of supervision in the monastic organization of duties but also, in a general sense, concerning all other members. According to the Rule of Saint Benedict, "[o]bedience is a blessing to be shown by all, not only the abbot but also to one another as brothers, because we know that it is by this way of obedience that we go to God" (Fry, 1981, p. 68). This means that those monks and nuns who admit that they experience their immediate superior as too "dominant" also recognize that such *feelings* are themselves problematic – even if they follow the directives of these superiors (see Sundberg, 2022, pp. 93–100, see also Americo et al., 2024, this volume, on emotional reflexivity in organization studies). In sum, Legion obedience is focused on the execution of specific commands and requests, whereas Cistercian monastic obedience extends to having a submissive approach to everything required, extending to both feelings and thoughts.

HOW CONCEPTIONS OF OBEDIENCE SHAPE CONDITIONS FOR UNDERLIFE

We have so far considered obedience primarily concerning work tasks, but "directives" of voluntary total institutions stretch beyond such activities. A key aspect of total institutions is the breakdown of the boundary between private and professional areas of life. How this plays out in practice differs depending on the total institutional arrangements, especially considering how private life can be maintained outside of residential quarters or through spontaneous activities; in other words, what the conditions for underlife are.

For new legionnaires, never-ending requests are central features of regimental life, meaning that they have little private time and difficulties in leaving regimental grounds. John, a legionnaire at the parachute regiment at Corse, said that there were "no freedom" and "no free time" at the beginning of his service. John explained:

> There's end of work but there's always something to do at the platoon. You can ask [the corporal] to go somewhere and he might say 'Yeah, what's the weight of the FAMAS [the type of rifle used]?' If you don't know, go to your room and revise. (...) There are loads of songs. You might have to learn these songs, so you don't really have time to do anything. Or you clean the whole weekend and things like that.

Consequently, official work hours can be over, but Legion regiments are also places of residence. For legionnaires, their life is very much taking place within their platoon. One salient aspect of platoon life is the persistent possibility of inspections, typically extending into nighttime and weekends. There were frequent complaints about how "unnecessary" this practice, referred to as *sketch*, is. "Sketch here is, for example, that they put so much time into inspecting your locker, if everything is properly ironed and your clothes are folded correctly, that's sketch. Perhaps it's not really needed but it's done anyway," Antonio, a corporal at the parachute regiment explained. Antonio continued:

> When [corporals] keep, during the weekend, doing a lot of stupid things with the guys, like checking lockers and I don't know what, all kinds of things, that's unnecessary, it's not needed. Because you don't learn anything, you only teach [legionnaires] to be quiet maybe.[9]

Expectations of silent obedience to authority extend beyond orders of command to all kinds of duties, and members are socialized into this through inspection practices. As indicated above, it does not imply agreement. Muttering to each other about superiors, tasks, equipment, work hours, etc. is common (so is also muttering about muttering!). This means that frustration with the system, "incompetent" superiors, and "stupid" orders are common topics of conversation, not something kept to oneself.

Interventions into more or less "free" time aside, all legionnaires can request permission to leave the regiment during evenings and weekends, *if* the document is filled out correctly and handed in on time, the uniform, boots, and white *képi* is impeccable, etc. Stories about how legionnaires have been banned from leaving because a crease was not in place or the white *képi* had a stain, abound. This is a good example of the bureaucratic organization of everyday life and the requirement to ask for permission to do things, at the same time as legionnaires circumvent these obstacles both individually and collectively. Sometimes legionnaires leave without permission, by themselves or in groups, if they have the opportunity to do so. For example, at the parachute regiments, it happens that members sneak out in civilian clothes through a hole in the fence surrounding the regiment. Such illicit activities may require special precautions to avoid negative consequences, however. Paul, a junior legionnaire offered an example:

> If you're going through the fence Friday night in civilian clothing you tell the corporal, "so you know I'm gone," kind of like that. If you know the corporal .... There's a sheet of paper showing how many we are; at night he signs you up.

This is but one example of how legionnaires engage collectively in illicit activities and/or rely on cooperation with other legionnaires to perform them. These secondary adjustments aim for instrumental, short-term gains; they represent frictions (Rubin, 2015) engaged in to make total institutional life more bearable, not understood as challenging the commitment to legionnaire identity or the system. They are probably also, to some extent, accepted by the system as loopholes for legionnaires to retain a sense of autonomy, remaining more disciplined when more important matters are at stake. All aspects of Legion life (i.e., regimental life) are just not to be taken too seriously, and while compliance with rules and regulations is preferable, it is acceptable to talk about how ridiculous some of them are. While this is a way to let steam off, it also legitimizes some circumvention of them and more confidence in bringing others along in doing so. Nevertheless, these activities constitute Legion underlife; collective adjustments that are often present as soon as superiors are out of sight and legionnaires are not requested to do anything or be anywhere specific.

In the context of the all-encompassing obedience of Cistercian monasteries, the distinction between more or less important tasks and requests is blurry due to the conception of tasks as *services* (Sundberg, 2022, pp. 89–92). One must also keep in mind that the "mission" of the OCSO is ultimately for Cistercian monks and nuns to maintain a relationship with, worshiping, and serving an omnipresent God. The common residence is a way to do so with others – there are no external "missions" beyond that. Even if monks and nuns occasionally ask for a couple of weeks of "vacation" to visit family or rest, it is simply incomprehensible that they would desire to leave the monastic grounds as soon as they had some "free time" – which they, in any case, have very little of. Consequently, their secondary adjustments do not concern such activities, and I will not discuss other specific secondary adjustments like those mentioned in the Foreign Legion either. In contrast, I draw attention to a key aspect shaping the fundamental *condition* for engaging in collective secondary adjustments in monasteries of the OCSO: The requirement to avoid conversations.

Silence is one of the principal monastic values of the OCSO. It is an assurance of solitude for the nun/monk in the community in relation to fellow members and a way for the member to engage in continual prayer and conversation with God. Silence "is to be observed especially in the regular places such as the church, the cloisters, the refectory and the scriptorium" (Constitution Part 2, C. 24, ST 24:A). Elsewhere, there may be legitimate reasons for speaking:

> Monks typically have three motivations to speak to one another: to get a particular work project carried out efficiently, to engage in a community discussion, or to discuss one's spiritual progress with a director or confessor. Sometimes, too, Trappists will enjoy friendly conversations with each other in a conversation room or nature. These different types of conversation are balanced with the discipline of fostering a general atmosphere of silence in the monastery. (Trappists, 2017)

"The monk must train himself to guard his tongue" (Merton, 2009, p. 175), not only concerning keeping quiet unless there is a good reason to speak but when talking, also carefully considering what to say and how (cf. Cummings, 1986, p. 143). No forms of muttering (neither silent nor aloud) or gossip are legitimate.

While restrictions on speech apply to both monks and nuns, there are nevertheless significant differences between what possibilities monks and nuns in the studied communities have to interact with one another (see Sundberg, 2022, Chapter 7, for details). The monks are entitled to ask each other for, at least occasional, private conversations in parlors, without asking their abbot for permission. They could also establish more long-term relationships with other monks by choosing them as their own personal "spiritual guide" and/or confessor (for the sacrament of reconciliation). Nuns are in principle expected to hold private conversations exclusively with their abbess and ask her for permission if they wish to talk in private – a permission which the abbess was entitled to decline. The only legitimate confidant for ordinary nuns, except for their confessor (the priest serving in their community) is their abbess. Nuns are expected to share their thoughts with and "open their hearts" to their abbess, something monks are much less expected to do to their abbots. Marie Rose explained the necessity of having meetings with the abbess:

> for what Saint Benedict calls opening of the heart, that means being able to say, because she represents Christ so … so the bond with the abbess is strong because … it's the bond of obedience to … and obedience has to be lived well (...) so it has to be very … that the relation with the abbess is really *clear … open* ….

Consequently, being open to the abbess is an aspect of obeying the abbess. Although they sometimes found sharing difficult, the nuns typically raised no criticism related to this expectation. There were exceptions, however. One untypically critical nun, Maribel, mentioned to me on repeated occasions her troubles with "authority" and said that she "refused" to talk to her abbess because she did not have a "very happy relationship with her." Illicitly, Maribel opened up to "a sister who is very discrete and who repeats nothing" instead. The "discrete" nun supposedly differed from the rest, who were suspected to report to the abbess: "*Everything* passes through the mother abbess and *everything*, everything, and a lot of our speech and our doings are repeated to the abbess," Maribel said. What Maribel said illustrates how nuns must be cautious about whom they (illicitly) chat with and what they tell them, not least because the reliance on the abbess as a conversation partner may result in a blurring between vertical reporting and horizontal gossip (cf. Scott, 2011) leading to her receiving more information about what is going on in the community than would otherwise be the case. In sum, expectations of an obedient mind-set and limited talk create poor conditions for maintaining an underlife among monks but even more so among nuns, where the required openness to the abbatial gaze may also lead to a sense of distrust among the ordinary nuns, making an underlife even less likely. Although the comparison of monks and nuns concerned a single type of total institution (contemplative monasteries), it suggests how total institutions offer the possibility to compare cases of organizations with an exceptionally high degree of similarity, *except* for in their gender composition. In other words, typically gender-segregated total institutions such as boarding schools, prisons, and monasteries offer valuable sites for exploring the gendering of organizations.

CONCLUDING REMARK

Goffman's (1961) demonstration of how the self is shaped and reshaped by patterns of interaction in specific institutional arrangements is well recognized in sociology. It has inspired many studies of identity formation and adjustments to the socialization conditions in, especially coercive, closed settings. In contrast, my ambition with this paper has been to show how *voluntary* total institutions are relevant sites of research for studying authority, not least since voluntary, rather than coercive, membership is the most common in modern organizations.

This paper has been limited to tracing ways to conceptualize obedience in two cardinal cases of voluntary total institutions, contemplative (cloistered) monasteries and professional armed force units, and linked this to how conditions for sustaining separate interaction contexts of collective adjustments (an underlife) differ there. The existence of differences is of course not surprising given the separate "functions" of the institutions. While pointing out some dimensions in which total institutions differ, Goffman (1961, pp. 113–123) did not present any detailed comparative analysis. The concept of the total institution applies to organizations of very different kinds and subsequent studies, whether they use the total institution concept or not, rarely treat them in tandem, but discuss them separately as organizations engaged in medical treatment, education, law enforcement, etc. One of the benefits of comparing cases of total institutions is that they are regarding certain aspects of organizational life extreme, regarding the scope of authority, for example. Yet at the same time, they also represent maximum variation cases within a specific, narrow category (cf. Flyvbjerg, 2006, pp. 229–230): The French Foreign Legion as a professional military force and Cistercian monasteries are both voluntary total institutions emphasizing obedience, but conceptions of obedience of the able body when needed in the Legion, on the one hand, contrast with a monastic form of total obedience present at all times, on the other hand. This shows the *multidimensionality* of obedience as a phenomenon.

Obedience in the Foreign Legion refers to external behavior. Soldiers should be executing and submitting to frequent and specific orders issued by a superior. Obedience does not extend much beyond that. There is a flourishing underlife, which serves to let "steam off," rather than challenge the organization, especially during long periods of regimental training (rather than military operations). Cistercian obedience is more of an internal affair; a form of inner state of generalized submissiveness, applying to all members. Everyone is responsible for upholding it for the sake of oneself, at all times and everywhere (cf. Sundberg, 2019). Not doing so would itself be contrary to the "aim" of the organization, which is to provide the premises for the *members* to develop and maintain a close relationship with God (cf. Sundberg, 2022). This undermines engagement in collective behaviors contrary to the monastic "mission," not least through restrictions on personal conversations. At the same time, one could view any collective secondary adjustment in monasteries as more defiant compared to the activities described among legionnaires, precisely because of the monastic conception of obedience as a form of total submission, encompassing behaviors, thoughts, *and* feelings. Although my analysis has not focused on interaction per se, it points to the importance of understanding constructions of the obedient self as linked to underlife, as a distinct interaction context of organizations, and hence, a key sociological dimension of the inner life of organizations.

NOTES

1. A great deal of research on various total institutions has been conducted without explicit reference to Goffman's concept (see also McEwen, 1980), or only briefly mentioning of it. In this paper, I primarily cite work that builds upon Goffman's (1961) concept and/or fundamental tenets.

2. The mortification process refers to the attempt to strip inmates of their past selves to take on the new role defined by the institution. The possibility to "kill" the self is related to Goffman's (1961, p. 168) understanding of the self "as something that resides in the arrangements prevailing in a social system for its members." Institutional arrangements "do not so much support the self as constitute it" (Goffman, 1961, p. 168).

3. The Cistercian order was founded in 1098 but split into two branches in 1892. In an attempt to follow the Rule of Saint Benedict more rigorously, the Order of Cistercians of the Strict Observance (OCSO), commonly known as Trappists, detached itself while Cistercians of the Common Observance remained loyal to the original form. I focus on OCSO, which is presently larger than the order of Common Observance. OCSO currently has a total of about 3,000 members and 157 monasteries in 45 countries around the world, 70 for nuns and 87 for monks (2021). For statistics, see https://ocso.org/monasteries/current-statistics/.

4. About half (83) of all the monasteries are located in Europe and 23 of those in France.

5. Punishment regimes are typically installed to enforce and maintain desirable behavior. For detailed analysis of the punishment regime of the French Foreign Legion, see Sundberg (2015b, Chapter 6) and for analysis of sanctions in Cistercian monasteries, see Sundberg (2022, Chapter 8).

6. Military orders can be different in scope and delivered verbally as well as in written form. I focus on verbal, direct orders.

7. The Foreign Legion comprises three principal groups. I refer to enlisted men as legionnaires. Legionnaires come from all over the world (they can be French) and typically live in lodgments at the regiment. Legionnaires can be promoted to non-commissioned officers and then live outside the regiment. Finally, there are officers on rotation from the French Army. A few selected NCOs are offered the possibility to serve as an "officer under foreign title" and enter the officer corps instead. Captain Faros is an example of such an officer.

8. The Rule was written for monks and thus men. Its relevance for nuns, thus women, was questioned during the early stages of Cistercian monastic development (see, e.g., Lawrence, 2015, p. 203), but this no longer seems to be an issue. Both monks and nuns spontaneously refer to the Rule during interviews, through specific citations and in a more sweeping manner, with no indication that it applies differently to the two member categories.

9. The expression *sketch* signifies that there is something unserious, almost funny, about it. This is reminiscent of Mouzelis' (1971, p. 116) discussion of obligatory military service in Greece, where the mortification processes during training should be seen as a joke or a game (and those who do take it seriously are considered foolish). Viewing them this way may be a way of coping, but in the Foreign Legion, inspections and other forms of *sketch*-activities are also a way to learn what is expected.

ACKNOWLEDGMENTS

I wish to thank the editors, the anonymous reviewer, Barbara Czarniawska, John Murray, and Adrienne Sörbom for valuable comments, remarks, and criticisms.

REFERENCES

Ahrne, G. (2021). *The construction of social bonds. A relational theory of globalization, organizations and society*. Edward Elgar.

Alvesson, M., & Willmott, H. (2002). Identity regulation as organizational control: Producing the appropriate individual. *Journal of Management Studies*, *39*, 619–644.

Americo, B. L., Clegg, S., & Carniel, F. (2024). Narrating the disjunctions produced by the sociological concept of emotional reflexivity in organization studies. In S. Clegg, M. Grothe-Hammer, & K. Serrano Velarde (Eds.), *Sociological thinking in contemporary organizational scholarship* (Research in the Sociology of Organizations, Vol. 90, pp. 227–252). Emerald Publishing.

Barnard, C. (1968). *The functions of the executive*. Harvard University Press.

Bennett, R. (1963). The meaning of institutional life. *The Gerontologist*, *3*, 117–125.

Clegg, S. R. (2006a). The heart of darkness. In S. R. Clegg, D. Courpasson, & N. Philip (Eds.), *Power and organizations* (pp. 143–189). Sage.

Clegg, S. R. (2006b). Why is organization theory so ignorant? The neglect of total institutions. *Journal of Management Inquiry*, *15*, 426–430.

Clegg, S. R., Pina, E., Cunha, M., & Rego, A. (2012). The theory and practice of utopia in a total institution: The pineapple panopticon. *Organization Studies*, *33*, 1735–1757.

Clot-Garrell, A. (2022). Boundaries in the making: Transformations in Erving Goffman's total institution through the case of a female Benedictine monastery. *Sociology*, *56*, 114–130.

Courpasson, D., & Dany, F. (2003). Indifference or obedience? Business firms as democratic hybrids. *Organization Studies*, *24*, 1231–1260.

Crewe, B., Warr, J., Bennett, P., & Smith, A. (2014). The emotional geography of prison life. *Theoretical Criminology*, *18*, 56–74.

Cummings, C. (1986). *Monastic practices*. Liturgical Press.

Flyvbjerg, B. (2006). Five misunderstandings about case-study research. *Qualitative Inquiry*, *12*, 219–245.

Fry, T. (Ed.). (1981). *The rule of Saint Benedict*. Vintage Books.

Fürst, H. (2022). Arrival to a fictional total institution. The Swedish Folk High School as a Liminal Space in Literature. *Sociologisk Forskning*, *59*, 321–340.

Goffman, E. (1961). *Asylums. Essays on the social situation of mental patients and other inmates*. Anchor Books.

Goldenberg, S., & Wekerle, G. R. (1972). From utopia to total institution in a single generation: The Kibbutz and the Bruderhof. *International Review of Modern Sociology*, *2*, 224–232.

Gubrium, J. F. (1997). *Living and dying at Murray Manor*. The University Press of Virginia.

Kirke, C. (2010). 'Orders is orders … aren't they?' Rule bending and rule breaking in the British Army. *Ethnography*, *11*, 359–380.

Lawrence, C. H. (2015). *Medieval monasticism: Forms of religious life in Western Europe in the middle ages* (4th ed.). Routledge.

Lopdrup-Hjorth, T., & du Gay, P. (2024). Facing up to the present? Cultivating political judgement and a sense of reality in contemporary organizational life. In S. Clegg, M. Grothe-Hammer, & K. Serrano Velarde (Eds.), *Sociological thinking in contemporary organizational scholarship* (Research in the Sociology of Organizations, Vol. 90, pp. 85–108). Emerald Publishing.

Manning, P. (2008). Goffman on organizations. *Organization Studies*, *29*, 677–699.

McCorkel, J. A. (1998). Going to the crackhouse: Critical space as a form of resistance in total institutions and everyday life. *Symbolic Interaction*, *21*, 227–252.

McEwen, C. A. (1980). Continuities in the study of total and non-total institutions. *Annual Review of Sociology*, *6*, 143–185.

Merton, T. (2009). *The rule of Saint Benedict. Initiation into the monastic tradition 4* (P. F. O'Connell (Ed.)). Liturgical Press.

Mouzelis, N. P. (1971). On total institutions. *Sociology*, *5*, 113–120.

Order of Cistercians of the Strict Observance (OCSO). (2018). *FAQs*. Retrieved February 27, 2018, from http://www.ocso.org/who-we-are/faqs/

Order of Cistercians of the Strict Observance (OCSO). (2021). *Current statistics*. Retrieved January 23, 2022, from https://ocso.org/monasteries/current-statistics/

Paterniti, D. (2000). The micropolitics of identity in adverse circumstance: A study of identity making in a total institution. *Journal of Contemporary Ethnography*, *29*, 93–119.

Reyes, V. (2018). Port of call: How ships shape foreign-local encounters. *Social Forces*, *96*, 1097–1118.

Rubin, A. T. (2015). Resistance or friction: Understanding the significance of prisoners' secondary adjustments. *Theoretical Criminology*, *19*, 23–42.

Scott, S. (2011). *Total institutions and reinventive identities*. Palgrave Macmillan.

Shenkar, O. (1996). The firm as a total institution: Reflections on the Chinese state enterprise. *Organization Studies*, *17*, 885–907.

Sundberg, M. (2015a). *A sociology of the total organization: Atomistic unity in the French Foreign Legion*. Routledge.

Sundberg, M. (2015b). Hierarchy, status and combat motivation in the French Foreign Legion. In A. King (Ed.), *Frontline: Combat and cohesion in Iraq and Afghanistan* (pp. 216–233). Oxford University Press.

Sundberg, M. (2022). *Fraternal relations in monasteries: The laboratory of love*. Routledge.

Tracy, S. J. (2000). Becoming a character for commerce – Emotion labor, self-subordination, and discursive construction of identity in a total institution. *Management Communication Quarterly*, *14*, 90–128.

Trappists (Brothers & Sisters, Cistercians of the Strict Observance). (2017). *Becoming a Trappist monk or nun*. Retrieved April 24, 2017, from http://www.trappists.org/becoming-trappist/vows

Van Maanen, J. (1978). People processing: Strategies of organizational socialization. *Organizational Dynamics*, *7*, 19–36.

Wästerfors, D. (2012). Analyzing social ties in total institutions, *Qualitative Sociology Review, 8*, 12–27.

Zurcher, L. A. (1965). The sailor aboard ship: A study of role behavior in a total institution. *Social Forces*, *43*, 389–400.

Organizing and Organization

WHY ORGANIZATION SOCIOLOGISTS SHOULD REFER TO TARDE AND SIMMEL MORE OFTEN

Barbara Czarniawska

University of Gothenburg, Sweden

ABSTRACT

This paper argues for an increased volume of references to Gabriel Tarde and Georg Simmel in the field of organization sociology. The text emphasizes the importance of these two sociologists in understanding the role of imperfection in organizing and the phenomena of fashion and imitation in contemporary organizations. Tarde's theory challenged the antinomy between continuity and discontinuity, considering finite entities as cases of infinite processes and stable situations as transitory. Simmel's theory of fashion explores the democratic and democratizing nature of fashion, which satisfies the demand for social adaptation and differentiation. They both saw fashion as a selection mechanism for organizational forms and managerial practices. Furthermore, referring to Tarde and Simmel can help counter the overemphasis on identity construction and the neglect of alterity in social sciences. The construction of identity often overlooks the inevitability of difference and alterity, which are essential aspects of collective projects. Lastly, this paper discusses Simmel's concept of the stranger and its relevance in analyzing the experiences of foreigners and their potential advantages as "double strangers" in academia and society. The conclusion is that Tarde and Simmel's contributions offer valuable

Sociological Thinking in Contemporary Organizational Scholarship
Research in the Sociology of Organizations, Volume 90, 273–286
ISSN: 0733-558X/doi:10.1108/S0733-558X20240000090011

insights for understanding the dynamics of management, organizing, and social interactions in contemporary organizations.

Keywords: Fashion; framing; identity terror; imitation; secret organizations; strangers

INTRODUCTION

I remember a conversation with my late friend, Swedish sociologist Inga Hellberg, who told me: "Barbara, you are not a sociologist. You do not quote Weber and Durkheim!"[1]

I've given that conversation a great deal of thought. Well, yes, I am not formally a sociologist. I am a transdisciplinary organization scholar and take inspiration not only from my original academic disciplines (psychology and economic sciences) but also from ethnology, narratology, and sociology. And it is the latter discipline that led me to Tarde and Simmel.[2] In what follows, I explain why those two scholars in my opinion require more attention, by giving examples of how they have been used in organization studies.[3] I do not intend to present their contributions in detail, because my hope is that this text will entice the readers to do it themselves. Instead, I begin with short biographies, to locate these authors in the historical context.

Gabriel Tarde (1843–1904)

Tarde was born in Sarlat, a town in the province of Dordogne, France. He studied law in Toulouse and Paris. From 1869 to 1894, he worked as a magistrate and investigating judge in the province, allegedly indulging in writing texts on criminology (Czarniawska, 2009). In 1894, he was appointed Director of Criminal Statistics at the Ministry of Justice in Paris. In 1900, both he and Henri Bergson were given chairs in modern philosophy at the Collége de France. (He asked that his title be changed to sociology but was refused.)

Tarde soon became known in English-speaking communities: His 1890 *Laws of Imitation* was published by Henry Holt in 1903 and reprinted in 1962. Macmillan published his 1897 *Social Laws: An Outline of Sociology* in 1899 and reprinted it in 1974. Tarde was among the authors that Robert E. Park and Ernest W. Burgess quoted most often in their 1922 *Introduction to the Science of Sociology*.

After the 1960s, however, the scientific fashion changed, and it was only Giles Deleuze and Niklas Luhmann who continued to read Tarde (Czarniawska, 2009). Then, more than 30 years passed, and in the late 1990s, a "Tardomania" exploded (Mucchielli, 2000), with reprints of Tarde's original works in several languages.

Why did Tarde come back into fashion? Many explanations have been offered. It seems that his work resonates well with that of many contemporary sociologists. (Almost) no one is surprised at the idea of connecting sciences to arts and philosophy; as Luhmann (2002) noticed and as everyone can see now, information can, in fact, increase ignorance. Also, Tarde's work preceded concepts of networks, cultural capital, and culture industry; reading him, one can have an impression that he is speaking of virtual reality (Irenius, 2002). It could also be that Tarde's voice better fits the present times of darkness. The 1970s were more optimistic ....

Georg Simmel (1858–1918)

Although the popularity of Tarde and Simmel is comparable, their careers differed. Simmel's father died when Georg was a boy, and a friend of the family was appointed his guardian (Wolff, 1950). He left Simmel a considerable fortune, which allowed him to lead the life of a scholar, despite his lack of proper university employment.

After graduating from the gymnasium (high school), Simmel started to study history at the University of Berlin, but he soon switched to philosophy. In 1881, he defended his doctoral dissertation on "The nature of matter according to Kant's physical monadology." Between 1885 and 1900, he was a "private docent" (a lecturer paid only via students' fees), and from 1900 to 1914, an "extraordinary professor" (still without salary) at the University of Berlin. It was only at age 56 that he became a full professor at Strasbourg University. A year later, he applied for a chair in Heidelberg but was refused – not for the first time.

> Applications, supported by most authoritative recommendations and a most impressive publishing record, were regularly turned down. It could be that the appointment committees and the assessors they approached to opine on Simmel's work resented his Jewish origin. (...) It is likely, however, that even more than Simmel's birth certificate the gatekeepers resented the substance of his sociology: so blatantly at odds with the standard sociological writings of the time, so different, so (...) *alien*, so *Jewish*. (Bauman, 1991, p. 185, italics in original)

In the United States, Simmel was seen as a sociologist rather than a philosopher. Many of his sociological writings were published between 1893 and 1910, particularly in *The American Journal of Sociology*. And like Tarde, Simmel was often quoted by Park and Burgess (2021) in their *Introduction to the Science of Sociology*. In the 1970s, however, interest in Simmel's work waned. According to Kurt H. Wolff (1950), the US sociologists had been trying to free themselves from the European influence even earlier and had chosen to redefine sociology as an "empirical and quantitative study" (p. xxiv). Interest in Simmel's writing returned in the 1990s, probably even earlier than did interest in Tarde's writing, judging from the words of Zygmunt Bauman in 1991: "It is only now that Simmel is beginning to be recognized as a most (perhaps *the* most) powerful and perceptive analyst of modernity ..." (p. 185).

Prophets of Imperfection

As to understanding the inevitability of imperfection and its role in organizing, there are few sociologists more aware of it than Tarde and Simmel were. As Vargas (2010) reminded his readers, Tarde's theory

> suspends (and puts in doubt) the antinomy between the uniform continuity and the punctual discontinuity or, more precisely, which considers the finite entities as peculiar cases of infinite

processes, the stable situations as movements of blockage, the permanent states as transitory agencies of processes to come (and not the opposite). (p. 214)

As to the necessity of imperfection in organizing, it cannot be put better than it was in Simmel's (1906) quote:

The strenuous organizing forms which appear to be the real constructors of society, or to construct society as such, must be continually disturbed, unbalanced, and detached by individualistic and irregular forces, in order that their reaction and development may gain vitality by alternate concession and resistance. (p. 448)

Alan Scott's (2009) comment regarding Simmel can be applied to both Simmel and Tarde: Their theories focus on "the unintentional unfolding of a logic inherent within a community of whose working actors are largely unaware. Such an approach is both anti-mechanistic and anti-rationalist" (p. 281).

So, why quote them now? What follows are only some examples of use of their theories in studies of organizing; I am sure a great many more are possible.

BECAUSE FASHION AND IMITATION ARE KEY PHENOMENA IN CONTEMPORARY ORGANIZATIONS

Fashion was long a phenomenon treated with disdain and neglect in social theory and organization studies (Czarniawska & Joerges, 1995). Blame is usually attributed to Thorsten Veblen (1899/1994), who claimed that fashion promoted "conspicuous consumption"; he contrasted it to valuable productivity (Czarniawska, 2005). He was probably unaware of the work of a French sociologist, 14 years his senior. Gabriel Tarde had, by then, claimed in his book, *Laws of Imitation*, that fashion was already a strong force in antiquity, although he admitted, in agreement with the later scholars, that it was the 18th century that "inaugurated the reign of fashion on a large scale" (Tarde, 1890/1962, p. 293, n. 2). Changes in fashion, he contented, were caused not by a search for perfection, but by boredom, which was in turn caused by customs:

In the case of industry and fine arts, it is for the pleasure of change, of *not doing* the usual thing, that the part of the public which is influenced by fashion adopts a new product to the neglect of some old one; then when the novelty has become acclimated and appreciated for its own sake, the older product seeks a refuge in the cherished habits of the other part of the public which is partial to custom and which wishes to show in that way that it also *does not* do the same thing as the rest of the world. (Tarde, 1890/1962, italics in original)

As it turned out, it was Simmel (1904/1971) who received the task of reviewing Tarde's book (Frisby & Featherstone, 1997, p. 13), and he expanded on the topic in his *Philosophy of Fashion*. He saw in fashion a democratic and democratizing phenomenon, which intensified with the progress of civilization, primarily because fashion connected two opposing tendencies: equalization and individualization:

Fashion is the imitation of a given example and satisfies the demand for social adaptation. ... At the same time, it satisfies in no less degree the need of differentiation, the tendency for dissimilarity, the desire for change and contrast. (Simmel, 1904/1971, p. 296)

Simmel's theory was embraced by Herbert Blumer (1969/1973), who postulated that fashion is a *selection mechanism* that influences the market and distorts the demand and supply curves, both using and serving economic competition. Its key element is a *collective choice* among competing tastes, things, and ideas; it is oriented toward *finding* but also toward *creating,* what is typical of a given time.

Sociologists interested in fashion emphasized its paradoxical character: It requires invention *and* imitation, variation *and* uniformity, distance *and* interest, novelty *and* conservatism, unity *and* segregation, conformity *and* deviation, change *and* status quo, revolution *and* evolution. It spreads via "diffusion by transformation" (Tarde, 1893/1999, p. 41), a process that later Tardeans called "translation" (Serres, 1974), to avoid being mixed with "diffusionists." Fashion would not be able to proceed without constant translation, which permits it to appear in many different guises in different times and places.

I have illustrated that understanding of fashion with a study of city management in three European capitals: Stockholm, Warsaw, and Rome (Czarniawska, 2002, 2004). Fashion there seemed to be the main selection mechanism of organizational forms and managerial practices; of problems and solutions. But I was hardly the first: F. Stuart Chapin, a US sociologist inspired by Tarde, attempted to analyze the causes or the motives and circumstances behind the fashion of the "city manager plan" in the US municipalities. Although first observed in 1908, it was similar to what I found in Rome in 1997. Chapin's (1928) explanation was inspired by Tarde and suggested

> [...] the rhythmical character of imitation. It diffuses from central models enjoying prestige, it spreads by geometric progression in many directions, in some cases it is refracted by its media more considerably than in other cases, it reaches a point of saturation, and the old model declines before some new model which has set up a wave of counter-imitation. (p. 208)

Thus, Tarde made it obvious that it is necessary to conduct processual studies of fashion if one wishes to capture the development of a fashion. Simmel (1904/1971) also criticized much of the history of fashion for its sole concentration on the development of its contents: It is necessary to report what is in fashion but also to inquire, "Why this? Why here? Why now?" A focus on time and space may help to redefine fashion – from a deviant irrationality on the part of erring managers, to the key to pattern recognition, to a better understanding of the dynamics of management and organizing (Czarniawska & Panozzo, 2008).

BECAUSE THEY WILL HELP TO COUNTER THE "IDENTITY TERROR"

> To exist is to differ; difference, in a sense, is the substantial side of things, is what they have only to themselves and what they have most in common. One has to start the explanation from here, including the explanation of identity, taken often, mistakenly, for a starting point. Identity is but a *minimal* difference, and hence a type of difference, and a very rare type at that, in the same way as rest is a type of movement and circle a peculiar type of ellipse. (Tarde, 1893/1999, p. 73)

If so, why, at present, is the focus of social and political sciences entirely on "identities," whereas "alterity" is a concept used by some anthropologists to denote "the Others"? Peter Brooks (2011) called it "an identity paradigm" and explained it with two developments central to the 19th century: urbanization and colonization. Newly arrived peasants, working people, and urban criminals needed to be *identified*, and so were the natives, perceived to be so similar to one another.

Although the issues of identity and alterity were born in relation to persons (originally, social psychologists such as G. H. Mead took it for granted that a "self" consisted of similarity and difference), they have, over time, been transferred, by analogy, to nation-states (Anderson, 1983/1991) and to such legal persons as corporations (Lamoreaux, 2003). Apparently, people grouped within the new borders needed to know what they had in common, as the differences were only too easy to demonstrate. The immigrant waves then encouraged people within the old borders to pay attention to their "traditional identity." Such "searches for identity" are, in the opinion of Ian Buruma (2002), behind most of the present world troubles.

Organization theory followed the fashion, and theorists began to pay attention to organizational identity construction (e.g., Hatch & Schultz, 2003; Schultz et al., 2000; Whetten & Godfrey, 1998). In social studies in general, it was mainly Giles Deleuze (1968/1997) who continued the Tardean tradition, and my colleagues and I used it in our studies of European capitals (see, e.g., Czarniawska, 2002, 2008).

We discovered that the cities were busy constructing their own difference, for which the Other was but a foil. Image construction, a truly significant work, consisted of a constant mix of identification, negation, and differentiation. Although some "Other" might have been constructed in this process, it was often no more than a prop, amorphous and shifting in adaptation to the image of "the City."

The need to distinguish between identity and alterity construction has been justified by the different places they occupy in various attempts in the construction of a collective image. Thus, if a discourse focuses on the cultural alterity of immigrants living in Sweden, the creation of "Swedishness" thus obtained is implicit; it is a byproduct of the construction of the Other. Such text *attributes* difference. The opposite can be said of a discourse aimed at discerning the "Swedish identity." Images of the Other are secondary to its primary aim – are its byproducts. Such text *affirms* difference. Whereas the attribution of difference has been granted a great deal of attention in recent social science writings, the affirmation of difference has not.

Another distinction we observed was that between opposition (as Deleuze called a degree of sameness) and alterity (an affirmation of difference): Stockholm is different from Oslo in a different way than it is different from Korpilombo,[4] whereas Warsaw and Rome are "unique." The general claim of city managers in Rome was that Rome differed from any other city; no image of the Other was necessary. Such an image does not emphasize the alterity of the Other but the alterity of the Self.

Still, the focus set on identity construction in organization studies is, in a sense, justifiable. Organizing means knotting together – people, things, actions. That is but one way of building associations. And, as Tarde (1893/1999) said, "to associate means to become similar, that is, to imitate." Each collective project requires as*simila*tion, however temporary. The problem begins when this temporality is overlooked (although projects, by definition, are temporary), and the inevitable re-production of difference and therefore of alterity is interpreted as a failure in the process of identity construction.

The subordination of identity to alterity or vice versa needs to be seen as a local and historical phenomenon. One can venture that the cities under study and most of the social sciences subordinate alterity to identity, at least partially because of the globalization of the media. But this was not the case always and everywhere. Tarde, speaking at the turn of the previous century, was aware that alterity of the self was fading from attention, perhaps as one of the victims of globalization. But because globalization is always met with resistance, alterity moves have never vanished completely. Bringing them to light can therefore aid in the interpretation of phenomena that are puzzling when explained only in terms of identity, just as they were puzzling to us in our studies of three cities.

BECAUSE STRANGERS ARE WITH US

In our article "The thin end of the wedge" (Czarniawska & Sevón, 2008), we analyzed biographies of the first European women professors, many of whom, it turned out, were foreigners who had immigrated to the country in which they worked. The observation that encouraged us to do this study was the fact that being "a double stranger" – to the academy and to the country – seemed to facilitate rather than obstruct their position. In our analysis, we were helped by Georg Simmel's (1909/1950) concept of the stranger:

> The stranger is ... not ... the person who comes today and goes tomorrow, but ... the person who comes today and stays tomorrow. He is, so to speak, the *potential* wanderer: although he has not moved on, he has not quite overcome the freedom of coming and going. He is fixed within a particular spatial group, or within a group whose boundaries are similar to spatial boundaries. But his position in this group is determined, essentially, by the fact that he has not belonged to it from the beginning, that he imports qualities into it, which do not and cannot stem from the group itself. (p. 402, italics in original)

To explain this concept further, Simmel added that the inhabitants of another planet are not strangers, as for the time being they do not even exist for us. And the natives of other countries are not strangers, as long as they stay in their own country.

Simmel's picture of the stranger has usually been interpreted as having been developed from the symbol of "the wandering Jew" and interpreted positively. It has been used, among others, by Rose Laub Coser (1999), in her study of immigrant Italian and Jewish women. She claimed that:

> He [the wandering Jew] may derive as much advantage from his partial belongingness as he may be disadvantaged by being an outsider at the same time that he is disadvantaged by having demands he cannot honor made on him by the new group. He may understand the group's shortcomings better than true insiders do, and he may be praised or hated for his objectivity. In any case he will have multiplied his opportunities – at the cost of secure belongingness – to form weak ties even with those with whom hostilities are customary. Although much pain ensued from this, advantages came from it as well. (Coser, 1999, p. 47)

We analyzed the biographies of four women, and although we emphasized that the reasons for their successes were many and interactive, including the politics and the culture of Europe at the turn of the previous century, Simmel's image of a stranger has been extremely helpful – gender aside. The point that we found especially relevant for women transgressing the "ordinary" by entering academia was the alleged "objectivity" of the stranger:

> He is not radically committed to the unique ingredients and peculiar tendencies of the group, and therefore approaches them with the specific attitude of "objectivity." But objectivity does not simply involve passivity and detachment; it is a particular structure composed of distance and nearness, indifference and involvement. (…) he is freer, practically and theoretically; he surveys conditions with less prejudice; his criteria for them are more general and more objective ideals; he is not tied down in his action by habit, piety and precedent. (Simmel, 1909/1950, pp. 404–405)

Relationships with the stranger, Simmel (1909/1950) continued, are also more abstract than are relationships with compatriots:

> [W]ith the stranger one has only certain *more general* qualities in common, whereas the relation to more organically connected persons is based on the commonness of specific differences from merely general features. (p. 405, italics in original)

This quote suggests that if the stranger is a woman academic, her womanhood may be overlooked because it does not correspond to the local standard of femininity. In her study of the way strangers are perceived, Margaret Mary Wood (1934/1969) made a summary of "the special sociological characteristics of the relationship of the stranger which Simmel presents" (p. 247): mobility, objectivity, confidence, freedom from convention, and abstract relations. Viewed together, these characteristics form a clear contrast to the stereotype of a woman, at least in European societies. Thus, if a woman were a stranger to academia, she would be a different kind of a stranger – a stranger in reverse, as it were. In Simmel's view, an intellectual was basically a stranger (Bauman, 1992). Indeed, his description of a stranger seems close to the stereotype of a scientist. But does his description agree with the common perception of present immigrants? After all, "from the perspective of the native majority, all strangers are identical" (Bauman, 1991, p. 72).

At present, Ansgar Thiel and Klaus Seiberth (2017) and Antonella Golino (2018), among others, believe that Simmel's analysis is highly pertinent. As Golino (2018) put it, "[h]is vision of the foreigner, in relation to the complex situation of the migration of people at war to Europe, appears extremely poignant today" (p. 190). The present fashion of "multiculturalism" ignores Simmel's observation that, as a reciprocal action, a conflict not only dissolves social relations but also generates them. Thus, though inspired by noble intentions, multiculturalism often reinforces ghettoization.

Although Golino emphasized the "objectivity" of the foreigner – someone who can therefore present the autochthons with a more correct image of their society – Simmel's observation can be used as an argument for going further than the integration of "strangers," to a general *hybridization* (Nederveen Pieterse,[5]

2006, 2015). After all, as Golino (2018) said, "[m]igration (...) constitutes a non-secondary source of social change ..." (p. 195).

But who could better understand and apply Simmel's idea of a stranger than Zygmunt Bauman (1991), who singled out the most difficult obstacle for a stranger's acceptance in another society – the striving for a perfect order:

> The stranger's unredeemable sin is (...) the incompatibility between his presence and other presences, fundamental to the world order; his simultaneous assault on several crucial oppositions instrumental in the incessant effort of ordering. It is this sin which throughout modern history rebounds in reconstitution of the stranger as the bearer and embodiment of *incongruity;* indeed, the stranger is a person afflicted with incurable sickness of *multiple incongruity.* The stranger is, for this reason, the bane of modernity. (pp. 60–61, italics in original).

Will postmodern societies be able to overcome "the horror of ambiguity" (Bauman, 1991), so necessary for successful albeit imperfect organizing, as demanded by James G. March (2010)? The present efforts at "organizing integration" (Diedrich & Czarniawska, 2023) reveal this constant fight between striving for the perfect order and accepting incongruities.

BECAUSE FRAMING PHOTOS IS NOT THE SAME AS FRAMING PICTURES

Erving Goffman's (1974) concept of "framing" has become immensely popular in social sciences and organization studies. Yet it is only scholars interested in film and photography who noticed that he meant by what in other languages (in French, for example) is called *encadrement* – choosing the focus and the limits of the background rather than putting a frame around a picture. The difference becomes obvious when reading Simmel's (1902/1994) article "The picture frame: An aesthetic study":

> What the frame achieves for the work of art is to symbolize and strengthen this double function of its boundary. (...) which exercise indifference towards and defence against the exterior and a unifying integration with respect to the interior (...). (p. 11).

Although Goffman's framing decides what is the focus and what is the context of a picture, Simmel's frame "defends" the picture from its surroundings. It is, indeed, an "ornamentation," as he called it. Such ornamentation is relatively well known in the world of management. One example (although the authors do not invoke Simmel) is to be found in the study of "wrapping," used by Japanese companies in their accounting reports (Sabelfeld et al., forthcoming). Indeed, managers often put frames around certain pieces of their work, and like many inexperienced art owners, they often choose a frame that is richer than the picture it surrounds. But those Japanese accountants do it intentionally.

In scientific analysis, however, Simmel's frame may not be of much use:

> [...] in more or less tasteful milieus, one no longer finds photographs from nature in frames. The frame is suited only to structures with a closed unity, which a piece of nature never possesses. Any excerpt from unmediated nature is connected by a thousand spatial, historical, conceptual

and emotional relationships with everything that surrounds it more or less closely, physically or mentally. (p. 14)

Thus, when studying "the nature of management and organizing," we unavoidably do "framing," but must not put the results into "a frame" (unless by it we mean a book cover – an "ornamentation").

BECAUSE SECRET ORGANIZATIONS ARE MANY, THOUGH RARELY STUDIED

Secret service organizations, such as intelligence agencies, are not often studied, as access to their doings is difficult. A possible solution is to rely on historical material (as has been done by Costas & Grey, 2014, 2016; Parker, 2018; Siebert & & Czarniawska, 2018; Stohl & Stohl, 2011). But Simmel (1906) was first: Although he studied secret societies, the organizing principles are similar in all secret organizations. So, although Sabina Siebert and I noted that building distrust is a common occurrence in both secret and non-secret organizations, Simmel (1906) had already stated that "[v]eracity and mendacity are (…) of the most far-reaching significance for the relations of persons with each other. Sociological structures are most characteristically differentiated by the measure of mendacity that is operative in them" (p. 445).

Simmel defined secrecy as "consciously willed concealment" (p. 449) and emphasized that it characterizes all commercial relationships:

> [...] all commerce of men with each other rests upon the condition that each knows something more of the other than the latter voluntarily reveals to him; and in many respects this is of a sort the knowledge of which, if possible, would have been prevented by the party so revealed. (p. 455)

Simmel also claimed that secrecy "is one of the greatest accomplishments of humanity" (p. 462):

> The historical development of society is in many respects characterized by the fact that what was formerly public passes under the protection of secrecy, and that, on the contrary, what was formerly secret ceases to require such protection and proclaims itself. (pp. 462–463)

Secrecy can be either highly moral (in case of intelligence agencies claiming the protection of their country as their purpose) or highly immoral (in case of criminal networks), though the boundaries are relatively unclear.

Many recent scandals follow the logic depicted by Simmel, according to which "with increasing telic [purposeful] characteristics of culture the affairs of people at large become more and more public, those of individuals more and more secret" (p. 468). The neighbors may not know your secrets, but the media can discover them, particularly if you are a public person.

This theoretical reasoning helped Simmel to characterize secret societies – groups that can extend "personal secrecy" to all their members. One condition is the reciprocal *confidence* of its members, which differentiates most secret societies from intelligence agencies, where general distrust is the rule (Siebert & & Czarniawska, 2018). On the other hand, the existence of intelligence agencies is known, although not of all their members or their actions are known. Simmel gave a similar description of Freemasons: What he called *"relatively* secret societies" (p. 471) have many advantages, especially their adaptability to change, and their ways of dealing with betrayals. But truly secret societies, Simmel suggested, emerge "as correlate of despotism and of police control" (p. 472).

Another condition for the survival of secret societies is "the ability to preserve silence" (p. 472), which must be reinforced by a threat of penalties when the oath or the promise of silence has been broken. Secret societies, like intelligence agencies, train their members' capacity for silence (Czarniawska & et al., 2023). This capacity, like the other conditions mentioned here, is one of the many reasons for members of secret organizations to see themselves as different from and better than other people (Scott, 2009, p. 277).

The only difference between Simmel's description of secret societies and our description of secret organizations is that, according to Simmel, secret societies are practically free of internal conflicts, whereas secret organizations seem to be rife with conflict (sometimes to the point of the members forgetting who their actual enemy is), probably because, as mentioned, the existence of intelligence agencies is publicly known, whereas the existence of secret societies can be only assumed or suspected.

> Since the secret society occupies a plane of its own – few individuals belong to more than one secret society – it exercises a kind of absolute sovereignty over its members. This control prevents conflicts among them, which easily arise in the open type of co-ordination. (Simmel, 1906, pp. 491–492)

BECAUSE THEY WROTE WELL, ACHIEVING BEAUTY WITHOUT PERFECTION ...

My purpose was to show that the works of Tarde and Simmel are far from being "a set of dead classics, which 'weigh like a nightmare on the brains of living'," to quote Marx after Jameson (1984, p. 7). To the contrary, they provide a good explanation for "the cultural logic of late capitalism,"[6] to continue quoting Jameson, or "fast capitalism" to quote Scott (2009, p. 281). Indeed, it has been suggested that Durkheim won the famous debate with Tarde in 1903 because, as an original thinker, well ahead of his time, Tarde was misunderstood (Candea, 2010). Moss Kanter and Khurana (2009) claimed that Simmel "may have been too far ahead of his time" as well (p. 304).

But it was not only because of *what* Tarde and Simmel said but also because of *how* they said it that they should be read more often today. It must be added that I am familiar with works of Tarde and Simmel mostly in their English translations, and as, for example, different translations of Niklas Luhmann's texts show, a translator can change the original text beyond recognition. Nevertheless, I am truly impressed by both the depth of their thought and the beauty of their language. Both were close to art and literature (Tarde was also a poet and fiction writer), and it shows in their sociological texts.

I began this text with a personal anecdote and will end it with another. Our paper on secret organizations (Siebert & Czarniawska, 2018) has been published by *Journal of Management Inquiry* (*JMI*) under the heading, "Non-traditional research." I wonder how *JMI* would react to receiving a submission from Tarde or Simmel? In other words, what do we understand by "tradition" in management and organization studies?

NOTES

1. For claims that the influence of Weber and Durkheim on organization studies is receding, see, for example, Lounsbury and Carberry (2005) and Candea (2010).
2. It was Bruno Latour who directed my attention to Tarde, and Bernward Joerges who pointed me toward Simmel. I am truly grateful to both.
3. By "organization studies," I do not mean studies of formal organizations only but studies of all kinds of organizing processes.
4. A small village in Northern Sweden, used in Stockholm discourse as "the Other."
5. Though Nederveen Pieterse (2006) evokes Simmel only as a historical predecessor.
6. Both Tarde and Simmel often allude to economic phenomena, fully realizing the central role of the economy in contemporary societies.

REFERENCES

Anderson, Benedict (1983/1991). *Imagined communities*. University of Chicago Press.
Bauman, Zygmunt (1991). *Modernity and ambivalence*. Polity Press.
Bauman, Zygmunt (1992). *Intimations of postmodernity*. Routledge.
Blumer, Herbert G. (1969/1973). Fashion: From class differentiation to collective selection. In Gordon Wills & David Midgley (Eds.), *Fashion marketing* (pp. 327–340). Allen & Unwin.
Brooks, Peter (2011). *Enigmas of identity*. Princeton University Press.
Buruma, Ian (2002). The blood lust of identity. *New York Review of Books*, *49*(6), 12–14.
Candea, Matei (2010). Revisiting Tarde's house. In M. Candea (Ed.), *The social after Gabriel Tarde. Debates and assessments* (pp. 1–24). Routledge.
Chapin, Francis Stuart (1928). *Cultural change*. Century.
Coser, Rose Laub (1999). Family structure: Some theoretical concepts. In Rose Laub Coser, Laura S. Anker, & Andrew J. Perin (Eds.), *Women of courage: Jewish and Italian immigrant women in New York* (pp. 39–48). Greenwood Press.
Costas, Jana, & Grey, Christopher (2014). Bringing secrecy into the open: Towards a theorization of the social processes of organizational secrecy. *Organization Studies*, *35*(10), 1423–1447.
Costas, Jana, & Grey, Christopher, (2016). *Secrecy at work: The hidden architecture of organizational life.* Stanford University Press.
Czarniawska, Barbara (2002). *A tale of three cities, or the glocalization of city management*. Oxford University Press.
Czarniawska, Barbara (2004). Gabriel Tarde and big city management. *Distinktion*, *9*, 81–95.
Czarniawska, Barbara (2005). Fashion in organizing. In Barbara Czarniawska & Guje Sevón (Eds.), *Global ideas: How ideas, objects and practices travel in the global economy* (pp. 129–146). Liber/CBS.
Czarniawska, Barbara (2008). Alterity/identity interplay in image construction. In Daved Barry & Hans Hansen (Eds.), *The Sage handbook of new approaches to organization studies* (pp. 49–67). SAGE.
Czarniawska, Barbara (2009). Gabriel Tarde and organization theory. In Paul S. Adler (Ed.), *Sociology and organization studies. Classical foundations* (pp. 246–267). Oxford University Press.
Czarniawska, Barbara, & Joerges, Bernward (1995). Winds of organizational change. How ideas translate into objects and actions. In Samuel B. Bachcrach, Pasquale Gagliardi, & Bryan Mundell (Eds.), *Research in the sociology of organizations* (Vol. 13, pp. 171–209). Emerald.

Czarniawska, Barbara, & Panozzo, Fabrizio (2008). Trends and fashions in management studies (I): Fashion in research. *International Studies of Management & Organization, 38*(1), 3–12.

Czarniawska, Barbara, & Sevón, Guje (2008). The thin end of the wedge: Foreign women professors as double strangers in academia. *Gender, Work and Organization, 15*(3), 235–287.

Czarniawska, Barbara, Siebert, Sabina, & McKay, John (2023). *Personnel management in secret service organizations*. Edward Elgar.

Deleuze, Giles (1968/1997). *Difference & repetition*. Athlone.

Diedrich, Andreas, & Czarniawska, Barbara (Eds.). (2023). *Organizing immigrants' integration. Practices and consequences in labour markets and societies*. Palgrave Macmillan.

Frisby, David, & Featherstone, Mike (1997). Introduction to the texts. In David Frisby & M. Featherstone (Eds.), *Simmel on culture* (pp. 1–28). SAGE.

Golino, Antonella (2018). Simmel's actuality in the light of migratory processes. *Italian Sociological Review*, 8(2), 187.

Goffman, Erving (1974). *Frame analysis: An essay on the organization of experience*. Harvard University Press.

Hatch, Mary Jo, & Schultz, Majken (Eds.). (2003). *Organizational identity: A reader*. Oxford University Press.

Irenius, Lisa (2002, March 26–27). Samhället består av sömngångare som imiterar varandra. *Axess*.

Jameson, Fredric (1984). Postmodernism, or the cultural logic of late capitalism. *New Left Review, I*(146), 53–92.

Lamoreaux, Naomi (2003). Partnerships, corporations, and the limits on contractual freedom in U.S. history. In K. Lipartito & D. B. Sicilia (Eds.), *Constructing corporate America* (pp. 29–65). Oxford University Press.

Lounsbury, Michael, & Carberry, Edward J. (2005). From king to court jester? Weber's fall from grace in organization theory. *Organization Studies, 26*(4), 501–525.

Luhmann, Niklas (2002). *Theories of distinction: Redescribing the descriptions of modernity*. Stanford University Press.

March, James G. (2010). *The ambiguities of experience*. Cornell University Press.

Moss Kanter, Rosabeth, & Khurana, Rakesh (2009). The significance of Georg Simmel's structural theories for organizational behavior. In Paul S. Adler (Ed.), *Sociology and organization studies. Classical foundations* (pp. 291–306). Oxford University Press.

Mucchielli, Laurent (2000). Tardomania? Réflexions sur les usages contemporains de Tarde. *Revue D'histoire des Sciences Humaines, 3*, 161–184.

Nederveen Pieterse, Jan (2006). Social capital and migration – Beyond ethnic economies. In Sara Radcliffe (Ed.), *Culture and development in a globalizing world. Geographies, actors, and paradigms* (pp. 127–149). Routledge.

Nederveen Pieterse, Jan (2015). *Globalisation & culture*. Rowman & Littlefield.

Park, Robert E., & Burgess, Ernest W. (2021). *Introduction to the science of sociology*. University of Chicago Press.

Parker, Martin (2016). Secret societies: Intimations of organization. *Organization Studies, 37*(1), 99–113.

Sabelfeld, Sabina, Dumay, Johannes, & Czarniawska, Barbara (forthcoming). Wrapping: An artistic device used for the integration of corporate reporting.

Schultz, Majken, Hatch, Mary Jo, & Larsen, Mogens Holten (Eds.). (2000). *The expressive organization: Linking identity, reputation, and the corporate brand*. Oxford University Press.

Scott, Alan (2009). Georg Simmel: The individual and the organization. In P. S. Adler (Ed.), *Sociology and organization studies. Classical foundations* (pp. 268–290). Oxford University Press.

Serres, Michel (1974). *Hermés III. La traduction*. Minuit.

Siebert, Sabina, & Czarniawska, Barbara (2018). Distrust: Not only in secret service organizations. *Journal of Management Inquiry, 29*(3), 286–298.

Simmel, Georg (1902/1994). The picture frame: An aesthetic study. *Theory, Culture & Society, 11*, 11–17.

Simmel, Georg (1904/1971). Fashion. In Donald N. Levine (Ed.), *Georg Simmel on individuality and social forms* (pp. 294–323). University of Chicago Press.

Simmel, Georg (1906). The sociology of secrecy and of secret societies. *The American Journal of Sociology, XI*(4), 441–498.

Simmel, Georg (1909/1950). The stranger. In Kurt H. Wolff (Ed.), *The sociology of Georg Simmel* (pp. 402–408). The Free Press.

Stohl, Cynthia, & Stohl, Michael (2011). Secret agencies: The communicative constitution of a Clandestine Organization. *Organization Studies*, 32(9), 1197–1215.

Tarde, Gabriel (1890/1962). *The laws of imitation*. P. Smith.

Tarde, Gabriel (1893/1999). *Monadologie et sociologie*. Institut Synthélabo.

Tarde, Gabriel (1899/1974). *Social laws: An outline of sociology*. Arno Press.

Thiel, Ansgar, & Seiberth, Klaus (2017). Migrant background, culture, and ethnicity: Sociological terms without explanatory value?! *European Journal for Sport and Society*, *14*(3), 183–185.

Vargas, Eduardo Viana (2010). Tarde on drugs, or measures against suicide. In M. Candea (Ed.), *The social after Gabriel Tarde. Debates and assessments* (pp. 208–229). Routledge.

Veblen, Torsten (1899/1994). *The theory of the leisure class*. Dover Publications.

Whetten, David. A., & Godfrey, Paul C. (Eds.). (1998). *Identity in organizations: Building theory through conversations*. Sage Publications, Inc.

Wolff, Kurt H. (1950). Introduction. In Kurt H. Wolff (Ed.), *The sociology of Georg Simmel* (pp. vii–xxvii). The Free Press.

Wood, Margaret Mary (1934/1969). *The stranger: A study in social relationships*. AMS Press.

ORGANIZATION SYSTEMS AND THEIR SOCIAL ENVIRONMENTS: THE ROLE OF FUNCTIONALLY DIFFERENTIATED SOCIETY AND FACE-TO-FACE INTERACTION RITUALS

Werner Schirmer

Vrije Universiteit Brussel, Belgium

ABSTRACT

Organizations are affected top-down by the overarching societies and bottom-up by foundational face-to-face encounters: societies provide norms, values, laws, institutions, beliefs, markets, political structures, and knowledge bases. What happens within organizations is done by people interacting with other people, arguing, discussing, convincing each other when preparing and making decisions. Organizations operate within social environments that leave their – however indirect – imprint on what is going on within organizations. This article argues that organizational sociology can benefit from an integrated theoretical framework that accounts for the embeddedness of organizations within the micro- and macro-levels of social order. The argument is developed in two main points: First, this article introduces the multilevel framework provided by Niklas Luhmann's systems theory to demonstrate how organizations are shaped by the functionally differentiated macro-structure of society. Organizations follow and reproduce the operational logics of societal domains such as the

Sociological Thinking in Contemporary Organizational Scholarship
Research in the Sociology of Organizations, Volume 90, 287–308

ISSN: 0733-558X/doi:10.1108/S0733-558X20240000090012

political system, the economy, science, law, religion, etc. Second, this paper demonstrates how organizations are shaped by micro-level dynamics of face-to-face interactions. Face-to-face encounters form a social reality of its own kind that restricts and resists the formalization of organizational processes. Here, this article draws on Erving Goffman's and Randall Collins' work on interaction rituals, emotions, and solidarity, which is inspired by Durkheimian micro-sociology. At the end, this article brings together all the elements into one general account of organizations within the context of their macro- and micro-structural social environments. This account can yield a deeper and more sociological understanding of organizational behavior.

Keywords: Functional differentiation; Goffman; interaction rituals; Luhmann; organizations; systems theory

INTRODUCTION

When we buy groceries in the supermarket, when we bring our children to school, when we take the bus to our workplace, when we file tax forms, when we get a parking ticket, when we stream videos, when we use our banking app, when we get our vaccinations, when we participate in meetings – in all of these situations we deal with organizations. What organizations do – organizing the supply of goods, education, transport, public administration, law enforcement, entertainment, finance, healthcare, business – has become indispensable for our lives in modern societies (Arnold et al., 2021, 2022; Bromley & Meyer, 2015; Perrow, 1991; Schimank, 2010; Simon, 1991). For tens of thousands of years of human history, social life was possible without organizations (Abrutyn & Turner, 2022; Boehm, 2009; Henrich, 2015), but modern, large-scale societies would end up in unimaginable chaos if all organizations were artificially removed.

Organizations are fundamental to the proper functioning of modern societies, both on the macro-societal level and on the micro-social level of everyday lives. At the same time, the very organizations that provide and sell supplies, educate us, transport us from A to B, regulate and administer us, etc. could and would not exist if they weren't highly affected top-down by the overarching societies and bottom-up by foundational face-to-face encounters: the societies provide norms, values, laws, institutions, beliefs, markets, political structures, and knowledge bases. Most of what happens within organizations is done by people interacting with other people, arguing, discussing, convincing each other when preparing and making decisions. Expressed differently, organizations operate *within social environments* that leave their – however indirect – imprint on what is going on within organizations: what goals are considered rational and desirable, and by which means these goals are to be achieved, how the relations between superiors and subordinates are regulated, what kind of talents and skills are available, what kind of products and services are in demand.

One of the major contributions of (neo-)institutional perspectives (DiMaggio & Powell, 1983; Scott, 2013) was to highlight the influence of macro-societal forces on organizations. Organizations tend to conform to societal norms, values, and expectations in order to gain legitimacy and support, and over time, organizations operating in the same domains start looking alike. Oriented toward the micro-level end of environmental influences on organizations, human resource (HR) perspectives (Boxall & Purcell, 2022; Wright et al., 2001) have emphasized social-psychological factors driving organizational behavior such as employee motivation, job satisfaction, leadership, as well as interactional dynamics within teams or between management and employees.

Both perspectives have increased our understanding of what happens within organizations. These two schools are examples of how micro- and macro-levels are studied apart and relatively isolated from each other. As I intend to demonstrate in this article, a sociological understanding of organizations can benefit from an integrated theoretical framework that accounts for the simultaneous embeddedness of organizations in the micro- and macro-levels of social order: face-to-face encounters on the micro-level and societal domains such as the political system, the economy, science, law, religion, and others, on the macro-level.

One such integrated theoretical framework is the theory of social systems by German sociologist Niklas Luhmann. Luhmann's oeuvre (1995, 1999 [1964], 2018) includes dedicated studies of organizations, but more importantly, it offers a general social theory that can be applied to the societal level (Luhmann, 2012, 2013), to organizations, *and* to the level of face-to-face interactions (Kieserling, 1999). Most importantly, it allows for an integration of all those levels within one and the same conceptual framework (Fuchs, 1989; Luhmann, 1982).

Over the years, there have been many recommendable and accessible efforts to introduce Luhmannian theory to an international audience of organization scholars (Grothe-Hammer, 2022; Nassehi, 2005; Seidl & Becker, 2006; Seidl & Mormann, 2015). Because these cater primarily to readers invested in studying organizational behavior and management, their focus is on Luhmann's rather unconventional approaches to the theory of organization, especially with regard to decision-making and formal structures. The attention of the introductory literature, hence, is on Luhmann's *organizational* sociology but less so on the embeddedness of the latter within Luhmann's general theory of social systems (Luhmann's *social* theory) and within Luhmann's theory of *society*. Luhmann's multilevel framework, thus, holds some untapped potential for the understanding of organizations within their micro- and macro-social environments.

There are two purposes of this article. *First*, the text can be read as a supplement to the existing introductory literature to an English-speaking audience in organization studies with a focus on Luhmann's theory of society (functional differentiation) and the integration of face-to-face interaction, organizations, and society within the same framework. *Second*, I propose an amendment to something I consider a weak spot in the Luhmannian tradition regarding face-to-face interaction. Deviating a little from the orthodox grounds of Luhmannian scholarship, I argue that some aspects highly relevant to the study of organizations (interaction rituals and solidarity) have been addressed better by the "micro-wing" of the Durkheimian tradition. From this tradition, I import insights by

Randall Collins (2004) and Erving Goffman (1967) that, in my view, can be made compatible with the Luhmannian link interaction–organization–society.

While I touch the question of what goes on within formal organizations[1] (such as decision-making, informal power struggles, conflicts of rationalities) only briefly, my emphasis is on organizations as social systems that operate *within a society*, surrounded by interaction systems. The structure of this paper is as follows: First, we look at how we can understand formal organizations from a Luhmannian framework. Second, we will invoke Luhmann's theory of functionally differentiated society in order to get a better understanding of how organizations are shaped by modern society. Third, we will look at how face-to-face encounters form a social reality of its own kind that restricts and resists the formalization of organizational processes. Fourth, we bring all the elements together into one general account of organizations within the context of their macro- and micro-structural social environments.

1. ORGANIZATIONS AS SOCIAL SYSTEMS

In his earlier work, Luhmann (1999 [1964]) was interested in the functions and consequences of formal organization systems. With focus on organizations as systems in an environment, Luhmann argued that the formalization of expectations reduces the enormous complexity in the environment. Members in organizations are expected to behave in certain (but not other) ways, report to certain (but not other) persons, and do certain (but not other) tasks. Unless they want to jeopardize their position in the organization, members need to adhere to these expectations. These expectations are formalized with regard to achieving the goals the organization has set. When goals shift, members are expected to support these changing goals. The difference between social order inside and outside of organizations is that many more behaviors are possible in the environment. By reducing this vast complexity through the formalization of expectations, organizations can build up their own, internal complexity that is necessary to "organize" the achievement of the set goals, such as building products or providing services.

One of Luhmann's key observations was that the formalization of behavioral expectations in a decision structure inevitably leads to informal structures that partly support and partly counteract the formal structures. This is so because formal structures are notoriously prone to goal conflicts, conflicts between means and ends where means can reify and turn into ends in themselves, as well as conflicting rationalities toward contradicting goals. In order to fulfill or integrate goal conflicts, informal expectation structures may emerge as parasites within the formal structure that ultimately become functional for achieving the formal goals in the first place. An example of the latter is an unofficially tolerated violation of safety rules in order to achieve production schedules (Bensman & Gerver, 1963).

With the increasing role of communication as a key concept of Luhmann's (1995) general theory of social systems, he also slightly shifted focus in his work on organizations. Notions of complexity reduction and the difference between formalized and informal expectations have lost some importance, and Luhmann focused more on organizations as communication systems that reproduce through decisions (for a detailed chronological overview of changes in Luhmann's organizational sociology, see, for instance, Seidl & Mormann, 2015). There are a few key elements of Luhmann's account that hold across different phases of his work. Importantly, Luhmann rejected the idea that social systems consist of human beings doing something together. In line with his general theory of social systems (Luhmann, 1995), he conceives organizations as communication systems, that is, emergent social orders that cannot be reduced to their constituent elements – for instance, interactions between people (Luhmann, 1992; Schirmer & Michailakis, 2019). Organization systems differentiate themselves from their environment through a recursive network of decisions and decision premises, and they distinguish members from non-members (Grothe-Hammer & Berthod, 2017; Luhmann, 2018). Membership is tied to formalized (and informal) behavioral expectations that apply within the system but not outside (Luhmann, 1999 [1964], 2018).

Decisions and membership are the lowest common denominators for any type of organization system, from barber shops to multinational concerns. Every organization has defined criteria for membership, and these criteria vary depending on the type of organization. The concept "decision" refers to the communication of a choice between alternatives of which one is selected, for instance, hiring candidate A instead of B, to find the defendant guilty or not guilty, to approve the export of high-precision artillery systems in order to support the territorial defense of an invaded country, to let a student just pass instead of fail in an exam. During the course of time, organizations build up a history of decisions, decision programs, and decision premises that define to a large degree what has to be done under which circumstances. Organizational structure is a "decided structure" (Grothe-Hammer et al., 2022).

Through its structure based on decision premises, an organization is capable of maintaining its operative difference toward the environment. At the same time, it can adjust past decision programs if changes in the environment (falling prices, new laws, new communication technology, outbreak of a pandemic) require new, more appropriate goals. This mix of variety and redundancy (Luhmann, 2018) allows organization systems to master contingency in and openness toward its social environment.

Organizations are social systems within which many elements of social life happen that we also find outside of organizations, a world full of social norms, conventions, coordination, cooperation, competition, and, more generally, communication. The functions and consequences of "formal organization," thus, are *different* in the way organizations are affected by their environment. As we will show throughout this paper, two levels of environment are particularly important: face-to-face interactions and the encompassing society. We resume with the latter in Section 2.

2. HOW FUNCTIONALLY DIFFERENTIATED SOCIETY AFFECTS ORGANIZATIONS

Luhmann conceptualizes organizations as *communication systems* and not – as the mainstream does – as assemblies of humans who get together to achieve joint goals. In the same manner, Luhmann argues that it makes sense to conceive of society not as a large group of people but as one complex communication system.[2] More specifically, Luhmann defines society as the encompassing social system that comprises all other social systems (= communication systems). Any face-to-face encounter, organization, or other social system is part of society, and thereby reproduces society as a whole. With the mere definition, we have not said much yet about society as such.

Luhmann's earlier conceptions of society stressed the function of complexity reduction. Society as an inner-social environment reduces the complexity for all other small-scale social systems such as organizations and face-to-face encounters. These same smaller social systems can rely to a large extent on the structures the encompassing society provides for them, such as norms, values, beliefs, legal and political structures, markets, knowledge, and skills. This is especially important for organizations that can focus on building up their internal decision-making structures within an already established societal environment.

As was the case with Luhmann's earlier writings on organizations, the notion of complexity reduction had been relegated to the background over time. The most important feature of Luhmann's account of society as the encompassing communication system is *differentiation*. This means that society is not a single, unitary entity but rather a conglomerate of different parts, realms, or subsystems. The notion of society as difference has a tradition in classical sociological theory, for instance, in Marxian conflict theories according to which society is characterized by difference in the form of conflict between ruling and oppressed classes (Marx & Engels, 2014 [1847]). Likewise, Max Weber (1968) rejected the notion of a societal unity in trade for difference through a plurality of "value spheres" such as politics, religion, art, ethics, science, love, and the erotic value sphere. These value spheres each operate according to different logics, rationalities, and values that cannot easily be substituted by or subsumed under the other: Art has a different telos than politics and love does not work like science – a fact that at least some of our colleagues are aware of.

2.1. What Is Functional Differentiation?

As I will demonstrate in the next paragraphs, Luhmann's approach is akin to Weber's (see also Bruun, 2008) but draws on another tradition of differentiation theory that has precursors in the works of Emile Durkheim (2012 [1893]) on the social division of labor and Talcott Parsons' earlier contributions to a systems theory of modern society (Parsons, 1951; Parsons & Smelser, 1956). Both Durkheim and Parsons describe modern society as *functionally differentiated*. For Durkheim (2012 [1893]), increasing complexity and competition forces different social groups to specialize, which, over time, lead to a differentiation of institutional spheres centered around societal functions. In modern society, there are several societal realms that are separate from each other by the function they fulfill for society as a whole. Parsons (1951) therefore calls these subsystems *function systems*. In his well-known AGIL scheme, he analytically distinguishes four of them by cross-tabulation of the two variables internal/external and consummatory/instrumental, which depict the relation of the system to itself and its environment, and to the present and the future, respectively. The functions are Adaption, Goal attainment, Integration, and Latent pattern maintenance. Parsons claimed that, in order to survive, each system needs to have these functions fulfilled by its subsystems (= function systems). For Parsons' (1977) general systems theory, society is just a special case of a social system that has its very own subsystems: the A-function is fulfilled by the *economy*, the G-function by the *polity*, the I-function by the *societal community*, and the L-function by what he calls the *fiduciary system*.

Luhmann's theory of modern society is an enhancement of this functionalist strand of differentiation theory. Like Durkheim and Parsons, he considers functional differentiation as the key characteristic of modern society. In contrast to Durkheim and Parsons, however, Luhmann neither assumed that all these function systems are well integrated into a coherent whole. Nor did he consider functional differentiation a societal division of labor that expresses a cross-societal solidarity built from mutual dependence of the parts. Luhmann was especially skeptical toward the notion that modern society is integrated by a special system. Likewise, Luhmann did not envision a special function for pattern maintenance, as Parsons did. According to Luhmann, the societal instances Parsons had in mind for pattern maintenance such as families, law, religion, and education, each form separate function systems fulfilling a different function.

While Parsons derived four functions analytically through cross-tabulation of two variables, Luhmann derived "his" function systems empirically and finds a much larger number of them. Luhmann himself and some Luhmannian scholars proposed the political system, the economy, science, religion, law, art, healthcare, education, mass media, love/family, social help, and sports.[3] For Luhmann, function systems solve a specific reference problem for society that arises with increasing complexity. To give some examples, the system of politics solves the problem of social order by providing the capacity to form and enforce collectively binding decisions through power (Luhmann, 2000). The economic system regulates the allocation of goods and services under the problem of scarcity. Science solves the problem of advancing knowledge. The modern function of religion is to handle the problem of meaninglessness by offering explanations of the unexplainable. The function of law is to stabilize normative expectations for future conflicts.

In contrast to pre-modern stratified societies, which had a center and an apex (represented by a royal court or some clerical leader), modern society has nothing of that sort. To be sure, there are national and supranational governments, usually organized strictly hierarchically and headed by prime ministers, presidents, or general secretaries. However, these are organizations of the global *political system* of society – not of society as such. Likewise, a globalized financial market is not a characteristic of an integrated society but of a globally operating economic system. Each of these systems has repercussions on other function systems. For instance, the financial markets will react if the government of a certain country falls or the government may fail to be re-elected because of a breakdown of some market. Luhmann's point here is that the political system reacts politically to events in the economic system, while the economic system reacts economically to events in the political system. The same is true for other function systems, of course. In general, function systems are autonomous, but they are not independent from each other. They react to events in their environment, but they do it "their way" (Schirmer & Michailakis, 2019).

2.2. How Functional Differentiation Works

One of the clues of Luhmann's notion of functionally differentiated society is that modern society is a paradoxical unity: its unity lies in the multiplicity of incongruent function system-specific views of it. The differentiation of functions and function systems is, according to Luhmann, not a societal division of labor in a Durkheimian sense postulating a cross-societal solidarity or position representing the unity from which the function could be delegated. Instead, the functions are operative logics or rationalities (comparable to Weber's value spheres) that – at some point in history – have started to differentiate from each other and observe society from their own emerging perspectives. Each function system operates with its distinct point of view that their rationality and logic enables them to see. For the economic system, everything is a potential commodity that can be bought and sold for the right price. For the political system, everything is a matter of power distribution, alliances, coalitions, and majorities in elections. For science, everything is a potential object of research, to be analyzed, explained, and predicted. For religion, everything is a matter of sin, sacredness, and supernatural forces.

Using a formulation coined by philosopher Gotthard Günther (1979), Luhmann describes modern society as *polycontextural*. Günther defined a contexture as a view of the whole world through a binary logic such as true/false or legal/illegal. Each function system creates its own contexture: its own limited sphere of relevance through a binary logic. For everything else that falls beyond this sphere of relevance and logic, function systems are blind. Polycontextural, then, means that there is a multitude of contextures, all of which are incommensurable to one another.

The relative blindness for other perspectives has implications for society as a whole, as Luhmann (1989) demonstrates in his book *Ecological Communication*. Lacking a central "Archimedean" standpoint, society can only get a grip on the increasing ecological self-endangerment via its function systems. The problem is that function systems can only react in the way their logics and rationalities allow them but not in some all-encompassing rationality such as "stop climate change or else the planet becomes unlivable." The economic system reacts in terms of prices: as long as raw oil is cheap and hydrogen too expensive, it will be hard to convince consumers and providers to shift. The legal system can only punish actors if they violate existing laws. As long as there are legal loopholes that allow to dump externalities that pollute the milieu, companies will continue doing it. Changing laws requires political support, but the political system is sensitive to public opinion. Drastic measures are unpopular and may cost elections. In the system of science, environmental problems offer plenty of opportunities for research and career, but successful scientific communication rests on truthfulness according to evidence, methodology, and accepted theories – a language that is not shared widely outside of academia. In order to have any impact, the scientific question "is it true?" has to be translated into "does it work?", "how much does it cost?", "is it legal?", "can we win elections with this?", "is it a sacrilege?" etc. None of this means that environmental progress is impossible – history shows the contrary – but the functionally differentiated structure of society prevents a direct pathway to solve such complex problems that transgress the boundaries of several function systems. The interdependence and autonomy of function systems entails conflicts about goal alignment, time frames, and mutually exclusive rationalities that need to be managed. An analysis grounded in functionally differentiated society casts doubt against simpleminded blaming of allegedly unwilling, greedy, and immoral groups of people and questions the effectiveness of protest actions by radical environmental movements such as Extinction Rebellion which are ignorant of the "multiperspectivity" (Nassehi, 2003) built into the structure of modern society.

2.3. How Functional Differentiation Affects Organizations

Now that we have presented Luhmann's analysis of modern society, we can address the question of what all of this has to do with organizations. The answer is threefold: (a) function systems are no agents but organizations are, (b) organizations are oriented to the operative logics of particular function systems, and (c) organizations need to console contradicting functional logics within their own operations.

(a) Function systems are communication systems, but they have no agential qualities. The economic system, for instance, operates and reproduces itself through economic transactions by processing payments that enable further payments through the use and circulation of money. Every payment that connects past payments to future payments reproduces the economic system, but the function system itself is not much more than the framework of meaning within which trades, payments, prices, money, merchandise, etc. make sense. The individual payments, however, have to be executed by concrete agents, such as individuals or organizations.

Like individuals, organizations have a communicative address, which means that they can participate in communication as subjects and recipients. The address is a name, such as John Doe or Harvard University, on the one hand, and a point of attribution for actions and communication, on the other hand. When a tech company launches a new smartphone on the market, when a social media platform changes its terms of service, when a state invades the territory of another state, when a scientific journal accepts a manuscript for publication, when a university awards a diploma to their students, we can be sure that an organization acted and communicated.

Having agential qualities entails being accountable for the actions or neglects thereof. When a sports apparel company fails to invest in safe work environments in their supply factories, or when a government fails to adjust its anti-pandemic lockdown measures resulting in social alienation and mental illness among its citizens, this will also be attributed as an action: the decision of not doing anything when something should have been done.

The ability of organizations to act and communicate collectively also comes at the price that they can be called out, claims can be directed at them, action can be demanded from them, all of which requires (communicative) reactions – refusal or silence will be attributed as communication, too (Watzlawick et al., 1967). The ability of collective communication of organizations becomes clear if we consider other types of social systems for comparison: informal groups, function systems, and society as a whole have no communicative address. We can try to direct claims at them but shouldn't wonder why nothing happens when we call for "the economy" or demand that "we as a society" have to act now. Well, only organizations and (collectives of) individuals can "do" something – function systems cannot. Function systems operate more as an inner environment for organizations and individuals participating in function-system-specific communication.[4] The problem is that organizations do not represent the function systems; they only represent themselves. For instance, governments *are* not *the* political system; banks and corporations *are* not *the* economic system. This brings us to the next point.

(b) Most but not all organizations are associated with a specific function system. "Associated with" is a careful formulation to address the circumstance that organizations and function systems are separate entities, and organizations are not part of "their" function systems (Schirmer & Michailakis, 2015). This thought is complicated and requires some explanation.

For starters, we associate the organization "government"[5] with the function system of politics. Next to the government, there are a number of other organizations that can also be associated with the political system, such as parliaments, parties, nongovernmental organizations (NGOs), political counseling organizations, lobby firms, and many more. To make things yet more complicated, there are states, regional states, international organizations such as the United Nations, supra-states such as the European Union, defensive organizations such as the North Atlantic Treaty Organization (NATO), the Organization for Security and Co-operation in Europe (OSCE), and others. All of these organizations are somehow associated with the system of politics because politics is their bread and butter. They are directly or indirectly involved in the function of collectively binding decisions – either on the side of policy-making, the opposition, or general formation of political will.

For an example of the economic system, we immediately think of business corporations and banks as typical organizations. Here, too, are other organizations that also deal with primarily economic affairs, such as central banks, venture capital investors, money transfer services, audit firms, rating agencies, cooperatives, and others. In the context of the system of science, there are universities and research institutes but also funding agencies, ethical review boards, disciplinary associations, journals and publishers, and others. In general, we find many other function systems that have "their" typical organizations. Examples for organizations of the educational system are schools, universities, and kindergartens; examples for organizations of religion are churches and congregations; examples of the legal system are courts and law firms; examples of the health-care system are hospitals, clinics, pharmacies, therapy centers, wellness spas, etc.

What all of these examples have in common is that the mentioned organizations are, as I called it earlier, "associated with" one specific function system.[6]

Revisiting the older Luhmannian notion of complexity reduction, we can keep in mind that functional differentiation reduces the enormous complexity of social reality. In the same manner as function systems are ignorant to the logics of other function systems, we can observe that organizations can also ignore large parts of what happens in their environments. However, this does not mean that they can just do what they want. Their decision premises are to a large part determined by the logics and rationalities of "their" function system. Businesses cannot ignore the logics of the market and profit, so they will have goals and rules that submit to cost-cutting and increase of revenue. Courts have to submit to the rule of law; hence, for executing the prime function, they will hire people trained in law who are capable to understand statute books rather than people who are good at social media marketing. Political organizations cannot ignore the logic of power, alliances, and formal procedures. Universities are directly associated with two function systems: education and science. As such, their decision rules need to reflect the logics of the educational system (grades, admissions, trajectories) and goal programs (subjects, curricula, aspired skill levels, etc.). Nor can they ignore the demands of scientific integrity through evidence, methodology, and argument.[7]

As these examples illustrate, we find the societal structure of functional differentiation represented in the multitude of organizations that help executing the functions of "their" systems. However, and that is why I spoke of "associated with," the situation is more complicated than that. On the one hand, much of what happens in the daily practice of the organization can have remarkably little to do with the high-level orientation to one (two in the case of universities) function system-specific code. We will address some of this in Sections 3 and 4. On the other hand, functionally differentiated society is an environment that strongly impacts organizations in yet another way, as we will see now.

(c) Organizations are operatively distinct from "their" function systems. As we said in Section 1, organizations are social systems that reproduce through decisions; function systems reproduce by operations that contribute to the functions they fulfill for society. So, while we can safely state that banks deal with different affairs than courts or churches – due to the logics and rationalities of different function systems, economy, law, and religion, all of them are organizations which means a number of commonalities apply to them: they have a couple of decision-making routines and rules about membership; the more complex they are, the likelier they will have formal hierarchies, differentiation into departments and subdivisions with different tasks and goals, and career paths with defined privileges. On the informal end, there will be factions and cliques with more or less influence to control uncertainty zones (Friedberg & Crozier, 1980), and there will be a decoupling of the daily practices and routines from the ceremonial and mythical representation of the organization (Meyer & Rowan, 1977). In sum, there are sociological phenomena that happen in any kind of organization, regardless of which function system they are associated with.

However, organizations have one advantage over function systems. Function systems are bound to their code that cannot be subsumed in another. One cannot observe politically from a scientific perspective or economically from a legal perspective. Although organizations are to some extent aligned with the respective codes of their function systems (as argued in b), they are – more precisely: they must be – able to switch the codes of different function systems. A business corporation cannot act economically only while disregarding legal rules for conduct and contracts; if it has an own R&D department, it will submit to scientific codes as well. The same is true if it has its own trainee program that needs to adhere to the educational code of passing or failing exams. Likewise, any none-business organization needs to household with its budget, even if there is no legal obligation to be profitable and to please shareholders. If they depend on public sources, they may regularly have to apply for funds and thereby submit to logics secondary to the main function. As many researchers know, contemporary requirements for securing funding of *scientific* projects are practical applicability, societal impact, and political desirability.

In sum, organizations have to take into account several functional perspectives at the same time. Systems theorists Andersen and Pors (2021) have argued that organizations, in contrast to function systems, are "heterophonic" because when producing decisions, they can draw from a multiplicity of function systems at the same time (Roth, 2014). It is important, however, that this doesn't happen at random. In most cases, there is a primacy of the function system (with which the organization is associated) under which all other logics are subordinated: while the R&D department of a business corporation follows scientific rules when researching new products or ways of production, the whole endeavor is subordinated the economic goal of profitability. In the long run, the research needs to lead to reduced production costs or higher profit margins or it will be shut down. Likewise, universities that are run under the premises of marketability or political impact while neglecting the telos of advancing basic knowledge independent from practical purposes may ultimately whither because they fail to attract talented researchers and students.

3. FACE-TO-FACE INTERACTIONS WITHIN ORGANIZATIONS

The previous section has focused on how organizations are (co)determined from "above" by their societal environment. We have looked in particular at how the functionally differentiated structure of society orients organizations toward contributing to the fulfillment of societal functions. In this section, we will see how organizations are influenced by social systems from "below": the level of face-to-face interactions. Interaction systems – sociologist Erving Goffman (1961) calls them encounters – are based on the (physical) copresence of two or more people who perceive each other and share joint attention on the present situation (Luhmann, 1982). Compared to organizations, interaction systems are ephemeral and can only process low complexity due to the funnels of turn-taking and limited attention capabilities of participants. As will be demonstrated in the following paragraphs, interaction systems form a distinct reality of social order that makes significant imprints on social life in organizations. This section starts with a brief detour about online meetings in order to address a number of features that are present in face-to-face encounters but absent in mediated communication. Drawing on work anchored in the Durkheimian tradition by Goffman and Randall Collins, I will demonstrate that the emotional and ritual aspects of interactions are highly important for life in organizations – something undertheorized in the Luhmannian tradition. At the end of the section, I show with Collins that power in organizations is often enacted through interactional rituals.

3.1. What Gets Lost in Mediated Interaction

Since the lockdown measures during the Covid pandemic, many of us had to participate in online meetings. From an administrative/managerial point of view, online meetings promise to be more effective than face-to-face meetings (Wu et al., 2022). They are supposed to be brief and on point; the technology affords screen- and file sharing for quick information exchange; automated calendar systems remind participants and prompt them to join the sessions with one click or tap. Another perk from a managerial perspective is that online meetings save costs for travel, catering, heating, and cleaning. Whether online meetings are for the benefit of the organization is an entirely different question, and research indicates mixed results (Angelova, 2020; Karl et al., 2022; Kreamer et al., 2021; Purvanova & Kenda, 2022).

From a micro-sociological perspective, however, the shift to online meetings has laid bare one thing in particular: much of what is important for the functioning of organizations cannot be formalized in rules and procedures (see again: Bensman & Gerver, 1963). It is so much more, and much of it is lost in mediated communication (Collins, 2020; Kalkhoff, Dippong, Gibson et al., 2020; Kalkhoff, Dippong, & Gregory, 2011). Most striking about online meetings is the inability to observe subtle changes in body language and facial expressions in the audience during presentations and discussions. When everybody except for the speaker has their microphone off, we cannot hear each other's murmurs and sighs that give off non-articulated attitudes. As every leader knows, perceiving such visual and auditory cues is very important when seeking support for controversial decisions. In online meetings, it is almost impossible to "read" the proverbial room, so presenters and leaders cannot feed their intuitions about how to engage their audience and sway them in the right direction.

A second aspect of online gatherings is the lack of casual interaction with your seatmates right before and after meetings, in breaks or while the presentation technology doesn't do what it is supposed to. It is here when you can quickly exchange information, rumors, and gossip or make brief informal pre-agreements with a colleague that should not be official yet. Online settings afford that everyone else can hear what you say even if it is intended only for your seatmate's ears – so you watch your tongue closely. But uttering any of the above things via email or messenger app would require to overcome a social-psychological threshold: it demands more intent and leads to more accountability. In oral communication, particularly when whispered, we can always assert that we didn't really say or mean it this way. Once it is written and sent on electronic media, however, it persists – and we cannot plausibly deny it anymore.

3.2. Interaction as Distinct Social Order

All of these examples, which most of us will recognize from their own experiences, demonstrate that much of what happens in organizations takes place on the micro-level of face-to-face interactions. Expressed in Luhmann's terminology, we need to distinguish organizations and interactions as two different levels of social systems. While the interaction system takes place (in the context of) the organization system, we cannot unequivocally say that the interaction is *within* the organization or that it is *part of* the organization – akin to the circumstance that organizations do not exactly operate within function systems but rather are associated with them. As for the case of interactions and organizations, the jokes and the gossip told during meetings are hard to separate from the more formal aspects of the meeting (Kieserling, 1999). They will not make it into the minutes underlying the decisions made and thus will not be part of the official organizational memory, but individual participants may remember them well afterward and may refer to them in future meetings.[8] It is these informal communicative actions that enact the reality of face-to-face encounters within the context of organizations.

A sociological account of organizations needs to acknowledge that interaction is a social order in its own right with its distinct dynamics (Goffman, 1983): What happens in organizations is, hence, much more than just preparing and making decisions and the work executed by the staff. Sociologist Randall Collins (2004) urges us to focus on the micro-sociological reality of the *situation* that occurs when people encounter one another. Hence, what also matters within organizations is what happens during encounters among the staff – whether the organization is a business or associated with any other function system.

3.3. Rituals and Emotion

Drawing on the works of Emile Durkheim and Erving Goffman, Collins has made a few theoretical points relevant to my argument. To begin with, Durkheim (2001 [1912]) analyzed the situation of primitive religious rituals when tribespeople gathered, chanted, and danced themselves into an extraordinary state of ecstasy or exaltation that Durkheim called "collective effervescence." In these rituals, people lose their sense of individuality and feel a strong bond and unity with the other participants. According to Durkheim, this is the origin of religious experience: the feeling of sacredness and divinity.

Generalizing from Durkheim's analysis of religious rituals, Collins argues that successful interaction rituals can also occur in other, non-religious contexts, as long as people gather physically, direct their attention and focus on the same object, and do something that lets them get rhythmically entrained, for instance, through synchronized body movements, chanting, and/or shouting. Typical examples are political rallies, rock concerts, techno parties, group exercise, audiences in popular sports such as football, carnival (Ehrenreich, 2007), but also intensive conversations in pairs or small groups. Neuro-sociological research (Kalkhoff et al., 2011; Kalkhoff, Thye, & Pollock, 2016) has shown that interacting people tend to synchronize speech rhythm, intonation, pitch, and body language with each other in conversations they experience as good.[9] The individuals participating in successful interaction rituals get "pumped up" with what Collins calls "emotional energy," a feeling of high self-esteem, happiness, and deep satisfaction.[10]

Goffman transported Durkheim's insights to the secular, profane world of interaction rituals in everyday life. He showed that everyday life is full of an emotionally charged moral order and of sacred objects (such as the "face" and status of individuals) that need to be worshiped. If the sacred objects are violated (e.g., by failure to greet somebody or addressing them with the wrong title), the moral order needs to be restituted through correction rituals (Goffman, 1967). When caught, perpetrators feel shame, while victims feel righteous anger after violation and satisfaction after restitution. When things go smoothly, interactants feel moderate levels of satisfaction as accepted members of the moral community.

Collins argues with Goffman that small, casual everyday rituals such as greetings and brief friendly verbal exchanges create feelings of solidarity between individuals. Compared to the highly intensive experience of collective effervescence, this everyday solidarity is light and low intensity but not shallow because it supplies people with the emotional energy that carries them through their days. It is no coincidence that some organizations foster casual interaction between employees from different teams who normally don't work together by placing espresso machines, watercoolers, and copying machines at strategic locations.[11] To the benefit of the company, this may help the spread of ideas across teams and divisions, but it also increases the odds that employees experience the time at work more positively and feel that they are part of a community.

An underestimated feature of face-to-face interaction in organizations is the possibility for experiencing intense emotions together. For an impressive example think of the cheers, cries, and hugs of joy when SpaceX successfully launched and landed their Falcon rockets. The collective experience of emotions is something that occurs frequently in organizational everyday life: joint cheering about accomplishments or swearing about failures. People also crave physical contact with their peers in less intensive situations, for instance, giving a high five or slap on the backs to encourage or express gratitude to each other.

3.4. Why Are Rituals and Emotions Important in Organizations?

Against that background, we can also understand better why seemingly irrelevant communicative acts such as jokes and gossip are important even in business meetings. It is not about the content of the jokes and gossip per se but the interactivity between tellers and audience. The laughter, murmurs, and smiles are a collective experience that creates a feeling of group solidarity. To get a glimpse of how natural and important this flow of casual interaction in organizations normally is, we can think of the period of forced telework during the Covid-related lockdowns (Brynjolfsson et al., 2020). The advantages of skipped commuting and no need to properly getting dressed were eaten up quickly by the lack of casual conversation and low-intensity interaction rituals, all of which in the course of months made many people more socially alienated and isolated (Lal et al., 2023; Yang et al., 2022).

Interestingly, in a recent trend that started already before the pandemic, there is an increasing number of dedicated remote-only companies that organize their whole operation with digital means. They double down on cost-effectiveness and productivity gains while attracting employees from a much larger talent pool than companies bounded by geography (Popovici & Popovici, 2020). However, the big micro-sociological challenge remote firms have to deal with is to create functional equivalents to the daily low-intensity interaction rituals that happen naturally in onsite organizations. A common strategy among remote working firms is to arrange annual retreats to exotic destinations in order to create group solidarity and social bonding among team members. As Collins (2004, 2020) argues with Durkheim, the "electricity" of collective effervescence that can occur in intensive teambuilding rituals pumps up the participants with emotional energy and creates a stronger group cohesion and identification with the firm. However, the social and emotional state of effervescence is precarious and withers away quickly unless it is repeated at regular intervals – something religious congregations are well aware of (Collins, 2004). The dilemma for remote working firms is that retreats are too costly to happen at high frequency, while the casual low-intensity rituals cannot occur naturally.

3.5. Power Rituals

Until now, we have emphasized the socially integrative aspects of face-to-face interaction in organizations. However, interactions also play a role in inequality. Organizations are the only types of social systems in modern society that allow legitimate socially unequal treatment based on rank (Luhmann, 2013; Nassehi, 2002). The formal structure of organizations is mostly hierarchical with discretionary power and privileges concentrated in the top positions. The formalized inequalities in organizations are expressed through what Collins (2000) calls "deference power,"[12] that is, the power to give orders. These inequalities are mainly enacted through power rituals during face-to-face interactions: "One person gives orders, in extreme cases with an imperious tone and demeanor, while the other acquiesces verbally and in bodily posture" (p. 33). A typical example is the Chief Executive Officer (CEO) who in front of everybody scolds a middle manager who failed to reach her target, making her look like a schoolgirl. Ritualistic display of deference power is socially significant as it marks the status differences between the superiors and subordinates (even high-ranking ones) and shapes the social relations among them: who can speak to whom in what way without getting punished.

Like other interaction rituals, power rituals require shared attention and mutual focus both by the superior and the subordinate, but they do not create much solidarity between the two unequal participants and usually have differential outcomes of emotional energy. Interaction rituals of deference power also produce sharp differences in social identity. Order-givers tend to identify more strongly with the organization and express this throughout official interactions, while the order-receivers rather feel "smouldering resentment and suppressed conflict" (Collins, 2000) and develop a cynical attitude toward the superiors (or the entire organization) which they can only express on a Goffmannian backstage among peers while the superiors aren't watching.

In sum, we can add to our previous diagnosis that much of what happens in organizations happens on the interactional level, that this is also true for enacting power and status differentials among members.

4. BRINGING IT ALL TOGETHER: INTERACTION, ORGANIZATION, AND SOCIETY

From a purely Luhmannian approach that fathoms organizations as "decision-machines" (Nassehi, 2005) whose sole reality exists in reproducing themselves through (the preparation and communication of) decisions (Luhmann, 2018; Seidl & Becker, 2006), much of what I described in the previous section cannot be adequately understood. However, if we consider the merit of Collins' (as well as Durkheim's and Goffman's) works in the analysis of what happens when co-present individuals engage in interaction with each other, we get a good insight into the importance of face-to-face interactions within organizations in a way that the Luhmannian vocabulary is less suited for.

On the other hand, Collins (2004) stretches his "radical microsociology" too far when he argues that society is not much more than chains of interaction rituals through which individuals move and that sociological phenomena on meso- and macro-levels can ultimately be reduced to and explained by micro-level dynamics of face-to-face encounters. In a worthwhile critique of this approach, Stephan Fuchs (1989) demonstrated that micro-approaches fail to adequately analyze the non-situational and non-ephemeral properties of organizations (such as formal structure, decision programs, organizational culture) and society (functional differentiation but also stock of shared knowledge, cultural values, social norms, semantics, and zeitgeist). Luhmann's general theory of social systems, by contrast, allows us to understand interactions, organizations, and society as emergent realities *sui generis* (Fuchs, 1989; Luhmann, 1982). As Fuchs (1989) puts it, "copresence is typical of interaction but not of 'macrosystems,' the latter differ in kind from the former and thus cannot be 'reduced to' or 'explained in terms of' interactions or microevents" (p. 180).

Thus, my suggested way to go for a deep sociological understanding of organizations within their micro- and macro-social environment is the integration of key insights from both Collins' micro-sociology and Luhmann's theory of social systems. Since Luhmann's theory is designed as a general theory of social systems, it can be applied with added value to analyze social systems on several levels. We have, in this paper, focused less on what all social systems have in common (they are self-referentially closed communication systems that, through their operations, differentiate themselves from an environment; see Luhmann, 1995) but rather what makes them distinct from each other: organizations are social systems that produce decisions; society is an encompassing social system and a differentiated unit of incommensurable function-specific rationalities; face-to-face interactions are small-scale social systems contingent on copresence.

A consequence of formal organization is that in organizational everyday life, all these system levels are invoked at the same time. To conclude this article, let us discuss a comprehensive example that brings everything together:

Imagine a meeting in the boardroom where a decision to purchase a production machine is prepared. First and foremost, it is a face-to-face interaction among real people. This means that the rules of copresence, such as turn-taking as well as norms of etiquette, demeanor, and politeness, apply. Furthermore, the co-present people will engage in Goffmannian impression management (Goffman, 1990 [1959]), ritualistically display their relative status and power, and they may become more or less emotionally energized from the interaction, contingent on their relative ownership of and identification with the issue at hand and the (verbal and subliminal) responses they receive from each other.

At the same time, every participant knows that this is a meeting within an organizational context – it is neither a dinner party nor casual chitchat. There is a defined topic and goal, there is possibly an agenda and a speaking order; participants have specialized roles such as CEO, Chief Financial Officer (CFO), Chief Technology Officer (CTO), project manager, which are known to everyone present without having to renegotiate every time anew. All of this is determined by the organizational programs and membership rules. In other words, these features are persistent beyond the here and now of the face-to-face interaction.

If the goal of the meeting is met, there will be a decision (buy or not buy the machine) which will be consequential for future decisions (more or less money available, precedents for similar situations, evaluations, future investments, etc.). Furthermore, the decision outcome of the meeting is enabled by a plethora of past decisions and decision premises (about product strategy, budget, space allocation, etc.) and documented work (research, market analysis, technical reports, etc.). While some of these aspects may have come about through past face-to-face interactions, they are stored, retrieved, and actualized on an emergent level of the organization system – irreducible to face-to-face interactions.

Finally, the meeting is about a purchase, which only makes sense in the context of the economic function system of society. The feasibility and utility of the purchase will be evaluated in light of prices for this machine and its alternatives, projected cost-saving and returns of investment, market evolution for the products the machine is supposed to produce, competitors in the market, and other business-related criteria. At the same time, the organization needs to take into account the operational logics of function systems other than the economy. Buying the machine does not only affect the business side (costs, profits, productivity gains), but it may require staff training to use the machine, it may trigger legal issues regarding safety and labor law, or it may have political repercussions because of shifting informal power dynamics between operators and maintenance personnel (Friedberg & Crozier, 1980). While the business organization in our example needs to be careful with regard to the rationalities of these other function systems, it is clearly the primacy of the economic logic that dominates all other operations in the system.

There is no simple causal pathway in how interaction systems and society determine organizational processes and vice versa. Every system level can affect another but is operationally closed and follows its own dynamics. A toxic collective mood in the meeting because of excessive deference power rituals may establish a culture of fear and yes-bias that leads to a suboptimal decision. Strict organizational rules may protect subordinates from too abrasive deference power rituals, and convoluted decision-making procedures may prevent too heated choices and actions. To stay in the above example, the purchase of a machine is curbed by the rationalities of the economic system, but it may, in turn, affect the economic system (albeit in a limited intensity) by putting pressure on prices, concentration of capital, shifting supply of goods, more or less jobseekers, etc.

To summarize, this paper has two main points: *First*, much of what happens in organizations is heavily affected by face-to-face interactions. Simultaneously, much of what happens in organizations follows and reproduces the operational logics and rationalities of societal function systems. In order to get this point across, I introduced the multilevel framework provided by Luhmann to account for social systems on the interactional, organizational, and societal levels. The *second* point is an amendment of what I consider a weakness in Luhmann's theory with key insights regarding the role of emotion and ritual from Durkheimian-inspired micro-sociology by Goffman and Collins. As I have demonstrated, Collins' "radical" micro-sociological approach on its own has its shortcomings because it cannot account for matters that are better compensated by Luhmann's comprehensive framework. Looking at the organizations as "decision machines" alone without simultaneously looking at system levels of society and interaction will forego much. The conjunction, however, will yield a deeper, stronger, and more sociological understanding of organizations.

NOTES

1. This text focuses on formal organization systems, such as registered companies, public authorities, universities, etc., that is, social systems that in legal terms are called corporate bodies. It is open for debate, but not the place to discuss here, whether the presented arguments also apply to informal organizations.

2. It is important to stress that Luhmann's conception of society as communication system is a definition for scientific purposes. Defining society as a communication system has a heuristic and epistemological value that allows for original hypotheses and research questions, but – regardless of Luhmann's intentions – it should not be read as an ontological claim about the "true" nature of society, contrasted with an allegedly "false" nature of society as an assembly of humans.

3. Among contemporary Luhmann scholars, there is a debate about whether some systems (such as sports, family, social help) should receive the status of a function system and whether there is something like a canon of function systems. See the special issue of *Cybernetics & Human Knowing* 2015/4 and in particular Roth and Schütz (2015).

4. One example of such an inner environment is the "market" in the economic system.

5. To be more accurate, the government is a conglomerate of several organizations.

6. Universities are an exception insofar as they are associated with science and education. In the former, they contribute to knowledge production in the quest for truth. In the latter, they are involved in the production of competences and skills in the quest for credentials.

7. Universities are not the only case of a dual (or multi-) function system relationship. Within the context of many function systems, we find organizations that are also business operations, for example, private hospitals, media corporations, or for-profit sports teams. While each of these need to submit their respective function system's code (health, news, sport success), they also adhere to the economic telos of profit maximization. At times, these function system-specific logics may be at odds. It is, then, difficult to determine which telos is more important for the survival and legitimacy of the organization. I thank the editors for this comment.

8. Jokes and gossip can become part of the official organization history, however, if some boundary transgressing behavior occurred that violates formal rules.

9. Conversely, interactions where this synchrony fails to establish are experienced as unpleasant and energy draining. This is the case if the interacting people dislike or mistrust each other but occurs also when digital glitches interrupt online talks due to poor network quality.

10. Social psychologist Jonathan Haidt (2012), who puts Durkheim's observations into an evolutionary context, speaks of a "hive switch" in our brains that, when activated through interaction rituals, makes us less selfish, more cooperative, and more unison with our group.

11. It is said that companies such as Google even reduce the speed of the waterflow in watercoolers to increase waiting times and, thereby, make more interaction with others likely.

12. Collins distinguishes "deference power" from "efficacy power," which indicates the means to make others do something in order to achieve goals for the whole collectivity. While the former is more akin to Weber's definition of power as having others execute your will, the latter is a non-zero-sum form more in line with Parsons' and Luhmann's understanding of power as a generalized medium of interchange/communication.

ACKNOWLEDGMENTS

I want to thank the anonymous reviewers and the editors for their helpful comments on a previous version of this article.

REFERENCES

Abrutyn, S., & Turner, J. H. (2022). *The first institutional spheres in human societies. Evolution and adaptations from foraging to the threshold of modernity.* Routledge.

Andersen, N. Å., & Pors, J. G. (2021). From self-evident norms to contingent couplings: A systems-theoretical analysis of changes in the relationship between schools and the function systems in Denmark. *European Educational Research Journal, 20*(6), 821–840.

Angelova, M. (2020). Indicators for effectiveness and efficiency of e-platforms for business meetings. In *2020 III international conference on high technology for sustainable development (HiTech)* (pp. 1–4).

Arnold, N., Hasse, R., & Mormann, H. (2021). Organisationsgesellschaft neu gedacht: Vom Archetyp zu neuen Formen der Organisation. *Kölner Zeitschrift für Soziologie & Sozialpsychologie, 73*(3), 339–360.

Arnold, N., Hasse, R., & Mormann, H. (2022). Organisationsgesellschaft>>reloaded<<. Organisationsweisen und Herausforderungen im 21. Jahrhundert. *Soziale Welt, 73*(3), 419–424.

Bensman, J., & Gerver, I. (1963). Crime and punishment in the factory: The function of deviancy in maintaining the social system. *American Sociological Review, 28*(4), 588–598.

Boehm, C. (2009). *Hierarchy in the forest: The evolution of egalitarian behavior.* Harvard University Press.

Boxall, P., & Purcell, J. (2022). *Strategy and human resource management.* Bloomsbury Publishing.

Bromley, P., & Meyer, J. W. (2015). *Hyper-organization: Global organizational expansion.* Oxford University Press.

Bruun, H. H. (2008). Objectivity, value spheres, and "inherent laws" on some suggestive isomorphisms between Weber, Bourdieu, and Luhmann. *Philosophy of the Social Sciences, 38*(1), 97–120.

Brynjolfsson, E., Horton, J. J., Ozimek, A., Rock, D., Sharma, G., & TuYe, H.-Y. (2020). *COVID-19 and remote work: An early look at US data.* https://www.nber.org/papers/w27344.

Collins, R. (2000). Situational stratification: A micro–macro theory of inequality. *Sociological Theory, 18*(1), 17–43.

Collins, R. (2004). *Interaction ritual chains.* Princeton University Press.

Collins, R. (2020). Social distancing as a critical test of the micro-sociology of solidarity. *American Journal of Cultural Sociology, 8*(3), 477–497.

DiMaggio, P. J., & Powell, W. W. (1983). The iron cage revisited: Institutional isomorphism and collective rationality in organizational fields. *American Sociological Review, 48*(2), 147–160.

Durkheim, É. (2001 [1912]). *The elementary forms of religious life.* Oxford University Press.

Durkheim, É. (2012 [1893]). *The division of labor in society.* Martino Fine Books.

Ehrenreich, B. (2007). *Dancing in the streets: A history of collective joy.* Granta.

Friedberg, E., & Crozier, M. (1980). *Actors and systems: The politics of collective action.* University of Chicago Press.

Fuchs, S. (1989). On the microfoundations of macrosociology: A critique of microsociological reductionism. *Sociological Perspectives, 32*(2), 169–182. htpps://doi.org/10.2307/1389095

Goffman, E. (1961). *Encounters: Two studies in the sociology of interaction.* Bobbs-Merrill.

Goffman, E. (1967). *Interaction ritual: Essays on face-to-face behavior.* Doubleday.

Goffman, E. (1983). The interaction order: American sociological association, 1982 presidential address. *American Sociological Review, 48*(1), 1–17.

Goffman, E. (1990 [1959]). *The presentation of self in everyday life.* Anchor Books.

Grothe-Hammer, M. (2022). The communicative constitution of the world. A Luhmannian view on communication, organizations, and society. In J. Basque, N. Bencherki, & T. Kuhn (Eds.), *The Routledge handbook of the communicative constitution of organization* (pp. 88–103). Routledge.

Grothe-Hammer, M., Berkowitz, H., & Berthod, O. (2022). Decisional organization theory: Towards an integrated framework of organization. In M. Godwyn (Ed.), *Research handbook on the sociology of organizations* (pp. 30–53). Elgar.

Grothe-Hammer, M., & Berthod, O. (2017). The programming of decisions for disaster and emergency response: A Luhmannian approach. *Current Sociology, 65*(5), 735–755.

Günther, G. (1979). *Beiträge zur Grundlegung einer operationsfähigen Dialektik II* Meiner.

Haidt, J. (2012). *The righteous mind: Why good people are divided by politics and religion.* Pantheon.

Henrich, J. (2015). *The secret of our success.* Princeton University Press.

Kalkhoff, W., Dippong, J., Gibson, A., & Gregory, S. W. (2020). Society in peril? how distance media communication could be undermining symbolic interaction. In R. Serpe, R. Stryker, & B. Powell (Eds.), *Identity and symbolic interaction* (pp. 317–338). Springer.

Kalkhoff, W., Dippong, J., & Gregory, S. W., Jr. (2011). The biosociology of solidarity. *Sociology Compass, 5*(10), 936–948.

Kalkhoff, W., Thye, S. R., & Pollock, J. (2016). Developments in neurosociology. *Sociology Compass, 10*(3), 242–258.

Karl, K. A., Peluchette, J. V., & Aghakhani, N. (2022). Virtual work meetings during the COVID-19 pandemic: The good, bad, and ugly. *Small Group Research, 53*(3), 343–365.

Kieserling, A. (1999). *Kommunikation unter Anwesenden. Studien über Interaktionssysteme.* Suhrkamp.

Kreamer, L., Stock, G., & Rogelberg, S. (2021). Optimizing virtual team meetings: Attendee and leader perspectives. American Journal of Health Promotion, *35*, 744–747.

Lal, B., Dwivedi, Y. K., & Haag, M. (2021). Working from home during Covid-19: Doing and managing technology-enabled social interaction with colleagues at a distance. *Information Systems Frontiers, 25*, 1333–1350.

Luhmann, N. (1982). Interaction, organization and society. In N. Luhmann (Ed.), *The differentiation of society* (pp. 69–89). Columbia University Press.

Luhmann, N. (1989). *Ecological communication.* University of Chicago Press.

Luhmann, N. (1992). What is communication? *Communication Theory, 2*(3), 251–259.

Luhmann, N. (1995). *Social systems.* Stanford University Press.

Luhmann, N. (1999 [1964]). *Funktionen und Folgen formaler Organisation.* Duncker und Humblot.

Luhmann, N. (2000). *Die Politik der Gesellschaft.* Suhrkamp.

Luhmann, N. (2012). *Theory of society. Volume 1.* Stanford University Press.

Luhmann, N. (2013). *Theory of society. Volume 2.* Stanford University Press.

Luhmann, N. (2018). *Organisation and decision.* Cambridge University Press

Marx, K., & Engels, F. (2014 [1847]). *The communist manifesto.* Penguin Classics.

Meyer, J. W., & Rowan, B. (1977). Institutionalized organizations: Formal structure as myth and ceremony. *American Journal of Sociology, 83*(2), 340–363.

Nassehi, A. (2002). Exclusion individuality or individualization by inclusion. *Soziale Systeme*, *8*(1), 124–135.

Nassehi, A. (2003). *Geschlossenheit und Offenheit. Studien zur Theorie der modernen Gesellschaft.* Suhrkamp.

Nassehi, A. (2005). Organizations as decision machines: Niklas Luhmann's theory of organized social systems. *The Sociological Review*, *53*(1), 178–191.

Parsons, T. (1951). *The social system.* Free Press.

Parsons, T. (1977). *The evolution of societies.* Prentice-Hall.

Parsons, T., & Smelser, N. (1956). *Economy and society.* Routlege.

Perrow, C. (1991). A society of organizations. *Theory and Society*, *20*, 725–762.

Popovici, V., & Popovici, A.-L. (2020). Remote work revolution: Current opportunities and challenges for organizations. *Ovidius University Annals Economic Science Series*, *20*, 468–472.

Purvanova, R. K., & Kenda, R. (2022). The impact of virtuality on team effectiveness in organizational and non-organizational teams: A meta-analysis. *Applied Psychology*, *71*(3), 1082–1131.

Roth, S. (2014). The multifunctional organization: Two cases for a critical update for research programs in management and organization. *TAMARA: Journal for Critical Organization Inquiry*, *12*(3), 37–54.

Roth, S., & Schütz, A. (2015). Ten systems: Toward a canon of function systems. *Cybernetics & Human Knowing*, *22*(4), 11–31.

Schimank, U. (2010). Die funktional differenzierte kapitalistische Gesellschaft als Organisationsgesellschaft– eine theoretische Skizze. In E. Martin & M. Thomas (Eds.), *Die Ökonomie der Organisation–die Organisation der Ökonomie*, 33–61. VS-Verlag für Sozialwissenschaften.

Schirmer, W., & Michailakis, D. (2015). The Luhmannian approach to exclusion/inclusion and its relevance to Social Work. *Journal of Social Work*, *15*(1), 45–64. htpps://doi.org/1468017313504607

Schirmer, W., & Michailakis, D. (2019). *Systems theory for social work and the helping professions.* Routledge.

Scott, W. R. (2013). *Institutions and organizations: Ideas, interests, and identities*: Sage Publications.

Seidl, D., & Becker, K. H. (2006). Organizations as distinction generating and processing systems: Niklas Luhmann's contribution to organization studies. *Organization*, *13*(1), 9–35.

Seidl, D., & Mormann, H. (2015). Niklas Luhmann as organization theorist. In P. Adler, P. du Gay, G. Morgan, & M. Reed (Eds.), *Oxford handbook of sociology, social theory and organization studies: Contemporary currents* (pp. 125–157). Oxford University Press.

Simon, H. A. (1991). Organizations and markets. *Journal of economic perspectives*, *5*(2), 25–44.

Watzlawick, P., Beavin, J., & Jackson, D. (1967). *Pragmatics of human communication. A study of interactional patterns, pathologies, and paradoxes.* Norton.

Weber, M. (1968). *Economy and society: An outline of interpretive sociology.* Bedminster.

Wright, P. M., Dunford, B. B., & Snell, S. A. (2001). Human resources and the resource based view of the firm. *Journal of Management*, *27*(6), 701–721.

Wu, J., Rajesh, A., Huang, Y.-N., Chhugani, K., Acharya, R., Peng, K., Johnson, R. D., Fiscutean, A., Robles-Espinoza, C. D., De La Vega, F. M., Bao, R., & Mangul, S. (2022). Virtual meetings promise to eliminate geographical and administrative barriers and increase accessibility, diversity and inclusivity. *Nature Biotechnology*, *40*(1), 133–137.

Yang, L., Holtz, D., Jaffe, S., Suri, S., Sinha, S., Weston, J., Shah, N. P., Sherman, K., Hecht, B., & Teevan, J. (2022). The effects of remote work on collaboration among information workers. *Nature Human Behaviour*, *6*, 43–54.

Printed in the USA
CPSIA information can be obtained
at www.ICGtesting.com
JSHW012259060924
69456JS00004B/36